Access to Justice in Arbitration

Access to Justice in Arbitration

Concept, Context and Practice

Edited by

Leonardo V.P. de Oliveira
Sara Hourani

Wolters Kluwer

Published by:
Kluwer Law International B.V.
PO Box 316
2400 AH Alphen aan den Rijn
The Netherlands
E-mail: international-sales@wolterskluwer.com
Website: lrus.wolterskluwer.com

Sold and distributed by:
Wolters Kluwer Legal & Regulatory U.S.
7201 McKinney Circle
Frederick, MD 21704
United States of America
Email: customer.service@wolterskluwer.com

ISBN 978-94-035-0691-3

e-Book: ISBN 978-94-035-0681-4
web-PDF: ISBN 978-94-035-0682-1

Editors

Leonardo V.P. de Oliveira is a Lecturer in Law at Royal Holloway, University of London. He has a PhD and LLM from University of Essex, England and he is a qualified lawyer in Brazil.

Sara Hourani is Senior Lecturer at the School of Law, Middlesex University London and Visiting Lecturer at the University of Aix-Marseille, France. Sara received an LLB degree from Grenoble Alpes University, an LLM in International Trade Law and a PhD in Law from the University of Essex, England. Sara was granted the UK AHRC PhD scholarship and was a John W Kluge Scholar at the Library of Congress in Washington DC which was also funded by the AHRC. Before joining Middlesex, Sara previously held a Lectureship in Law at the Law Department and CIPPM at Bournemouth University, United Kingdom and also taught at the University of Essex, England and the University of East Anglia, United Kingdom. Sara's research focuses on the use of new technologies in arbitration and online dispute resolution.

Contributors

Avani Agarwal is a final year law student at NALSAR University of Law, India. She has worked on arbitration disputes as an intern at various domestic and international law firms. She has a strong interest in the intersection between international arbitration and policy considerations, and has contributed to several articles and blog-posts about it.

Dr Crina Baltag is Senior Lecturer in International Arbitration at Stockholm University, Sweden and qualified attorney-at-law since 2004, with extensive practice in various aspects on international dispute resolution, private and public international law. Crina regularly sits as arbitrator (ICC, LCIA, SIAC, etc.) and advises on investment arbitration cases.

Prof Dr Ian Blackshaw is an International Sports Lawyer, Academic, Author and a member of the Court of Arbitration for Sport, Lausanne, Switzerland and a member of the WIPO (World Intellectual Property Organization) Arbitration and Mediation Center, Geneva, Switzerland.

Ramona Elisabeta Cirlig is an attorney-at-law in Bucharest, Romania focusing her practice on international commercial arbitration, a PhD Candidate in Private International Law (University of Bucharest, Romania), magna cum laude graduate of the LLM in International and European Law (Institute for European Studies, Vrije Universiteit Brussels). Prior to joining the Bucharest Bar, she gained valuable experience while working for the United Nations Population Fund (UNFPA).

Berk Demirkol is an Associate Professor at Galatasaray University, Turkey. He teaches Private International Law, International Investment Law and Arbitration and International Economic Law. Berk is also a Partner and the Co-Head of the Arbitration department at Yüksel Legal. Berk holds his PhD degree from the University of Cambridge, United Kingdom. His monograph on 'Judicial Acts and Investment Treaty Arbitration' was awarded the International Chamber of Commerce (ICC) Institute Prize in 2017 and was published by Cambridge University Press in 2018.

Dr Youseph Farah is an Associate Professor in international dispute resolution at the University of East Anglia, United Kingdom. He is widely published on business and human rights with focus on access to justice. Youseph is an expert on International commercial arbitration, business and human rights, Contract law and Private International Law. Outside academia Youseph advises law firms and corporations with focus on arbitration disputes in the Middle East and in the UK.

Duarte Henriques is a lawyer and arbitrator based in Lisbon, Portugal. Since 1990, he has acted as both counsel and arbitrator in a number of litigation and arbitration cases related to investment disputes, banking & finance, corporate, commercial, distribution and construction disputes. He is a member of the ICC Task Force on Financial Institutions and International Arbitration and of the Task Force on Third-Party Funding in International Arbitration of the International Council for Commercial Arbitration (ICCA) & Queen Mary University of London Law School, London.

Johanna Hoekstra is a Lecturer in the School of Law at the University of Essex, England. She has a PhD from the University of Essex and master degrees from the University of Bordeaux (France) and Birkbeck College (United Kingdom). She previously worked at the University of Greenwich (London). Her research is in the areas of Private International Law, arbitration and business and human rights focusing on international contracts and she is currently finalising her monograph on the legal authority of non-state rules in international commercial contracts.

Clotilde Jourdain-Fortier, Dr. iur., is Professor of Private Law and Criminal Science and Director of the CREDIMI (Research Centre on Global Markets and International Investment Law) at the University of Burgundy, France. She is also Co-Editor-in-chief of the Revue Internationale de Droit Economique and Vice President of the Association Internationale de Droit Économique, an international francophone scientific association. Her main fields of research are international trade law, international and comparative contract law and arbitration.

Carolina da Rocha Morandi is a lawyer qualified in Brazil, Secretary General of AMCHAM Brazil Arbitration and Mediation Center and Chair of INOVARB-AMCHAM. Carolina holds a bachelor's degree in law from the University of São Paulo (Brazil) and an LL.M. degree in International Commercial Arbitration Law from Stockholm University (Sweden).

Joao Ilhão Moreira is a Lecturer at the University of Macau, Faculty of Law, chairing Civil Procedure Law and a DPhil candidate in Law at the University of Oxford, United Kingdom, working on the regulation of international commercial arbitration. Previously, João lectured on and Regulation at University of Oxford (2016-2019) and International Law in the University of Coimbra (2011-2015). He further worked as a lawyer in the arbitration team of law firm PLMJ (2010-2015).

Dr Aislinn O'Connell is a Lecturer in Law in the Department of Law and Criminology at Royal Holloway University of London. She joined Royal Holloway in 2018. She has previously held positions in the School of Management and Law at St Mary's University, Twickenham, after completing her PhD at UCL on the impact of the digital shift on copyright for publishers. She is the secretary of the Association of Law Teachers and a Freeman of the Worshipful Company of Stationers and Newspaper-Makers. Her research covers copyright and intellectual property, focusing on online issues.

Mirèze Philippe is Special Counsel at the Secretariat of ICC International Court of Arbitration, Co-Founder of Arbitral Women and Board member, member of Equal Representation in Arbitration Steering Committee, member of ICCA Diversity Task Force, member of the Council of the American Bar Association (ABA) Section of Dispute Resolution, member of Arbitrator Intelligence's Board of Advisors, member of Association Arbitri's Advisory Board, member of International Journal of Online Dispute Resolution's Editorial Board, fellow of National Centre for Technology and Dispute Resolution (NCTDR), International Council for Online Dispute Resolution's Board member (ICODR).

Christine Sim is an Associate, Herbert Smith Freehills New York LLP. She holds an LLM from MIDS and an LLB from National University of Singapore. She represents parties in international arbitrations. Previously, she represented commercial clients in courts and clerked for arbitrators in investment disputes. She has also presented her public international law research and published articles on provisional measures, investment valuation, maritime boundaries and law of the sea dispute settlement.

Aysem Diker Vanberg is a Senior Lecturer at the University of Greenwich, School Law and Criminology. Her research interests lie in which lie in Competition Law, Information Technology law and Data Protection Law and the regulation of digital technologies. Prior to joining the University of Greenwich (London), she taught at Anglia Ruskin University and at the University of Essex (England). Before moving to the UK, she qualified as a lawyer in Turkey and worked as a lead in-house counsel for multinational companies. She holds a PhD in Competition Law from the University of Essex. Aysem has authored six articles that were published in refereed journals in the area of competition law and IT law. She is currently working on her monograph on the application of EU competition law to digital markets.

Summary of Contents

Table of Contents

Foreword

Reimagining Justice in Arbitration

This book brings together a multifaceted array of scholars discussing 'access to justice in arbitration.' At first glance, one may ask: Is it even possible to provide 'justice' in arbitration? In certain contexts, such as consumer and employment cases, arbitration has gained a reputation for serving the 'big guy' 'repeat-player' companies as they seek to cut off class claims and effectively limit access to remedies in smaller dollar claims.

As I have argued, pre-dispute arbitration clauses have been particularly powerful in the US to perpetuate differential access to remedies and justice in business-to-consumer dealings, producing a 'squeaky wheel system' in which only the most sophisticated squeaky wheels are sufficiently proactive in pursuing their complaints to get the limited assistance, remedies and other benefits that companies provide.[1] Meanwhile, the majority of consumers remain silent because they lack the knowledge, experience, or resources to artfully and actively pursue their interests.[2] Moreover, it is generally not worth the cost for an individual to pursue a required arbitration in smaller dollar claims. As a result, the individuals who already enjoy disproportionate bargaining power due to social or economic status are usually the 'squeaky wheels' that receive the benefits.[3]

However, as authors note in this book, ideas of 'justice' and 'access to justice' can be quite complex. As Rebecca Sandefur noted, not all problems are legal and the meaning of 'justice' depends on how one frames the problem to be solved.[4] As she notes:

---

1. Amy J. Schmitz, *Access to Consumer Remedies in the Squeaky Wheel System*, 39 Pepperdine Law Review 279, 280 (2012).
2. *Ibid.*, 282–283.
3. *See* Peter A. Alces & Jason M. Hopkins, *Carrying a Good Joke Too Far*, 83 Chicago-Kent Law Review 879, 895–96 (2008). *See generally* Amy J. Schmitz, *Secret Consumer Scores and Segmentations: Separating Consumer 'Haves' from 'Have-Nots,'* Michigan State Law Review 1411 (2014).
4. Rebecca L. Sandefur, *Access to What?*, 148 Dædalus 49, 51 (2019).

> When the relevant substantive and procedural norms govern resolution, that resolution is lawful and we have access to justice, whether or not lawyers are involved in the resolution and whether or not the problem comes into contact with any kind of dispute-resolving forum. Access to justice is a good in itself. Its effects reach powerfully into people's lives.[5]

Context matters. What is 'just' in one case may not be 'just' in another, and policymakers and practitioners can shape arbitral processes to better 'fit the forum to the fuss' and help advance access to justice. Creating more accessible and user-friendly means for obtaining justice can have ripple effects that further social justice.

Indeed, technology has provided immense fuel for fashioning procedures to advance access to justice. Some of us have long argued that ODR, including problem diagnosis tools, as well as online negotiation, mediation, arbitration, community courts and variations thereof, provides promise for opening new avenues to remedies due to its low cost, accessibility and ease of use.[6] When properly designed, ODR allows individuals to resolve disputes quickly and cheaply, without the cost or hassle of travel or time away from work. Online processes may also help ease the stress of entering a courthouse and facing a judge or a prosecutor face to face.

Of course, that does not mean that online arbitration is perfect. Online processes may ignore due process and become 'click-through' sifters that may not feel like the type of just resolutions we crave in a system that is largely legal.[7] However, some may argue that quick online arbitrations may provide a type of rough justice that is appropriate for consumers who do not think of their problems as legal and simply want easy access to assistance without needing to consult lawyers or spend time negotiating.[8] Certainly, in the case of crowdsourced Blockchain resolutions, cryptographers 'trust the math' more than they would trust judges in a traditional courthouse. Furthermore, we now see wide variations in online arbitration, especially in the wake of COVID-19 as everything moves online. In many cases, online arbitration is the only means to a remedy with courts mainly closed, or themselves moving online. Even before COVID-19, courts were moving online.[9]

We should use the COVID-19 momentum toward creativity to advance access to justice, with an aim toward using technological and non-technological means for *reimagining* processes that advance access to justice – not for merely *repeating* traditional procedures in an online world. We can imagine how AI may expand chatbots and guided procedures that help, for example, self-represented litigants who

5. *Ibid.*
6. *See generally* Amy J. Schmitz & Colin Rule, The New Handshake: Online Dispute Resolution and the Future of Consumer Protection (ABA, Section of Dispute Resolution, 2017); Amy J. Schmitz, 'Building on OArb Attributes in Pursuit of Justice', *in* Maud Piers & Christian Aschauer (eds), *Arbitration in the Digital Age: The Brave New World of Arbitration* (Cambridge University Press 2018) 182.
7. Rebecca L. Sandefur, *The Fulcrum Point of Equal Access to Justice: Legal and Nonlegal Institutions of Remedy*, 42 Loyola of Los Angeles Law Review. 949, 950–54 (2009).
8. *See* Jean Braucher, *An Informal Resolution Model of Consumer Product Warranty Law*, Wisconsin Law Review 1405, 1405–1406, 1413–1447 (1985).
9. *See* Amy J. Schmitz, *Expanding Access to Remedies Through E-Court Initiatives*, 67 Buffalo Law Review 89, 101–163 (2019).

cannot afford the time and costs of hiring an attorney to assess their cases and assist them with in-person processes. Furthermore, problem diagnosis tools built into ODR programmes may prevent disputes from escalating into lawsuits, and online negotiation and mediation may lead to consensual resolutions. This saves the courts from the administrative burden of trial proceedings and may generate greater process satisfaction.[10]

Congratulations to the authors of this book! This book is foundational for these discussions, as we reimagine arbitration and how it may better advance access to justice. Again, arbitration need not fit one formula. It is uniquely subject to contractual creation and contextual design. To that end, let us all continue the quest to 'fit the forum to the fuss' as we reimagine arbitration in the key of justice.

Amy J. Schmitz
Elwood L. Thomas Missouri Endowed Professor of Law,
University of Missouri School of Law

10. *Ibid.*; *see also* Amy J. Schmitz, *A Blueprint for Online Dispute Resolution System Design*, Journal of Internet Law 3, 3-11 (January 2018); Amy J. Schmitz, *There's an "App" for That: Developing Online Dispute Resolution to Empower Economic Development*, 32 Notre Dame Journal of Law, Ethics and Public Policy 1, 1-45 (2018).

List of Abbreviations

AAA	American Arbitration Association
ADR	Alternative Dispute Resolution
BIT	Bilateral Investment Treaty
CAS	Court of Arbitration for Sport
CEO	Chief Executive Officer
CETA	EU-CANADA Comprehensive and Economic Trade Agreement
CJEU	Court of Justice of the European Union
EC	European Commission
ECHR	European Convention of Human Rights
ECtHR	European Court of Human Rights
EU	European Union
FTA	Free-trade agreement
HKIAC	Hong Kong International Arbitration Centre
IBA	International Bar Association
ICC	International Chamber of Commerce
ICJ	International Court of Justice
ICSID	The International Centre for Settlement of Investment Disputes
IIA	International investment agreement
IP	Intellectual Property
ISDS	Investor-State Dispute Settlement
LCIA	London Court of International Arbitration
Model Law	United Nations Commission on International Trade Law Model Law on International Commercial Arbitration
NYC	1958 New York Convention on Enforcement of Arbitral
ODR	Online Dispute resolution

OECD	Organisation for Economic Co-Operation and Development
OHADA	Organisation pour l'Harmonisation en Afrique du Droit des Affaires
PCA	Permanent Court of Arbitration
SCC	Stockholm Chamber of Commerce Arbitration Institute
SGD	Singapore Dollar
SIAC	The Singapore International Arbitration Centre
TFEU	Treaty on the Functioning of the European Union
UDHR	Universal Declaration of Human Rights
UK	United Kingdom
UN	United Nations
UNCITRAL	United Nations Commission on International Trade Law
UNCITRAL Rules	Arbitration Rules of the United Nations Commission on International Trade Law
UNCTAD	United Nations Conference on Trade and Development
US	United States of America
USD	US Dollars
WIPO	World Intellectual Property Organization

Acknowledgements

This book is a result of ideas developed through seven years in academia doing research and teaching the subject of arbitration. In this small period, we could see that arbitration expanded, and it continues to expand, into areas outside the so called commercial circle. As a result, discussions about fairness and access justice in arbitration, especially in areas where arbitration is not ordinary, became a common topic in our research, which now is reflected in one book.

The journey to make this book started with an idea followed by the initial stage, which was a conference about this topic held at Royal Holloway, University of London, in June 2019. In this conference, several of this book's contributors came together for a rainy day in Egham to talk about access to justice in arbitration. First, we would like to thank the conference participants that joined us in June 2019. Second, we are grateful to Royal Holloway, University of London and University of Middlesex for financing the event. At Royal Holloway, we are would like to thank the support given by Professor Matthew Humphreys, Professor David Denney, Professor Jill Marshal, Mr Robert Jago and Ms Maria Right. At Middlesex University we are grateful for the support given by Professor Erica Howard, Professor Alan Durant, Professor Sarah Bradshaw, Ms Christiana Rose, Ms Joanne Nunn and Professor Laurent Pech.

We would like to thank Wolters Kluwer for giving us an opportunity to publish our work, especially Eleanor Taylor and Kiran Gore. Thank you for your support and patience. In relation to Kluwer, we really appreciate the indication made by Dr Crina Baltag who, from the beginning thought the topic of this book was a good idea and thus, made a bridge between us and Wolters Kluwer.

We gratefully acknowledge the help of all contributors to this edited book. Without you, this title would not be here. Thank you for your contribution.

Leonardo particularly thanks his parents, Professor Licia do Prado Valladares and Dr Icaro Pacheco Alves the Oliveira. You have always been there for me and I am forever thankful for your support. Moreover, Leonardo would like to express gratitude to Dr Caroline Rook. You give me support, love, kindness and you put up with my foolish idiosyncrasies.

Sara would like to dedicate this work to the soul of her mother Floarea Naciu who always believed in the power of knowledge and would like to thank Yasar for his continuous love and support.

Introduction

Leonardo V.P. de Oliveira & Sara Hourani

Access to justice is not a new topic. Since Mauro Cappelletti and Bryant Garth's survey of different methods to promote access to justice was published,[1] making access to justice cheaper and effective has become a legal policy.[2] One of Cappelletti and Garth's ideas was that there were three waves of access to justice. The third wave, called 'The Access to Justice Approach', stated that arbitration would play a significant role in fomenting access to justice. The idea was that people would seek alternatives to the regular court system.

Arbitration has grown exponentially since the publication of Cappelletti and Garth's work, reaching disputes that were traditionally only decided by courts. The guarantee of adequate access to justice is now generating questions about the impact of this expansion. For purely commercial arbitration, such as one between two multinational companies represented by multinational law firms, relaxing the approach to some rights of access to justice might not create a problem to the fairness in the arbitral procedure. However, in a dispute in which the inequality of power is evident, for arbitration to be fair and also a trustworthy sustainable dispute resolution method, relaxing access to justice rights might be a disservice to arbitration.

Taking the example of employment disputes, if the employee is in a high position, such as a CEO, there is a likelihood that this person will able to negotiate their employment contract and afford legal counsel to review the contract. In such cases, CEOs might want to have an arbitration clause in their contract to enjoy the confidentiality feature of arbitration.[3] However, when the employee is not in an advantageous position, imposing arbitration clauses in employment contracts can provide a dispute resolution system aiming at reducing the employee's right to access to justice. The lack of consent when agreeing to 'in or out' arbitrations clauses takes away from the

1. Mauro Cappelletti & Bryant Garth, *Access to Justice: The Newest Wave in the Worldwide Movement to Make Rights Effective*, 27 Buffalo Law Review, 181 (1978).
2. *See* Chapter 1, §1.02.
3. Randall Thomas, Erin O'Hara & Kenneth Martin, *Arbitration Clauses in CEO Employment Contracts: An Empirical and Theoretical Analysis*, 63(4) Vanderbilt Law Review, 959 (2010).

employee its right to access to court. This does not mean that the employee will not have access to some form of justice in arbitration, but if the employee is forced into arbitration without knowing that access to justice in arbitration does not reflect the exact access to justice that they would be entitled in court, such approach might not be helpful to arbitration. Here, there are two different scenarios. The CEO will opt for arbitration because of its features whereas the lower level employee will not have such choice.[4] Also, a public hearing is an inherent feature of access to justice in courts, thus, submitting disputes to arbitration takes away this principle of access to justice. The issue has been highlighted in the US where congresswoman Cherri Bustos introduced in the House of Representatives a bill that 'prohibits a pre-dispute arbitration agreement from being valid or enforceable if it requires arbitration of a sex discrimination dispute'.[5] If an employee sings an employment contract stating that all conflicts during their employment will be solved by arbitration, including cases of sexual harassment, and arbitration will be confidential, the result might be that arbitration will, indirectly, shield sexual predators.

Access to justice has also been expanding via the Internet and emerging technologies. The use of ODR has been particularly popular for dealing with consumer disputes arising from e-commerce. ODR has expanded from being used by e-commerce companies such as eBay and PayPal to being adopted by State judicial systems such as England and Wales and British Columbia for low-value claims.[6] The EU has also enacted Regulation No 524/2013 of the European Parliament and of the Council of 21 May 2013 on online dispute resolution for consumer disputes. According to Article 1 of this text, the aim of the Regulation is to

> contribute to the proper functioning of the internal market, and in particular of its digital dimension by providing a European ODR platform ('ODR platform') facilitating the independent, impartial, transparent, effective, fast and fair out-of-court resolution of disputes between consumers and traders online.

The benefits of consumer ODR are that on one hand, through technology consumers can have access to remedies in a timely and convenient manner.[7] On the other hand, traders will also be able to minimise their costs with a functional dispute resolution system that not only guarantees access to justice to the parties in a dispute but it also puts an end to the dispute.

The expansion of ODR has not stopped there and is undergoing continuous growth. The use of ODR and online arbitration has been gaining ground in business-to-business disputes as technological advancements are increasingly facilitating the

4. Theodor J.St. Antoine, *Labor and Employment Arbitration Today: Mid-Life Crises or New Golden Age?*, 32(1) Ohio State Journal of Dispute Resolution, 1 (2017).
5. The new law, if enacted, will be called Ending Forced Arbitration of Sexual Harassment Act. *See* https://www.congress.gov/bill/116th-congress/house-bill/1443?r=38&s=1 (accessed 18 June 2020).
6. *See* Amy J. Schmitz & Colin Rule, *The New Handshake: Online Dispute Resolution and the Future of Consumer Protection* (American Bar Association, 2017). *Also see* Ethan Katsh & Orna Rabinovich-Einy, *Digital Justice: Technology and the Internet of Disputes* (OUP, 2017).
7. Amy J. Schmitz, *'Drive-Thru' Arbitration in the Digital Age: Empowering Consumers Through Binding ODR*, 62 Baylor Law Review 178 (2010).

resolution of such disputes. For example, the use of Blockchain technology for facilitating arbitration procedures in smart contracts is an emerging field that has been attracting high interest due to its potential in improving access to justice for certain low-value business-to-business disputes. The question though is whether such procedures actually ensure access to justice against the backdrop of the current legal framework.

The topic of access to justice in arbitration is also of particular current interest in Investor-State arbitration. Some new trade agreements are running away from the traditional ISDS system. CETA, for instance, has taken steps towards an investment court to handle disputes arising under the free trade agreement. This has also been epitomised in the case of *Slovak Republic v. Achmea*[8] where it was held by the CJEU that it is incompatible with EU law to include arbitration clauses in intra-EU BITs. The legitimacy crisis revolves around the issue of how to ensure a fair and equitable procedure where a private investor and a State are involved in a dispute. One of the main problems affecting the procedure is that private individuals are given the power to issue arbitral awards against State parties. This problem raises issues related to how to ensure adequate access to justice for investment disputes for both the private investor and the State.

As it can be seen from the three examples addressed above and discussed in this book, the role of access to justice in arbitration has become extremely relevant. As arbitration progresses and policies to facilitate dispute resolution are implemented, the impact of access to justice in arbitration is fundamental to examine its effect in society. Arbitration provides a final binding decision that can be challenged on very limited grounds; thus, with arbitration settling disputes that were originally a prerogative of the judiciary, securing fairness in such procedures is paramount to the survival of arbitration. By not embracing embrace access to justice, distrust will grow on how efficient arbitration, as a mechanism of dispute resolution, is. If arbitration is going to be a substitute for litigation so the court workload can be reduced, it needs to guarantee access to justice.

With the above ideas in mind, this book aims at presenting a collection of studies about access to justice in arbitration. The book is not going to produce an exhaustive examination of all aspects relating to access to justice in arbitration, this would be counterproductive. The idea of the edited collection is to present, for the first time, in one single title, an analysis of the role access to justice plays in arbitration. In doing so, the book initiates a focused debate about access to justice in arbitration that would enable a larger public discussion about the specific role of access to justice in arbitration. It makes a unique contribution to the current international research and practice of arbitration as it looks at the conceptual contribution to the notion of access to justice in arbitration; and it provides a picture of how access to justice works in various types of arbitration. The book is designed to assess how access to justice can be guaranteed in arbitration, generating awareness about the proper use of arbitration to solve disputes. In five parts, the book will show the concerns about access to justice in

8. Case C-284/16 (CJEU, Judgment of 6 March 2018).

arbitration, how they are materialised in a practical scenario and finally, how it is applied in arbitral institutions.

The book's first part brings a conceptual contribution to the notion of access to justice in arbitration and deals with theoretical and conceptual gaps in this area. Leonardo V.P. de Oliveira starts with a conceptual analysis of access to justice and how it should be applied in arbitration. Clotilde Fortier looks at consent as the central part of arbitration and how it relates to access to justice. Joao Ilhão Moreira examines if arbitration can provide a fair, independent and accessible dispute resolution mechanism outside large contractual disputes and Ramona Elisabeta Cirlig assesses the interaction between courts and arbitral tribunals as a guarantor of access to justice.

The second part of the book discusses two specific points in investment disputes. Berk Dermikol looks at the possibility of bringing an autonomous claim based on the NYC in investment treaty arbitration as a form of access to justice. Crina Baltag evaluates the issue of access to justice and non-disputing parties - *amici curiae*- in investment law and arbitration.

In the third part, access to justice in specific types of disputes submitted to arbitration is scrutinised. Carolina Morandi presents a case study of access to justice in labour and employment arbitration in light of the Brazilian and the US experiences. Ian Blackshaw looks at how sports disputes submitted to CAS have been dealing with the question of access to justice. Johanna Hoekstra and Aysem Diker Vanberg examine access to justice with regards to competition law in the EU with a view to determine whether arbitration can lower barriers. Lastly, Youseph Farah addresses the use of unilaterally binding arbitration as a mechanism to improve access to justice in business-related human rights violations.

Part four reports on two aspects of technology and access to justice. Mirèze Philippe looks at ODR as a method to guarantee access to justice whilst Sara Hourani investigates how Blockchain-based arbitration can be used to improve access to justice.

Lastly, the book presents the view of how two arbitral institutions deal with the question of costs and access to justice, and how the rules of one arbitral institution provide access to justice guarantees. Aislinn O'Connell assesses access to justice under WIPO's Arbitration Rules whilst Christine Sim examines costs at SIAC and Duarte Henriques and Avani Agarwal do the same in relation to ICSID.

The book has dealt with a number of crucial issues facing the right of access to justice and its connection to arbitration. At this tumultuous time of change, the assessment of the legitimacy of arbitration and the extent to which arbitration offers the opportunity for access to resolve disputes is of utmost importance. The book has provided the perspectives of academics, practitioners and practitioners who work in arbitral institutions from all corners of the world on these issues. This rich and diverse contribution enabled the book to bring critical and innovative discussions of the topic from a theoretical, contextual and practical outlook.

Part I Theoretical Aspects of Access to Justice in Arbitration

CHAPTER 1
To What Degree Should Access to Justice Be Secured in Arbitration?

Leonardo V.P. de Oliveira[*]

Access to Justice is not a new theme in legal theory and practice, it is a topic that has been subject of extensive academic and policy debate. However, the degree to which access to justice should be secured in arbitration is lacking examination. As arbitration becomes a more popular method of dispute resolution, expanding beyond the commercial circle, it is imperative to look at access to justice in arbitration more widely. Thus, this chapter looks at the general meaning of access to justice to evaluate if and how it can be guaranteed in arbitration. The study is done by scrutinizing the concept of access to justice and contextualizing it to the nature of arbitration. As arbitration is a procedure used to obtain justice, when the discussion about access to justice is taken within arbitration, procedural justice becomes a foundation to evaluate the degree in which access to justice can be guaranteed in arbitration. Therefore, procedural justice is also assessed together with the concept of access to justice and the nature of arbitration. At this point, a case is made that for access to justice to be guaranteed in arbitration, some form of procedural justice needs to be secured and the degree in which this is assured, will depend on the position and consent given by the parties in the arbitral process.

§1.01 INTRODUCTION

Access to justice is not a new theme in legal theory and practice; it is a topic that has been the subject of extensive academic and policy debate.[1] However, the degree to

* The author would like to thank Dr Ryan Hill and Dr Sufyan El Droubi for the comments on the early draft of this chapter. All mistakes of interpretation and translations are the author's own.
1. *See* §1.02 and §1.03.

which access to justice should be secured in arbitration is lacking examination. The analysis of access to justice in arbitration has mainly focused on specific types of arbitration,[2] without a theoretical basis to scrutinize the degree in which access to justice should be implemented generally in arbitration, be it domestic or international.

As arbitration becomes a more popular method of dispute resolution, expanding beyond the commercial circle, it is imperative to look at access to justice in arbitration more widely. Hence, this chapter will provide a conceptual analysis of access to justice to examine what is required in arbitration if access to justice is to be guaranteed. Access to justice is not just having physical or digital access to a system of adjudication, but also having a procedure securing a fair process. This leads the way to two components of access to justice: first the existence of means to have access; and second, fairness in the process adopted for adjudication, that is, procedural justice. Because arbitration is a procedure used to obtain justice, when the discussion about access to justice is taken within arbitration, procedural justice becomes a foundation to evaluate the degree in which access to justice can be guaranteed in arbitration.

Therefore, in this chapter, the case will be made that in arbitration, some form of procedural justice is essential if access to justice is to be secured in the arbitral process. To reach this conclusion, the chapter will start by looking at the development of access to justice as a concept in the context of the conventional system of law and adjudication at court. This will first be done by looking at the background of access to justice, and the modern foundations for its concept will be defined after. Once the conceptual understanding of access to justice has been explained in the context of adjudication in court, a distinction between court adjudication and arbitration will be discussed to set the scene for the analyses of the nature of arbitration. This will be done by describing the theoretical underpinnings that provide ways in which we might understand the nature of arbitration. At this stage, the debate will shift to a discussion of procedural justice where its theoretical aspects will be examined. The chapter will conclude that access to justice in arbitration should be guaranteed in different ways depending on the position and consent given by the parties in the arbitral process.

§1.02 BACKGROUND FOR THE DEVELOPMENT OF ACCESS TO JUSTICE

Historically, features of access to justice, such as the right to access to court, can be found in early legal instruments, going all the way back to the Magna Carta.[3] Other features, such as the right of an individual to effectively challenge a criminal charge in

2. For instance, *see* Jonnette Watson Hamilton, Pre-Dispute Consumer Arbitration Clauses: Denying Access to Justice?, 51 McGill Law Journal, 693 (2006); Francesco Francioni, Access to Justice, Denial of Justice and International Investment Law, 20(3) The European Journal of International Law, 729 (2009), Mark D. Gough, 'Employment Lawyers and Mandatory Arbitration: Facilitating or Forestalling Access to Justice?', in David Lewin and Paul Gollan (eds) Managing and Resolving Workplace Conflict, Advances in Industrial and Labor Relations vol. 22 (Emerald Group Publishing Limited 2016) and Omri Ben-Shahar, The Paradox of Access Justice, And Its Application to Mandatory Arbitration, 83 University of Chicago Law Review 1755 (2016).
3. Clause 40 of the Magana Carta stated that: '[t]o no one will we sell, to no one deny or delay right or justice.'

court was secured already in the Sixth Amendment of the US Constitution 1791, which provides that anyone accused of a crime has the right to a trial and the '[a]ssistance of Counsel for his defence'.[4] Similarly, the French Constitution of 1791 stated that all citizens had the '[l]iberty to address individually signed petitions to the constituted authorities'.[5] These early examples were the beginning of a process to both furnish and regulate features of access to justice. They provided some principles of access to justice such as access to court and the right to be represented by counsel. However, at the time such instruments came into force, not all citizens were treated the same way and only certain classes of citizens had access to such rights.[6]

By the twentieth century, however, a shift was happening over both the place of justice within legal systems and its substantive requirements. For example, guarantees that those unable to afford legal representation will be able to have such representation given to them, free of charge, was being more broadly applied. In England, for example, the development started with the Poor Prisoners Defence Act 1903 which provided a *right* of legal aid for qualifying prisoners but restricted such right to trials on indictment. Seventeen years later, the Poor Prisoners' Defence Act 1930 expanded the reach of legal aid to preliminary inquiries and to cases heard summarily before magistrates' courts. Three years later, the Summary Jurisdiction (Appeals) Act 1933 regulated legal aid rights for criminal cases and sixteen years later, the law went beyond the criminal sphere. The Legal Aid and Advice Act 1949 created a system of legal aid in civil courts and civil proceedings in magistrates' courts. At this stage, in England, parties in criminal and civil cases were guaranteed the right to have legal representation supported by the state when they did not have the funds for it.

At the international level, in 1948, the UN General Assembly approved the Universal Declaration of Human Rights which calls for the right to court and a fair trial.[7] The right also appeared in the 1950 European Convention of Human Rights,[8] the 1966

4. The full wording of the amendment states: 'In all criminal prosecutions, the accused shall enjoy the right to a speedy and public trial, by an impartial jury of the State and district wherein the crime shall have been committed, which district shall have been previously ascertained by law, and to be informed of the nature and cause of the accusation; to be confronted with the witnesses against him; to have compulsory process for obtaining witnesses in his favor, and to have the Assistance of Counsel for his defence.'
5. Title I of the 1791 Constitution. Original in French: 'La Constitution garantit pareillement, comme droits naturels et civils: ... La liberté d'adresser aux autorités constituées des pétitions signées individuellement.'
6. For instance, slaves were not treated as citizens and women were not equal to men.
7. Article 8 of the Declaration states: 'Everyone has the right to an effective remedy by the competent national tribunals for acts violating the fundamental rights granted him by the constitution or by law.' Article 9 of the Declaration says: 'Everyone is entitled in full equality to a fair and public hearing by an independent and impartial tribunal, in the determination of his rights and obligations and of any criminal charge against him.'
8. Article 6(1) of the convention provides: 'In the determination of his civil rights and obligations or of any criminal charge against him, everyone is entitled to a fair and public hearing within a reasonable time by an independent and impartial tribunal established by law. Judgment shall be pronounced publicly but the press and public may be excluded from all or part of the trial in the interests of morals, public order or national security in a democratic society, where the interests of juveniles or the protection of the private life of the parties so require, or to the extent strictly necessary in the opinion of the court in special circumstances where publicity would prejudice the interests of justice.'

International Covenant on Civil and Political Rights,[9] the 1969 American Convention of Human Rights[10] and the 1981 African Chart on Human and Peoples Rights.[11] Access to court, in these documents, did not simply refer to have means to access a court. They also carried within them conditions needed to ensure that any trial was fair, that justice is served through the outcome of the disputes, but also through the path to reach the outcome. As such, the conditions for fairness included such things as an independent and impartial tribunal, a public hearing, the right to present your case, the right to be heard and the right to be assisted by legal counsel. Notably, the documents clearly viewed ensuring justice as central to the trial purpose and process.[12]

This led the way to more fully defining the requirements of the right to access to justice and also, under what circumstances the right can be secured. The development of the right to access to justice consolidated the view that such a right is fundamental to promote democracy and fairness. A society cannot be just if its members are not able to seek remedies for the violation of their rights. In this sense, it is also relevant to mention that access to justice is part of sustainable development. The UN, in 2015, adopted the 2030 Agenda for Sustainable Development which 'provides a shared blueprint for peace and prosperity for people and the planet, now and into the future'.[13] The Agenda for Sustainable Development has seventeen goals, with number sixteen being to '[p]romote peaceful and inclusive societies for sustainable development, provide access to justice for all and build effective, accountable and inclusive institutions at all levels'.[14] On a domestic level, it is common to find within state constitutions a provision guaranteeing access to justice as a fundamental right.[15]

9. Article 14(1) of the Covenant says: 'All persons shall be equal before the courts and tribunals. In the determination of any criminal charge against him, or of his rights and obligations in a suit at law, everyone shall be entitled to a fair and public hearing by a competent, independent and impartial tribunal established by law. The press and the public may be excluded from all or part of a trial for reasons of morals, public order (*ordre public*) or national security in a democratic society, or when the interest of the private lives of the parties so requires, or to the extent strictly necessary in the opinion of the court in special circumstances where publicity would prejudice the interests of justice; but any judgment rendered in a criminal case or in a suit at law shall be made public except where the interest of juvenile persons otherwise requires or the proceedings concern matrimonial disputes or the guardianship of children.'
10. Article 8(1) of the convention says: 'Every person has the right to a hearing, with due guarantees and within a reasonable time, by a competent, independent, and impartial tribunal, previously established by law, in the substantiation of any accusation of a criminal nature made against him or for the determination of his rights and obligations of a civil, labor, fiscal, or any other nature.'
11. Article 7(1) of the Chart provides: 'Every individual shall have the right to have his cause heard. This comprises: 1 The right to an appeal to competent national organs against acts of violating his fundamental rights as recognized and guaranteed by conventions, laws, regulations and customs in force; 2 The right to be presumed innocent until proved guilty by a competent court or tribunal; 3 The right to defence, including the right to be defended by counsel of his choice; 4 The right to be tried within a reasonable time by an impartial court or tribunal.'
12. Article 6(3)(c) of the ECHR states that everyone has the right 'to defend himself in person or through legal assistance of his own choosing or, if he has not sufficient means to pay for legal assistance, to be given it free when the interests of justice so require'.
13. https://sustainabledevelopment.un.org/sdgs (accessed 16 June 2020).
14. https://sustainabledevelopment.un.org/sdg16 (accessed 16 June 2020).
15. For instance, the Angolan Constitution, Article 29(1) states: 'Everyone shall be ensured access to the law and the courts in order to defend their legally protected rights and interests, and justice shall not be denied to anyone due to a lack of financial means.' Similar provisions can be

Additionally, different government's bodies adopt policies to promote access to justice. In the US Department of Justice, there is an Office for Access to Justice.[16] It was established in 2010 with its goal to 'help the justice system efficiently deliver outcomes that are fair and accessible to all, irrespective of wealth and status'.[17] The EU has a similar approach and its Agency for Fundamental Rights has as one of its themes access to justice.[18] The agency 'seeks to provide evidence-based advice to policymakers at EU and National levels in order to improve awareness of and access to justice'.[19] In the UK, an important moment for the reassessment of access to justice came in 1996 when Lord Woolf published his report on Access to Justice.[20] The report aimed at changing civil procedures rules, reducing costs of litigation and excluding complexities, all of which were made to improve access to justice. The question of reducing costs was paramount and innovative, however, its effects were subjected to doubts.[21] A method to improve case management was to encourage the resolution of disputes through alternative dispute resolution (ADR) before they reached litigation.[22] The report does not specify the type of ADR, giving the idea that ADR should encompass all its different types of dispute resolution methods. Furthermore, it has been argued that access to justice should be a central concern of legal education.[23] Although universities are now providing some type of assistance to the public through law clinics, it is not common for the subject to be addressed as a core topic in the teaching curriculum.[24]

By recognizing justice as an entitlement owed to everyone, access to justice became an essential element of the rule of law.[25] In explaining the requirements

found in the Constitution of Bhutan (Article 21(1)); The Cape Verde Constitution (Article 20(1)); The Ecuadorian Constitution (Article 75); the Mexican Constitution (Article 17); The Finish Constitution (Section 21); The Dutch Constitution (Article 17); The Indian Constitution (Section 39A); and the Japanese Constitution (Article 32).

16. In https://www.justice.gov/archives/atj (accessed 04 April 2019).
17. *Ibid.*
18. In https://fra.europa.eu/en/theme/access-justice (accessed 04 April 2019).
19. *Ibid.*
20. Harry Wolf, Access to justice final report to the Lord Chancellor on the civil justice system in England and Wales (HMSO 1996).
21. There was a possibility that even if the recommendations were implemented, lawyers would still be able to use litigation for profit, diminishing the impact of the report. *See* A.A.S. Zuckerman, *Lord Wollf's Access to Justice: Plus Ça change...*, 59 MLR 773 787 (1996): 'Although Lord Woolf seeks to confer a power on lay clients to resist lawyers' tendency to push up costs, clients are unlikely to be more successful in this regard than they are at present...Clients find it difficult to resist costs, not for lack of information about costs but because they cannot judge for themselves whether any proposed investment in procedure is worthwhile. For making such a judgment they will, of necessity, continue to depend on their lawyers, and no improvement in information as to how the costs are calculated will change this.'
22. Wolf (*supra* n. 20) Section 2, Chapter 1 7(d) and 16(c).
23. Donald Nicolson, Legal Education, Ethics and Access to Justice: Forging Warriors for Justice in a Neo-Liberal World, 22(1) International Journal of Legal Profession, 51, 52 (2015).
24. Deborah L. Rhode, *Whatever Happened to Access to Justice*, 42 Loyola of Los Angeles Law Review, 869, 905 (2009).
25. Hazel Genn, *What is Civil Justice For? Reform, ADR, and Access to Justice*, 24 Yale Journal of Law & the Humanities, 397, 411 (2012). The assessment of access to justice and the rule of law is also employed by the UN in the United Nations and the Rule of Law (in https://www.un.org/ruleoflaw/thematic-areas/access-to-justice-and-rule-of-law-institutions/access-to-justice/ (accessed 04 April 2019).

deriving from the rule of law, Lord Bingham argued that access to a procedure was the sixth principle of the rule of law because 'means must be provided for resolving, without prohibitive cost or inordinate delay, bona fide civil disputes which the parties themselves are unable to resolve'.[26] Moreover, '[Q]uestions of legal right and liability should be resolved by the application of the law and not by the exercise of discretion'.[27] The link between access to means of redress and the rule of law was debated in *R (On the application of Unison) v. Lord Chancellor*.[28] Deciding the case, the UK Supreme Court ruled that fees imposed by employment tribunals and employment appeals tribunals restricted access to justice. Lord Reed asserted that access to court, as a part of access to justice, was a constitutional right 'inherent in the rule of law'.[29] He explained that the meaning of rule of law is not always clear and there is an assumption that when the judiciary administer justice, it is merely providing a service to users; and 'the provision of those services is of value only to the users themselves and those who are remunerated for their participation in the proceedings'.[30] Rejecting this assumption, Lord Reed argued that access to courts is a mechanism to maintain the rule of law irrespective of litigants involved in specific cases. Laws are made by Parliament and, together with the common law, their applicability is assured by courts. Therefore, if there is no access to courts, 'laws are liable to become dead letter, the work done by Parliament may be rendered nugatory, and the democratic election of Members of Parliament may become a meaningless charade'.[31] Accordingly, access to court, which is part of access to justice, is in the centre of the rule of law. It not only provides a path for parties to seek justice, but it has an *erga omnes* effect. Decisions made by courts will guide society on how the law is applied; therefore, restricting access to courts diminishes the rule of law and it removes from access to justice one of its basic principles. If courts cannot decide quarrels in society, it defeats the purpose of the rule of law and therefore there is no access to justice. Other relevant features in Bingham's analysis of the rule of law include that 'judicial procedures should be fair and open'.[32] Inherent, therefore, in the rule of law is an independent and impartial judiciary along with any procedural guarantees in the judicial process necessary to ensure justice can be delivered.

§1.03 UNDERSTANDING ACCESS TO JUSTICE

Access to justice means more than just getting a day in court. It also secures that justice will be an essential part of the procedure in court. In this sense, it is not enough to provide means for legal aid, it is also important to have a procedure shaped in a way that mitigates disadvantages between the parties. This inequality of arms between

26. Tom Bingham, *The Rule of Law* (Penguin Books 2011) 85.
27. *Ibid.*
28. *R (On the application of Unison) v. Lord Chancellor* [2017] UKSC 51. Though the case did not assess access to justice per se, it evaluated one of its main dimensions, the access to court.
29. *Ibid.*, paragraphs 65 and 66.
30. *Ibid.*
31. *Ibid.*, paragraph 68.
32. Bingham (*supra* n. 26).

parties demands a qualitative balance in the procedure and not merely getting through the courtroom door. Therefore, it is important for parties to have their day in court, but it is paramount that such 'day' will be following a procedure that is employed in a fair manner. This is the guarantee of procedural justice which makes the process fair and protects the right to access to justice regardless of the dispute's result.[33] To understand the concept of access to justice, this section will first look at the survey on access to justice made by Mauro Cappelletti [A]. From this evaluation, a critical analysis of its concept will be made [B] to set up the context of access to justice for its later study in arbitration.

[A] Cappelletti's Access to Justice Survey

The Florence Access to Justice Project, led by Mauro Cappelletti, provided a world survey about access to justice, with reports from twenty-three jurisdictions.[34] In this survey, Cappelletti evaluated how access to justice was being employed, at the time, through a comparative study based on data provided by the twenty-three reports. When defining access to justice, Cappelletti argued that it 'served to focus two basic purposes of the legal system',[35] being equal access to all and 'results that are individually and socially just'.[36] Proper access to justice, that is, an equal and just access, emerged from a new class of 'social rights'[37] which 'presupposes mechanisms for their effective protection'.[38] Access to justice needed to be effective and achieving such effectiveness was not simple.[39] Therefore, Cappelletti looked at barriers to access to justice gathered from the collected data and identified common obstacles. These included costs of litigation, capability of parties and problems with diffuse interests, such as consumer and environmental protection.[40]

To overcome these barriers, he proposed three major steps called waves of access to justice. The first wave was to foment access to justice to the poor.[41] If society was to secure equality of arms, access to legal remedies must be affordable to all. With legal aid, everyone, in theory, could have their day in court. However, this does not suffice. It is also necessary to have an adequate representation so a party could obtain a fair

33. *R (On the application of Unison)* (*supra* n. 28), paragraph 29, Lord Reed asserted: 'More fundamentally, the right of access to justice, both under domestic law and under EU law, is not restricted to the ability to bring claims which are successful. Many people, even if their claims ultimately fail, nevertheless have arguable claims which they have a right to present for adjudication.'
34. Mauro Cappelletti and Bryant Garth, Access to Justice: The Newest Wave in the Worldwide Movement to Make Rights Effective, 27 Buffalo Law Review, 181 (1978).
35. *Ibid.*, 182.
36. *Ibid.*
37. Such rights were reflections of the acceptance and positive consolidation of the international human rights instruments enacted before the production of the report.
38. Mauro Cappelletti, *Access to Justice: Comparative General Report*, 40 Rabel Zeitschrift für ausländisches und internationales Privatrecht, 669, 672 (1976).
39. *Ibid.*, 673. The meaning of effectiveness in this context is to provide a 'complete equality of arms', which is utopian.
40. Cappelletti (*supra* n. 34) 186-196.
41. *Ibid.*, 197.

result to their claims. The second wave addressed diffuse interests, that is, not just the interest of the poor but the interest of anyone affected by a violation of a legal right.[42] This was to be done through the types of procedures encompassing several parties, such as class actions, in which collective rights are examined at the same time instead of each individual, on its own, starting a claim. The last wave, named access to justice approach,[43] analyses the implementation of the two waves, but it goes further. For the two waves to be effective, new legal procedures are required to facilitate disputes, and even prevent them from materializing. The proposals were to reform litigation procedures with more specialized courts and the use of ADR mechanisms, such as arbitration.[44]

The work of Cappelletti is commendable and it was the first of its kind. The first wave became one of the ways to analyse access to justice, but it is important to emphasize that access to justice has social and philosophical dimensions. Moreover, a critique needs to be made if one looks at access to justice solely in relation to those who cannot afford to pay for legal services, as if access to justice was only a problem of the less fortunate.[45] This is not an invalid view as it can appear that access to justice is only a problem if one of the parties is poor.[46] However, access to justice is not limited to being able to afford legal fees. It also embodies a proper and *effective* access to a court with a procedure that ensures certain fundamental conditions for justice, such as the rule of law. This can be seen in Cappelletti's idea of the third wave where effective access to justice requires an effective mechanism to provide justice in a fair manner. Other guarantees, such as due process, the right to present your case, and to challenge claims made against a person are paramount to assure access to justice and are thus, implicit components of access to justice.

---

42. *Ibid.*, 209.
43. *Ibid.*, 223.
44. *Ibid.*, 232.
45. Catherine R. Albiston and Rebecca L. Sandfur, *Expanding the Empirical Study of Access to Justice*, Wisconsin Law Review, 101, 110 (2013).
46. Instruments with the label access to justice tend to give such impression. For instance, the Hague Conference on International Private Law in its 1980 Convention on International Access to Justice that regulates legal aid. Article 1 of the convention states: 'Nationals of any Contracting State and persons habitually resident in any Contracting State shall be entitled to legal aid for court proceedings in civil and commercial matters in each Contracting State on the same conditions as if they themselves were nationals of and habitually resident in that State. Persons to whom paragraph 1 does not apply, but who formerly had their habitual residence in a Contracting State in which court proceedings are to be or have been commenced, shall nevertheless be entitled to legal aid as provided by paragraph 1 if the cause of action arose out of their former habitual residence in that State. In States where legal aid is provided in administrative, social or fiscal matters, the provisions of this Article shall apply to cases brought before the courts or tribunals competent in such matters.' The same approach is taken by the Access to Justice Act 1999 in the UK. *See also* Deborah L. Rhode, *Access to Justice* (Oxford University Press 2004) 3, and Maurice Hayes, *Access to Justice*, 99 (393) Studies: An Irish Quarterly Review, 29, 30-31 (2010).

[B] Conceptualizing Access to Justice

Access to justice is not a straightforward concept. Cappelletti thought that access to justice should be equal access for all with just results. Such access derived from the emergence of social rights. Thus, the more social rights individuals have, the greater the need for a process that guarantees an adequate path to attain justice. Lord Bingham saw access to justice as a feature of the rule of law. His point was not far from Cappelletti's in the sense that it is imperative for means to be implemented, in a timely and cost-effective manner, and for disputes to be resolved fairly, when parties are unable to solve quarrels without the interference of a third party. As a result, one interpretation is that access to justice needs expansion to secure the protection of social rights, whereas the other view is that access to justice is paramount for the operation of the rule of law. Additionally, access to justice engages with public interest, as it is in the interest of the public to have the capacity to seek redress for violation of their rights. Another complication with the concept of access to justice is that its features cannot be mixed with its main idea. Access to court is part of access to justice but the latter is larger than the former. From the discussion so far, it can be said that access to justice has two main areas of concern: access to some form of procedure for dispute resolution; and conditions that the procedure adopted for dispute resolution will be able, as far as possible, to produce a just outcome.

Starting with the first area of concern, access to justice secures that parties will have access to the dispute resolution procedure. This means that parties must be able to have access to courts, whether physically or, in modern times, in a digital format. The adjudication process should be available to all if they would like to access it. That is when access to justice looks at legal aid. Legal representation is needed to claim such right and legal fees are not cheap, hence, means should be provided for individuals to have funds to obtain access to courts. This is when legal aid, normally supported by the state, comes to play as one of the sources to assure poor parties can have their right to access some form of procedure for dispute resolution. In this sense, a distinct approach to how access to the courts should be achieved is presented by Cornford[47] where he argues that 'the work of private legal profession would have to be socialized'. [48] This claim he supports through a comparison with access to the National Health Service (NHS) in the UK. The right to health is a social right, hence, it is the government's duty to provide healthcare that is accessible to all. The UK approach is that this is achieved by, among other things, ensuring that access to the NHS is free. Using the same argument, the implementation of the socialized access to justice would have to be done by socializing the Bar, 'turning it into a salaried public service'.[49] Cornford also argues that the solicitor's profession would be socialized and in a similar structure as the

47. Tom Cornford, 'The Meaning of Access to Justice', in Ellie Palmer, Tom Cornford, Audrey Guinchard and Yseult Marique (eds), *Access to Justice Beyond the Policies and Politics of Austerity* (Hart 2016).
48. *Ibid.*, 36.
49. *Ibid.*

socialized Bar, there would be free advice for actions such as 'mediation, conveyancing, writing wills, notarization of documents, etc'.[50] This view is about funding access to courts and as a result, providing access to justice free at the point of delivery. The idea has its merit, but Cornford recognizes that achieving the socialization of the legal profession is unlikely.[51]

The second area of concern deals with procedural conditions to assure a just outcome. Here access to justice involves a number of basic rights which are essential for justice to be achieved. There is initially, a requirement of a legal system conforming to the rule of law. As ramification of the rule of law, the procedure must deliver guarantees of natural justice and the right to a fair trial. In that sense, due process must be in place by giving the parties the opportunity to have participation rights such as right to be heard, right to call witnesses, right to challenge any charge against one, right to have an impartial adjudicator, to be able to understand the process (transparency) and, in a timely manner, to have a decision for their dispute. Additionally, it is important to remove obstacles that can be used in the procedure to shake the balance between the parties. If there is evidence of inequality of arms between the litigants, access to justice should secure that procedure tools can be used to bring procedural balance to the parties in the dispute. A weaker party might be able to have access to court but if in court, such party is not protected, it will be pointless to just get through the courtroom door.

Access to justice involves the support of access to courts, financial care for legal representation, the rule of law and due process. A legal system providing these things through its adjudication processes, therefore, would meet the requirements of access to justice for those making use of this avenue of dispute resolution. What, however, of ADR mechanisms? Is the situation the same or the requirements identical to ensure these too deliver access to justice? To answer such questions, the differences between court litigation and arbitration need to be addressed.

§1.04 ARBITRATION AND COURT LITIGATION

In this section, a summary of the differences between arbitration and court litigation will be made. The aim is not to cover every aspect of arbitration and court litigation but to contextualize both forms of dispute resolution in relation to access to justice. This is started by answering the following question: Are the same conditions appropriate for ensuring access to justice where arbitration, rather than adjudication at court, is the chosen method to resolve a dispute?

At first sight, the answer would be 'why not'! The common factors between arbitration and litigation in court would lead to the conclusion that the same conditions should be present in both mechanisms of dispute resolution. Both systems require access to a procedure, the possibility of an outcome in favour of either party (not a

50. *Ibid.*
51. *Ibid.*, 38. Cornford states: 'Socialisation of the legal profession will not happen because there is no political will to do it and, what is simply the reverse side of the same coin, political opposition to it would be strong.'

predetermined outcome) and the need to deliver what a reasonable person can identify as justice (even if a party is not happy with the outcome). Nevertheless, when the differences in arbitration and litigation in court are highlighted, the 'why not' might not be an obvious answer. Characteristics of the arbitral procedure have the potential to interfere with or displace some of the procedural requirements expected at court litigation, yet these features are, in many cases, key reasons people choose arbitration over adjudication.

Litigation in court is the standard form of dispute resolution. Understanding how access to justice operates in court can normally be found by reference to case law, legislation and various procedural rules relating to different aspects of law, such as civil, criminal, family, etc. Also, constitutions will secure access to justice to parties as well as the rights deriving from access to justice. As a result of this constitutional right, policymakers will implement measures indorsing and guaranteeing access to justice. Thus, in court, access to justice is assured to the parties by law. A good example can be found in the Fourteenth Amendment of the US Constitution when it states that '[n]o state shall make or enforce any law which shall abridge the privileges or immunities of citizens of the United States; nor shall any state deprive any person of life, liberty, or property, without due process of law'. The due process clause is there to assure a fair process and that parties in court litigation, will be entitled to procedural safeguards. A process in court is covered by standards giving the parties a day in court with a public hearing and a right to a remedy. Once a claim is triggered, the adjudicator has to follow the procedures established by law and they cannot deviate from access to justice guarantees.

In arbitration the sources of access to justice are not entirely the same. The arbitral case law does not have an effect of a binding precedent. It can have a persuasive character; nevertheless, it is not the same as a court case embodied by the principle of *stare decisis*. Additionally, confidentiality is an attractive feature of arbitration, making the content of the decisions unavailable to the public. The features of access to justice in arbitration can also be found in domestic or international legislation. In domestic legislation, it is common for an arbitration act to state that parties will be treated equally, that they will have the opportunity to present their case, that arbitrators have to be impartial and independent and that decisions should be reasoned.[52] In the international arena, for example, the same rights can be found in the Model Law[53] and the OHADA Uniform Act on Arbitration.[54] Furthermore, if the arbitration is institutional, it is likely that the rules of the institution will provide for the matching safeties found in domestic and international legislation.[55] Be that as it may,

52. *See* for instance: Sections 1036, 1042(1), 1046 and 1054(2) of the German Code of Civil Procedure; Articles 18 (1)(ii), 25 and 39(2) of the Japanese Arbitration Act 2003 and Article 15(3), 26 and 43(2) of the Egyptian Arbitration Act 1994.
53. Articles 12, 18 and 21(2) of the Model Law.
54. Articles 7, 9 and 20 of the OHADA Uniform Act on Arbitration.
55. At least this can be seen in well-known arbitral institutions such as: ICC Arbitration Rules 2017 Articles 11, 22(4) and 32(2); LCIA Arbitration Rules 2014 Articles 5.3 and 14.4(i) and SIAC Arbitration Rules 2016 Articles 14.4 and 32.4.

access to justice in arbitration differs from access to justice in courts because arbitration originates from the agreement of the parties. If the parties decide that court adjudication is not how their disputes will be solved and, thus, they agree on an arbitral procedure to settle their impasses, they will have the opportunity to influence more the process adopted in arbitration as opposed to the one in court. In arbitration, parties have more input in the arbitral process with, for instance, the capacity to choose the arbitrators, agree upon deadlines, apply a law different from the jurisdiction where the arbitration is taking place and decide how evidence will be assessed.

State courts are bound by due process. The same should be said about arbitration, but the differences between litigation in court and in arbitration could not, at first sight, lead to the conclusion that access to justice in courts is employed in the same manner in arbitration. While litigation in courts and arbitration fulfil the same goal (that is, to provide a binding mechanism to solve disputes) when a conflict is submitted to court, the procedure adopted does not enjoy the same flexibility if the dispute would have been submitted to arbitration. In arbitration, parties can decide upon the procedural measures to be adopted by the tribunal,[56] if there should be hearings in the procedure[57] and that the award does not need to be reasoned.[58] Such differences would indicate that the way access to justice is applied in courts could not follow the same steps in arbitration. After all, the flexibility of arbitration could reduce the degree in which access to justice is guaranteed. This is not entirely accurate: access to justice should be respected in arbitration. However, this cannot be done by adopting the identical procedural dimensions of access to justice in a court procedure. What is better, is to attune the access to justice perspective to the different nature of arbitration, which is a private method of dispute resolution and rooted in the consent of the parties. Although arbitration and litigation in court deliver a procedure by which disputes can be resolved, the procedure is not the same. Consequently, access to justice in arbitration will have similar parameters to that in court but it might not be employed in the same manner.

Furthermore, relying solely on court litigation is no longer sustainable.[59] As the world population increases, more disputes will arise, and other forms of conflict

56. This is the case of Article 22(2) of the ICC Arbitration Rules 2017: '(2) In order to ensure effective case management, the arbitral tribunal, after consulting the parties, may adopt such procedural measures as it considers appropriate, provided that they are not contrary to any agreement of the parties.'
57. This is the case of Section 52 of the Hong Kong Arbitration Act (Arbitration Ordinance (Cap. 609): 'Article 24 of UNCITRAL Model Law (Hearings and written proceedings) Article 24 of the UNCITRAL Model Law, the text of which is set out below, has effect – "Article 24. Hearings and written proceedings (1) Subject to any contrary agreement by the parties, the arbitral tribunal shall decide whether to hold oral hearings for the presentation of evidence or for oral argument, or whether the proceedings shall be conducted on the basis of documents and other materials. However, unless the parties have agreed that no hearings shall be held, the arbitral tribunal shall hold such hearings at an appropriate stage of the proceedings, if so requested by a party.'
58. This is the case of Section 1054(2) of the German Code of Civil Procedure: '(2) The award shall state the reasons upon which it is based, unless the parties have agreed that no reasons are to be given or the award is an award on agreed terms under section 1053.'
59. *See* for instance Vivek Maru, *Access to Justice and Legal Empowerment: A Review of World Bank Practice*, https://openknowledge.worldbank.org/bitstream/handle/10986/18102/518430NWP0Acce10Box342050B01PUBLIC1.pdf?sequence=1&isAllowed=y (accessed 10 May 2019).

resolution should be used to ensure a timely resolution of disputes. This was predicted by Capelletti's third wave and that is where arbitration initially found a place in the access to justice debate. At the time of the access to justice project, arbitration was not as popular as it is today. Also, arbitration was seen as a quicker and cheaper process to solve disputes,[60] hence, promoting it as an alternative to court was a good solution to foment access to justice. Nevertheless, arbitration is no longer perceived to be fast or cheap; on the contrary, it has become an expensive form of out-of-court litigation.[61] Today, purely commercial disputes, such as one between two multinational companies represented by multinational law firms are ordinary in arbitration. As a result, because the parties are well represented and making a clear choice of how their dispute resolution system will be employed, they are aware that access to justice in arbitration might not be applicable in the same manner as in court litigation. To better understand this proposition, it is necessary to look at the nature of arbitration.

§1.05 THE NATURE OF ARBITRATION

Arbitration is not a new technique, in fact, arbitration has even been traced back to ancient Roman law, albeit within a different framework.[62] Its function is to provide a mechanism to settle disputes outside of court. Ultimately, arbitration, just as litigation in court, aims at providing justice. A feature of arbitration that sheds light into its nature is that it allows a private arbitral tribunal to provide a final and binding decision to the parties' quarrel. But being a private tribunal, it cannot enforce its decisions. It needs a court to assure that its awards will be enforced. However, to decide, an arbitral tribunal needs to have authority to do so. The capacity to arbitrate originates from an agreement between the parties stating that disputes arising out of a transaction will be submitted to arbitration. The agreement is made by the parties and it gives them freedom to decide the format of the arbitral process by choosing the applicable law, selecting the arbitrators, assigning a seat for the arbitration, etc. Moreover, it allows the parties to remove the exclusive jurisdiction of the judiciary to solve disputes. If this agreement is breached and one of the parties seeks relief in court, the innocent party can challenge the jurisdiction of the court based on the agreement. These features are necessary for the functionality of arbitration. As a mechanism opposing litigation in court, arbitration has to provide a system that is not only attractive for parties but is also efficient. This is when arbitration, in the international scenario, becomes appealing. The possibility of subjecting a dispute arising out of an international contract to a private tribunal instead of a domestic court, in a neutral venue, gives the parties some security. It is common for parties not to trust the judiciary of a foreign country.

---

60. Bruce L. Benson, *To Arbitrate or to Litigate: That is the Question*, 8 European Journal of Law and Economics, 91, 94 (1999).
61. *See* Jennifer Kirby, *Efficiency in International Arbitration: Whose Duty is It?*, 32 Journal of International Arbitration, 689 (2015) and Louis Flannery, Gautham Chandrakumar, Krystal Lee and Alastair Kwan for GAR, Arbitration costs compared, https://globalarbitrationreview.com/editorial/1178433/arbitration-costs-compared (accessed 22 February 2019).
62. Alan Redfern and Martin Hunter, *Law and Practice of International Commercial Arbitration* (England, Sweet and Maxwell 2007) 4.

As such, the nature of arbitration can be seen to be contractual and private. It is contractual because it comes out of an agreement between the parties and it is private because the dispute is not solved by a public entity. But for arbitration to take place, it is necessary to have a law regulating the arbitral activity and guaranteeing that arbitral decisions will be enforced in court. Thus, arbitration needs to be allowed within a territory of a jurisdiction. Also, if arbitration is international, different laws can be used as the applicable law and it can take place in a neutral forum. The result is that arbitration becomes delocalized and, perhaps, it creates a legal system of its own, independent from courts.

The attachment or detachment between courts and arbitral tribunals is the essence for understanding the nature of arbitration. On the one hand, the state will allow parties to submit disputes to arbitration, and therefore the arbitrator will resolve the impasse; that is, the arbitrator exercises a public function by putting an end to a dispute. On the other hand, arbitration originates from a contract in which parties agree to submit their dispute to arbitration, demonstrating a private and contractual angle to arbitration. The discussion about the nature of arbitration seems very academic,[63] and conceivably with minor implication in practice, but, analysing the different theories regarding the nature of arbitration is necessary to clarify in what way access to justice should be applied in arbitration.

When looking at how the nature of arbitration has been studied, Lew, Mistelis and Kroll identified four theories.[64] The first theory, called the jurisdictional theory, determines that arbitration is permitted if the jurisdiction in which arbitration is taking place has the power to regulate it.[65] This signifies that arbitration is allowed because there is a law establishing its function; a specific jurisdiction permits a private tribunal to administer justice and therefore, the legal nature of arbitration is jurisdictional. The arbitrator has a similar role to a judge, and they will apply the local law. The second theory opposes the jurisdictional approach. The contractual theory argues that arbitration has a contractual character depending completely on the parties' agreement; that is, the consent of the parties.[66] It is irrelevant if a state is regulating arbitration as it originates from the parties' intention to have a dispute arbitrated. Its root is freedom of contract, the contract being the arbitral cornerstone. Without it, there is no arbitral procedure. The arbitrator will be the authority to find a solution to the dispute and their power emanates from the contract which opted to exclude the solution of disputes from the judiciary. The third approach, the mixed or hybrid theory, combines the jurisdictional and the contractual theory as arbitration depends on both features of the two theories.[67] It is a fact that arbitration comes out of a contract, however, it cannot function alone. To make sure that arbitration is effective, there is a need for jurisdictional support, not only by regulating arbitration, but also to assist in the enforcement of the arbitral decisions. Last comes the autonomous theory stating that arbitration

63. Julian D.M. Lew, Loukas A. Mistelis and Stefan M. Kröll, *Comparative International Commercial Arbitration* (Kluwer Law International, 2003) 72.
64. *Ibid.*
65. *Ibid.*, 74.
66. *Ibid.*, 77.
67. *Ibid.*, 79.

developed independent from a jurisdiction or a contract and it can operate outside the jurisdictional limitations of a legal system.[68] This theory presents arbitration as a system of its own, independent from constraints of any legal system. Arbitration will start with the parties' agreement but once the process commences, it has its own rules, dynamics and procedures, all delocalized and detached from a legal system. Under this theory, arbitration is seen as having grown into a non-national and transnational procedure, reflecting what is sought by its users; that is, an autonomous system unchained from national or international legal systems.

Another format used is to address the legal foundations of arbitration.[69] Paulsson presents four propositions for the legal foundations: 'the territorial thesis, the pluralistic thesis, the autonomous legal order and arbitration independent of national law or judges'.[70] The territorial thesis has the same idea as the jurisdictional nature of arbitration. It preaches that arbitration cannot have effect if there is no permission for it to materialize.[71] The pluralistic thesis goes beyond the territorial limitations and sees arbitration as combination of legal orders insuring its efficacy. Despite the confusion that a multitude of orders can create, 'an unknown set of potentially relevant legal orders corresponds to the reality of international life'.[72] The third of Paulson's proposals is that arbitration has produced a legal order of its own, not depending on a territorial basis or on a combination of legal orders. It has developed its own unique system with its own rules and principles. The last proposal, like the autonomous theory of the nature of arbitration, embraces an arbitral system but it preaches that, from time to time, some help from the judiciary is needed. Arbitration would work mainly, but not solely, on its own, akin to 'private social systems which secure the enforcement of rights and obligations defined by its constituting groups'.[73]

When assessing the judicialization, governance and legitimacy of arbitration, Sweet and Griesel present another viewpoint to the nature of arbitration.[74] They looked at three models of arbitral governance to assess the judicialization of arbitration: contractual, judicial and pluralist-constitutional.[75] The idea was that agency plays a role in the models, thus, the contractual model has a principal giving power to an agent, the former being the parties and the latter being the arbitrators.[76] This has a contractual nature but it is a peculiar form of agency as the arbitrators – the agents – have power over the principals, being more like a trusteeship.[77] The judicial model states that the arbitrator is an '[a]gent of a larger arbitral legal order, which is comprised of transnational firms, investors, arbitration houses, states and other

68. *Ibid.*, 81.
69. Jan Paulsson, *The Idea of Arbitration* (Oxford University Press 2013).
70. *Ibid.*, 30.
71. *Ibid.*, 32-33.
72. *Ibid.*, 38.
73. *Ibid.*, 45.
74. Alec Stone Sweet and Florian Grisel, *The Evolution of International Arbitration* (Oxford University Press 2017).
75. *Ibid.*, 24-25.
76. *Ibid.*, 26.
77. *Ibid.*

stakeholders'.[78] Again, agency is present but this time on a larger scale, breaking the contractual limitation and reaching beyond privity of contract. The pluralist-constitutional model looks at transnational governance, assessing how arbitration is not attached to one legal system but a myriad of systems, being national, international and transnational.[79] The constitutional aspect of the model relies on two facts, the first is that some instruments employed in international arbitration, such as the NYC and the ICSID convention have been ratified by many countries and they 'perform inherently constitutional functions'; the second is that the same instruments 'are foundational elements of an evolving international economic constitution grounded in general principles and fundamental rights'.[80]

The different perspectives offer similitudes. Jurisdictional, judicial and territorial approaches are all based on the idea of a positive law regulating and allowing arbitration to take place within a sovereign state. This follows a legal positivist perception such as Hart's rules of adjudication whereby individuals 'who are to adjudicate' can be recognized, *and* the procedures followed in adjudicating can be demarcated.[81] The fact that arbitration originates from a contract cannot be ignored but to see the contract as the sole source of arbitration is to disregard the fact that arbitration might depend on local courts to be effective. There is merit in saying that arbitration is completely autonomous as it has created a body of precedents gathering principles from diverse jurisdictions; nevertheless, it is hard to see arbitration completely detached from the machinery of a state. At the very least it needs a local court to enforce its decisions.[82] Ignoring completely the jurisdictional character of arbitration can be concerning because, in an extreme scenario, it could completely exclude the application of rights that, for instance, guarantee access to justice to the parties. The hybrid theory, the pluralist-constitutional model and Paulsson's last foundation of a system that depend on the judiciary from time to time but are independent, present a reasonable concept. This context provides legitimacy to arbitration as it is grounded by rules enacted to ensure its application.

For a rule to be legitimate, reference must be made to 'a community's evolving standards of what constitutes a right process'.[83] Legitimacy of rules can be achieved if it presents four indicators: 'determinacy, symbolic validation, coherence and

78. *Ibid.*, 25.
79. *Ibid.*, 30.
80. *Ibid.*, 31. The authors assert that there are 'constitutional understandings of the international legal system which presuppose a substantive body of higher law norms that are binding on all international judges, including arbitrators'. As a result, the common elements of this higher norm are '*jus cogens* norms, human rights, including property rights and procedural guarantees associated with due process and access to justice.'
81. H.L.A. Hart, *The Concept of Law* (3rd ed., Oxford University Press 2012) 97.
82. There is a possibility of even excluding the participation of a court during the enforcement if the parties in arbitration have an independent contract guarantee to pay for the amount established in the award. For a theoretical framework of such possibility *see* Cristián Gimenez Corte, *Lex Mercatoria, International Arbitration and Independent Guarantees: Transnational Law and How Nation States Lost the Monopoly of Legitimate Enforcement*, 3(4) Transnational Legal Theory, 345 (2012).
83. Thomas Franck, *Fairness in International Law and Institutions* (Oxford University Press 1997) 26.

adherence'.[84]The first indicator requires the rule to be clear and transparent so 'one can see through the language of a law to its essential meaning'.[85] Once arbitration is regulated by the state or arbitral bodies, using international rules with a constitutional character recognized by the international community, the procedure is likely to be transparent or at least based on rules accessible to all. The second indicator relates to authorities. A rule has a symbolic validation by showing that authority 'is being exercised in accordance with right process that it is institutionally recognized and validated'.[86] The authority will be the acceptance that the arbitral tribunal is constituted by the agreement of the parties, protected by law and applied in a manner that combines different approaches. The third indicator requires that a rule 'whatever its content, be applied uniformly in every similar and applicable instance'.[87] The combination between the contract and the jurisdiction would lead to a coherent application of the rules; moreover, arbitration has also been subject to the pluralist view whereby rules from different legal systems have constituted a body of law proper to arbitration. Last, the adherence indicator makes the connection between a primary rule, which establishes the obligation, and the secondary rules, which govern the execution of the obligation in a community.[88] Merging the theories would create the adherence and would fulfil the last stage of its legitimacy.

The debate about the nature of arbitration explains how this method of dispute resolution gained so much relevance and continues to expand in application.[89] The purely commercial context of disputes is no longer a monopoly in arbitration and, although the autonomous theory is a well-established concept, the development of arbitration to other fields of law such as consumer, employment, family disputes and sports disputes, where equal footing between the parties is not clear, might not welcome the independence enjoyed in commercial disputes, principally when it comes to guaranteeing access to justice.

§1.06 ACCESS TO JUSTICE AND ARBITRATION

So far, this chapter has analysed the concept of access to justice to establish that it requires access to some form of dispute resolution procedure and throughout this procedure, certain conditions should be met to ensure, as far as possible, a just outcome. After looking at the concept of access to justice, the differences between arbitration and court litigation were addressed to contextualize the assessment of the nature of arbitration. It was shown that the court system is established by law and in

84. *Ibid.*, 30.
85. *Ibid.*
86. *Ibid.*, 34.
87. *Ibid.*, 38.
88. *Ibid.*, 41.
89. *See* for instance the 2018 International Arbitration Survey: The Evolution of International Arbitration, made by the School of International Arbitration at Queen Mary, University of London, in http://www.arbitration.qmul.ac.uk/media/arbitration/docs/2018-International-Arbitration-Survey---The-Evolution-of-International-Arbitration-(2).PDF (accessed 22 February 2019), where '97% of respondents indicate that international arbitration is their preferred method of dispute resolution'.

this sense, it is rather rigid when compared to arbitration. Also, arbitration, which derives from a contract, has its focus on the parties' agreement and liberty to determine a procedure to be applied in the dispute resolution mechanism. This gives the parties more flexibility when compared to court litigation. Such flexibility can be seen in the theories underpinning the nature of arbitration. Although flexibility is one of the reasons for arbitration to be an attractive method of dispute resolution, it can have a potential to interfere or displace procedural requirements that would be expected in court. Because arbitration is a procedure employed to deliver justice, and access to justice requires a procedure, before looking at access to justice in arbitration, we will first examine the debate about what procedural justice is [A]. Once procedural justice has been theoretically conceptualized, this section will finally propose how access to justice should be secured in arbitration [B].

[A] Procedural Justice

Studies on procedural justice have been done through legal theory and legal and social psychology. In relation to legal theory, this section will look at the work of Rawls in his assessment of pure procedural justice [1]. Concerning legal and social psychology, the work of several psychologists will be examined in relation to their studies about how lay people perceive procedural justice [2].

[1] Rawls Pure Procedural Justice

In legal theory, Rawls provides us with a concept of pure procedural justice which, in his view, to be understood, first needs an analysis of the distinction between perfect and imperfect procedural justice.[90] For Rawls, perfect procedural justice would require 'an independent standard for deciding which outcome is just and a procedure guaranteed to lead to it'.[91] Rawls exemplifies this view with a division of cake where the person dividing the cake will do this in an equal manner, making the largest share possible and getting for themselves the last piece.[92] The example demonstrates two characteristics of procedural justice. The first is 'an independent criterion for what is a fair division, a criterion defined separately from and prior to the procedure which is to be followed'.[93] The second is that 'it is possible to devise a procedure that is sure to give the desired outcome'. [94] Rawls concludes that perfect procedural justice 'is rare, if not impossible, in cases of much practical interest.'[95] Moving to imperfect procedural justice, Rawls argues that it would have the same independent standard as perfect procedural justice but, in this variant, 'there is no feasible procedure which is sure to

90. John Rawls, *Theory of Justice* (Harvard University Press 1971) 85.
91. *Ibid.*
92. *Ibid.*
93. *Ibid.*
94. *Ibid.*
95. *Ibid.*

lead to it'.[96] An illustration of imperfect procedural justice is a criminal trial that, despite having rules governing the trial, the proceedings can generate a wrong result such as a guilty person walking free or an innocent person being found guilty.[97] Rawls next envisages what he calls pure procedural justice. This version excludes the independent standard for the outcome; 'instead there is a correct or fair procedure such that the outcome is likewise correct or fair, whatever it is, provided that such procedure has been properly followed'.[98] This can be seen, for example, with gambling, where several individuals will make a bet and the distribution of money, when the game ends, is fair, or at least not unfair, because the rules of the game were followed and the established procedure was carried out rigorously.[99] In other words, '[i]t is as if the procedure by itself makes the outcome just'.[100]

[2] Procedural Justice in Legal and Social Psychology

In legal and social psychology, the first examination of procedural justice was made by Thibaut and Walker who concluded that, in legal proceedings, parties are as concerned about the procedure employed as opposed to the outcome to be obtained.[101] Individuals that could take part in deciding the procedure, having some control over it, would ultimately consider that the result of the dispute would be fair.[102] The participation in the process which produces the outcome of the dispute gives the impression that, regardless of the result, as long as the process is accepted by the parties, the result is just. Later on, Leventhal outlined that for a procedure to be considered fair, six procedural justice rules would need to be met: consistency rule, bias-suppression rule, accuracy rule, correctability rule, representativeness rule and ethicality rule.[103] The rules are based on perceptions of individuals in the procedure. Thus, lack of consistency would lead the individual to see the procedure as unfair. This rule is connected to the principle of equality of opportunity.[104] Bias needs to be avoided because a person 'is likely to believe that procedural fairness is violated when there is unrestrained self-interest or devotion to doctrinaire views'.[105] The process must be founded in a decision with quality and accuracy, informed by proper sources and competent

96. *Ibid.*, 86.
97. *Ibid.*
98. *Ibid.*
99. *Ibid.*
100. William Nelson, *The Very Idea of Pure Procedural Justice*, 90(4) Ethics, 502, 503 (1980).
101. John Thibaut and Laurens Walker, *Procedural Justice: A Psychological Analysis* (John Wiley & Sons Inc. 1975).
102. *Ibid.*, 118.
103. Gerald Leventhal, 'What Should Be Done with Equity Theory', in Kenneth J. Gergen, Martin S. Greenberg and Richard H. Willis (eds), *Social Exchange Advances in Theory and Research* (Plenum Press 1980) 39.
104. *Ibid.*, 40.
105. *Ibid.*, 41.

authorities.[106] Correctability means the opportunity to rectify errors during the process.[107] Representativeness is the ability that parties should have in the decision-making process and, the ethical rule declares that 'allocative procedures must be compatible with the fundamental moral and ethical values accepted by that individual.'[108] Last, Lin and Tyler introduced the concepts of group-value model[109] and the relational model.[110] The first model outlines that a procedure should be created on the basis of the values adopted by a group.[111] As the procedure is based on the values of the group, the procedure will be accepted as fair, even though the parties in the procedure will not take an active role in the decision-making. Thus, an individual would be more concerned about the procedure in itself as opposed to the outcome obtained by the procedure.[112] The second model states that although the procedure will have sources in group values, the group transfers the power to an authority to make decisions. The procedure in itself will give a structure to the authority to decide, thus, the authority to decide moves from the group to one individual.[113] This signifies that fairness in the procedure is linked by perceptions between the authority and the parties subject to the authorities' decision. This relation is based on features of the procedure such as 'judgments of neutrality, trust and dignity'.[114]

[B] Can Access to Justice Be Secured in Arbitration?

Access to justice and arbitration are not incompatible. On the contrary, for the smooth operation of arbitration, guaranteeing access to justice is essential.[115] Access to justice is not just being given the opportunity to have a dispute decided by a third party, be that an adjudicator belonging to a judiciary or an arbitrator. It is having the 'day in court' together with guarantees that the procedure to be followed will assure procedural justice and, from that, a just outcome.

The concern regarding arbitration is that access to justice might appear to be at odds with the nature of arbitration or, at least, not an essential requirement. For example, arbitration, due to its contractual nature and its autonomous stance, could be an arena to disregard access to justice. That is to say, if arbitration is contractual, up to what point can or should the parties in the contract be able to restrict access to justice by reducing its features? This becomes very relevant where there is an imbalance of power between the two parties. For example, a stronger party, through an arbitration

106. *Ibid.*
107. *Ibid.*, 42-43.
108. *Ibid.*, 43-46.
109. E. Allan Lind and Tom R. Tyler, *The Social Psychology of Procedural Justice* (Springer Science + Business Media 1988).
110. Tom R. Tyler and E. Allan Lind, 'Relational model of authority in groups', in Mark P. Zanna (ed.), *Advances in Experimental Social Psychology* vol. 25 (Academic Press 1992).
111. E. Allan Lind and Tom R. Tyler, *The Social Psychology of Procedural Justice* (Plenum 1988) 231.
112. *Ibid.*, 1.
113. Tyler (*supra* n. 110) 117.
114. *Ibid.*, 143.
115. Mauro Cappelletti, *Alternative Dispute Resolution Processes within the Framework of the World-Wide Access-to-Justice Movement*, 56(3) Modern Law Review, 282, 287 (1993).

agreement in a contract, could impose upon a weak party the idea of a mandatory day in court (in this case, a hearing in the arbitral procedure), but with a procedure that is one-sided. If the nature of arbitration is of a system of its own, the guarantee that access to justice will be respected relies on the users of the system and what they agreed upon. If the balance of power in the system does not have a requirement of equity in any arbitration agreement to be decided, again, access to justice can be removed at the discretion of the stronger party. If arbitration has some reliance on a court system, similar to Paulsson's idea that arbitration is an independent system that from time to time needs the help of a judiciary, this can be mitigated by the chance to challenge a lack of access to justice in the arbitral procedure. This would also be in line with the pluralist-constitutional model as the instruments applied in arbitration protect features of access to justice.

A delocalized arbitral framework might work well for commercial disputes involving business to business. Under Rawls' perspective of pure procedural justice, the procedure will make the result just, as long as the parties have agreed and have followed it. In arbitration, parties might have an option to choose the procedure to be adopted, but this choice is not unlimited; there are laws guaranteeing features of access to justice even when the procedure is private.[116] Moreover, if the parties have chosen an arbitral institution, the rules of such institutions will provide for assurances of access to justice such as the right to be heard and an independent and impartial tribunal.[117] However, due to the freedom that arbitration offers the parties to choose the rules to settle the dispute, it appears that arbitration could apply several independent standards to decide if the result obtained is just. Be that as it may, the independent standards in arbitration should not be based on unfair procedures. That would defeat the purpose of arbitration. If the parties have freely agreed the method for the procedure to be followed, and such method is considered fair, the outcome should be fair because the procedure would also be fair. This could be seen in traditional commercial arbitration. If the parties are financially able to be represented by a counsel who clarifies the implications of arbitrating disputes, the parties will be aware of the ramifications generated by removing the exclusive jurisdiction of courts. In doing so, if the parties follow a procedure they have established and accept that in this procedure access to justice is not secured in the same way as it is in court litigation, the result is likely to be fair. This will not necessarily generate unfairness in how justice is being delivered. On the contrary, it will respect the parties' intention and freedom of contract which is translated into the method that parties have contracted to solve a dispute. It will be imperative that minimum principles of access to justice will be present, such as

116. For instance, section 33(1) of the 1996 English Arbitration Act that imposes the tribunal to 'act fairly and impartially as between the parties, giving each party a reasonable opportunity of putting his case and dealing with that of his opponent', Article 594(2) of the Austrian Code of Civil Procedure which stated that 'parties shall be treated fairly. Each party shall have the right to be heard'; and Article 18 of the Chilean International Arbitration Act (Ley 19971/2004) which guarantees that parties should be treated equally and that 'each one of them should be given full opportunity to assert their rights.'

117. *See* SCC Arbitration Rules 2017 Articles 18 and 23(2) and SIAC 2016 Arbitration Rules 14 and 24.1.

having an impartial adjudicator and the parties being be able to present their case, but at same time, parties can agree on how strict the application of such principles will be. The main aspect of a fair process here is that the parties decided together the procedure to be adopted.

Compared to Rawls' theory, the studies in psychology seem more objective since they touch on how the participants in the procedure perceive the process which was used to achieve justice. This shows one of the biggest differences between arbitration and court proceedings, namely, the choice dimension. Parties must have confidence in the system they are choosing, whereas, with the courts, confidence is assumed by its monopoly/structure in spite of the fact parties have neither say in the make-up of the court or its procedures, nor is there need for any contractual agreement to comply with the findings as the court has automatic jurisdiction irrespective of the parties' agreement.

The psychological approach has also been considered in the context of ADR and arbitration.[118] Even when the examination is about ADR, there is a view that arbitration fits the psychological perspective better than other ADR procedures. For example, if procedural justice is about the parties having some ownership over the procedure, mediation would meet the rules proposed by Leventhal. Nevertheless, Collet argues that in an example of divorce, if one party agrees to submit the dispute to mediation and the settlement obtained was heavily influenced by the other divorcing party, it would not matter that there was participation in the process as one of the parties would still feel that there was no procedural justice.[119] However, in arbitration, even though the parties contribute to the process, the decision is made by a third party and not simply mediated through a third party. Therefore, instead of being disappointed and consequently seeing the decision as unfair, the dissatisfaction will be directed at the arbitrator or the arbitration process instead of the other party.[120] In this sense, looking at the relational approach, the outcome might be disappointing but not the process in itself. Moreover, arbitration is a form of ADR which closely mirrors court litigation. In court litigation, the fairness in the adopted procedure is essential for the parties to understand the court system but also to interpret this experience 'into a subjective valuation of the court system as a whole'.[121]

For the parties in arbitration to feel that the arbitral process is fair, it is suggested, therefore, that factors used to assess procedural justice in courts should be applied to

118. For ADR, *see* Neil Vidmar, *Procedural Justice and Alternative Dispute Resolution*, 3(4) Psychological Science, 224 (1992) and Rebecca Hollander-Blumoff and Tom R. Tyler, *Procedural Justice and the Rule of Law: Fostering Legitimacy in Alternative Dispute Resolution*, Journal of Dispute Resolution, 1 (2011). For arbitration, *see* Jaunius Gumbis and Miglé Petkevičiene, 'Application of selected elements of procedural justice in arbitration', in Marianne Roth and Michael Geistlinger (eds) *Yearbook on International Arbitration and ADR* vol. V (Neuer Wissenschaftlicher Verlag 2017).

119. Jessica L. Collett, *Is Procedural Justice Enough? Affect, Attribution, and Conflict in Alternative Dispute Resolution*, 25 Justice, 267, 275 (2015).

120. *Ibid.*, 276 and 278.

121. Kevin Burke and Steve Leben, *Procedural Fairness: A Key Ingredient in Public Satisfaction*, 44(1-2) Court Review, 4, 6 (2007-2008).

arbitration, such as neutrality and trustworthiness of the decision-maker, the opportunity to present your case and courtesy.[122] However, this simple transfer of factors from court to arbitration may not be sufficient. For example, the elements of procedural justice in court were described as 'judicial protection, impartiality, guarantee of court instances and respect for previously formed precedents'.[123] Because of the private nature of arbitration, it would fail to meet at least three of these elements. When a dispute is submitted to arbitration, judicial protection is somehow waived. Although parties can resort to court to assist in some aspects of arbitration, it is not the local judiciary that will decide the dispute. Furthermore, arbitration is not subjected to appeals; the attractiveness of arbitration is that it will provide a final binding decision. Last, arbitration has no link to the principle of *stare decisis*, thus, precedents are non-binding. While there is a lot of debate to the way impartiality is employed in arbitration,[124] this requirement is fairly guaranteed in arbitration.

Be that as it may, arbitration cannot be used as a tool to restrict people from seeking redress or from achieving justice.[125] To do so would make arbitration worthless as a dispute resolution procedure. Expanding the same situation mentioned above, if traders impose arbitration clauses on consumers without their consent, and create an arbitral procedure that is one-sided, can there be proper access to justice? For example, in the UK, when a person parks their car in a private car park, be it a residential or commercial car park, and a parking ticket is issued, depending on the operator of the car park, the person can submit an appeal to the Independent Appeals Service (IAS).[126] The IAS ADR rules for appeals are arbitration rules for consumer disputes.[127] The procedure is online, which saves time and makes it easy for consumers to access it. Nonetheless, there is nothing in the IAS ADR rules stating that the arbitrator has to act impartially. Rule 5.2 states that '[a] single Arbitrator will claim the Arbitration using the IAS' automated "case queue" and confirm to the IAS that he has no conflict of interest in the matter in dispute'. Having no conflicts does not, however, create an obligation to act impartially. Moreover, there is no hearing as the process is done

122. Hollander-Blumoff (*supra* n. 118) 14.
123. Gumbis (*supra* n. 118) 43.
124. *See* Drew J. Hushka, *How Nice to See You Again: The Repetitive Use of Arbitrators and the Risk of Evidence Partiality*, 5 Penn State Yearbook on Arbitration and Mediation, 325 (2013); Catherine A. Rogers, *A Window into the Soul of International Arbitration: Arbitrator Selection, Transparency and Stakeholder Interests*, 46 Victoria University Wellington Law Review 1179 (2015); Thomas Schultz, *Arbitral Decision-Making: Legal Realism and Law & Economics*, 6 Journal of International Dispute Settlement, 231 (2015); Van Harten, Gus, *Arbitrator Behaviour in Asymmetrical Adjudication: An Empirical Study of Investment Treaty Arbitration*, 50(1) Osgoode Hall Law Journal, 211 (2012) and Nancy A. Welsh, *What Is '(Im)Partial Enough' in a World of Embedded Neutrals?*, 52 Arizona Law Review 395 (2010).
125. *See* this discussion in Chapters 2, 3, 5 and 6.
126. Their service is provided online. *See* https://www.theias.org/home (accessed 21 February 2020).
127. Rule 2.1 of the IAS Arbitration (ADR) General Rules And Procedures provides: '2.1 Where an Initial Appeal is made against a Trader and where that trader has indicated to the consumer and the IAS that they are willing to engage in Arbitration, the Trader is joined in Arbitration under these Rules automatically.' In https://www.theias.org/the-ias-arbitration-adr-general-rules-and-procedures (accessed 21 February 2020).

online.[128] The absence of a hearing is not a limitation to access to justice, but in the case of consumers, this should be made clear from the beginning so that the consumer would have a choice whether or not to venture into a documents-only dispute resolution system. Otherwise, in such circumstance, because the parties in the dispute are not familiar with the procedure that has been imposed on them, they might perceive it as unfair. [129] Viewing the procedure as fair is essential when there is no equal footing in a dispute.[130]

The same question has also been addressed outside the consumer sphere. The Canadian Supreme Court, in *Uber Technologies Inc. v. Heller*,[131] had to decide if Uber drivers can be considered employees under the Ontario's Employment Standards Act 2000. The service agreement between Uber and its drivers, which was a standard form imposed to all Uber drivers, had an ICC mediation-arbitration clause with the seat of arbitration in Amsterdam and Dutch law as the contractual governing law. To start the dispute resolution process, it was required an upfront administrative and filing fees of US$14,500, in addition to legal fees and cost of participation. The fees reflected most of the claimant's annual income. The claimant argued that the arbitration agreement was

128. Rule 2.4 of the IAS Arbitration (ADR) General Rules and Procedures says: '2.4 Arbitrations will be conducted on a documents only basis and there will not be an oral hearing.'
129. Margaret Jane Radin, in *Access to Justice and Abuses of Contract*, 33 Windsor Yearbook of Access to Justice 189-190, 177 (2016), presents several reasons why consumers would have aversion to mandatory arbitration clauses: 'first, the arbitrators are repeat players for the firms, and it is at least widely suspected that they rule in favour of the firm most of the time; second, arbitration is private and secret, so that if a firm were to lose a waiver case to a consumer, it could still deploy the same waiver with every other consumer; third, arbitration creates no precedent, so that even if Consumer A wins an arbitration case and succeeds in disallowing a waiver, the firm can still deploy the same arbitration clause against Consumers B through Z; and, fourth, as interpreted by the US Supreme Court, arbitration must be strictly between the individual and the firm, so aggregative actions are prohibited. This means that many injuries – those that depend on aggregative actions for redress just cannot be remedied. The US Supreme Court, in effect, said that it is just too bad.'
130. In *Seidel v. TELUS Communications Inc.* 2011 SCC 15, the majority of the Canadian Supreme Court decided that an arbitration clause in a consumer contract was void according to Section 3 of the British Columbia Business Practices and Consumer Protection Act 2004. Such provision makes it void any agreement waiving rights, benefits or protections in the Act. As the claim was based on Section 172 of the Act, which allows the parties to directly petition the Supreme Court, staying proceedings because of the arbitration clause would restrict the right under Section 172. The interest aspect of the decision in relation to access to justice can be found in the dissenting opinion of the court. Although the prevailing opinion, at paragraph 22, starts by saying that '[t]he underlying issue in this appeal is access to justice', the reasoning concentrates in the interpretation of the above mentioned provisions and does not develop the access to justice question. The dissenting opinion, on the contrary, argues that arbitration preserves access to justice. At paragraph 54 the decision states: 'Given the current structure of consumer protection legislation in British Columbia, submitting a consumer's dispute with their mobile phone service provider to arbitration is entirely consistent with the important public purposes of protecting consumers, vindicating their rights and promoting access to justice.' And at paragraph 149 it says: 'Our colleague argues that in the consumer context, the principles of access to justice require a public form of relief that is not limited to the parties to the consumer transaction in issue, and also require that the claims themselves be adjudicated in only one public forum: the courts. We would respond to this argument by observing that access to justice is protected both by the broad powers given to arbitrators and by the representative action provided for in the BPCPA.'
131. 2020 SCC 16.

not valid whilst Uber stated that the claim should be settled by arbitration. The majority of the Canadian Supreme Court understood that the clause was not valid.[132] It started by looking into the application of the Ontario International Commercial Arbitration Act or the Ontario Arbitration Act to the dispute. It concluded that the case was about a labour dispute which is not covered by the Ontario International Commercial Arbitration Act but by the Ontario Arbitration Act. Therefore, under Section 7(2)(2) of the Ontario Arbitration Act, a refusal to stay proceedings can be done if the arbitration agreement is invalid. From this point, applying the doctrine of unconscionability, the Supreme Court did not stay proceedings because the arbitration clause in the service agreement was invalid. They stated that '[t]here was clearly inequality of bargaining power between Uber and Mr. Heller',[133] and that the service agreement was an in or out contract, with no other option given to the claimant. Moreover, the court asserted that '[t]here was a significant gulf in sophistication between Mr. Heller, a food delivery man in Toronto, and Uber, a large multinational corporation',[134] and at no moment, the claimant was made aware of the costs incurred into agreeing to have any dispute arbitrated in the Netherlands. As a result, the conclusion was that '[b]ased on both the disadvantages faced by Mr. Heller in his ability to protect his bargaining interests and on the unfair terms that resulted, the arbitration clause is unconscionable and therefore invalid'.[135] Brown J agreed that the clause was invalid but under a different perspective. His view was that the arbitration agreement was not valid because it undermines 'the rule of law by denying access to justice, and are therefore contrary to public policy'.[136] He asserted that

> [a]ccess to civil justice is a precondition not only to a functioning democracy but also to a vibrant economy, in part because access to justice allows contracting parties to enforce their agreements. A contract that denies one party the right to enforce its terms undermines both the rule of law and commercial certainty.[137]

The *obiter* makes a clear statement that a clause imposing arbitration where inequality of bargaining power is evident, restricts access to justice. Therefore, the clause is against public policy because it limits the capacity to have access to adjudication and also access to a fair procedure to solve the dispute.[138]

A similar setting can be found in sports arbitration. Athletes wishing to participate in a competition might have to sign an agreement that any sports' dispute will be

132. Wagner C.J. and Abella, Moldaver, Karakatsanis, Rowe, Martin and Kasirer JJ formed the majority. Brown J agreed with the majority but in different terms and Côté J. dissented in favour of staying the proceedings.
133. *Ibid.*, at 93.
134. *Ibid.*
135. *Ibid.*, at 98.
136. *Ibid.*, at 101.
137. *Ibid.*, at 112.
138. Brown J at 115 said: 'None of this is to say that public policy requires access to a court of law in all circumstances. As this Court has recognized, "new models of adjudication can be fair and just" (*Hryniak*, at paragraph 2). But public policy does require access to *justice*, and access to justice is not merely access to a resolution. After all, many resolutions are *un*just. Where a party seeks a rights-based resolution to a dispute, such resolution is *just* only when it is determined *according to law*, as discerned and applied by an independent arbiter.'

submitted to arbitration at CAS. It is an 'in or out' agreement because non-adherence would result in not joining the competition. This question has reached the ECtHR in *Mutu et Pechstein v. Switzerland.*[139] The cases were about challenges to CAS decisions. Pechstein and Mutu questioned CAS awards that restricted the two athletes from competitions due to doping. The challenges to the awards reached the ECHR where it was concluded that arbitration clauses in sports agreements between athletes and sporting bodies are compulsory and therefore, the arbitral procedure should provide the guarantees established in Article 6(1) of the ECHR.[140] At this point, the, Strasbourg Court asserted that CAS was a tribunal established by law for the purposes of Article 6(1) and that compulsory arbitration is only valid as long as it respects that article. The interesting aspect of this decision is that arbitration in sports disputes without consent is not necessarily unlawful, but it needs to secure the principles of Article 6(1); that is, 'a fair and public hearing within a reasonable time by an independent and impartial tribunal established by law'. What the ECHR provided is that basic features of access to justice should be guaranteed in sports arbitration. The reason for this is clear, in sports disputes; on one side there will be an athlete and on the other side there will be a sporting body on which the athlete heavily depends, otherwise, the athlete cannot perform their trade. Thus, where the inequality of power is evident, to assure proper access to justice, the standards in Article 6(1), which are applied in courts, must equally be respected in sports arbitration.

In this context, Rawls' pure procedural justice might not be the best approach for disputes with inequality of arms, that is, when arbitration is imposed on parties. Parties in such conflicts are not familiar with arbitration and for them to trust the system, a strong guarantee of procedural justice should be made. In this sense, Lin and Tyler's relational model can be useful. The fairness in the procedure is based on the relationship between the authority and the parties. To do that, robust principles of access to justice must be present. In arbitration, parties will contribute to the process used to solve the dispute. Nonetheless, if parties are not in equal footing, they need to trust that the system being used will mitigate this. If parties can participate in the procedure by presenting their case, having an impartial tribunal, being heard and treated cordially, the likelihood will be that they will see the process as fair. Inequality of arms does not mean that if parties submit a dispute to arbitration, there is no access to justice. Yet, to ensure that access to justice is provided in such cases, access to justice cannot be subjected to much flexibility, it will need safeguards in place like those that seek to achieve access to justice in court. Moreover, some benefits to the weak party should be made part of the arbitration rules. For example, where there is ambiguity in an agreement, interpretation should be analysed to favour the party that did not draft the ambiguous rule and the onus of proof should favour the weak party. Additionally,

139. App no. 40575/10 and no. 67474/10 (ECHR, 02 October 2018). The case is also addressed in Chapters 2, 4 and 8.
140. (*Supra* n. 8).

where a party cannot afford the costs of the arbitration, some form of legal aid needs to be in place to assist the less fortunate party.[141]

There will always be an individual that, regardless of the fairness in the procedure, will feel that the result of the dispute is unfair if they are the losing party. This, however, does not render the procedure unjust. You can compare this feeling with seeing the team you support in a sports event. If the team loses in a fair game because they did not perform well, although you might be unhappy, the result will be perceived as acceptable. Conversely, if the team loses because the referee did not detect a violation of the rules of the game by the opposing team, which then led to that team winning, you feel cheated.

§1.07 CONCLUSION

When thinking about access to justice, there should not be a 'box ticking' approach adopted; that is, if you get your day in court it is fine and the access to the justice box is ticked. It is common that parties, after experiencing court proceedings, will not 'feel that justice has been done'.[142] Access to justice should be more than just assuring that parties have their day in court. It requires that they have a fair day in court in which the outcome is neither predetermined nor manipulated in favour of one party over the other. Securing that parties can get to a court is a fundamental guarantee, but if it is done proforma, it will be a disservice to the right of access to court.

Arbitration is similar to litigation in court as both forms of dispute resolution aim at providing a solution to a dispute. However, as it has been shown, they are not bound by the same rules. Moreover, they should not be subject to the same rules as this would defeat the purpose of arbitration. Arbitration is a form of ADR, and following Cappelletti's proposal, it is a tool for the third wave of access to justice. It is a private method to solve disputes that, although it resembles court litigation, it provides the parties with certain benefits not available in court.[143] At the same time, access to justice in arbitration functions as a procedural justice guarantor. The expansion of arbitration will generate disputes with inequality of arms between parties, thus, a differential approach is required. This perspective will focus on the parties in arbitration. If the nature of arbitration will be completely delocalized, this approach might not work for disputes where there is a presumption of inequality of arms. When individuals are involved in disputes, their perception of the dispute and associated feelings are essential to determine how they will conclude that the process is fair. Hence, when an

---

141. Furthermore, Jill I. Gross, in *Arbitration Archetypes for Enhancing Access to Justice*, 88 Fordham Law Review, 2327, 2319 (2020), proposes four conditions to enhance access to justice in arbitration, she says: 'In order for a subtype of arbitration to enhance parties' access to justice ... it is critical that the process: (1) cost less and take less time than litigating the same claim in court; (2) result in a published, explained award; (3) does not strip the rights of the parties to assert any claim, remedy, or procedure that would be available in court; and (4) permit the parties to be represented.'
142. Deborah L. Rhode, *Access to Justice*, 69 Fordham Law Review, 1785, 1786 (2001).
143. Parties can choose the arbitrators, they can choose the seat of the dispute, the language of the dispute and the rules guiding the procedure of the dispute.

arbitral dispute involves parties that are not on equal footing, a stricter view of access to justice is required. This view will be mirroring access to justice applied in courts and there should be little room for reducing access to justice. But if it is a business-to-business dispute, where the parties are well informed about the consequences of arbitration, a flexible approach to access to justice need not be unfair. On the contrary, it might reinforce the view that the parties' intentions were recognized and respected. There is no reason for arbitration to reject access to justice; quite the reverse, the flexibility of arbitration permits it to embrace access to justice.

Currently, institutions, parties, legislators and all users of arbitration should assure that disputes submitted to arbitration will respect the rights deriving from access to justice. The expansion of arbitration should be welcomed and not feared. Nevertheless, if such growth does not guarantee effective access to justice, the work devoted to the promotion of arbitration might backfire, rendering an important method of dispute resolution obsolete. Perhaps, with the development of technology and artificial intelligence, in future, conceivably a machine will guarantee the right of access to justice when there is clear inequality between parties.[144] But for now, when disputes are submitted to arbitration, the arbitral procedure should secure the preservation of access to justice, so it generates more public trust in this method of dispute resolution.

144. For the role of artificial intelligence in arbitration *see* Christine Sim, *Will Artificial Intelligence Take Over Arbitration?*, 14(1) Asian International Arbitration Journal 1 (2018) and Maxi Scherer, *Artificial Intelligence and Legal Decision-Making: The Wide Open?*, 36(5) Journal of International Arbitration 539 (2019).

CHAPTER 2

Access to Justice and Arbitration: Is Consent to Arbitrate Still at Stake?

Clotilde Jourdain-Fortier

Access to justice has gradually been established, in Europe and elsewhere, as a fundamental right. It is a widely recognized right, not easy to define precisely, but at least understood as the right of access to a court to any person. It is up to States to guarantee and organize this access, to enable individuals to obtain the remedy to which they claim to be entitled to. Freedom implies that States may rather prefer to organize access to a private judge, to an arbitrator, or to offer an alternative to a State judge. It is then up to the parties to express their choice of forum, which is expressed by the agreement to entrust an arbitrator with the task of settling their dispute, and by which they accept in advance the loss of freedom to contest the validity of the decision thus rendered. This situation calls for a general reflection on the force of consent and its scope, regardless of the type of arbitration (commercial, investment, sports, etc.). For several years, consent to arbitration has been presented as declining, to such an extent that it would gradually be reduced to a shambles skin; some even wonder whether it has not become a 'pure legal fiction'. In fact, many cases presented as 'mandatory arbitrations' seem to be emerging in Europe and elsewhere. This chapter questions the very notion of arbitration and try to distinguish between hypotheses, depending on whether arbitration is required by law or by the co-contractor. It is questionable whether arbitration could be imposed in the absence of consent of the parties, which raises the question of the necessary coincidence between arbitration and consent. In other words, is arbitration necessarily a consensual justice or can there be cases of arbitration without consent?

§2.01 INTRODUCTION

Access to justice has gradually been established, in Europe and elsewhere,[1] as a fundamental right: a right of constitutional value in the United States ('right to be heard in court') based on the original principles of natural justice,[2] a fundamental right of constitutional value and non-waivable in English law ('the right of access to the courts'),[3] a human right enshrined in the ECHR (Article 6 § 1), etc. It is a widely recognized right, not easy to define precisely, but at least understood as the right of access to a court to any person, natural or legal. It is up to States to guarantee and organize this access, to enable individuals to obtain the remedy to which they claim to be entitled.

However, the right of access to a court does not necessarily imply, the ECtHR has pointed out, 'the right to have access to a court of law of the classic kind, integrated within the standard judicial machinery of the country'.[4] In other words, there is no right of access to a State judge. Freedom implies that States may rather prefer to organize access to a private judge, to an arbitrator, or to offer an alternative, a choice for individuals between private and public justice. According to the ECtHR, '[a]rticle 6 does not therefore preclude the establishment of arbitral tribunals in order to settle certain pecuniary disputes between individuals'[5]. In the event of alternative jurisdiction, it is then up to the parties to express their choice of *forum*, which is expressed by the agreement to entrust an arbitrator with the task of settling their dispute, and by which they accept in advance the loss of freedom to contest the validity of the decision thus rendered.

This situation calls for a general reflection on the force of consent and its scope, regardless of the type of arbitration (commercial, investment, sports, etc.). If States have the freedom to organize access to an arbitral tribunal, it is questionable whether they might not exercise this freedom and prohibit arbitration, despite the consent of the parties which would then be ineffective. Conversely, it is questionable whether they could impose arbitration in the absence of the consent of the parties, which raises the question of the necessary coincidence between arbitration and consent. In other words, is arbitration necessarily a consensual justice or can there be cases of arbitration without consent? But in that last case, would it still be arbitration?

1. Article 8 UDHR; Article 14 § 1 International Covenant on Civil and Political Rights: '... everyone shall be entitled to a fair and public hearing by a competent, independent and impartial tribunal established by law'.
2. *Bounds v. Smith*, 430 U.S. 817 (1977), No. 75-915.
3. *Bremer Vulkan Schiffbau v. South India Shipping Corp ltd* (1981) 1 ALL ER 289. At 977, Lord Diplock declared: 'every civilised system of government requires that the state should make available to all its citizens a means for the just and peaceful settlement of disputes between them as to their respective legal rights. The means provided are courts of justice to which every citizen has a constitutional right of access in the role of plaintiff to obtain the remedy to which he claims to be entitled in consequence of an alleged breach of his legal or equitable rights by some other citizen, the defendant. whether or not to avail himself of this right of access to the court lies exclusively within the plaintiff's choice; if he chooses to do so, the defendant has no option in the matter; his subjection to the jurisdiction of the court is compulsory...'.
4. *Mutu and Pechstein v. Switzerland* nos. 40575/10 and 67474/10 § 94 (ECHR 2 October 2018).
5. *Ibid.*

To the first question, that is whether a State could prohibit arbitration without ignoring the right of access to a court, the answer seems *a priori* positive. If we follow the reasoning of the ECtHR, it appears that access to justice requires States to guarantee access to a court for individuals, which is characterized by its jurisdictional function, which meant determining matters within its competence by applying the law and after conducting proceedings in a prescribed manner.[6] A State could thus very legitimately fulfil its duties by setting up traditional judicial structures (i.e. organizing access to a State judge), without guaranteeing access to parallel private justice. What is required is to guarantee the existence of a way of access to a court, but nothing seems to impose on the State to offer on within its jurisdiction the choice of an alternative jurisdictional mechanism. Thus, strictly speaking, there is no guarantee of access to arbitration.

Some will oppose this conclusion, at least as it is formulated in general terms, arguing that States can only limit the arbitrator's right of access and not prohibit it. There are two arguments for this. The first is the idea that while the right of access to a court is not absolute and can be legitimately limited by States, the restriction imposed must not go so far as to infringe this right 'in its very essence', i.e. to make it disappear.[7] The statement is obviously valid but inoperative as long as access to a court is guaranteed. The second is the respect of individual liberty and freedom of choice, which are at the root of the consent of the parties to contract and then to decide to set up a private person as a 'judge' to adjudicate their dispute. States should therefore not be able to prohibit arbitration, but only to regulate it 'minimally' namely 'only' for general interest purposes (some disputes being unsuitable for arbitration, limits can be set by law on their arbitrability). While we are not fully convinced by this argument, it is especially important to note its highly theoretical nature, as arbitration is nowadays the subject of an almost universal practice (*favor arbitrandum*) because of its many recognized advantages for States and/or individuals. Almost all States in the world now recognize the existence of this alternative method of dispute resolution.[8]

Regarding the second question formulated above that is whether a State could impose arbitration in the absence of the litigant's consent, the answer also seems positive even if it is controversial: consent is deeply rooted in the collective conception of lawyers as inseparable from arbitration; it is the essential condition 'to any process of dispute resolution outside national courts'.[9] Consent has always been accepted and reaffirmed as the cornerstone of arbitration, essentially in the form of a convention.[10] Moreover, the existence of an arbitration agreement, and therefore the consent of the

6. *Julius Kloiber Schlachthof GmbH and others v. Autria*, nos 21565/07, 21572/07, 21575/07 and 21580/07 (ECHR 4 April 4 2013).
7. *Mutu and Pechstein* (*supra* n. 4) at 93.
8. One hundred and sixty States are parties to NYC. To our knowledge, North Korea is one of the few countries that prohibits arbitration on its territory.
9. Nigel Blackaby, Martin Hunter, Constantine Partasides, Alan Redfern, *Redfern and Hunter on International Arbitration* (Oxford University Press, 2009), paragraph 2-01.
10. 'The existence of an agreement between the parties to submit any dispute between them to arbitration is the cornerstone of international commercial arbitration law. In the absence of an arbitration agreement, there can be no international commercial arbitration', Eric Loquin, *L'arbitrage du commerce international* 10 (Joly Lextension éditions, 2015).

parties, is a prerequisite for the application of many international texts relating to international commercial arbitration, in particular the NYC.

However, if we still discuss the European human rights system, a positive answer is needed, for the same reasons as those set out above: States are free to organize access to justice on their territory as they wish. Only the existence of a remedy is relevant, and an arbitral tribunal is likely to be considered as a tribunal within the meaning of Article 6 § 1 of the convention – even if the legal regime of a compulsory arbitration differs from a voluntary one as we will see. The only condition stated would be that the tribunal is 'established by law',[11] which presupposes that it is permanent in nature. 'This means that States are obliged to adopt specific laws establishing and then managing the functioning of national courts. This requires permanence, which excludes bodies that exercise a judicial function on the basis of an agreement between the parties to a case'.[12] However, arbitration can have these qualities: it can be required by law and then present a permanent nature, which leads to a distinction between so-called mandatory arbitration and voluntary arbitration, which one is an alternative, non-exclusive and consensual form of justice, while in the case of mandatory arbitration, 'the parties have no option but to refer their dispute to an arbitral tribunal'.[13] Therefore, it seems possible to consider that a State would fully implement its obligations with regard to ensuring access to justice by choosing access to an arbitral tribunal to adjudicate certain disputes of a pecuniary nature between individuals rather than to an ordinary tribunal.

The hypothesis of a mandatory arbitration, exclusive of any consent from the litigant, seems therefore to have been validated by the ECtHR. The coincidence between arbitral justice and consensual justice would then not be total, as this was previously highlighted by Diallo in his PhD thesis on consent in international arbitration.[14] But one important thing is that cases of mandatory arbitration can only be reduced to those required by law. They are the only ones that can be considered as legal and therefore valid, which undoubtedly invites us to distinguish between the many cases of so-called mandatory arbitrations that are now being carried out. For several years, consent to arbitration has been presented as declining, to such an extent that it would gradually be reduced to a shambles skin; some even wonder whether it has not become a 'pure legal fiction'.[15] In fact, many cases presented as 'mandatory arbitrations' seem to be emerging in Europe and elsewhere, for instance in the US where a majority of employment contracts now contain an arbitration agreement imposed by the employer on the employee, depriving the latter of the possibility of bringing an action before an ordinary court.[16]

11. *Suda v. the Czech Republic*, no. 1643/06, § 49 (ECHR 28 October 2010).
12. European Union Agency for Fundamental rights, *Handbook on European Law Relating to Access to Justice* (Publications Office of the European Union, 2016) 31.
13. *Mutu and Pechstein* (*supra* n. 4) § 95.
14. Ousmane Diallo, *Le consentement des parties à l'arbitrage international* (PUF, The Graduate Institute Publications, 2010).
15. Benson Lim, Adriana Uson, *Relooking at Consent in Arbitration*, http://arbitrationblog.kluwerarbitration.com/2019/02/12/relooking-at-consent-in-arbitration/ (accessed 22 October 2019).
16. See below §2.03.

While one can obviously question the legitimacy of this phenomenon with regard to the matter of access to justice, it is undoubtedly necessary to distinguish between hypotheses, depending on whether arbitration is required by law or by the co-contractor. Moreover, if consent does not necessarily form the basis of arbitration like in a real compulsory one, then what is it? Compulsory arbitration raises questions about the very notion of arbitration. What fundamentally characterizes arbitration and distinguishes it from State justice? What is the root of arbitration? To address these questions, three points will be questioned in this chapter.

In a first point, the consubstantiality of consent to arbitration will be discussed. Can arbitration be required by law, including at the international level through treaties or conventions, and then be imposed on the litigant without his consent? And in this case, can it still be called arbitration?

In a second point will be raised the question of whether quickly so-called mandatory arbitrations can actually constitute real cases or whether a distinction should be drawn between mandatory arbitration and mandatory consent. In that last case, it will be necessary to consider the legitimacy of a consensual arbitration in which the consent of the litigant would appear to have been forced by the co-contractor.

In a third point the different forms of consent will be examined, in a critical perspective on the need for an arbitration agreement to qualify arbitration. Is consent likely to be expressed otherwise than in an agreement, without calling into question the existence of genuine arbitration?

It will be possible, at the end, to answer the final question as to whether consent is still at stake in arbitration.

§2.02 QUESTIONING THE CONSUBSTANTIALITY OF CONSENT TO ARBITRATION

Mandatory arbitration means arbitration that is required by law. If rare, this type of arbitration has always existed in domestic law: the legislator may impose an exclusive jurisdiction of an arbitral tribunal with a specific composition and operating rules to settle a dispute of a particular nature, most often sensitive, excluding ordinary courts' jurisdiction. For instance, in French law, the arbitral commission of journalists is the only body competent to rule on disputes relating to employment contracts involving professional journalists, excluding the jurisdiction of State Labour Court.[17]

Can we consider in this case that access to justice would be denied to the litigant who is deprived of access to the ordinary courts? The question was submitted to the French Conseil Constitutionnel which replied negatively, considering that although the Arbitral Commission decisions could certainly not be appealed, they could nevertheless be challenged as it is usually the case in arbitration, that is why they did not,

17. Commission established by a law of 29 March 1935, codified in Article L. 7112-4 of the Labour Code. For other examples of mandatory arbitration in comparative law, *see* Diallo (*supra* n. 14) 59-61.

therefore, ignore the right 'to an effective judicial remedy'.[18] Such a solution, although controversial,[19] is in accordance with the ECtHR case law.[20]

This situation is much more complicated at the international level as long as sovereign States are equal, which means that neither of them can unilaterally impose international arbitration on each other; arbitration could only have legitimacy if it was instituted by means of a treaty – bilateral, plurilateral or multilateral. But that situation would raise another question: could such a treaty require the subjects of signatory States to refer their disputes to the established arbitral tribunal rather than to another court, in particular a State court? Assumptions are rare and very controversial.

The question arose in a case in which a contract had been concluded between two companies, one Romanian and the other Lebanese, containing an arbitration clause giving jurisdiction to the Court of Arbitration of the Chamber of Commerce and Industry of Romania. However, a bilateral treaty had been concluded between Romania and Lebanon, providing that private disputes between the nationals of these two States should be settled by arbitration before the ICC Court of Arbitration in Paris. On the basis of this agreement, one of the parties had referred the matter to the Paris Chamber of Commerce, which had recognized its jurisdiction since the bilateral treaty made arbitration mandatory in the event of a dispute arising between legal persons of the two signatory countries concerning contracts concluded on the basis of the treaty. The award was nevertheless annulled by the Paris Court of Appeal on the ground that, in the absence of the consent of the parties, the jurisdiction of the arbitral tribunal constituted under the Paris ICC's aegis was unfounded.[21] The solution seems to be open to criticism.[22] The jurisdiction of the Paris' ICC Court of arbitration was based on the bilateral treaty concluded between the States of which the litigants were nationals. A treaty creates obligations towards the States party to it, but it may also, sometimes, exceptionally, create rights or impose obligations on the subjects of the signatory States. We know that some international treaties or conventions have a direct effect, or a horizontal direct effect, that allows them to apply to relations between private

18. The validity of this mandatory arbitration was confirmed by the Conseil Constitutionnel when deciding *Société Yonne Republicaine and others*, No. 2012-243/244/245/246 QPC of 14 May 2012, particularly point 13 on the absence of infringement of the right to an effective judicial remedy. *See* no. 13-27759, Soc., 15 April 2015.
19. The Italian Constitutional Court declared the unconstitutionality of mandatory arbitration in Decision No. 177 of 14 July 1977, reaffirmed in a decision of May 9, 1996, *Mortini v. Comune di Alidone, Foro pad*, case law cited by Diallo (*supra* n. 14) 62.
20. *Mutu and Pechstein* (*supra* n. 4) at 94.
21. No. 99-19878, Civ. 1st, 19 March 2002: 'Only the common will of the parties to a contract has the power to vest the arbitrator with his jurisdictional power; … the Court of Appeal, which retained the lack of common consent … at the disposal of the Interstate Agreement of December 6 1980 providing for ICC arbitration, correctly deduced from this, whatever the mandatory nature of this Agreement in the Romanian internal order from which it had nevertheless been derogated from in the 1985 contract, the absence of an arbitration agreement within the ICC framework'.
22. *See* the opposing views on this issue between Brigitte Stern, Revue Arbitrage, 403 (2000) and Eric Loquin, Journal de Droit International, 370 (2000). *See* also Eric Loquin, *Des difficultés posées par l'application du principe de l'origine nécessairement conventionnelle du tribunal arbitral en matière... d'arbitrage forcé*, Revue Trimestrielle de Droit Commercial, 664 (2002).

persons, for example the ECHR.[23] Was this the case with the bilateral trade treaty between Romania and Lebanon? In any case, the text of the treaty expressly envisaged its application to contracts concluded between companies of the contracting States. For this reason, arbitration could here be considered as a mandatory one, valid without the consent of the individuals potentially parties to it, and without any violation of their fundamental right of access to justice. In theory (the hypothesis is rare in practice, almost a textbook case), an international treaty could undoubtedly institute a mandatory arbitration which would be binding on the nationals of the signatory States not because of their consent, but of an act of sovereignty.

This case can be compared with the well-known Iranian-American Dispute Tribunal in The Hague, established by the Algiers Agreements between the US and Iran which require nationals of both countries to act before that court to settle certain types of disputes, to the exclusion of any other judge, including a State judge.[24] The question of the true nature of this jurisdiction has given rise to the strongest oppositions, without a consensus being reached.[25] Nevertheless, it is not convincing that the nationals' lack of consent would be sufficient to make the established procedure lose its status of an *ad hoc* arbitration.[26] Arbitration being one way of access to justice among others, may be imposed by an act of legitimate sovereignty of the States concerned over their subjects, including at the international level. It follows that the characteristics of arbitration would not be limited to the consent of the parties alone,[27] and that other characteristics such as the parties' possibility to designate their arbitrator(s), or the special procedure applicable to arbitration, are all elements that can make it possible to define this method of dispute settlement.[28]

---

23. Béatrice Montel, *L'effet horizontal" de la Convention européenne des droits de l'homme en droit privé français*, thèse de l'Université de Limoges (2006).
24. The Declaration of the Government of the democratic and popular republic of Algeria,19 January 1981, www.iusct.net/General%20Documents/1-General%20Declaration%E2%80%8E.pdf (accessed 22 October 2019) provides: 'It is the purpose of both parties... to terminate all litigation as between the government of each party and the nationals of the other, *and to bring about the settlement and termination of all such claims through binding arbitration*. Through the procedures provided in the declaration relating to the Claims Settlement Agreement, the United States agrees to terminate all legal proceedings in United States courts involving claims of United States persons and institutions against Iran and its state enterprises, to nullify all attachments and judgments obtained therein, to prohibit all further litigation based on such claims, and to bring about the termination of such claims through binding arbitration ...'.
25. David D. Caron, *The Nature of the Iran-United States Claims Tribunal and the Evolving Structure of International Dispute Resolution*, 84(1) American Journal of International Law 84 (1990).
26. *Contra* recommendation No. 1 made by the Working Group of the Club of Jurists chaired by Professor Thomas Clay in its report *Online Arbitration* (7-8 April 2019), http://www.leclubdesjuristes.com/wp-content/uploads/2019/04/Online-Arbitration.pdf (Accessed on 20 October 2019).
27. Jean-Michel Jacquet, preface to Diallo (*supra* n. 14) XVIII declared: 'State, which still has the power to judge, can perfectly guide the parties towards a justice different from that rendered by its own courts, without distorting arbitration, the characteristics of which are not limited to the consent of the parties'.
28. Diallo (*supra* n. 14) 81 stated: 'Thus, it is clear that, in the final analysis, the difference between arbitration and judicial settlement does not lie so much in the legal (for the judge) or conventional (for the arbitrator) basis of their jurisdiction as in their way of proceeding. Flexibility and the important role of the will of the parties in the arbitration procedure are increasingly a determining factor in the identity of arbitration'.

In any event, it must be recognized that mandatory arbitration can only be understood as arbitration imposed by an act of sovereignty (a national law or a treaty) on which it is based, which fundamentally distinguishes it from consensual arbitration, an alternative to State justice which can only be based on the consent of the parties, but which States may sometimes limit to certain persons or object matters.

It is therefore always important to determine whether individuals have an option or not, if the established tribunal is mandatory or not, so that to determine whether consent is consubstantial with the arbitration in question. This question arises in the field of the CETA which envisages a mechanism for the resolution of ISDS.[29] The text of the agreement provides that investors 'may' – not must – bring a claim against the host State,[30] before the tribunal constituted under the treaty – of a hybrid nature, halfway between State and arbitral justice.[31] Does this mean that this competence would not be mandatory for investors? Could the latter prefer bringing their dispute before another traditional arbitral tribunal, rather than before the ISDS? In such a case, if the host State accepts the jurisdiction of that other tribunal, it could be subject to infringement proceedings brought by the European institutions. But should this arbitral tribunal decline jurisdiction when both parties to the dispute have given their consent? In reality, two interpretations of the treaty seem to be possible.[32] Either the jurisdiction of the tribunal constituted is considered as optional for the investor whose consent is logically required, but it would then be necessary to consider the scope of the option offered to him by the text between State courts and/or traditional arbitral tribunal. Either the jurisdiction of the tribunal constituted is mandatory and in that case the question is to know how to interpret the consent. It could be required only under the procedure applicable before the tribunal. Indeed, a distinction must be made between the constituting conditions of a mandatory arbitration and the regime of this one, in particular the question of the possibility for the tribunal's awards to benefit the NYC regime (which requires consent). The issue does not seem to be clearly resolved today.

Nevertheless, the expression of 'compulsory arbitration', kind of a 'curiosity' because of its rarity, can only refer to a hypothesis of arbitration imposed either by law or by a treaty, to the exclusion of all others wrongly qualified as such. Some of these last cases need now to be examined to determine whether the shift from forced arbitration to forced consent would result in the disappearance of consent.

---

29. *See* the favourable opinion given by the CJEU to the creation of this mechanism in the opinion 1/17 30 April 2019.
30. Article 8.18.1 says: 'An investor of a Party *may* submit to the Tribunal constituted under this Section a claim that the other Party has breached an obligation…' and Article 8.23.1: 'If a dispute has not been resolved through consultations, a claim *may* be submitted under this Section…'.
31. The tribunal should be composed of judges appointed not by the parties but by the States (see Article 8.27 CETA). The awards of that tribunal should benefit from the favourable regime of the New York Convention, but they also should be subject to appeal (see Article 8.28 CETA).
32. Article 8.22: '1. An investor may only submit a claim pursuant to Article 8.23 if the investor: (a) delivers to the respondent, with the submission of a claim, its consent to the settlement of the dispute by the Tribunal in accordance with the procedures set out in this Section;'.

§2.03 THE REALITY OF A FORCED CONSENT IN ARBITRATION

We have just seen that arbitration can be forced when it is imposed by an act of sovereignty. This is the only hypothesis in the light of access to justice in which consent could be dispensed with. In all other cases, as long as States offer to litigants an alternative between a judge and an arbitrator, only the willingness of the parties can invest a private person with the power to settle their dispute. The power to judge, which is not exclusively reserved to States, can only be vested in a private person if the litigants consent to it. Thus, while the arbitrator's function is jurisdictional, its basis is contractual. The rules of contract law apply to the arbitration agreement resulting from the freedom of contract.[33] Decisions of national courts and international arbitral awards frequently recall that 'arbitration is a matter of contract and a party cannot be required to submit to arbitration any dispute which he has not agreed so to submit'.[34] Therefore, as with any other contract, this agreement will only be considered validly formed if the consent of the parties exists and presents certain characteristics as recalled by the ECtHR. This latter requires that the waiver of ordinary courts' jurisdiction and its guarantees must be 'free, lawful and unequivocal'.[35]

But we will see from the ECtRH's case *Mutu and Pechstein*[36] related to CAS sports arbitration that consent might be forced sometimes, which tends, moreover, to multiply in other types of arbitration. However, this hypothesis of forced consent in arbitration is not equivalent to that of forced arbitration from the point of view of access to justice. Indeed, a forced consent may sometimes be legitimate, sometimes not, and when it is it can be considered, in our view, that the parties have expressed a willingness to invest a private person of the jurisdictional function. Access to justice does not appear to be compromised.

In the case of Ms Pechstein, a professional skater, the arbitration clause opposed to her was inserted in the sports regulations of the international federation of her discipline. In order to have the right to participate in international competitions, Mrs Peichstein had to adhere to these rules, i.e. to the arbitration agreement contained therein giving exclusive competence to the CAS – which can be seen as an arbitration clause 'by reference' –, which she had done by signing a declaration of acceptance.[37] The problem in the present case was that, because of the federation's monopoly on international sports competitions, Mrs Pechstein had in reality no choice: either she adhered to the said regulation or she had to 'completely renounce earning a living by practising her discipline at such a level'.[38] On this basis the ECtHR concluded that she

33. *See* Alan Scott RAU, *The Culture of American Arbitration and the Lessons of ADR*, 40 Texas International Law Journal 478 (2005), who discusses the two models of arbitration, the contractual model and the jurisdictional model, and links American international arbitration law to the contractual model and arbitration to the family of contracts.
34. *United Steelworkers of America v. Warrior & Gulf Nav Co* (1960) 363 US 574, 582.
35. *Mutu and Pechstein* (*supra* n. 4) at paragraph 103.
36. *Ibid.*
37. *Ibid.*, at paragraphs 84 and 85.
38. *Ibid.*, at paragraph 113.

did not freely accept the waiver of the ordinary courts' jurisdiction in favour of the CAS, and that this arbitration therefore constituted a 'mandatory' one.

This last qualification is open to criticism: what seems to be imposed here is not CAS arbitration as the court says, but rather the athlete's consent. Although existing, it was forced.

Obviously, CAS arbitration is not imposed by a law or a treaty, by a legitimate act of sovereignty. The court itself acknowledges this, stating that the CAS arbitration clause constituted a mandatory arbitration even though it 'had not been imposed by law'.[39] It is generally included in the regulations or statutes of sports federations which are associations, i.e. legal persons governed by private law, in the registration forms for a sports competition issued by these federations or in the athletes' contracts (for example in the employment contract which bound Mr Mutu to his football club).[40] In other words, the arbitration clause is issued from acts made by private persons, not from State acts, which does not prevent the court from validating this arbitration considered as being in accordance with the ECHR.[41] We can note here an extension of the field of mandatory arbitration, without the court justifying it. In reality, it implicitly equates sports law with State law, sports power with public power, probably because of the hierarchical and unbalanced relationship within the sports legal order between an athlete and their federation;[42] one is in a situation of strength, the other in a situation of weakness or even of economic dependence (as of Mrs Peichstein). Therefore sport 'law' would impose arbitration on athletes (so that is mandatory arbitration). But the assimilation to an act of public authority is questionable.

In fact, the discussion here is more about the quality of the athlete's consent than about his or her existence. In reality, consent can be seen as given without any State constraint, either by Mrs Peichstein by signing a declaration of acceptance or by Mr Mutu by signing his employment contract – it is all the more true for Mr Mutu since, unlike Mrs Peichstein, the rules of his sports federation, in this case FIFA, did not impose the CAS arbitration but left the choice of dispute settlement mechanism to the contractual freedom of clubs and players. Hence, neither the law nor the FIFA regulation required Mr Mutu to accept the arbitration clause.[43] We will later see that

39. *Ibid.*
40. Mr Mutu had signed an employment contract in which he agreed to abide by the rules of the International Football Federation (FIFA) 2001, Article 42 of which gave jurisdiction – non-exclusive – to CAS arbitration. *Mutu and Pechstein* (*supra* n. 4) at paragraph 80.
41. According to the decision, two types of CAS arbitration are now likely to coexist: consensual arbitration and forced arbitration, the difference between the two being less in their nature than in their legal regime. The parties having been forced to accept CAS arbitration would not have accepted the exclusion of the procedural guarantees offered by Article 6 § 1 of the ECHR, unlike those having granted them, which the court recognizes the right to voluntarily renounce certain rights guaranteed by the convention, *Mutu and Pechstein* (*supra* n. 4) at paragraph 95. In practice, CAS has since amended its arbitration rules to extend procedural guarantees to all its consensual and forced arbitrations, the difference between the two now appears very small.
42. Franck Latty in *CAS scores points before the ECHR*, 192, Jurisport, 31-36, 33 (December 2018) states that: 'The *lex sportiva* produces binding effects on the athlete that are very similar to those of its national law'. On the notion of 'sporting power', see Gérald Simon, *Puissance sportive et ordre juridique étatique*, (LGDJ, 1990) 1-430.
43. *Mutu and Pechstein* (*supra* n. 4) at paragraph 116.

according to Mr Mutu the inequality of bargaining power between him and the club made arbitration compulsory, which is however not the case.

It is obviously possible to consider that the athlete's real willingness to resort to arbitration is in fact ignored, so the non-acceptance of arbitration is associated with a sanction; if the athlete refuses the clause, he cannot join the federation and is denied access to sporting competitions. The federation, a private person, thus makes athletes' membership of its group conditional on compliance with the operating conditions it itself has predefined. But should we consider the real, internal intention of the parties, or the declared one?[44] The declared intention has well been expressed; the athlete has expressed consent.

However, consent does not systematically meet the usual requirements. It appears more or less forced depending on the degree of constraint on the athlete, which varies from case to case. Mr Mutu for instance has not been considered as having been placed in a situation of constraint equivalent to that of Mrs Peichstein, who opposed the International Skating Federation (ISF) which had previously been condemned by the European Commission for anticompetitive practices because of its regulations prohibiting skaters from taking part in sporting events organized by independent third parties (i.e. not by the ISF).[45]

One athlete's situation does not appear to be fundamentally different from that of other social categories, such as that of employees vis-à-vis employers or that of consumers vis-à-vis traders. What can be said about the employee who is required by the employer to accept an arbitration clause, or even a clause waiving in advance any collective action against them, as a condition for the conclusion of their employment contract? Admittedly, it could be considered, as the ECtHR did in the Mutu case, that the employee is free to choose another employer and therefore free not to conclude the employment contract containing the said arbitration agreement. But when more than 50% of employers in the United States adopt the same behaviour, is the employee really free to refuse?[46]

In reality, it is not so much a mandatory arbitration in these situations than a forced consent of the person to whom the arbitration clause is opposed; consent exists because an acceptance is declared, but it results from a constraint exercised by a person who is strong in bargaining power: an international federation, an employer, a trader,

44. The voluntary tradition of French law whereby the internal intention, if proven, takes precedence over the declared one, appears to be isolated at the international level. In German law or in *common law*, the intention of the parties is assessed through the terms of the contract and not through what their mindset was when concluding the contract.
45. *AT.40208 – International Skating Union's Eligibility Rules*, C(2017) 8240 final (European Commission 8 December 2017). An action for annulment of this decision was brought before the Court of First Instance of the European Union on 19 February 2018 (*International Skating Union v. Commission*, T-93/18).
46. Alexander J.S. Colvin, in *The growing use of mandatory arbitration, Economic Policy Institute* (6 April 2018), https://www.epi.org/files/pdf/144131.pdf (accessed on 22 October 2019), stated: 'In a trend driven by a series of Supreme Court decisions dating back to 1991, American employers are increasingly requiring their workers to sign mandatory arbitration agreements… Since the early 2000s, the share of workers subject to mandatory arbitration has more than doubled and now exceeds 55 percent'.

etc. In these circumstances, the question is to know whether the coercion is legitimate and thus whether consent can be considered as validly given, or not.

Coercion may indeed be considered legitimate in some cases. A person who needs to drive a car, in particular to carry out his or her work, is required to take out an insurance contract. Although forced, consent to the insurance contract remains valid because it is justified by imperatives of general interest (in this case, protecting the person against himself but also protecting third parties against the risks to which he exposes them as a result of his activity).

More generally, many contractual relationships are found to be unbalanced due to inequality between the parties, when one is in a situation of weakness or economic dependence on the other. It is not uncommon when there is no equality of arms for one party to take advantage of his situation to impose their will on others, and in particular the insertion of an arbitration clause. However, the agreement cannot be void or voidable only due to this imbalance alone, which is often inherent in economic relations. It can be only from a protective legislation (e.g. in European consumer law, legislation to combat unfair terms)[47] or from a case of duress. However, under French and English law, in order for duress to be characterized, it is required for the coercion to be unlawful, i.e., the conduct of a party acting violently has to obtain a 'manifestly excessive advantage'[48] from this situation.

But how should such an excessive advantage in the case of an arbitration agreement that is a procedural agreement be characterized? The latter does not create any substantive rights. In order to obtain its invalidity, it would have to be shown that arbitration is a form of justice in principle more favourable to the person in a strong bargaining position than would an ordinary court, which seems highly unlikely,[49] except possibly if the composition of the arbitral tribunal cast suspicion on its independence.

There are doubts about the chances of success of such a reasoning in the case of CAS. Indeed, the ECtHR recognizes that 'there is a definite interest' in the fact that disputes arising in the context of professional sport at international level may be submitted to it: not only is the CAS a 'specialized' court, 'able to rule quickly and economically', which 'facilitates a certain procedural uniformity and strengthens legal certainty',[50] but its independence from the sports organizations which it is called upon to judge (federations) is regularly recognized by various courts.[51] Thus, although

47. *See Mostaza Claro* Case C-168-05 (ECJ 26 October 2006); *Asturcom*, Case C-40:08 (ECJ 6 October 2009).

48. Article 1143 of the French Civil Code: 'Violence also occurs when a party, abusing the state of dependence in which its co-contractor is dependent on it, obtains from it a commitment which it would not have entered into in the absence of such coercion and derives a manifestly excessive advantage from it'. In *Pao On v. Lau Yiu Long* (1980) AC 614 it was held that for a contract to be voidable for economic duress there must be a threat or pressure which is *illegitimate* and that pressure or threat must amount to a coercion of will that vitiates consent'.

49. *See* Civ. 1re civ., n° 03-19692 (1 February 2005) ruling that, in connection with a clause inserted in a consumer contract (syndic's contract) and requiring prior conciliation in the context of a dispute between the syndic and a co-owner, it was free of any significant imbalance to the detriment of the consumer and that it was therefore not in itself unfair.

50. *Mutu and Pechstein* (*supra* n. 4) at paragraph 98.

51. *Mutu and Pechstein* (*supra* n. 4) at paragraph 157.

sometimes forced, consent to CAS arbitration would nevertheless be valid since the constraint exercised on the athlete is not illegitimate - procedural guarantees being then granted to the athlete[52].

The question is more controversial regarding the arbitration clauses included in employment contracts in the United States. A study published in 2018 revealed that an increasing number of companies are demanding that their employees, or consumers,[53] agree in advance to waive recourse to a State court if a dispute arises between them.[54] This can be seen, as in the case of sports arbitration, as a hypothesis where the consent of the employee or consumer has been given but under duress - what some authors probably more accurately call arbitration 'adhesionary' or 'disparate-party' arbitration.[55] In the name of the existence of this consent, the US Supreme Court validated these arbitration agreements. It even ruled, in *Epic Systems Corp. v. J. Lewis*,[56] decided on 21 May 2018, that when this arbitration clause was coupled with an advance waiver by the employee to participate in a class action, it remained valid, and therefore enforceable, under the Federal Arbitration Act, despite section 7 of the National Labour Relations Act 1935, which protects the right of employees to participate in concerted (collective) activities. The existence of consent seems indisputable from our point of view. But still, has it been given freely? American arbitration law allows, as with any contract, to challenge the validity of an arbitration agreement, particularly for duress or unconscionability.[57] However, it must be noted that the Supreme Court did not consider these clauses invalid because of duress or inequality of bargaining power contrary to common fairness.

52. Diallo (*supra* n. 14) 57.
53. In the United States, most consumer contracts contain an arbitration clause. Julia A. Scarpino, *Mandatory Arbitration of Consumer Disputes*, 10(3) Journal of Gender, Social Policy & the Law 679 (2002).
54. Colvin (*supra* n. 46). A 1991 Supreme Court decision, *Gilmer v. Interstate/Johnson Lane*, 1991, 500 US 20, upheld the enforceability of mandatory employment arbitration agreements. Then, a series of court decisions have subsequently broadened the scope of the 1991 Court decision so that in recent years, the use of mandatory arbitration in employment has been upheld. Colvin (*supra* n. 46) declared: 'These decisions have likely encouraged employers to require these agreements, expanding the use of mandatory arbitration. In two key decisions, *AT&T Mobility LLC v. Concepcion* (2011) (563 U.S. 333) and *American Express Co. v. Italian Colors Restaurant* (2013) (133 S. Ct. 594), the Supreme Court held that class action waivers in mandatory arbitration agreements were broadly enforceable'.
55. Thomas E. Carbonneau, *Arguments in Favor of the Triumph of Arbitration*, 10 *Cardozo J. Conflict Resol* 398 (2009).
56. 138 S. Ct. 1612 (2018). The plaintiffs were employees who had agreed in employment agreements to individually arbitrate any disputes arising out of their employment and to waive any class or collective claims. Despite these agreements, plaintiffs brought class or collective actions in federal court asserting wage and hour violations related to overtime pay under the Fair Labor Standards Act (FLSA). *Epic Systems Corp. v. J. Lewis*, 584 US (2018); Cherine Foty, *U.S. Supreme Court Holds That Individualized Employer-Employee Arbitration Agreements Must Be Enforced as Written*, http://arbitrationblog.kluwerarbitration.com/2018/06/29/u-s-supreme-court-holds-individualized-employer-employee-arbitration-agreements-must-enforced-written-2/ (accessed 22 October 2019).
57. Also, for fraud.

However, the legitimacy of these clauses can be challenged, as some authors have shown that the arbitration agreement favours the company when the implementation of the employee's substantive rights proves to be more difficult procedurally in the context of arbitration than before the State judge:

> [r]esearch has found that employees are less likely to win arbitration cases and they recover lower damages in mandatory employment arbitration than in the courts. Indeed, employers have a significant advantage in the process given that they are the ones who define the mandatory arbitration procedures and select the arbitration providers.[58]

But the evidence of duress is probably too difficult.

The question of legitimacy in consent imposed by the stronger party as a condition for concluding a contract with a weaker party or for access to a service, etc., is a sea snake under US law. Until now, no answer has been found due to political disagreements[59] that have led to the repeated failure of bills regularly tabled over the years to combat this type of arbitration.[60]

Whilst many countries make arbitrability a condition on the parties to the arbitration agreement to enable negotiation on equal terms in order to protect the integrity of consent, French law, for instance, is now adopting a third way. The solution it provides appears to respect contractual freedom (disputes in labour or consumer law are no longer non-arbitrable by nature) and to protect the weak party to whom the arbitration clause is opposed. In 2016, an act was enacted[61] to make it possible to insert an arbitration clause in contracts (domestic and international),[62] in which the parties are dealing with disposal of rights, which covers all contractual matters, i.e. consumer and employment contracts. As in US law, arbitration clauses are in principle valid in employment or consumer contracts. But a very important safeguard has been put in place for consumers,[63] which already existed for employees.[64] When they contract with a trader or an employer, the arbitration clause that has been included in their consumer contract (in general terms and conditions in particular) or employment contract, is

58. Katherine V.W. Stone and Alexander J.S. COLVIN, *Mandatory arbitration deprives workers and consumers of their rights*, The arbitration epidemic, paper 414 (December 7, 2015), https://www.epi.org/files/2015/arbitration-epidemic.pdf (accessed 22 October 2019).
59. Carbonneau (*supra* n. 55) 400 declared: 'The left is preoccupied with the unfairness associated with a contract imposed unilaterally *by* the stronger party upon the weaker party on a take-it-or-leave-it basis... The right propounds a position based upon the sanctity and freedom of contract. Parties in the marketplace should be at liberty to agree to any exchange to which they mutually consent and which complies with the minimal requisites of public policy'.
60. Many legislative proposals have been regularly filed since the *Arbitration Fairness Act of 2007*, up to *The Forced Arbitration Injustice Repeal Act* ('FAIR Act'), February 28, 2019, Senate bill S. 610; HR 1423, https://www.congress.gov/bill/116th-congress/house-bill/1423/text (accessed 22 October 2019).
61. Act No. 2016-1547 of 18 November 2016 on the modernization of twenty-first century justice.
62. This was already the case in international consumer contracts since the *Jaguari* case (no. 95-11427, Civ 1st, 21 May 1997).
63. Article 2061 paragraph 2 of the Civil Code ('The arbitration clause must have been accepted by the party to whom it is opposed, unless the latter has succeeded to the rights and obligations of the party who initially accepted it (para. 1). Where one of the parties has not entered into a contract in the course of his professional activity, the clause may not be invoked against him (para. 2)').

unenforceable against them if they do not wish to implement it. In other words, the law offers them an option of protective jurisdiction. When a dispute arises, the consumer[65] or employee can choose between resorting to arbitration or preferring to bring the matter before the State judge. The trader or employer shall not have the same right of choice if they are given their consent to the insertion of an arbitration clause in the contract. Favour is given to the weak party.[66]

This solution appears to fully respect the consensual nature of the arbitration as it decouples the arbitration offer from its acceptance over time. To be valid, the arbitration clause included, for example, in the trader's general conditions must present this offer of jurisdiction to the consumer, who can only undertake, at the time the contract is concluded, to make a choice of forum once the dispute has arisen and therefore to 'exercise the option' of the arbitration clause if he so wishes. At that sole moment, he will be able, in complete freedom, to choose the path of arbitration after having usefully inquired about its cost, the payment of his procedural costs, his place, etc.[67] The effects of this 'optional' clause,[68] also called 'unilateral effect',[69] are suspended from its unilateral will. Consent does exist, and it is also fully informed, which reinforces the consensual nature of arbitration. The solution must be approved. As one author notes, 'as long as the option is stipulated in favour of the party who needs protection from the likely abuses of his partner, the consent conveyed by unilateral arbitration clauses is in no way questionable'.[70] In the present case, the fact that the option derives here from the law, and not from the agreement of the parties, proves to be protective and justifies the acceptance in this case of this type of clause, whose validity is otherwise much more questionable in the light of the principle of equality between the parties – like asymmetric arbitration clauses.[71]

---

64. In an international employment contract since a decision no. 96-40643, Soc. 16 February 1999, including when it is performed abroad (no. 99-43288, Soc., 9 October 2001). Then in an internal employment contract since no. 11-12905, 11-12905 and 11-1290, Soc. 30 November 2011, *BW Deloitte*.
65. Jean-Georges Betto, *Arbitration, a new consumer weapon?*, JCP 426 (2017). Also, Thomas Clay, *Les arbitrages des conflits du travail*, Cahier du CNB, 38 (3rd ed., 2017).
66. Jean-Baptiste Racine, *Droit de l'arbitrage* 149 (Thémis, 2016).
67. As Professor Jean-Baptiste Racine points out: 'the arbitration agreement appears to be harmful whenever its purpose or effect is to prevent or make access to justice for consumers (by geographical distance, cost, etc.) much more difficult', *ibid.*, 187.
68. Philippe Fouchard, Emmanuel Gaillard, Berthold Goldman, *Traité de l'arbitrage commercial international*, 288 (Litec, 1996). In this case, if the weaker party chooses to bring the case before the Court, the effects of the arbitration clause are neutralized, hence the sanction of unenforceability.
69. Also 'one-sided arbitration agreement', 'asymmetric arbitration agreement', 'unilateral option clause'... In the US law, the validity of 'Unilateral Option Clauses' remains susceptible to a great deal of uncertainty and debate. Courts that uphold their validity rely on party autonomy. Courts that reject such validity rely on a wide array of arguments. For a critical presentation of the arguments used by courts to reject their validity, *see* Youssef Nassar, *Are Unilateral Option Clauses valid?*, http://arbitrationblog.kluwerarbitration.com/2018/10/13/are-unilateral-option-clauses-valid/ (accessed 22 October 2019).
70. Diallo (*supra* n. 14) 111.
71. Because one party is firmly committed to arbitration, the other is not. On this principle, Loquin (*supra* n. 10) 261-265. This could be different in the case of a bilateral optional clause. See,

We saw that hypotheses quickly qualified as 'mandatory arbitrations' are very diverse and questionable. Most of the time, consent is forced, which means that it exists, which is why we can say that the consensual basis of arbitration remains in most of cases where alternative jurisdiction is offered by the State to private persons. Consent is very largely consubstantial with arbitration and hence with access to justice. The arbitration agreement voluntarily confers jurisdiction, in the sense that the parties waive the jurisdiction of the State courts to vest a third party with a jurisdictional task, i.e. with the power to decide their dispute knowing that his decision will be binding on them. When consent to the arbitration agreement appears to be forced by one of the parties, the mandatory jurisdiction of the arbitral tribunal results from a private act, not from the exercise of sovereignty. It may however sometimes prove illegitimate.

Once the reality of consent in arbitration has been established, its form must be addressed. It takes different forms, according to the needs for efficiency of the arbitration, which also sometimes raises questions about its true existence.

§2.04 CONSENT, THE 'HARLEQUIN' OF ARBITRATION

As noted previously, access to justice may mean access to an arbitral tribunal which requires, apart from cases of mandatory arbitration, the characterization of consent. The form that such consent must take is not an incidental or trivial matter in view of the confusion that has arisen. Indeed, in recent years, the turmoil has set in because consent in arbitration would have declined, to such an extent that some authors question whether it is still the basis of arbitration. This raises the idea of a decline in will in arbitration law. Professors Kaufmann-Kholer and Henry Peter wrote:

> More and more, the classical concept of arbitration based on consent is being supplemented by other concepts of arbitration which largely ignores this requirement. This is especially in the areas of sport, consumer transactions, and investment arbitrations based on treaties or national statutes.[72]

We would thus see 'a growing new category of arbitration without consent'.[73] We are not convinced by such a conclusion. Consent remains the cornerstone of arbitration, but its form evolves into a functional approach to arbitration.

All national and international laws converge on the point that consent is a condition for the validity of arbitration – except in the case of mandatory arbitration.

---

however, Bas van Zelst, *Unilateral Option Arbitration clauses: An unequivocal choice for arbitration under the ECHR?*, 25(1) Maastricht Journal of European and Comparative Law 77 (2018).

72. Gabrielle Kaufmann-Kholer and Henry Peter in *Formula 1 Racing and Arbitration: the FIA Tailor-Made System for Fast-Track Dispute Resolution*, 17(2) Arbitration International 186 (2001) argued that: 'One may choose to cling to the dogma of consent and when no true and meaningful consent exists, rely on a fiction of consent. But if we merely preserve the appearance of consent, this justification for arbitration is no longer compelling. Indeed, it may be more accurate and intellectually honest to simply admit that arbitration without consent exists. Having made that admission, one can then investigate the requirements that have come to replace consent. Are there any? What are they? Simply the fairness of the process? Or others? Which ones?'.
73. *Ibid.*, 186.

Traditionally, this consent is expressed in an arbitration agreement (arbitration clause or compromise), which requires to characterize both an offer and an acceptance. To promote informed consent to the arbitration agreement, some laws impose formal requirements. While a distinction is usually made between the substantive requirements and the formal requirements of the arbitration agreement, both are in reality linked, in the same way as the formal requirements imposed by European Law on the validity of the jurisdiction clause intended to ensure that the consent of the parties is actually given.[74] Form serves here the essential substantive requirement: namely, informed consent to the arbitration clause.

Most European Conventions and laws thus require a written form of consent, sometimes for validity purposes, sometimes as evidence only. This is the case with the NYC, which specifies (Article II) that writing must expressly characterize the common consent of the parties. But some countries, notably France,[75] New Zealand, Scotland, Sweden and Denmark, do not have any formal requirements.[76] The validity of the arbitration agreement is then based solely on the consent of the parties, whose evidence may be more freely provided. As for England, not only does the Arbitration Act of 1996 (section 5) define the concept of writing very broadly, but case law accepts that an agreement made without writing, in particular orally, but referring to written conditions is equivalent to an agreement in writing.[77]

The evolution of arbitration law is interesting on this point because it shows that the condition of consent is interpreted more and more broadly, flexibly in its form, in favour of a consent qualified by some as 'functional', i.e. in the service of a greater possible efficiency of arbitration. In many cases, the basis of the arbitration agreement may indeed become increasingly objective, but the condition of consent never actually disappears.

Consent to arbitration is likely to be expressed in several ways. In particular, the meeting of consents may not always be simultaneous, as the acceptance of the arbitration clause is sometimes dissociated, decoupled, from the offer - as in consumer or labour arbitration under French law where the weaker party can decide to opt for arbitration at the time the dispute arises. The choice of option then retroacts to the day of conclusion of the contract and becomes effective (it produces legal effects). The arbitration agreement comes into existence at that point.

---

74. Article 25 § 1 of the Brussels I *bis* Regulation (former Article 23).
75. Article 1507 NCP: 'The arbitration agreement is not subject to any formal requirements'.
76. Hong-Lin Yu, *Written Arbitration Agreements — What Written Arbitration Agreements?*, 32(1) Civil Justice Quarterly 68 (2012).
77. In *Zambia Steel & Building Supplies Ltd. v. James Clark & Eaton Ltd*, [1986] 2 Lloyd's Rep. 225 the English sellers had sent to the Zambian buyers a quotation which was no more than an invitation to make an offer and which contained an arbitration clause. The contract was concluded orally in Zambia on the terms of the quotation. The Court of Appeal held that the buyers had orally assented to the written terms and that therefore there existed an agreement in writing to submit to arbitration within the meaning of section 7 of the English Arbitration Act 1975.

More delicate and contested is the case of consent to investment arbitration. The majority doctrine agrees that the host State, in a convention, law or treaty,[78] would make a permanent, general and impersonal offer of arbitration, which the private investor would accept when initiating the arbitration procedure. Consent would be tacit here since it results from conduct: by referring the dispute to the arbitral tribunal, the investor agrees to have it decided by a private judge rather than by a State judge and an arbitration agreement is formed between the parties. But another part of the doctrine contests the existence of an arbitration agreement, considering that investment arbitration has opened the door to another type of arbitration, some to forced arbitration,[79] others to voluntary arbitration, whose name varies ('unilateral transnational arbitration',[80] 'arbitration without privity', etc.) *but not based on an arbitration agreement* – the jurisdiction of the arbitral tribunal (in particular ICSID) not being based on a direct agreement between the parties to the dispute (consents are not expressed in the same *instrumentum*).[81] In the case of *Société générale de surveillance S.A. v. Philippines*, the arbitral tribunal stated:

> The parties have consented in writing to ICSID arbitration. It is generally accepted that consent to ICSID jurisdiction may be given in any one of the following ways: by a direct agreement...; by a provision in the host State's investment legislation which is accepted by the investor; or by an offer made by the State in a treaty which is thereafter accepted by an investor of the other contracting State...[82]

The form of consent seems to be at the heart of the discussions here; acceptance not only appears to be time-delayed in relation to the offer but is also tacitly expressed by the behaviour of the private investor. Does this disqualify the exchange of consents? *A priori* no. Many authors then highlighted the originality of the agreement thus

---

78. Provided that the State decides to make such an offer in a bilateral or multilateral convention, law or treaty on investment protection.
79. The qualification is open to criticism for at least two reasons: the first is that States do give free consent to arbitration, the second is that almost all instruments do not establish exclusive jurisdiction for arbitration but offer an option to the investor between public and private justice. The latter therefore also gives its consent. On this point, *see* Sébastien Manciaux, *Foreign Investments and Arbitration between States and nationals of other States. Thirty years of ICSID's activity*, 194, (CREDIMI, Litec, 2004).
80. Walid Ben Hamida, *Unilateral transnational arbitration – Reflections on a procedure reserved for the initiative of a private person against a public person*, thesis University Panthéon-Assas (Paris II) (2003).
81. Jacques Werner in *The Trade Explosion and Some Likely Effects on International Arbitration*, 14 Journal of International Arbitration 5 (1997) declared that '[w]e enter the era of arbitration without contractual relationship' and Antonio R. Parra in *Provisions on the Settlement of Investment Disputes in Modern Investment Laws, Bilateral Investment Treaties and Multilateral Instruments on Investment*, 12 ICSID Review of Foreign Investment Law Journal, 287 (1997) stated that '[w]ith the huge and still growing number of highly generalized consents by States, this puts the requirement of mutual consent in a new light, quite far removed from traditional contractual conceptions of arbitration', *See* also Geneviève Burdeau, *Nouvelles perspectives pour l'arbitrage dans le contentieux économique intéressant les Etats*, 1 Revue d'Arbitrage, 9 (1995).
82. 'According to SGS, in the present case the parties' consent to refer the dispute to ICSID arbitration was given pursuant to the third method. It arises out of two separate instruments: the BIT between Switzerland and the Philippines, and the SGS's letter of 22 April 2002, received by the Philippines on 24 April 2002', ARB/02/6, http://icsid.worldbank.org (accessed 22 October 2019).

created, a so-called mixed agreement, halfway between the arbitration clause (on the State side) and the compromise (on the investor side, which only accepts arbitration once the dispute has arisen). But whether or not[83] the meeting of consents is qualified, it is at the very least necessary to admit their existence, putting forward the hypothesis that they would then express themselves in a convergent and therefore original way.

However, not all forms of consent to arbitration are exhausted by these assumptions. It is also necessary to mention the case of the arbitration clause by reference or the statutory clause.[84]

The first, the reference clause, is a clause that is not contained in the main contract but in a separate document to which reference is made; the rules of an international sports federation,[85] general conditions of sale, a standard contract, etc. Has the clause thus contained in an attached document been accepted by them? The answer is more or less delicate depending on whether the reference to the appended document is explicit or implicit.[86] When it is explicit (for example, when a clause in the contract expressly refers to the general terms and conditions of one of the parties), the issue does not raise any real difficulty from the point of view of consent. But when the reference is implicit, i.e. when the contract does not mention the reference document and/or the arbitration clause it contains, the situation is more delicate. It then depends on whether the parties were or should have been aware of the said clause, which depends on the circumstances of the case. The usual business relations between them, the practices of the branch, may play a role in proving consent.[87] But the more or less broad admission of this evidence will depend on the formal requirements imposed by national laws, French law being particularly liberal.[88] It is also important to note that such a clause is usually considered compatible with international texts, in particular

83. Diallo (*supra* n. 14) rejects it, considering that the State grants by law or treaty a - non-contractual - right to the investor, which it is the investor's responsibility to implement if he so wishes.
84. On the question of the legality of mandatory arbitration clauses in shareholder agreements, Avani Agarwal and Aditi Ramakrishnan, *Mandatory Shareholder: Moving the Debate to India*, http://arbitrationblog.kluwerarbitration.com/2019/09/01/mandatory-shareholder-arbitration-moving-the-debate-to-india/(accessed 22 October 2019).
85. It is not uncommon for the statutes of the national federation to which athletes belong to simply refer to those of the international federation which contain a clause giving exclusive competence to the CAS. However, this arbitration clause by reference is examined 'with benevolence' by the Swiss Federal Court: 4A_246/2011 (Federal Court, 7 November 2011), recital 2.2.2. and 13 February 2012, 4A_428/2011, *Wickmayer/Malisse*, recital 3.2.3.
86. Jean-François Poudret, Sébastien Besson, *Droit comparé de l'arbitrage international* 176 (Bruylant, 2002).
87. *Tradax Export S.A. v/ Amoco Iran Oil Company*, ATF 110 II 54, (Swiss Federal Court, 7 February 1984) YCA 1986, 532.
88. *Bomar Oil*, No. 91-15194, Civ. 1st, 9 November 1993: 'Whereas in international arbitration proceedings, the arbitration clause by written reference to a document containing it, for example the general conditions or a standard contract, is valid, in the absence of a reference in the main agreement, when the party to whom the clause is opposed was aware of the content of that document at the time the contract was concluded, and has, even if by its silence, accepted the 'incorporation of the document into the contract'. Subsequently, the French court removed the requirement of a 'written reference' to the document containing the arbitration clause (No. 95-17603, Civ. 1st, 3 June 1997).

with Article II of the NYC.[89] As Professor Racine points out, 'the only thing that matters is the existence in fact of consent to the arbitration clause...Whatever its mode of expression, the essential thing is that consent to the clause has been given'.[90]

Some assumptions are nevertheless probably more problematic than others. The question of whether the consent given by one of the parties can be 'extended' to others, who are not signatories to the contract, appears to be particularly thorny and complex. Arbitrators may hear claims brought or against third parties who have not 'signed' the arbitration agreement. In principle, privity of contract prohibits a third party to acquire rights under or enforce the provisions of that contract or rely on them. But some of them are in a particular situation vis-à-vis of the parties, which would justify a 'particular influence'[91] of the arbitration agreement towards them, either through its transmission or its extension. Two hypotheses must be distinguished.[92]

Can the arbitration agreement be extended to third parties (joining non-signatories)? It is often the existence of implicit consent that is put forward to justify such an extension.[93]

Thus, in an ICC *Dow Chemical v. Isover* award,[94] the arbitral tribunal held that a parent company could benefit from the effects of an arbitration agreement inserted in the contract concluded by one of its subsidiaries to which it was a third party if, by its conduct, it resulted that the parent company had 'adhered' to that clause. For domestic laws that do not need any formal requirements of the arbitration agreement, for example French international arbitration law, it is possible to accept that consent may be inferred from a tacit acceptance of the agreement, or even from a presumed acceptance,[95] resulting from the conduct of the third party, and more precisely from its interference or involvement in the negotiation, conclusion, performance or termination

89. Poudret (*supra* n. 86) 189.
90. Racine (*supra* n. 66) 198-200 and 258-259.
91. Christophe Seraglini, Jérôme Ortscheidt, *Droit de l'arbitrage interne et international*, 215 (Domat droit privé, Montchrestien, 2013).
92. Eric Loquin, *Differences and convergences in the regime of the transmission and extension of the arbitration clause before the French courts*, 157 Gaz. Pal., 7 (2002).
93. William W. Park in 'Non-signatories and international contracts: an arbitrator's dilemma', in *Multiple Parties in International Arbitration*, Permanent Court of Arbitration, paragraph 1.10 (Oxford 2009) says that: 'In determining whether a non-signatory should be joined to international proceedings, arbitrators usually look to theories related to implied consent and lack of corporate personality... Verbal formulae vary from one legal system to another. However, most explanations of joinder relate to either implied consent or disregard of corporate personality. In each case, an agreement to arbitrate must exist. However, the effect of that agreement extends beyond the named signatories, by virtue of behavior that either suggests acceptance of the agreement by someone else or justifies going beyond the corporate form of the signatory entity.'
94. Sentence CCI *Dow Chemical*, n° 4131, JDI, 899 (1983), obs. Yves Derains: 'Considering, in particular, that the arbitration clause expressly accepted by certain of the companies of the group should bind the other companies which, by virtue of their role in the conclusion, performance, or termination of the contracts containing said clauses, and in accordance with the mutual intention of all parties to the proceedings, appear to have been veritable parties to these contracts or to have been principally concerned by them and the disputes to which they may give rise'. Jean-François Poudret, Sébastien Besson (*supra* n. 86) 229.
95. CA Paris, 7 December 1994: 'In international arbitration law, the effects of the arbitration clause extend to the parties directly involved in the performance of the contract as soon as their situations and activities give rise to a *presumption that they were aware of the existence and scope of the clause* so that all economic aspects of the dispute could be brought before the arbitrator'.

of the contract containing the arbitration agreement. It is not uncommon, as Professor Derains writes, 'for a company that was not originally a party to a contract to become a party to it in the course of execution by implementing acts expressing its accession or ratification'.[96] The 'common intention of the parties' characterized by court would have allowed the extension of the arbitration agreement. France then generalized this solution in *ABS* case,[97] which now applies to complex situations of groups of contracts or various contractual groups (related, complementary or ancillary contracts, subcontracts, framework contracts and implementing contracts, etc.).[98] Most countries also use this criterion especially for rights transfers.[99]

But the *ABS* case[100] raised a doubt about the role of consent in the application of the mechanism for extending the arbitration agreement. The criterion of 'direct involvement' of the third party in the performance of the contract containing the arbitration clause is formulated without any further reference to the will, even tacit, of the third party to adhere to it. The doctrine has thus raised the question of whether this should be seen as the advent of a purely objective criterion. The direct involvement of the third party is a factual notion, which requires an objective analysis of the links between the various contracts (the one containing the arbitration clause and the others that do not). Above all, what consequence can be drawn from the ignorance, if any, invoked by the third party to the arbitration agreement included in the main contract that they have accepted by conduct? If their consent is not indifferent, proof of their ignorance (and therefore of their non-acceptance of the arbitration agreement) should be able to free them. If not, their consent could be considered as half-forced (half only because by their direct participation in the main contract they have expressed their consent to it), although probably justified by other considerations - like by the requirement of a proper administration of justice (the ABS case makes it possible to unify the legal treatment of disputes which are connected or indivisible), or by the effectiveness of the arbitration agreement.[101] A so-called half-forced consent therefore. Hence the question is to know if the *ABS* case law will have eliminated the need for the will of the parties, and therefore for their consent. While Professor Racine considers that the subjective element is not eliminated but only put in the background,[102]

96. Sentence CCI *Dow Chemical* (*supra* n. 94).
97. *ABS*, no. 04-20842, Civ. 1st, 27 March 2007: 'the effect of the international arbitration clause extends to the parties directly involved in the performance of the contract and the disputes that may result from it'.
98. See, for example, the case law cited by Xavier Boucobza, Yves-Marie Serinet, *Varia on the existence of consent to arbitration*, 3 Rev. des contrats, 386 et seq. (2018).
99. Austria, England, Germany, Switzerland, USA... See Stavros Brekoulakis, *Rethinking Consent in International Commercial Arbitration: A General Theory for Non-signatories*, 8 Journal of International Dispute Settlement 610, 613-614 (2017).
100. *ABS* (*supra* n. 97).
101. Racine (*supra* n. 66) 250.
102. *Ibid.*, 248-249: 'The involvement of the third party, an objective element, is the basic condition... It seems to us that this involvement reveals (necessarily and automatically) the third party's adherence to the arbitration agreement, and therefore its acceptance. In other words, involvement implies acceptance. This is a form of irrefutable presumption... If the need for consent to the arbitration agreement is strongly watered down, it is not completely removed. The subjective element, once first, has clearly become second...'.

Professor Loquin considers that the solution can be based on the mechanism of ratification of the arbitration agreement. He states that 'ratification implies that a third party to an agreement, with the agreement of the initial parties, accepts to be bound by this agreement. In doing so, this third party will also be bound by the arbitration clause it contains'.[103] The reasoning is convincing. It is difficult to see how a third party could participate in the conclusion or performance of a contract to which it is not a party without wanting to, without consenting to it, and therefore without consenting to the arbitration agreement included in that contract. Such a scenario seems to be confirmed by a decision of the Swiss Federal Court of 17 April 2019, which considered that a party who intervenes continuously in the performance of a contract containing an arbitration clause also accepts the latter by implicit consent.[104] Consent must, in our opinion, underline the solutions on the extension of the arbitration agreement with regard to its effects which are that the litigant renounces State justice, which severely restricts his or her right to appeal against the decision rendered. This justifies that, in the absence of will, the mechanism of extending the arbitration clause to non-signatories should not apply, as the latter remain third parties to the contract.

Sometimes the willingness to engage in arbitration is not strong, and it must then be interpreted, which can lead to different decisions.[105] This emphasis on interpretation should make it possible to take into account the field and its specificities. If it is easier to admit half-forced consent in international commercial arbitration, it is because this type of dispute settlement has gradually established itself as the common law justice of international commercial affairs. One author notes that 'the contractual and bilateral nature of arbitration is often unable to accommodate modern business transactions that are typically multifaceted, multiparty and multi-contract'.[106] The extension of the arbitration agreement should therefore be encouraged, in the interest of the efficiency of international commercial arbitration. But out of this field, the voluntarist foundation of arbitration should, in our opinion, recover more vigorous colours.

That need requires limits to be placed on the recognition of the transmission of the arbitration agreement, a hypothesis distinct from the previous one insofar as it does not cover hypothesis of the addition of a new debtor, but substitution of one debtor for another. Subjects of rights receive already born rights that are transmitted to them (typically through an assignment of a claim, a personal subrogation, a novation, a

103. Loquin (*supra* n. 10) 156.
104. Swiss Supreme Court, 4A_646/2018, April 17 2019: confirmed for the first time that an arbitration clause may validly bind also a party which had not signed the main contract under the NYC, which does not constitute any bar to an implied prolongation of an arbitration clause by the parties' conduct.
105. See *Dallah v. Government of Pakistan*, in which the French judges agreed with the arbitrators that they had extended the arbitration agreement to the Pakistani State (an agreement concluded by a trust created by it), on the ground that it had acted 'as if the contract were its own' (Court of Appeal Paris 17 February 2011), while the English judges reached the opposite solution (UK Supreme Court, 3 November 2010, *RA* 2012, p. 427; Pierre Mayer, *The Extension of the Arbitration Clause to Non-Signatories – The Irreconciliable Positions of French and English Courts*, American University International Law Review, 831 (2012); Brekoulakis (*supra* n. 99) 622-623.
106. Brekoulakis (*supra* n. 99) 611.

chain of contracts). The mechanism here is 'purely objective, the arbitration agreement is automatically transmitted to an initial third party to the contract, without any expression of will, even inferred from conduct on its part'.[107] Arbitration laws are favourable in many cases, considering in particular that the assignment of rights entails the assignment of the arbitration clause, unless otherwise agreed. However, as Professor Racine points out, while it is possible to accept the automaticity of such a transmission in international commercial arbitration where this 'dispute resolution mechanism exceeds, by its usefulness, the person of potential litigants', this is not the case in cases where the person against whom the arbitration agreement is invoked is a non-professional (for example in contract chains, where the final purchaser would be a consumer)[108]. The latter should then be able to invoke his ignorance of the arbitration agreement as proof of his lack of consent.

§2.05 CONCLUSION

In conclusion, to the question of whether consent is still the basis of arbitration or whether its clothes appear so worn out that it is time to change them, the answer varies according to the type of arbitration. First, arbitration is not limited to consent, as evidenced by cases of mandatory arbitration imposed by law or treaty. The essence of arbitration is also reflected in the flexibility of the mechanism, the important role of the will of the parties in the procedure applicable to resolve the dispute between the parties, etc. Second, if arbitration as an alternative to States' justice realizes access to justice, consent is needed because it is necessary to legitimize the exclusion of State justice. As one arbitrator writes: '[y]et consent (even implied from circumstances) remains the cornerstone of arbitration, at least by arbitrators who value intellectual rigor and analytic integrity'.[109] Third, it must also be recognized that consent can have multiple faces, different according to the type of arbitration - sports, commercial, investment - each responding to different issues and specificities. In particular, consent is probably not reducible to an arbitration agreement in international investment arbitration, or even in international commercial arbitration. The 'needs of international trade' may justify the almost automatic extension of arbitration clause to 'non-signatory third parties', who were not parties to the original contract but became in a way or another involved in the development of the project afterwards, their delated unilateral act creating legal effects. But in all these cases, consent is and must still be at stake.

107. Racine (*supra* n. 66) 252. No 95-14330, Civ. 1st, 8 February 2000: 'The international arbitration clause is binding on any party entering into the rights of one of the contracting parties'.
108. *Ibid.*, 252-257.
109. Park (*supra* n. 93) paragraph 1.03. *Contra*, Brekoulakis (*supra* n. 99) 612 and 630: 'Under the proposed theory, what matters is not whether a non-signatory can demonstrate consent for arbitration, but whether it is *inextricably implicated in a dispute which is the subject matter of an arbitration*'.

CHAPTER 3

The Limits to Voluntary Arbitration in Establishing a Fair, Independent and Accessible Dispute Resolution Mechanism Outside Large Contractual Disputes

Joao Ilhão Moreira

Arbitration has become the de facto standard system of solving large transnational disputes. This success has, however, not extended to smaller domestic disputes. This article explores the idea that voluntary commercial arbitration, as currently understood, while well suited for large disputes between sophisticated parties, is not competitive in smaller disputes. It argues that the bargaining and information gathering costs inherent to setting up and operating a voluntary dispute resolution process tend to outstrip the gains of a more efficient dispute resolution system when the dispute is small. In this context, national courts usually provide a more beneficial option for parties. Finally, this article explores the idea that in the context of asymmetric levels of sophistication, arbitration might be selected by the parties as in those circumstances bargaining and information gathering costs are reduced. Arbitration in this context, might, however, give rise to concerns regarding the fairness and impartiality of the proceedings as the more experienced party might explore its knowledge edge and repeating-player status to its advantage.'

§3.01 INTRODUCTION

In their 1978 article 'Access to Justice: The Newest Wave in the Worldwide Movement to Make Rights Effective', Mauro Cappelletti and Bryant Garth projected arbitration as one of the techniques to expand access to justice.[1] Since then, arbitration has truly become a key dispute resolution mechanism, playing an increasingly prominent role. Following a string of legislative reforms in the 1980s, commercial arbitration became not only the dominant mechanism of solving transnational disputes but also captured a significant share of high-value domestic contractual disputes.[2] Still, for the most part, classical voluntary arbitration has not attracted mass adoption. Typically, most small and micro disputes – for example, private renting or second-hand selling – are still solved by recourse to judicial courts, amicably settled or simply not solved at all.[3]

When writing their article, Cappelletti and Garth, while acknowledging that arbitration had the potential to be 'a relatively quick and inexpensive process', noted that, in reality, it was often a high-cost process.[4] Since then voluntary commercial arbitration has been increasingly criticized in some circles as having become gradually an expensive, slow and adversarial system.[5] Still, the ease of enforcing arbitral awards across borders, neutrality and specialization has allowed it to maintain its prominent role in transnational disputes and some domestic disputes.[6] The ability to avoid national courts often perceived as having even more drawbacks has also certainly contributed to the flourishing of arbitration.

This chapter explores why, despite this, voluntary commercial arbitration, as currently designed, has considerable difficulties in expanding access to justice – in the sense of providing both an affordable and just forum for solving grievances – outside large disputes by parties with vast resources. It will do so by, first, exploring why voluntary commercial arbitration is able to provide a neutral and effective, albeit often costly, dispute resolution forum, when parties are well resourced, informed and can pay the costs of effective legal support. It will then explore why, conversely, voluntary arbitration has difficulties to be an effective alternative to small claims and in regard to parties with limited resources and information. It will then discuss the possible interventions to remediate this. While no exact hard border can be drawn to distinguish a 'large' from a 'small' claim, the key idea is that the less valuable and complex a

1. Bryant G. Garth and Mauro Cappelletti, *Access to Justice: The Newest Wave in the Worldwide Movement to Make Rights Effective*, 27 Buffalo Law Review 181, 232 (1978).
2. In the words of Lew: 'International arbitration, before neutral arbitrators, in a third country, with non-national or international procedures being followed, has become the essential mechanism for the settlement of all kinds of international business disputes.' Julian D.M. Lew, *Achieving the Dream: Autonomous Arbitration*, 22 Arbitration International 179, 185 (2006). *See also*, Thomas E. Carbonneau, *Law and Practice of Arbitration* (5th ed., Juris Publishing, Inc. 2014) xiii; Karl-Heinz Böckstiegel, *Past, Present, and Future Perspectives of Arbitration*, 25 Arbitration International, 295 (2009).
3. Civil justice statistics in the UK for example show total civil proceedings started to be over 2 million See, Civil Justice Statistics Quarterly: January to March 2019. Tables available at https://www.gov.uk/government/statistics/civil-justice-statistics-quarterly-january-to-march-2019 (accessed 10 July 2019). Albeit not an apple to apples comparison, cases on the largest arbitral institutions are numbered in the hundreds.
4. Garth and Cappelletti, *supra* n. 1, 232.
5. *See* Gary Born, *International Commercial Arbitration* (Kluwer Law International 2009) 85.
6. *See*, for all, QMUL/White and Case, 2018 International Arbitration Survey: The Evolution of International Arbitration, available at http://www.arbitration.qmul.ac.uk/media/arbitration/docs/2018-International-Arbitration-Survey---The-Evolution-of-International-Arbitration-(2).PDF (accessed 10 July 2019).

dispute is, the smaller is the likelihood of arbitration being the forum where the dispute will be solved.

From there, the text will explore the difficulties in guaranteeing fairness, independence and impartiality of voluntary commercial arbitration when there is significant asymmetry of resources and information between the parties. It will do so by discussing the situations where, despite asymmetric power positions, the 'stronger' party might still offer arbitration and/or other forms of alternative dispute resolution that increase the 'weaker' party access to justice. It will then discuss situations where the converse might happen and the possible interventions to mitigate these risks. Finally, this chapter will briefly delve into the situation where a platform may provide arbitration as a dispute resolution mechanism for transactions operated within it.

§3.02 WHY ARBITRATION CAN BE AN EFFECTIVE SYSTEM OF DISPUTE RESOLUTION WHEN BOTH PARTIES HAVE SIGNIFICANT RESOURCES AND THE DISPUTE IS LARGE

The popularity of arbitration clauses in large contracts both at the transnational and the national level is a strong indication that parties perceive arbitration and arbitrators as being able to provide a neutral and fair forum for solving disputes. This is the case due to the fact that: [A] arbitral institutions and arbitrators have, in most circumstances, an interest in being independent, impartial and fair deciders; [B] well-resourced parties have the capacity to monitor and select impartial deciders; and [C] finally, in this kind of cases, parties have strong incentives to detect and the ability to react through the justice system against miscarriages of justice within arbitral proceedings. These ideas will be explored in turn.

[A] Incentives for Arbitrators and Arbitral Institutions to Be Independent and Impartial Deciders

One of the reasons why commercial arbitration works derives from the fact that arbitral institutions and arbitrators have, in most circumstances, long-term incentives to be impartial and independent. In the case of arbitral institutions, since they rely on being selected by both sides, they have to maintain, amongst other characteristics, a reputation of being neutral and even-handed.[7] With regard to arbitrators, in the case of a sole arbitrator tribunal, parties will only agree on an arbitrator they both perceive as not biased in favour of the opposing party. Even in the case where parties select their own arbitrator, they have an interest in selecting an arbitrator who has a reputation of being independent and impartial, as an excessively partisan arbitrator will have a lower influence over the remaining members of the panel.[8]

7. *See* Dolores Bentolila, *Arbitrators as Lawmakers* (Wolters Kluwer 2017) 151.
8. In the oft-cited words of Martin Hunter: 'When I am representing a client in arbitration, what I am really looking for in a party-nominated arbitrator is someone with the maximum predisposition towards my client, but with the minimum appearance of bias.' Martin Hunter, *Ethics of the International Arbitrator*, 53 Arbitration 219, 223 (1987).

In more general terms, the way that the arbitration market works leads arbitrators to depend heavily on reputation and networking to succeed in the market. One of the elements of reputation that arbitrators seek to express is to be viewed as neutral and independent. As explained, in most circumstances, assuming an image of independence and impartiality not only makes arbitrators a more likely choice for parties but also for arbitral institutions and co-arbitrators. These actors, which are responsible for a significant percentage of arbitral nominations, [9] also have, in most instances, incentives to appoint neutral arbitrators as part of their own strategies to project their own images of neutrality and independence.

[B] Incentives of Well-Resourced Parties to Obtain Information on the Quality, Independence and Neutrality in Large Disputes

An important aspect of why arbitration works for well-informed and well-resourced parties in potentially large disputes relates to the relatively low-cost of gathering information on the 'quality' of arbitral institutions and arbitrators vis-à-vis the value of the dispute and the cost of litigation. Typically, jurisdiction is attributed to arbitral tribunals at the moment a contract is established. Parties do so by establishing a pre-dispute binding agreement where they usually establish that all the disputes related to their contract will be finally submitted to arbitration. They normally also define which arbitral institution will be responsible for organizing the proceedings or, conversely, if the arbitration will have an ad-hoc nature – i.e., with the arbitral tribunal undertaking the functions of an arbitral institution.

In the context of significant commercial transactions, contracts are typically signed by parties with the support of legal specialists, either externally hired and/or in-house. In these cases, the cost of deploying such resources is often vastly inferior to the risks of completing a transaction without legal support. Albeit it is frequently noted that the negotiation of dispute resolution clauses plays a minor role in large contract negotiations,[10] it is reasonably accessible for these parties, directly or through their counsel, to obtain information as to whether arbitration can provide a fair and effective forum for their potential disputes, which arbitral institution – if any – should be selected; and how their arbitration clause should be drafted.

In a similar fashion, after a dispute has started, well-resourced parties in the context of large disputes also have a strong incentive and the ability to obtain information regarding the quality of the arbitrator when making a selection. 'Quality' in this context means selecting an arbitrator that conforms to several conditions such as technical expertise and reputation as a legal or industry expert. A party may also seek to strategize the selection of an arbitrator to have a member of the panel more

---

9. In the context of ICC administered arbitrations, for around 56% of the nominations. ICC, *2014 ICC Dispute Resolution Statistics* (2015). To the same effect, LCIA's 2015 statistics indicate that parties accounted for slightly less than 50% of the nominations. LCIA, *2015 Registrar's Report*, available at https://www. lcia.org/ lcia/reports.aspx (accessed 28 September 2019).
10. Dispute resolution clauses are, in this sense, sometimes referred as 'midnight clauses' due to their tendency to be relegated to last minute negotiations. *See* Ewelina Kajkowska, *Enforceability of Multi-Tiered Dispute Resolution Clauses* (Bloomsbury Publishing 2017) 223.

willing to favour their position and/or influence the panel to obtain a favourable position. However, due to the lack of a credible system of control of the party in regard to the arbitrator, any attempts to 'capture' an arbitrator are not easy to develop.[11]

In any case, well-informed and well-resourced parties have the ability to: i) influence the selection of the arbitral tribunal to guarantee, at least, that such tribunal as a whole is not biased towards their opponent; ii) exclude from their range of selection arbitral institutions that they perceive as possibly biased towards the other party; and iii) ultimately, self-exclude themselves from arbitration if they perceive it as inappropriate and/or not fair by not establishing further arbitration clauses. In a context where there are high stakes for the parties, they will have a strong incentive to acquire information about arbitrators and arbitral institutions, with the costs of acquiring such information being typically considerably low compared to the risks of unacceptable dispute resolution forums.

[C] The Adversarial Nature of International Arbitration and the Ability to Detect and React to Unfair Proceedings in Large Disputes

Aside from the self-interest of arbitrators in international commercial arbitration, there are other safety mechanisms to prevent miscarriages of justice. In the context of sufficiently large disputes, parties have a strong incentive to monitor the behaviour of arbitrators and arbitral institutions and respond to any procedural violations. As a reaction, the party will typically have, amongst other means, the right to challenge an arbitrator and the right to challenge the arbitral award and resist enforcement. In certain more limited circumstances, a party can also seek to sue an arbitrator and/or an arbitral institution for damages related to serious wrongdoing undertaken by one of these actors.[12]

Exercising these rights is, however, often a costly endeavour as it implies navigating complex legal rules, which requires specialized guidance. In the context of large commercial arbitration cases, where parties are usually already supported by specialized legal counsel, and the stakes are high, they can overcome these barriers. In any case, conceivably, the simple fact that parties have a serious possibility of identifying and exercising these rights can already be a deterrent to serious deviations by arbitrators or arbitral institutions from their independence and impartiality obligations.

11. A particular important point to note in this regard is the limitations on repeated appointments of an arbitrator by the same company, group of companies and law firms. *See*, for all, the IBA Guidelines on Conflicts of Interest in International Arbitration. As parties cannot dangle the 'promise' of future appointments to an arbitrator their leverage to influence their behaviour is also limited in this way.
12. To this effect it should be noted that different jurisdictions and contractual arrangements often limit arbitrators' and arbitral institutions' liability. For an overview *see*, amongst others, *The Arbitrator's Liability Report from the Club des Juristes*, Ad-hoc Committee, June 2017, available at https://www.leclubdesjuristes.com/wp-content/uploads/2017/06/CDJ_Rapports_Responsabilit%C3%A9-de-l%C2%B9arbitre_Juin-2017_UK_web.pdf (accessed 10 July 2019).

§3.03 WHY VOLUNTARY ARBITRATION HAS DIFFICULTIES IN ESTABLISHING ITSELF AS AN EFFICIENT AND FAIR SYSTEM IN SMALL DISPUTES

As discussed above, a number of underlying incentives lead both arbitrators and arbitral institutions to act independently and fairly, and parties to remain vigil and react to wrongdoing. On top of this, a number of legal safeguards further keep the system in check guaranteeing means of response when partial behaviour takes place. In smaller and micro disputes, the incentives and safeguards also exist to an extent. Still, a number of reasons contribute to the difficulties of voluntary commercial arbitration in establishing itself as a competitive alternative for small and micro contractual disputes. These include: [A] the existence of significant information gathering and bargaining costs;[13] [B] the strong competition provided by national courts due to the subsidization of their activity by the state; and [C] the safeguards provided by addressing these disputes within national courts.

[A] Information Gathering and Bargaining Costs as a Barrier to Voluntary Arbitration in Small Disputes

One of the difficulties of voluntary commercial arbitration establishing itself as a competitive method for solving small and micro disputes relates to the difficulties of parties agreeing and operating an arbitral agreement. The first of these difficulties relates to obtaining information regarding the comparative quality of different dispute resolution mechanisms. Acquiring information as to whether arbitration, court litigation or mediation should be chosen, and, if arbitration is chosen, which arbitral institution to choose and how to draft an arbitration clause is a costly process. In the context of small transactions, that would frequently involve either hiring legal support or exploring a complex web of information. While perhaps self-evident for those familiar with arbitration, much of this information is rather opaque for those who are outside the field.

Further to this information gathering costs, it is also important to consider the bargaining costs parties would have to undertake to agree on a dispute resolution mechanism. Even if one of the parties or, more rarely, both of the parties were familiar with different dispute resolution mechanisms, they would have to agree on the one applicable to their transaction. However, often parties to the transaction will disagree on what dispute resolution mechanism should be chosen. In fact, parties may have a different perception as to what the best option is objectively or, more cynically, parties may want to select the dispute resolution forum that benefits themselves the most. While through bargaining parties can oftentimes find an equilibrium point, in the context of small and micro-transactions, the time spent in agreeing on such issues is

13. On the concept of information gathering and bargaining costs as a part of a larger category of transaction costs, *see* Carl J. Dahlman, *The Problem of Externality*, 22 The Journal of Law & Economics 141, 148 (1979).

often too substantial when compared to the benefits of an optimized dispute resolution system.

Bargaining costs are a relevant point that should not be overlooked. In the context of large transactions, parties often have enough resources and experience to navigate these issues. Further, the larger the transaction the more rational it is to invest in hiring legal counsel who will advise and negotiate on their behalf. The larger the dispute the more likely it is that the benefits that the parties accrue from an optimal dispute resolution will outweigh the costs of negotiating a dispute resolution clause. However, the smaller the transaction the less rational and/or feasible it is to address these issues. First, the smaller a transaction is, equally smaller is the likelihood of the emergence of a dispute worth escalating to a formal dispute resolution mechanism. Second, the gains from a marginally better dispute resolution system will usually be less significant the less sizeable the dispute is.

In practice, the reason why in the context of 'small' and 'micro' transactions parties do not agree on a dispute resolution mechanism prior to the dispute is the same that lead parties to often not establish this kind of contractual relationships in writing or, when a written contract is established, many possible aspects of the contractual relationship are not regulated. The costs of agreeing on all those issues would outweigh the advantages of a fully set contractual relationship. In the particular case of dispute resolution, parties, however, will most times not agree on establishing a dispute resolution, as, frequently, due to strained relationships, agreements between the parties will be difficult to establish at this stage; and the defaulting party will often drag their feet and avoid accepting a quick award to their dispute.[14]

[B] The State-Subsidized Competition Provided by National Courts as a Barrier to Voluntary Arbitration in Small Disputes

Closely connected to the ideas above, it is also important to note that national courts have a number of important competitive advantages. First, they typically work as the default option for solving disputes. In case parties have not agreed on a different system, their disputes will usually be subject to the jurisdiction of the competent national court according to applicable legislation. Since information gathering and bargaining costs often make selecting an alternative system difficult, courts have an innate advantage. The smaller the dispute is, the more likely it is that it is not worth for the parties to select a different system but rather rely on the default mechanism provided by national legislation.

Furthermore, courts have another important competitive advantage in regard to small claims as they are usually financed by taxes leading to the subsidization of litigating parties by the state budget. In private dispute resolution, parties typically have to pay the full costs of those providing the service – i.e., in the case of arbitration, parties have to pay the fees of arbitrators and arbitral institutions. In the case of

14. *See* William M. Landes and Richard A. Posner, *Adjudication as a Private Good*, 8 The Journal of Legal Studies 235 (1979).

national courts, while parties are often required to assume a cost in using the court system, there are usually significant transfers from public money to the justice system.[15] These transfers of money help making national courts a competitive alternative in terms of costs in regard to small claims - especially in cases where states provide a specialized forum for minor disputes.[16]

It should also be noted that sometimes a level of cross-subsidization takes place, with money charged to parties in large disputes being used to subsidize smaller disputes to a certain extent.[17] This occurs due to the fact that court fees are usually correlated to the size of the dispute - i.e., typically courts charge in a system where the larger the dispute is, the higher the court fees are, in a way that does not mimic perfectly the increased costs undertaken by the court.[18] In turn, typically, courts heavily undercharge smaller disputes - by not charging court fees or charging a value that is only a very small portion of the actual cost of providing the service. This, naturally, makes the national public court system attractive for small claims in comparison with private options, and the national judicial system frequently prescribes specialized chambers or courts for 'smaller' disputes.

[C] The Protections Afforded by the Judicial System as a 'Competitive' Advantage over Arbitration

The other reason that explains why the judicial system is a competitive forum for small and micro disputes relate to a number of safeguards that it provides. It was noted above that if well-resourced parties have several different mechanisms to pre-emptively evaluate the different dispute resolution mechanisms available to them and detect and react against miscarriages of justice within arbitral proceedings. If, on a macro-level, reputational mechanisms can, in theory, work as a proxy for quality, independence and impartiality, it is less certain that less sophisticated parties would be capable to obtain enough information regarding the 'quality' of the service provided and react to deviations.

---

15. For example, in the UK, taxpayer financing accounted around 80% of the Ministry of Justice expenses with the justice system with fees and fines accounting for the remainder 20%. *See* Martin Chalkley, *Funding for Justice2008 to 2018: Justice in the Age of Austerity*, published for the Bar Council of England & Wales, November 2018, https://www.nucleus.org.uk/justice-week/ (accessed 10 July 2019).
16. In the EU, most member states provide specialized arrangements for small claims. For an overview, *see* World Bank Group / Kingdom of the Netherlands, *Fast-Tracking the Resolution of Minor Disputes: Experience from EU Member States*, available at http://documents.worldbank.org/curated /en/670181487131729316/pdf/Fast-tracking-the-resolution-of-minor-disputes-experience-from EU-Member-States.pdf (accessed 10 July 2019).
17. *See* Gerhard Wagner, 'Dispute Resolution as a Product: Competition Between Civil Justice Systems' in Horst Eidenmüller (ed.), *Regulatory Competition in Contract Law and Dispute Resolution* (Bloomsbury Publishing 2013) 386.
18. *Ibid.* Heterogeneous national realities make generalizations regarding this point difficult. The fee structure in different countries varies greatly. For example, France emphatically subscribes to the principle of '*gratituité de la justice*', while Germany courts impose substantial fees which rise in proportion to the dispute.

In this sense, and albeit, due to wide variance, any generalizations are difficult to make, courts may benefit from having institutional arrangements that guarantee independence and impartiality of the judiciary. This may lead parties to be comfortable with resorting to solving disputes within national courts as it will not require investigation on the particular decider of the disputes.[19] It is also important to note that litigating in national courts usually allows some forms of support for those in financial need, which may include a waiver of court fees and/or legal aid that usually do not exist in arbitration.[20]

Altogether, there are strong reasons why arbitration is not usually established for 'everyday' small and micro contractual disputes. Indeed, the more well-known arbitral institutions seem to be designed to deal with rather large disputes.[21] While there is a movement to adapt proceedings to better deal with 'smaller' disputes, these are still usually envisioned to be reasonably large – not the kind of everyday contractual arrangements 'ordinary' citizens enter into.[22] Less well-known or smaller arbitral institutions do sometimes try to get a foothold within the arbitral market by catering to 'smaller' disputes. Even in these cases, however, arbitral institutions are rarely looking to establish themselves as a forum for small and micro everyday disputes. In this sense, there seems to be generally a lack of interest by the market to provide dispute resolution mechanisms for these disputes.

§3.04 POSSIBLE INTERVENTIONS TO MAKE VOLUNTARY ARBITRATION A MORE SOUGHT-AFTER MECHANISM FOR SMALL AND MICRO DISPUTES

If for the reasons set out above, voluntary arbitration, in its current form, is not a particularly suitable forum for small and micro disputes between 'unsophisticated' parties, the question is whether the system can be modified to make arbitration a more competitive alternative for this particular set of disputes. In this subchapter, I will explore some of these possibilities, namely: [A] making arbitration mandatory; [B] increasing the level of information regarding arbitration; and [C] levelling the competition between arbitration and national courts. As it will be seen however all these possibilities have severe limitations and/or drawbacks that potentially make them either largely fruitless or even counterproductive. These possibilities will be analysed in turn.

---

19. Surveys in the EU, for example, indicate that more than half of all respondents (56%) rate their justice system – in terms of the independence of courts and judges – as good. Survey conducted by TNS political & social at the request of the European Commission, Directorate-General for Justice and Consumer available at: http://ec.europa.eu/commfrontoffice/publicopinion/index.cfm/ResultDoc/download/DocumentKy/82970 (accessed 10 July 2019).
20. *See* Bernhard Berger and Franz Kellerhals, *International and Domestic Arbitration in Switzerland* (2nd ed., Hart Publishing 2015) no. 572.
21. As an example, ICC Statistical Report for 2015 indicates the average value of the disputes referred to the ICC to be USD 84 million.
22. For example, ICC expedited procedure is available for disputes up to USD 2,000,000.

[A] The Possibility of Making Arbitration Mandatory and Its Drawbacks

If one of the difficulties of arbitration establishing itself as a competitive dispute resolution system for small and micro relates to the high information and bargaining costs that in turn lead parties to not establish an arbitration clause, this could be, in theory, partially solved by determining that arbitral tribunals would have jurisdiction over a dispute even in the absence of an agreement to arbitrate. This could be done, for example, by inverting the presumption regarding the agreement to arbitrate - i.e., determining that unless parties expressly agreed on the jurisdiction of national courts, they would be presumed to have agreed to arbitrate; or, by determining concurrent mandatory jurisdiction of national courts and arbitral tribunals - i.e., allowing the parties to select where they would prefer to start their proceedings, making it mandatory to the counterparty.

The advantage of such a system would be to allow parties to avoid the information gathering and bargaining costs in defining their dispute resolution mechanism, while at the same time, allowing them to enjoy the purported advantages of arbitration, namely, its finality, flexibility, neutrality and, more controversially, cost-efficiency. Details of such a system would, however, be complex to work out. It could, in theory, either determine that a party would have the ability to initiate proceedings in an ad-hoc style arbitration or, alternatively, allow a party to start proceedings within a list of predetermined arbitral institutions. Legislation could also determine the possibility of recourse to arbitration without a previous agreement in general terms or only for a subset of disputes, such as those of small value.[23]

Such a system would obviously have a number of drawbacks. Depending on how the system would be designed, it could be argued that any such system of mandatory arbitration would represent too much of a restriction on the right to access courts. Also, such a system would run against the voluntary nature of arbitration, one of the tenets of the field, giving rise to doubts with regard to the legitimacy of such a system. While statutory arbitration is increasingly prescribed in some fields, a more general system would not necessarily be easy to conform to the current legal system and would certainly attract heavy opposition and legal challenges.[24]

But even if such legal constraints and opposition could be overcome, such a system would have the risk of producing a number of unwanted effects. One particular risk would be that of the system being manipulated by one of the parties to produce inequitable or inefficient results. That would be a particular risk if such a system would allow forum shopping by one of the parties - i.e., allowing one party to select where to start the dispute. The party could, in such circumstance, select not the most equitable option but the one it would perceive as giving it the greater chance of success.

23. An example to be noted is the Indian Micro, Small and Medium Enterprises Development 2006 Act, which prescribes statutory arbitration in regard to payment disputes owed to a micro, small or medium enterprise, with a facilitation council either acting as an arbitration tribunal or referring the matter to an arbitral institution.

24. *See* Dwight Golann, *Making Alternative Dispute Resolution Mandatory: The Constitutional Issues*, 68 Oregon Law Review 487, 491(1989).

Some of these drawbacks could, in theory, be partially addressed by regulating the arbitral institutions and/or arbitrators providing these services. A state could, for example, establish criteria to authorize and oversee arbitral institutions and/or arbitrators with the aim of guaranteeing that all alternative forums would conform to minimum requirements of independence, impartiality and due process. Such interventions, aside from having a cost, could also put at stake the flexibility that gives arbitration an edge in speed and access over national courts.

[B] The Possibility of Increasing Information Regarding the Availability of Arbitration

If one of the difficulties of establishing arbitration as a competitive system to solve small and micro disputes relates to the costs of gathering information regarding the quality of different dispute resolution options, a state could simply intervene by making more information available. A state could, for example, simply increase awareness of arbitration as a whole, hoping that would prompt parties to investigate which arbitral institutions they should choose and how to draft arbitration clauses. Alternatively, a state could provide further information, by endorsing a set of arbitral institutions, recommending standard clauses or inviting parties to submit their disputes to arbitration instead of courts when parties commence court proceedings.

Such measures, despite lacking the bluntness of making arbitration mandatory, would not, however, be cost-free. Advertising arbitration, arbitral institutions or draft models comes with a cost. Depending on how successful the campaign was and the exact efficiency gains, if any, from the increased usage of arbitration, such endeavours could be worthy or not. It should also be noted that when the state endorses arbitration or specific arbitral institutions for mass adoption, this would also likely involve some form of regulation of these structures. As discussed above, undertaking such interventions in the market can diminish the capability of arbitration providing gains of cost-efficiency.

[C] The Possibility of Levelling the Playing Field Between Courts and Arbitration

As discussed above, the reason why courts often end up being the preferred forum where small and micro disputes are decided does not relate only to the costs of the parties in obtaining information, transacting and the courts' usual position as the default dispute resolution forum. Courts also typically enjoy the advantage of public financing and cross-financing from large amount disputes to small amount disputes. In a certain way, national courts can be seen as undertaking a peculiar form of below-cost pricing. By making the cost to the user of the system lower than the actual cost of providing the service, the disputing parties are being subsidized by either taxpayers or other litigants.

To make arbitration more competitive, one approach could be changing the way how courts fees are calculated so its amount would reflect the actual cost incurred by the judicial system to solve the dispute. However, this kind of revision of the court fees system would be highly problematic.[25] There are extremely valid reasons why states may decide to finance the resolution of disputes. These include the wish to maintain public peace and order and discourage the private settling of disputes through non-legal means. Indeed, increasing the cost of dispute resolution would ultimately run against the core of the principles of access to justice.[26]

Alternatively, the opposite approach could be undertaken: states could finance directly and/or indirectly the costs of parties accessing arbitration. They could do so, for example, by directly shouldering totally or partially the operational costs of the arbitral institution and/or arbitrators; or reimbursing totally or partially the costs incurred by the parties. States could, in theory, further boost the attractiveness of arbitration by financing access by, for example, providing legal aid in arbitration. While at first view such options might look attractive, difficulties must be considered. In assuming costs, depending on the exact arrangement, states might endanger incentives for cost-efficiency and might even open the door for fraud by, for example, incentivizing artificially created demand.

§3.05 THE PARTICULAR CASE OF ASYMMETRIC KNOWLEDGE, POWER AND ACCESS TO JUSTICE IN ARBITRATION

A variation of the discussion above – i.e., small and micro disputes between parties without particular knowledge about arbitration – is the situation where the parties are significantly asymmetric in terms of resources and knowledge about arbitration. We are talking about, for example, consumer arbitration where one of the parties is usually a 'repeat-player' and has access to large resources for dispute resolution and the other will often not have the same level of information and/or the same level of resources in the dispute arena.[27] Other areas of arbitration, albeit with specificities, have similar asymmetric structures such as employer-employee arbitration.[28]

In these cases, there are often no difficulties regarding information gathering and bargaining costs. One of the parties, due to its resources, previous experiences and/or ability to rely on legal counsel, is often well informed about the different options of dispute resolution at its disposal. Also, the way how contracts in this asymmetric relation are established frequently leads to very low bargaining costs in establishing alternative dispute arrangements. Often, the most well-informed and resourced party will present a contract that will detail a dispute resolution mechanism to the other,

25. *See* Landes and Posner, *supra* n. 14, 241.
26. *See* for example Nathy Rass-Masson and Virginie Rouas, *Effective Access to Justice*, European Parliament Directorate-General for internal Policies, p. 25 available at http://www.europarl. europa. eu/RegData/etudes/STUD/2017/596818/IPOL_STU(2017)596818_EN.pdf (accessed 10 July 2019).
27. For an overview of arbitration and other forms of consumer ADR in Europe, *see* Christopher Hodges, Iris Benöhr and Naomi Creutzfeldt, *Consumer ADR in Europe* (Bloomsbury Publishing 2012).
28. For an overview of labour and employment arbitration in the US, *see* Theodore J. St. Antoine, *Labor and Employment Arbitration Today: Mid-Life Crisis or New Golden Age*, 32 Ohio State Journal on Dispute Resolution 1 (2017).

typically less-resourced and informed party, who will only have the option to either accept or reject the contract.

In one sense, by providing arbitration in this kind of contracts, it is sometimes possible to increase access to justice. If the option chosen is more efficient both in terms of providing a lower-cost and/or fairer forum to address these situations, it will allow both parties to exercise their rights.[29] However, this is not necessarily the case. The strongest party may not select a fair system but instead the one that is more likely to favour it. Also, the strongest party may not select the lowest cost dispute resolution forum. Instead, if it perceives that the most likely situation is that the weaker party will probably be the one to look for redress, as it will be often the case in business-consumer relationships, it might elect a high-cost dispute resolution so as to discourage the commence of proceedings.

[A] Preliminary Point: Competitive Pressures as Incentivizing the Establishment of Fair Dispute Resolution

An important point to note is that even in the cases where one of the parties has considerably more resources and knowledge than its counterparty, it might still be highly incentivized to voluntarily select a fair dispute resolution forum. This will be particularly the case where the party faces considerable competitive pressures. In such circumstances, the party may decide that in order to preserve reputation and/or get a competitive edge over competitors, it may be interested in offering bolstered access to dispute resolution. As information about companies' practices gets progressively easier to be obtained and compared, they may be increasingly more interested in providing such ancillary options.

It should be noted, however, that, often this will not be the option voluntarily undertaken by the stronger party. In some cases, there will be not enough competitive pressure to incentivize the stronger party to provide a fair dispute resolution system. In other situations, the weaker party, even facing highly competitive providers, will not be in a position to fully evaluate the costs and risks of an unfair dispute resolution system.[30] Indeed, often consumers are not in a position to incorporate into their decision-making uncertain events. These situations create a case for intervention to avoid that arbitration is used as a barrier to accessing justice. This will be analysed next.

29. *See* Jean R. Sternlight, *Creeping Mandatory Arbitration: Is It Just*, 57 Stanford Law Review 1631, 1633 (2004).
30. *See* Llewellyn Joseph Gibbons, *Creating a Market for Justice; a Market Incentive Solution to Regulating the Playing Field: Judicial Deference, Judicial Review, Due Process, and Fair Play in Online Consumer Arbitration*, 23 Northwestern Journal of International Law & Business 1, 6 (2002).

[B] State Interventions to Guarantee the Fairness of Dispute Resolution in Asymmetric Relationships

In order to guarantee that the usage of arbitration does not represent a limitation to the 'weaker' party to access justice, a state may limit its usage. A first approach could be to simply not allow arbitration in regard to contractual disputes where parties are understood to be systematically in asymmetric positions. These prohibitions could extend to certain kind of disputes (such as business-consumer disputes or employer-employee disputes) or certain sectors perceived as being particularly conducive to arbitration being abused. In less blunt approaches, a state could determine that while arbitration clauses would be valid, that would not preclude the 'weaker' party from selecting national courts if it so chooses and/or add further guarantees to assure the 'weaker' party is fully informed of the implications of selecting arbitration.

Aside from determining limitations on the forum to be chosen or allowing the 'weaker' party to undertake some level of forum shopping, a state may also intervene in other ways. It may, for example, intervene by determining rules to guarantee that the arbitral process provides a fair and accessible forum for the 'weaker' party.[31] That can be done by, amongst other measures, creating, pre-authorizing and/or regulating arbitral institutions that will provide a neutral and fair forum, and determining that only such institutions can be used for such disputes.[32] The state can further increase accessibility by supporting directly the costs or determining that the costs have to be supported by the 'stronger' party or, in another variation, the sector that the 'stronger' party belongs to.

Again, however, these solutions are not without drawbacks. Outright limiting access to arbitration can have a detrimental effect, being often difficult to distinguish in abstract terms the situations in which arbitration increases access to justice from the situations where it restricts it. Regulating and/or pre-authorizing arbitral institutions may further limit the level of flexibility that arbitral institutions need to innovate and be a competitive dispute resolution forum. Shifting costs from the 'weaker' party to the state or the 'strong' party may lead to inefficient results by over encouraging the submission of weak claims and/or, depending on the particular arrangements, subsidizing over-litigious parties. Making the sector bear the cost as a whole may lead to a cross-subsidization from complying companies to non-complying ones.

§3.06 THE PARTICULAR CASE OF ARBITRATION OF TRANSACTIONS THROUGH LARGE WELL-RESOURCED PLATFORMS

An interesting variation of the situation described above is when a well resourced and well informed party provides arbitration not for it to solve disputes directly with a weaker party, but rather for solving disputes between two parties using its network to

31. With this aim *see*, for example, Directive 2013/11/EU – 'Consumer ADR Directive'.
32. *Ibid.*, 5.

conduct contractual relationships. Through technological developments, such situations have become more and more common. Think of companies like Amazon, eBay or Airbnb. The platform can do that in several different ways. It can, for example, determine the power to settle the dispute itself, operating in this way as an arbitrator of sorts.[33] It can alternatively establish a process through which a third party will settle the dispute. Such dispute settlement might or might not be binding upon parties. In practice, these platforms often offer a combination of dispute resolution mechanisms mostly undertook online.

It should be noted that, while, as referred above, at first sight, the platform may have an interest in providing a fair and accessible system of dispute resolution, it cannot be guaranteed that it will do so. A particular possible concern is when there are considerable differences between the costs of acquiring, buyers and sellers. In such situations, the platform might have an incentive of favouring a party that in its view may be more important to keep content, rather than offering a fair, independent and impartial dispute resolution. This again gives rise to an argument to be made for some intervention in the regulation of the dispute resolution undertaken in this kind of contractual relationships.

It should be noted that, in this particular scenario, competitive pressures will most often lead the platform to self-correct any biased dispute resolution mechanisms. In the vast majority of situations, a platform will strive for equilibrium, as most often it will not want for either buyers or sellers to systematically exclude themselves from it. In most cases, the underlying transaction price of the goods and services will tend to be set at a value that will attract buyers and sellers in a matching way. In this sense, this kind of arbitration through platforms offers the most potential as a form of alternative dispute resolution that increases both access to a low-cost and fair process of adjudication.

§3.07 CONCLUSION

This text identifies how the attractiveness of arbitration as a dispute resolution system correlates with the size of the underlying disputes and the sophistication of the disputing parties. It shows why arbitration, as currently designed, is not a dispute resolution system thought for everyday disputes, but it is rather mostly appropriate only for a small subset of high-value complex disputes, especially those with a transnational element. To fully explore the advantages of arbitration, parties need to gather information regarding the quality and fairness of different services providers, overcome bargaining difficulties as well as having the ability to credibly use the legal mechanisms that assure the good functioning of arbitration.

Due to the competition provided by national courts, which are often publicly financed, and the transaction costs of pre-establishing a dispute resolution mechanism, arbitration has never truly taken off as an industry for everyday disputes. While those

33. An example is for example *eBay Resolution Centre* which resolves disputes between e-commerce parties. For an overview, *see* Colin Rule, *Designing a Global Online Dispute Resolution System: Lessons Learned from EBay*, 13 University of St. Thomas Law Journal 354 (2017).

more optimistic may see opportunities in technological innovations for arbitration to expand its attractiveness, the difficulties of escalating arbitration as the typical system of dispute resolution are more systematic. Arbitration is not truly competitive when disputes are too small, and parties are inexperienced. Furthermore, arbitration is fraught with risks when one of the parties is a repeated and sophisticated player and the other is not. While regulatory interventions may be attempted to solve this dilemma, nevertheless, it is hard to overcome the problem as to how to maintain the incentives that ultimately lead arbitration service providers to offer their services in an efficient and fair way in everyday small disputes.

CHAPTER 4

The Interplay Between Courts and Tribunals Assures Access to Justice

Ramona Elisabeta Cirlig

The international dispute settlement system is a network of courts and tribunals between which there are different degrees of interaction. Arbitral tribunals have their special place within this system, and they interact both with other international courts or tribunals, as well as with domestic courts. The umbrella question for both categories of interactions is whether such interplay contributes to ensuring access to justice or, on the contrary, it hinders it and diminishes its effectiveness. Under the first limb, the analysis will focus on benefits and positive contributions that the interplay between arbitral tribunals and other international courts and tribunals brings to access to justice: cross-referencing to case law and legal interpretations, the wider coverage of legal matters and larger availability of legal remedies, more choices for parties, more checks and balances. As regards the downsides, the main aspects explored will be competing/overlapping jurisdictions, contradictions in the interpretation and application of international legal concepts, and the prolongation and complication of the proceedings. The practical examples will come from the interplay between the International Court of Justice, the European Court of Human Rights, the Court of Justice of the European Union, on the one hand, and arbitral tribunals, on the other hand. Moreover, the interplay between parallel commercial and treaty-based arbitrations will also be addressed. Under the second limb, the interplay between arbitral tribunals and national courts, the analysis will focus on the national courts' measures supporting arbitration, the interim and conservatory measures, the setting aside proceedings and the recognition and enforcement of the arbitral awards. Does this interplay with the national courts contribute to the access to justice in any way or, on the contrary, it only complicates and uselessly prolongs the proceedings?

§4.01 INTRODUCTION

The international dispute settlement system is a network of courts and tribunals between which there are different degrees of interaction. Arbitral tribunals have their special place within this system, and they interact both with other international fora, as well as with domestic courts. By categorizing the various types of interactions and looking at different examples, the current chapter will try to answer the question whether such interplay contributes overall to ensuring access to justice, whether it increases the standards and safeguards attached thereto or, on the contrary, it hinders it and diminishes its effectiveness.

Access to justice will be considered as a whole, including all the guarantees and safeguards that actually ensure a procedure that can objectively be considered fair by an outsider third party, and that hopefully can be perceived as fair also by all the parties involved. The ideal is to have the losing party satisfied that he/she/it was treated fairly and maybe even to accept and understand the grounds for the outcome of the case from a very clear, pertinent and persuasive reasoning.

While the conclusions of the chapter will be based on the views of a law practitioner, it would be truly revealing to grasp the users' perceptions on whether the interplay between courts and tribunals improves access to justice. Some sociological research in this area of users' perceptions on access to justice would definitely be interesting, but it goes beyond this chapter's boundaries.

Without any sociological research in the background, and based purely on personal observations, in practice, depending on which side of the dispute each party is situated (winning or losing), one party will be very annoyed, and the other truly delighted by any possibility of interaction between the arbitral tribunal and any other forum. For one party any further referral to another court will be an unacceptable hurdle and prolongation, while for the other party, this will be a last resort before accepting defeat, putting all the hopes and expectations in that other court as the saviour and protector from any procedural evil and gross substantive injustice.

In this chapter, the focus will be directed towards the interactions between arbitral tribunals and some other courts and tribunals, more precisely the ICJ, ECtHR, the CJEU and domestic courts. The interaction between commercial arbitration and investment arbitration will also be tackled.

All these interactions will be categorized in three different forms of manifestation of the interplay: cross-referencing to case law and legal interpretations, competing or overlapping jurisdictions and various checks and balances. These forms of interaction will also make up the subsections of the current chapter. Relevant examples will be provided for each form of interplay, and some conclusions will be reached, both intermediary as regards each interaction, and finally over the whole analysis.

The analysis starts from the assumption that the main benefits brought by this interplay as regards access to justice are the wider coverage of legal matters and more legal remedies, more options for parties. The main downsides would be the potential contradictions in the interpretation and application of legal concepts, and the prolongation and complication of the proceedings, which impede the timely, efficient and effective resolution of disputes, criteria that are part of the access to justice under the case law of the Strasbourg court. This assumption will be tested below by looking at various relevant examples of interplay in order to boil down a conclusion corresponding to a very simple yes or no answer to this chapter's question.

§4.02 CROSS-REFERENCING TO CASE-LAW AND LEGAL INTERPRETATIONS

Cross-referencing to case law and legal interpretations arises consistently in the interplay between ICJ and investment arbitration tribunals. Alain Pellet, in a very comprehensive analysis of the ICJ case law in investment arbitration, concluded that investment tribunals' attitude towards the case law of the ICJ 'range from polite indifference to compelling authority'.[1]

The areas where investment tribunals refer to the jurisprudence of the ICJ regard especially the general principles of treaty interpretation, the sources of international law, the existence of a rule of customary international law, general principles of state responsibility, the competences of the state, the jurisdiction of international courts and tribunals, the junction of the preliminary objections to the merits, incidental proceedings, the burden of proof, in absentia proceedings.[2] Although the case law of the ICJ is useful for determining some procedural issues or some aspects of general international law, as regards specific investment matters and investment protection standards, investment tribunals do not find very useful resources in the jurisprudence of the ICJ since the ICJ rarely deals with such issues.[3]

Cross-referencing to case law, legal interpretations arise as well in the interplay between the ECtHR and investment arbitration tribunals. The right to property, as enshrined in Article 1 Protocol 1 to the ECHR, and as interpreted and developed in the case law of the Strasbourg Court, is many times invoked in investment arbitration in support of an expropriation claim.[4] For instance, in *Ronald Lauder v. Czech Republic*,[5] *Azurix v. Argentina*,[6] *ADC v. Hungary*[7] the case law of the ECtHR has been used by arbitrators when dealing with the expropriation claims. For example, the arbitrators sought guidance in the case law of the ECtHR for determining the conditions for qualifying expropriation,[8] the applicable standard for assessing the damages to be

1. Alain Pellet, *The Case Law of the ICJ in Investment Arbitration*, 28 ICSID Review, 223, 233 (2013).
2. *Ibid.*
3. *Ibid.*
4. United Nations Conference on Trade and Development, *Selected Recent Developments in IIA Arbitration and Human Rights*, IIA MONITOR No. 2 (2009) International Investment Agreements, 4, https://unctad.org/en/Docs/webdiaeia20097_en.pdf (accessed 14 June 2019).
5. *Ronald Lauder v. Czech Republic* (UNCITRAL, Final Award, 3 September 2001), https://www.italaw.com/cases/documents/611 (accessed 14 June 2019).
6. *Azurix Corp. v. Argentine Republic*, Case No. ARB/01/12 (ICSID, Award of 14 July 2006) https://www.italaw.com/cases/118 (accessed 14 June 2019).
7. *ADC Affiliate Limited and ADC and ADMC Management Limited v. Republic of Hungary*, Case No. ARB/03/16 (ICSID, Award of 2 October 2006) https://www.italaw.com/cases/41 (accessed 14 June 2019).
8. *Azurix Corp. v. Argentine Republic*, Case No. ARB/01/12 (ICSID, Award of 14 July 2006) 111 https://www.italaw.com/cases/118 (accessed 14 June 2019).

awarded for expropriation,[9] as well as for delineating formal expropriation from de facto expropriation.[10]

Furthermore, besides the right to property, there is a recent trend to bring up also other human rights in arbitration proceedings. Investors invoke human rights breaches when they complain about the actions of the host states to abuse their criminal investigation powers, harass, threaten, retain or apply inhumane and degrading treatments directed towards the investor himself or his employees. Such actions are usually also invoked as reasons to request provisional measures. Nevertheless, arbitral tribunals are very cautious in dealing with human rights violations if these do not fall under their jurisdiction. For example, in *Biloune v. Ghana,*[11] the investor was arrested for thirty days without any charge and afterwards he was deported. Consequently, in the investment arbitration proceedings, the investor put forward a distinct head of claim, besides expropriation, requesting damages for human rights violations. Although the arbitral tribunal confirmed that under customary international law states should ensure foreign citizens on their territory a minimum standard of treatment and that international law grants all individuals inviolable human rights, it also explained that this situation does not lead automatically to the conclusion that the arbitral tribunal has jurisdiction to deal with any human rights violation. The tribunal concluded that although it does not have jurisdiction over an independent claim regarding human rights violations, to the extent that such violations impact the investment, they will fall under the arbitral tribunal's jurisdiction.

In another case, which is currently pending, *Al Jazeera Media Network v. Egypt,*[12] one of the investor's complaints was that the state breached its obligations deriving from international conventions on human rights, namely from the freedom of expression and the right not to be subject to inhumane or degrading treatment. The factual background is that Al Jazeera's headquarters in Egypt, and its journalists, have been attacked by the Egyptian army and police, as well as by some groups supporting the military government. In the end, the operating licence of the media network was also withdrawn. It will be interesting to see how the tribunal deals with the investor's human rights claims, and whether it will follow the reasoning in *Biloune v. Ghana,* namely that as long as human rights violations do not impact the investment, the tribunal does not have jurisdiction over an independent claim regarding human rights.

In the end, considering the international origin and character of investment arbitration, it is only natural for investment tribunals to turn to the case law of the ICJ for guidance on general international law matters. Similarly, when faced with aspects regarding human rights, it is only natural to turn to the case law of the courts

9. *ADC Affiliate Limited and ADC and ADMC Management Limited v. Republic of Hungary,* Case No. ARB/03/16 (ICSID, Award of 2 October 2006) 93 https://www.italaw.com/cases/41 (accessed 14 June 2019).
10. *Ronald Lauder v. Czech Republic* (UNCITRAL, Final Award, 3 September 2001), 43. https://www.italaw.com/cases/documents/611 (accessed 14 June 2019).
11. *Biloune and Marine Drive Complex ltd v. Ghana Investments Centre and the Government of Ghana,* 95 ILR 184 (UNCITRAL, Award on jurisdiction and liability of 27 October 1989) in Monique Sasson, *Substantive Law in Investment Treaty Arbitration: The Unsettled Relationship Between International and Municipal Law* (Wolters Kluwer 2010) 91.
12. *Al Jazeera Media Network v. Arab Republic of Egypt* (ICSID No. ARB/16/1).

specialized in dealing with human rights disputes. The Strasbourg court was used as an example in the current chapter given the author's familiarity with the interplay between ECtHR and international arbitration, but the interaction does arise also with other fora specialized in human rights.

From the access to justice perspective, such cross-reference contributes to ensuring some degree of coherence between legal interpretations for the users of the international dispute settlement system. Moreover, it enriches the legal toolbox with which arbitrators operate by bringing in the criteria, checklists and best practices developed over time by another court in similar or identical matters. Very pragmatically, from the disputants' perspective, there is more legal ammunition available to construct and deconstruct legal arguments. All these aspects contribute to a more coherent international dispute settlement system overall, and therefore to better access to justice.

§4.03 COMPETING OR OVERLAPPING JURISDICTIONS: MORE DOORS TO ACCESS JUSTICE

Several competing or overlapping jurisdictions can be identified in the international dispute resolution landscape. What does this mean for access to justice? Access to more or alternative courts means more options for potential claimants, and therefore increased access to justice, at least from a quantitative standpoint.

The multiplication of international courts and tribunals offers more options of dispute resolution to potential parties in litigation and arbitration. Nikolaos Lavranos considers that it is a good sign in the sense that 'states are prepared to use courts and tribunals more often for settling their disputes rather than using armed forces'.[13] Nevertheless, some problems may arise in respect of overlapping jurisdictions and there is a risk of conflicting decisions since there is no 'hierarchical legally binding relationship between all these courts and tribunals'.[14]

This form of interplay, competing or overlapping jurisdictions, can be found between ECtHR and investment arbitration tribunals. Take for example the famous Yukos saga, where Yukos' former majority shareholders brought arbitration proceedings for alleged breaches of the Energy Charter Treaty,[15] while Yukos, in its own name, initiated proceedings before the Strasbourg court[16] invoking among others the violation of Article 1 Protocol 1 (the right to property). Russia raised the issue of parallel proceedings before the Strasbourg Court and asked for the discontinuance of the case

13. Nikolaos Lavranos, *Regulating Competing Jurisdictions Among International Courts and Tribunals*, 68 ZaöRV, 575, 576 (2008).
14. *Ibid.*
15. PCA Case no. AA 227, *Yukos Universal Limited v. The Russian Federation*, case information and documents available at https://pca-cpa.org/en/cases/61/ (accessed 14 June 2019).
16. *OAO Neftyanaya Kompaniya Yukos v. Russia*, Application no. 14902/04 (ECtHR, Judgment of 20 September 2011).

pursuant to Article 35(2)(b) of the Convention.[17] The court first looked into the purpose of Article 35(2)(b), noting that:

> the situation where several international bodies would be simultaneously dealing with applications which are substantially the same [...] would be incompatible with the spirit and the letter of the Convention, which seeks to avoid a plurality of international proceedings relating to the same cases.[18]

Subsequently it explained the method that should be applied in order to determine similarity: 'The assessment of similarity of the cases would usually involve the comparison of the parties in the respective proceedings, the relevant legal provisions relied on by them, the scope of their claims and the types of the redress sought.'[19] And finally, the court concluded that the arbitration proceedings and the human rights proceedings concern matters which are not substantially the same, because 'the claimants in those arbitration proceedings are the applicant company's shareholders acting as investors, and not the applicant company itself'.[20]

Considering the criteria adopted by the Strasbourg Court for assessing the matters that are 'substantially the same', the conclusion is a positive one for investors and their companies, which have more doors to access justice, and unfortunate for respondent states, which will have to defend themselves before two fora for the same set of actions.

The CJEU also takes part in the game of competing and overlapping jurisdictions, both with interstate arbitration, and, more recently, also with investment arbitration derived from intra-EU BITs. In interstate arbitration, the *Mox Plant* case is a good example of this interplay. The dispute arose between Ireland and the UK and concerned some radioactive discharges into the Irish Sea by Mox Plant.[21] The dispute unfolded in two arbitration proceedings (under the Convention for the Protection of the Marine Environment of the North-East Atlantic (OSPAR) and under the United Nations Convention on the Law of the Sea (UNCLOS)) and an infringement case before the Luxembourg Court,[22] brought by the Commission against Ireland precisely for initiating the proceedings against UK outside the Community legal order, without considering that the European Community was also a party to UNCLOS, and thus violating the exclusive jurisdiction of the European court as well as the duty of loyal co-operation. While the OSPAR arbitral tribunal did not bother with the applicable European Community rules, and the UNCLOS arbitral tribunal decided to stay the proceedings

17. Article 35(2)(b): 'The Court shall not deal with any individual applications submitted under Article 34 that:...

    (b) is substantially the same as a matter that has already been examined by the Court or has already been submitted to another procedure of international investigation or settlement and contains no relevant new information.'

18. *OAO Neftyanaya Kompaniya Yukos v. Russia*, Application no. 14902/04 (ECtHR, Judgment of 20 September 2011) paragraph 520.
19. *Ibid.*, paragraph 521.
20. *Ibid.*, paragraph 524.
21. Lavranos (*supra* n. 10) 578.
22. *Commission v. Ireland*, C-459/03, ECR I-4635 (ECJ, Judgment 30 May 2006), ECLI: EU:C:2006:345.

until it is established whether the European court had jurisdiction, the Luxembourg court upheld the infringement action brought by the Commission.[23]

The court explained that the Law of the Sea Convention is a mixed agreement, having the same status in the Community legal order as agreements concluded by the European Community alone. The court further explained that 'an international agreement cannot affect the allocation of responsibilities defined in the Treaties and, consequently, the autonomy of the Community legal system'[24] and that 'the provisions of the Convention in issue in the dispute concerning the Mox plant come within the scope of Community competence which the Community exercised by acceding to the Convention, with the result that those provisions form an integral part of the Community legal order'.[25]

As regards investment arbitration derived from intra-EU BITs, the position of an investment arbitral tribunal as to the interplay with the Luxembourg court is well reflected in *Eurêko v. The Slovak Republic.*[26] The Slovak Republic raised an 'Intra-EU Jurisdictional Objection' arguing that the Slovak Republic's membership in the EU deprives the tribunal of its jurisdiction.[27] Moreover, the European Commission asked for a suspension of the arbitration proceedings until any doubts were solved by the European court, similarly to Mox plant case, arguing that there was a risk of contradictory decisions between the arbitral tribunal and the pending infringement case.[28] The arbitral tribunal retained jurisdiction and noted that:

> The argument that the ECJ has an "interpretative monopoly" and that the Tribunal therefore cannot consider and apply EU law, is incorrect. The ECJ has no such monopoly. Courts and arbitration tribunals throughout the EU interpret and apply EU law daily. What the ECJ has is a monopoly on the final and authoritative interpretation of EU law: but that is quite different. Moreover, even final courts are not obliged to refer questions of the interpretation of EU law to the ECJ in all cases. The acte clair doctrine is well-established in EU law.[29]

As regards to Commission's request for suspension in order to avoid contradictory decisions, the arbitral tribunal dismissed it at the jurisdictional stage, but it did not totally reject the idea of a potential suspension should the relationship between the two sets of proceedings prove to be closer than initially anticipated.[30]

Such a position as the one adopted by the arbitral tribunal in *Eurêko v. The Slovak Republic* was strongly contested by the European Commission in numerous intra-EU investment arbitration cases and, in the end, in the *Achmea case*,[31] the CJEU supported

23. Lavranos (*supra* n. 10) 578, 581-583.
24. *Commission v. Ireland* (*supra* n. 17) paragraph 123.
25. *Ibid.*, paragraph 126.
26. *Eurêko v. The Slovak Republic,* PCA Case no. 2008-13 (UNCITRAL, Award on Jurisdiction, Admissibility and Suspension, 26 October 2010. *See also* Laurence Boisson de Chazournes, *Plurality in the Fabric of International Courts and Tribunals: The Threads of a Managerial Approach*, 28 European Journal of International Law 13 (2017).
27. *Ibid.*, paragraph 19.
28. *Ibid.*, paragraph 194.
29. *Ibid.*, paragraph 282.
30. *Ibid.*, paragraph 292.
31. *Slovak Republic v. Achmea B.V.*, Case C-284/16 (CJEU, Judgment of 6 March 2018).

the view that investor-state arbitration in intra-EU BITs is incompatible with EU law. Thus, the Luxembourg court stepped in aggressively in this interplay and put in place fences delineating more clearly its exclusive jurisdiction. Such a step was unwelcomed by investors, who felt that one door of their access to justice was unfairly blocked, but was welcome by the EU Member States which, more and more often, found themselves as losing respondents before investment tribunals because of the measures adopted in consideration of their EU membership.

Finally, competing or overlapping jurisdictions also arise in the interplay between commercial and treaty-based arbitration. A dispute between the same two contractual parties regarding the same set of facts could fall under both the contractual dispute resolution mechanism, and under the investment treaty protection mechanism.[32]

On the one hand, this brings more options for the parties, but on the other hand, the distinction is not always clear cut and therefore different problems arise in practice which prolong and complicate the proceedings. Sometimes there may be an overlap between the jurisdictions of the contractually established tribunal and the treaty-based tribunal because of the wording of the clause representing consent to jurisdiction. For instance, consenting to arbitration for 'any investment dispute' (which may include contract claims) as opposed to jurisdiction for 'treaty violations'. Moreover, there are also the so-called umbrella clauses, under which states have the obligation to comply with any obligation undertaken with respect to the investment, and which may open the door for contract breaches into the investment disputes.[33] For example, in *SGS v. Pakistan*[34] there were exhaustive debates between the parties as regards the interplay between contract claims and treaty claims at the jurisdictional stage of the proceedings, which obviously prolonged the overall proceedings. More precisely, the arbitral tribunal had to address whether it had jurisdiction over BIT claims, over contract claims or over both. [35] While retaining jurisdiction, the arbitral tribunal noted that:

> As a matter of general principle, the same set of facts can give rise to different claims grounded on differing legal orders: the municipal and the international legal orders. BIT claims and contract claims appear reasonably distinct in principle. Complexities, however, arise ... particularly where, as in the present case, each party claims that one tribunal ... has jurisdiction over both types of claims which are alleged to co-exist.[36]

The competing and overlapping jurisdictions as a form of interplay between international courts and tribunals bring in more options, more doors of access to justice for the claimant, and burden the respondent with defending the same set of actions before two or more fora. From all the interactions presented above, the CJEU seems to

32. Christoph Schreuer, 'Interactions of International Tribunals and Domestic Courts in Investment Law', in *A. W. Rovine* (ed.), *Contemporary Issues in International Arbitration and Mediation: The Fordham Papers 2010* (Brill 2011) 71 and 81.
33. *Ibid.*, 82.
34. *SGS Société Générale de Surveillance S.A. v. Islamic Republic of Pakistan*, Case No. ARB/01/13 (ICSID Decision of the Tribunal on Objections to Jurisdiction, 6 August 2003).
35. *Ibid.*, paragraph 146.
36. *Ibidc*, paragraphs 147-148.

be the most committed to defend its exclusive jurisdiction and exclude any competing forum, thus limiting the parties' options for having access to justice.

§4.04 CHECKS AND BALANCES

The interplay between courts and tribunals leads to a set of checks and balances, which contribute to assuring access to justice at higher standards. In Europe, the main checks and balances appear in the interplay between the ECtHR, CJEU, domestic courts, on the one hand, and arbitral tribunals, on the other hand. Each interplay will be duly presented in the following pages.

[A] Checks and Balances in the Interplay Between the ECtHR and Arbitral Tribunals

In the states parties to the ECHR the interplay between the ECtHR and commercial arbitration gives rise to a set of checks and balances, which protect access to justice at certain standards, and protect the finality of arbitration awards.

On the one hand, the standards imposed by Article 6(1) of the ECHR permeate arbitral proceedings by means of the threat that the arbitral award may be set aside or refused enforcement in states that are parties to the ECHR. Therefore, this interplay improves access to justice qualitatively, namely procedural guarantees and standards are better complied with in arbitral proceedings. On the other hand, by considering that an arbitral award is protected by Article 1 in Protocol No 1 to the ECHR, the ECtHR contributes greatly to protecting the finality of an arbitral award. Ensuring compliance and enforcement of arbitral awards improves access to justice because without appropriate mechanisms for the enforcement of awards, the whole arbitration proceedings would be meaningless, and access to justice would be an illusory and void concept. First, by voluntarily signing an arbitration agreement parties waive the right to a state court and the right to a public hearing, under Article 6(1) of the ECHR, but the guarantees of a fair trial are not affected. Their right to a fair hearing, the right to be heard, the equality of arms and the right to an independent and impartial tribunal will continue to be applicable in arbitration proceedings.[37]

Therefore, in the signatory states to the *ECHR* the arbitral procedure may be reviewed by state courts as regards to its compliance with fundamental guarantees under art. 6(1) ECHR, especially because by confirming an arbitral award a state court triggers the responsibility of the state for compliance with the Convention. In this respect, although the actions of an arbitral tribunal cannot by themselves trigger the responsibility of a state signatory of the Convention, since they are not state organs and are not exercising state power, art. 6(1) ECHR gives rise to two categories of obligations for a signatory state as regards arbitration: the negative obligation of abstaining from

37. *See* Juan Carlos Landrove, 'The European Convention on Human Rights' Impact on Consensual Arbitration: An État des Lieux of Strasbourg Case-Law and of a Problematic Swiss Law Feature', in S. Besson, M. Hottelier, F. Werro (eds), *Human Rights at the Center* (Schulthess, 2006) 90. *See also* D. St. J. Sutton, J. Gill, M. Gearing, *Russel on Arbitration* (Sweet & Maxwell, 2007) 17-18.

enforcing or giving effect in any other way to an arbitral award obtained through proceedings breaching fundamental guarantees under art. 6(1), and the positive obligation to ensure, through state courts, the appropriate procedural mechanisms to check compliance with fundamental guarantees under art. 6(1).[38]

Moreover, the procedural guarantees under art. 6(1) ECHR are already considered so fundamental that almost all national arbitration laws and international conventions on arbitration provide for their observance, and they are usually considered as part of the public policy of the signatory states.[39]

Consequently, if they wish to render an award which is enforceable in a country which is a party to the Convention, arbitral tribunals will pay attention to the non-waivable procedural guarantees under art. 6(1) because any violation might be sanctioned by a domestic court either by setting aside, or by refusing enforcement of the arbitral award.[40]

Furthermore, even if the award survives the domestic courts, their failure to set aside or refuse enforcement of a tainted award may be further brought before the ECtHR. To take a recent example, in *Mutu and Pechstein v. Switzerland*[41] the Court found a violation of art. 6(1) because domestic courts failed to set aside an award rendered in breach of the right to a public hearing. The court established that consent to arbitration before the CAS was not freely given by Mrs Pechstein, that it was a compulsory arbitration, and therefore there was no waiver of the right to a public hearing. This was true for Mrs Pechstein, but not for Mr Mutu whose contract allowed him to choose the jurisdiction of the state courts. The court decided that her explicit request to have a public hearing has been refused without any good justification.

Separately, the Strasbourg court plays an important role also in protecting the finality of arbitral awards. Without appropriate mechanisms to assure the enforcement of awards, the whole arbitration proceedings would be meaningless, and access to justice would be an illusory and void concept. In *Marini v. Albania,*[42] the court noted

38. Georgios Petrochilos, *Procedural Law in International Arbitration* (Oxford University Press, 2004) 112-113, 154.
39. Landrove (*supra* n. 33) 97.
40. *Ibid.*, 92.
41. *Mutu and Pechstein v. Switzerland*, Application no. 40575/10 and 67474/10 (ECtHR, Decision of 2 October 2018). *See also* Adam Thew, *ECHR Releases its Judgment in the Pechstein case: What does this Mean for the Court of Arbitration for Sport?*, 11 October 2018, https://www.lexology.com/library/detail.aspx?g=bee3263b-b473-442b-a645-ba606ca4a52e (accessed on 14 June 2019). Nathalie Voser, Benjamin Gottlieb, How the European Court for Human Rights Interferes in (Sports) Arbitration, 19 December 2018, http://arbitrationblog.kluwerarbitration.com (accessed on 14 June 2019). *Cathérine Van de Graaf, Mutu and Pechstein v. Switzerland: Strasbourg's Assessment of the Right to a Fair Hearing in Sports Arbitration*, 30 November 2018, https://strasbourgobservers.com/2018/11/30/mutu-and-pechstein-v-switzerland-strasbourgs-assessment-of-the-right-to-a-fair-hearing-in-sports-arbitration/ (accessed on 14 June 2019). Edith Wagner, *Putting an End to Forced Arbitration Behind Closed Doors: The Need for a Public Hearing Before the Court of Arbitration for Sport*, 8 November 2018, https://blogdroiteuropeen.com/2018/11/08/putting-an-end-to-forced-arbitration-behind-closed-doors-the-need-for-a-public-hearing-before-the-court-of-arbitration-for-sport-by-edith-wagner/ (accessed on 14 June 2019).
42. *Marini v. Albania*, Application no. 3738/02 (ECtHR, Judgment of 18 December 2007).

that access to justice under art. 6(1) ECHR would be illusory if a final and binding decision cannot be enforced in a timely manner:

> Execution of a judgment given by any court must therefore be regarded as an integral part of the "trial" for the purposes of Article 6. A delay in the execution of a judgment may be justified in particular circumstances. But the delay may not be such as to impair the essence of the right protected under Article 6 § 1.[43]

In that case the court found a violation of art. 6(1) of the Convention and art. 1 of Protocol No. 1 because 'proceedings exceeded the reasonable time requirement and that the decision in the applicant's favour had not been enforced for a period of time, preventing him from enjoying his property'.[44] *In concreto*, some final and binding decisions of the State Arbitration Commission, upheld by domestic courts in final decisions, were not enforced by the authorities for ten years without any satisfactory explanation.[45] In the same vein, in *Regent Company v. Ukraine*,[46] a company complained under art. 6(1) of the Convention about the non-enforcement of an arbitration award on account of an omission by the State Bailiffs' Service and the enactment of a law introducing a moratorium on the forced sale of property.[47] The court found that 'the continued non-enforcement of the judgment debt at issue constituted a violation of art. 6 § 1 of the Convention'.[48]

Second, the ECtHR established that an arbitral award is a 'good' protected by art. 1 in Protocol No 1 to the ECHR.[49] In *Stran Greek Refineries and Stratis Andreadis v. Greece*[50] the Court found a violation of art. 1 of Protocol No.1, noting that 'the legislature upset [...] the balance that must be struck between the protection of the right of property and the requirements of public interest'.[51] Moreover, the court noted that:

> The applicants' right under the arbitration award was "pecuniary" in nature, as had been their claim for damages allowed by the arbitration court. Their right to recover the sums awarded by the arbitration court was therefore a "civil right" within the meaning of Article 6 whatever the nature, under Greek law, of the contract between the applicants and the Greek State.[52]

43. *Ibid.*, paragraph 126.
44. *Ibid.*, paragraph 186.
45. *Ibid.*, paragraphs 131, 134, 135.
46. *Regent Company v. Ukraine*, Application no. 773/03 (ECtHR, Judgment of 3 April 2008).
47. *Ibid.*,' paragraph 3.
48. *Ibid.*, paragraph 60.
49. Landrove (*supra* n. 33) 78.
50. *Stran Greek Refineries and Stratis Andreadis v. Greece*, Application no. 13427/87 (ECtHR, Judgment of 9 December 1994).
51. *Ibid.*, paragraph 74.
52. *Ibid.*, paragraph 40.

[B] Checks and Balances in the Interplay Between the CJEU and Arbitral Tribunals

Checks and balances also arise in the interplay between the CJEU and commercial arbitration, by means of defining the content of the public policy. For instance, in *Eco Swiss,*[53] the Luxembourg court started its reasoning by showing that art. 81 of the Treaty establishing the European Community[54] constitutes a fundamental provision which is essential for the accomplishment of the tasks entrusted to the European Union and, in particular, the functioning of the internal market,[55] and therefore it indicated that, where domestic rules give the possibility of annulment of an arbitration award on grounds of public policy, it must also give it for failure to comply with the prohibition laid down in art. 81(1).[56] Moreover, the court showed that this conclusion is compatible with the New York Convention and that the provisions of art. 81 should be regarded as a matter of public policy within the meaning of the New York Convention.[57]

In *Asturcom,*[58] the enforcing court asked for a preliminary ruling whether the Unfair Terms Directive must be interpreted as meaning that a national court, hearing an action for enforcement of an arbitration award which has acquired the force of res judicata and was made in the absence of the consumer, is required to determine of its own motion whether an arbitration clause in a contract concluded between a consumer and a seller or supplier is unfair, and to annul the award. The Luxembourg court instructed that the provision of consumer law was so fundamental as to have to be treated equally to national public policy.[59] In *Mostaza Claro*[60] the court showed that the consumer protection provision constitutes such an essential rule for the Union that a national court must determine whether the arbitration agreement is void and annul that award where that agreement contains an unfair term, even though the consumer had not pleaded that invalidity during the arbitration proceedings.[61]

By delineating the content of public policy, which is relevant for the setting aside and the recognition and enforcement proceedings carried out in the European Union, the CJEU is indirectly ensuring compliance with EU fundamental values and mandatory substantive rules even in arbitral proceedings. Such values or norms have mostly a protective role. For instance, in the cases quoted above, the rules qualified by the CJEU as public policy aim to protect the functioning of the internal market and to

53. *Eco Swiss China Time Ltd v. Benetton International NV*, Case C-126/97 (ECJ, Judgment of 1 June 1999).
54. Articles 81 and 82 of the Treaty establishing the European Community (EC Treaty) currently correspond to Articles 101 (concerted practices that restrict competition) and 102 (abuse of dominant position) of the Treaty on the Functioning of the European Union (TFEU).
55. *Ibid.*, paragraph 36.
56. *Ibid.*, paragraph 37.
57. *Ibid.*, paragraphs 38-39.
58. *Asturcom Telecomunicaciones SL v. Cristina Rodriguez Nogueira*, Case C-40/08 (ECJ, Judgment of 6 October 2009).
59. *Ibid.*, paragraph 52.
60. *Elisa María Mostaza Claro v. Centro Móvil Milenium SL*, Case C-168/05 (ECJ, Judgment of 26 October 2006).
61. *Ibid.*, paragraphs 37-39.

protect the consumers. How does this affect access to justice? By qualifying some mandatory substantive rules as public policy, a concept so relevant to arbitral tribunals, the CJEU is safeguarding these rules also in 'private justice' proceedings, not only in 'state justice' proceedings. By safeguarding some mandatory substantive rules in arbitral proceedings, the CJEU is indirectly improving access to justice from a qualitative standpoint. A justice that ensures protection of consumers and protection of fair competition on the internal market is better justice.

Therefore, as opposed to the ECtHR that impacts access to justice in arbitral proceedings mostly from a procedural perspective, the CJEU impacts arbitral proceedings mostly from a substantive law perspective.

[C] Checks and Balances in the Interplay Between Domestic Courts and Arbitral Tribunals

Finally, checks and balances are also present in the interplay between arbitral tribunals and domestic courts. Although international arbitration is regarded as a dispute resolution mechanism alternative to the national courts, in fact it still maintains some ties with national systems, without which it cannot function properly. As also noted by other scholars, under the current framework, arbitration 'cannot survive, much less prosper, without the active and effective support of the national court systems'[62] since 'arbitral tribunals lack many of the vital powers held by courts which give the adjudicative process real bite'.[63] In the same vein, it was held that 'arbitration is totally dependent on the courts, and therefore on access to justice and the rule of law, for its efficacy. Without an effective court system to enforce their procedural directions and awards, arbitrators would be toothless'.[64]

The conditions for and the extent of court assistance for and control over the arbitration proceedings are usually provided for in the national arbitration laws.[65] Measures in aid of arbitration may be obtained from the courts at the seat or even from domestic courts in another state, depending on the relevant national law. Schaefer offers a good example by pointing to section 1050 of the German Code of Civil Procedure, allowing a party in an arbitration seated outside Germany to apply to the German court for assistance in ordering the witness domiciled in Germany to appear before the state court and give testimony to be used subsequently in arbitration.[66]

The assistance from national courts is needed in various situations, either before, during or after the arbitration proceedings: interim and conservatory measures before the constitution of the arbitral tribunal; help with the constitution of the arbitral

62. Jacques Werner, *Should the New York Convention Be Revised to Provide for Court Intervention in Arbitral Proceedings?*, 6 Journal of International Arbitration 113 (1989).
63. John Templeman, *Towards a Truly International Court of Arbitration*, 30 Journal of International Arbitration 197, 220 (2013).
64. David Neuberger, *Keynote Speech: Arbitration and the Rule of Law*, 17 Asian Dispute Review 180 (2015).
65. Jan K. Schaefer, *Court Assistance in Arbitration: Some Observations on the Critical Stand-by Function of the Courts*, 43 Pepperdine Law Review 521, 534 (2016).
66. *Ibid.*, 535.

tribunal when one party refuses to appoint an arbitrator; preservation of evidence; one party's refusal to comply with the arbitration agreement; production of evidence if not produced voluntarily; enforcement of interim and conservatory measures; challenges of arbitrators; setting aside the arbitral award; recognition and enforcement of awards.

Some of the points above, where court assistance was needed, are currently covered by arbitral institutions, which can now help with the constitution of the arbitral tribunal, [67] the challenge of an arbitrator,[68] replacement of the arbitrator[69] and the appointment of an emergency arbitrator.[70]

Nevertheless, special attention should be awarded to interim measures. Before the constitution of the arbitral tribunal, interim measures may prove to be essential when there is a serious risk of dissipation of assets. Without fast pre-arbitration interim measures, the whole arbitration may become futile, and the concept of access to justice becomes void. More recently, precisely in order to cover this important aspect of dispute resolution, more and more arbitral institutions modified their rules and added provisions regarding the emergency arbitrator.[71] The problem is that interim measures ordered by emergency arbitrators or arbitral tribunals are not self-executing since the arbitrators lack coercive powers. Therefore, when the emergency arbitrator or arbitral tribunal orders some interim measures, there are two possibilities; either the party complies voluntarily with the measures fearing potential negative inferences, or the beneficiary of the interim measures must obtain their enforcement before the state court.[72]

The matters get even more complicated when differentiating between enforcement at the seat of arbitration and enforcement of interim measures ordered by an arbitral tribunal seated abroad. Recognition and enforcement of interim measures under the New York Convention is problematic under a very optimistic perspective. In the best-case scenario, the state court will distinguish between interim measures that are final on that particular issue, and those that are provisional and reversible, allowing enforcement only for the first category.[73] Therefore, for enforcing interim measures, either at the seat or abroad, which sometimes is essential for preserving the essence of access to justice, domestic courts are indispensable in the current framework.

As regards setting aside and enforcement proceedings, the interplay between arbitral tribunals and national courts is often considered a source of annoyance, supplementary costs and delay. Moreover, the enforcement mechanism under the New

67. Article 12 of the ICC Rules of Arbitration, Article 5 of the LCIA Arbitration Rules, Rule 9 of the SIAC Rules (2016), Article 17 of the SCC Arbitration Rules (2017).
68. Article 14 of the ICC Rules of Arbitration, Article 10 of the LCIA Arbitration Rules, Rules 14, 15, 16 of the SIAC Rules (2016), Article 19 of the SCC Arbitration Rules (2017).
69. Article 15 of the ICC Rules of Arbitration, Article 11 of the LCIA Arbitration Rules, Rule 17 of the SIAC Rules (2016), Article 21 of the SCC Arbitration Rules (2017).
70. Article 29 and Appendix 5 of the ICC Rules of Arbitration, Article 9B of the LCIA Arbitration Rules, Rule 30 and Schedule 1 of the SIAC Rules (2016), Article 37 and Appendix II of the SCC Arbitration Rules (2017).
71. *Ibid.*, 526.
72. Régis Bismuth, *Anatomy of the Law and Practice of Interim Protective Measures in International Investment Arbitration*, 26 Journal of International Arbitration 773 (2009).
73. *Ibid.*

York Convention, although much applauded, can often, depending on the country of enforcement, be rather long and full of surprises, especially concerning the public policy exception under art. V.2(b) of the New York Convention.[74] Nevertheless, these mechanisms ensure a check as regards compliance with fundamental principles and values, and for some parties they are the last resort when the arbitration is tainted by injustice. This does not exclude the situations when these same mechanisms were used abusively by state courts for political and nationalistic reasons. There is a very fine equilibrium between a good faith check and an abusive interference, and some risks must be assumed in order to avoid others. *Saipem v. Bangladesh*[75] is an example of both how domestic courts may abusively interfere with the arbitration process, thus hindering access to justice, and how such abuse may be sanctioned thanks to the interplay between courts and tribunals. The object of the investment arbitration was precisely the fact that Saipem's access to commercial arbitration was hindered by the local courts. The respondent in the commercial arbitration proceedings (Petrobangla) asked the local court to revoke the ICC's authority to deal with the case and applied for an injunction to stay the arbitration proceedings. Despite the injunction, the ICC tribunal continued the proceedings and rendered an award in Saipem's favour. During the annulment proceedings, the local court deemed that the ICC arbitration proceeded illegally and therefore there was no award to be set aside. Consequently, Saipem initiated ICSID arbitration and the investment tribunal concluded that 'the Bangladeshi courts abused their supervisory jurisdiction over the arbitration process'[76] and 'thus violated the internationally accepted principle of prohibition of abuse of rights'[77] and that 'the revocation of the arbitrators' authority was contrary to international law, in particular to the principle of abuse of rights and the New York Convention. [78]

§4.05 CONCLUSION

The analysis started from the assumption that the main benefits brought by this interplay as regards access to justice are the wider coverage of legal matters and more legal remedies, more doors for parties to access justice. While the main downsides would be the potential contradictions in the interpretation and application of legal concepts, and the prolongation and complication of the proceedings, which impede the timely, efficient and effective resolution of disputes.

After categorizing the interactions between courts and tribunals in three different forms of manifestation: cross-referencing to case law and legal interpretations, competing or overlapping jurisdictions and various checks and balances, and after looking at various examples, the answer to this chapter's question is yes, the interplay between courts and tribunals assures access to justice.

74. Templeman (*supra* n. 59).
75. *Saipem Spa v. the People's Republic of Bangladesh*, Case No. ARB/05/07 (ICSID, Award of 30 June 2009). *See also* Francesco Francioni, *Access to Justice, Denial of Justice and International Investment Law*, 20 European Journal of International Law, 729, 737 (2009).
76. *Ibid.,*' paragraph 159.
77. *Ibid.,*' paragraph 161.
78. *Ibid.,*' paragraph 170.

Cross-referencing to case law and legal interpretations contributes to ensuring some degree of coherence between legal interpretations for the users of international dispute settlement system. Moreover, it enriches the legal toolbox with which arbitrators operate by bringing in the criteria, checklists and best practices developed over time by another court in similar or identical matters. Very pragmatically, from the disputants' perspective, there is more legal ammunition available to construct and deconstruct legal arguments. All these aspects contribute to a more coherent international dispute settlement system overall, and therefore to better access to justice.

The competing and overlapping jurisdictions as a form of interplay between international courts and tribunals bring in more options, more doors of access to justice, for the claimant, but at the same time they burden the respondent with defending the same set of actions before two or more fora. The CJEU stepped in aggressively in this interplay and put in place fences delineating more clearly its exclusive jurisdiction. Such a step was unwelcomed by investors, who feel that one door of their access to justice was unfairly blocked, but was welcomed by the EU Member States which, more and more often, found themselves as losing respondents before investment tribunals because of the measures adopted in consideration of their EU membership.

Checks and balances protect access to justice at certain standards and protect the finality of arbitration awards. In the current framework in which international arbitration operates domestic courts have an important supervisory role in ensuring that arbitration proceedings are conducted fairly, and in giving teeth to the measures adopted by the arbitrators. However, it is expected that they interfere as little as possible with the arbitral process because there is a very fine equilibrium between a good faith check and an abusive interference.

PART II Access to Justice and Investment Arbitration

CHAPTER 5

Access to Justice Through Investment Arbitration in Cases of Refusal of Enforcement of Commercial Arbitration Awards: Is There Any Room for Autonomous Claims Based on the New York Convention?

Berk Demirkol[*]

One of the causes of action that has become quite popular in investment treaty arbitration involves a violation of the obligations undertaken in the Convention on the Recognition and Enforcement of Foreign Arbitral Awards (New York Convention). That is to say, foreign investors have been more frequently invoking in their investment claims the responsibility of the state for its failure either to give effect to an arbitration agreement or to refuse the recognition or enforcement of an award rendered by international commercial arbitration tribunals. This subject, in parallel to the development of the case law in investment treaty arbitration, has attracted the attention of academic writings. This chapter seeks to explore how investment treaty arbitration can be used as a means of access to justice in cases where the enforcement of an arbitral award is wrongfully denied by the domestic courts of the host state in an attempt to safeguard the interests of a debtor state entity or a company that is a national of the host state. While such investment claims might require the consideration of a number of jurisdictional and substantive issues, the main focus of this chapter is on the possibility of bringing an autonomous claim based on the New York Convention in investment treaty arbitration. This is a rather under-investigated aspect that deserves further elaboration. The key question is thus whether an investor

* This work was supported by the Scientific Research Projects Commission of Galatasaray University (Istanbul / Turkey) under grant number: Research Project No. 18.200.002. I would like to express my sincere gratitude to Galatasaray University for providing me with such support.

can directly invoke the violation of the New York Convention without basing its claim on an investment treaty undertaking, such as the fair and equitable treatment or the effective means standards.

§5.01 INTRODUCTION

Commercial arbitration, including international commercial arbitration, is most of the time subject to domestic laws and to what national jurisdictions decide on the matter of arbitration. State courts can intervene with arbitration proceedings declaring that the underlying arbitration agreement is invalid, revoking the authority of one or more arbitrators, issuing an anti-arbitration injunction, annulling the award rendered by the arbitral tribunal, or at the stage of enforcement, refusing the enforcement of a foreign arbitral award.

It is trite to indicate that these outcomes could come out as a normal, fair, just and legal consequence of the legal relationship between the parties (e.g. the parties might not have concluded a valid arbitration agreement or the arbitrator appointed by the parties might not fulfil the conditions of independence and impartiality) or as per the hostility of domestic courts towards arbitration. This kind of hostility towards arbitration may emerge more often in some jurisdictions when it comes to the interests of the state, state entities or nationals of that state (for instance, companies owned by individuals having tight connections with politicians).

Assume an international construction contract between a foreign commercial party and a ministry of a government, which includes an arbitration clause. Assume a dispute arises out of this contract and the commercial party resorts to commercial arbitration. At that point, assume that domestic courts of the host state declare that the arbitration clause is invalid for a reason that does not seem sound and supported by law. By the same token, domestic courts at the home state could have rejected for equally implausible reasons the enforcement of foreign arbitral awards that are against the interests of their nationals. This would lead to a problem of access to justice regarding the foreign party's interests. Despite having concluded an international arbitration agreement, the foreign party might not enforce its procedural rights – let alone the substantial ones – against the local company, ministry, or other governmental organization.

The last ten to fifteen years have witnessed a new line of cases in investment arbitration.[1] Investors, disappointed with the domestic courts' intervention with the commercial arbitration, resorted to investment arbitration and invoked international

1. *See Saipem S.p.A. v. The People's Republic of Bangladesh*, ICSID Case No. ARB/05/7, Decision on Jurisdiction and Recommendation on Provisional Measures, 21.03.2007 / Award, 30.06.2009; *Romak S.A. v. The Republic of Uzbekistan*, PCA Case No AA 280, Award, 26.11.2009; *ATA Construction, Industrial and Trading Company v. The Hashemite Kingdom of Jordan*, ICSID Case No. ARB/08/2, Award, 18.05.2010; *Frontier Petroleum Services v. The Czech Republic*, UNCITRAL, Final Award, 12.11.2010; *GEA Group Aktiengesellschaft v. Ukraine*, ICSID Case No. ARB/08/16, Award, 31.03.2011; *White Industries Australia Limited v. The Republic of India*, UNCITRAL, Final Award, 30.11.2011; *Marco Gavazzi and Stefano Gavazzi v. Romania*, ICSID Case No. ARB/12/25, Decision on Jurisdiction, Admissibility and Liability, 21.04.2015; *Anglia Auto Accessories Limited v. The Czech Republic*, SCC Arbitration Case V (2014/181), Final Award, 10.03.2017.

responsibility of the state for the inappropriate judicial conduct towards the underlying arbitration process. The availability of resort to investment arbitration provides access to justice to those who qualify for protection under the investment arbitration regime. The current practice accepts that judicial decisions making the commercial arbitration process ineffective could lead to a breach of one of the investment treaty standards (especially the breach of the fair and equitable treatment standard).

The protection granted under this investment treaty regime is however limited. The limits of this regime necessitate the discussion of what constitutes an investment in this context, whether the host state or a state entity needs to be a party to the underlying arbitration agreement, whether the investor should exhaust the local remedies, and more importantly the breach of which standards could be invoked in case domestic courts annul, or reject the enforcement of, arbitral awards. These issues have been discussed in the academic writing mostly since the beginning of 2010s.[2]

These more general questions do not constitute the focus of this chapter. This chapter rather treats a more specific issue that is the possibility of bringing an autonomous claim based on the NYC [3] in investment treaty arbitration. This is a rather under-investigated aspect that deserves further elaboration. The key question is thus whether an investor can directly invoke the violation of the NYC without basing its claim on the breach of an investment treaty undertaking, such as the fair and equitable treatment or the effective means standards.

To be more precise, the NYC encompasses two major operative clauses. The first one is Article II, where the Contracting States undertake to recognize an arbitration agreement (Article II(1)) and refer the parties to arbitration upon the request of one of the parties when the other party has brought a domestic court proceeding despite the arbitration agreement (Article II(3)). The second main obligation that Contracting States undertake under the NYC is the recognition and enforcement of foreign arbitral awards (Article III) under the conditions laid down in Articles IV and V of the Convention. This chapter discusses whether it would be possible to hold a Contracting State to the NYC responsible in investment treaty arbitration for the failure to abide by one of these obligations without further referring to the breach of one of the investment treaty standards. In other words, the question is whether investors could bring investment claims for the responsibility of the state for domestic courts' failure either to give effect to an arbitration agreement or to reject the recognition or enforcement of an award rendered by international commercial arbitration tribunals. The discussion of whether the obligations in the NYC could serve as autonomous grounds for a self-standing claim in investment treaty arbitration would relieve the investor from the

2. W. Michael Reisman & Heide Iravani, *The Changing Relation of National Courts and International Commercial Arbitration,* 21 American Review of International Arbitration 5 (2010); Gabrielle Kaufmann-Kohler, *Commercial Arbitration Before International Courts and Tribunals – Reviewing Abusive Conduct of Domestic Courts* 29(2) Arbitration International 153 (2013); Stephen Fietta & James Upcher, *Public International Law, Investment Treaties and Commercial Arbitration: an emerging system of complementarity?* 29(2) Arbitration International 187 (2013); Loukas A. Mistelis, *Award as an Investment: The Value of an Award or the Cost of Non-Enforcement,* 28(1) ICSID Review 64 (2013); Berk Demirkol, *Enforcement of International Commercial Arbitration Agreements and Awards in Investment Treaty Arbitration,* 30(1) ICSID Review 56 (2015).
3. Concluded on 10 June 1958, entered into force on 7 June 1959, 330 UNTS 38.

burden of further establishing that the breach of the NYC in a given case meets at the same time the threshold of the breach of investment treaty standards, which is usually higher than the threshold of establishing the violation of the NYC.

Bringing such claim directly based on the NYC requires that an NYC dispute could be heard by an investment treaty tribunal. This chapter will thus address first the question of whether investment treaty tribunals have jurisdiction to hear these claims. The second issue pertains to the substance of the dispute and deals with the possibility to hold the state responsible for the misapplication of the NYC before an investment treaty tribunal. As a third point, this chapter will elaborate on the question of whether it is required for the investor to exhaust local remedies before invoking state responsibility for the breach of the NYC. Finally, this chapter will draw its conclusion on the practical implications of the approach suggested in this chapter.

§5.02 JURISDICTION OF INVESTMENT TREATY TRIBUNALS TO HEAR NYC DISPUTES

Contracting states to investment treaties provide their consent to resolve a category of disputes between host states and investors before arbitral tribunals constituted pursuant to the dispute settlement clause of the relevant treaty. The wording used in the dispute settlement clause identifies which category of disputes can be submitted to investment arbitration. This determines the scope of the state's consent to international arbitration and thus the jurisdiction of the investment treaty tribunals.

The examination of the terms of the dispute settlement provision in the applicable treaty is essential in determining the jurisdiction of a particular international adjudicatory mechanism as underscored by the International Court of Justice (ICJ) in the *Application of the Convention on the Prevention and Punishment of the Crime of Genocide* case.[4] The jurisdiction provided by the treaty may either confine to disputes in relation to the interpretation and application of that treaty or disclose a different intention providing broader or even more restricted consent. The same principle applies to the dispute settlement provisions incorporated in investment treaties as well.[5]

A survey carried out by Douglas reveals four prototype provisions in investment treaties that record host states' consent to international arbitration.[6] Two major categories among these four prototype provisions are dispute settlement provisions which record states' consent for disputes arising from the obligations undertaken in the applicable investment treaty and the ones which allow investors to submit *any*

4. *Application of the Convention on the Prevention and Punishment of the Crime of Genocide (Croatia v. Serbia)*, ICJ Judgment, 3 February 2015, paragraph 88.
5. On the scope of the dispute settlement provisions in investment treaties, *see* further Mara Valenti, *The Scope of an Investment Treaty Dispute Resolution Clause: It is Not Just a Question of Interpretation*, 29(2) Arbitration International 243 (2013).
6. Zachary Douglas, *The International Law of Investment Claims* (Cambridge University Press, 2009), 234.

investment dispute to international arbitration.[7] The jurisdiction of a tribunal established under the former model would be limited to hearing claims arising out of the breach of one of the investment treaty standards. The breach of the NYC could be brought to investment arbitration under this prototype dispute settlement provision only if this breach constitutes at the same time a breach of one of the investment treaty standards.

An investment treaty tribunal established under the latter model, however, would have jurisdiction to hear any claim relating to the investment regardless of the source of responsibility. As pointed out by the annulment committee in *Vivendi v. Argentina*, this category of dispute settlement clauses 'do[es] not necessitate that the Claimant allege a breach of the BIT itself: it is sufficient that the dispute relate to an investment made under the BIT'.[8] In this case, the investor may invoke a breach of an investment treaty undertaking, as well as the breach of another rule applicable between the parties – which could be a rule of international law, a rule of national law or a contractual obligation.[9] The tribunal's jurisdiction would extend to any investment claim arising from any breach infringing investor's rights. No restriction applies upon the source of obligations, which form the basis of the claim.[10]

This type of dispute settlement provisions provides investors with a greater access to justice: for investors to resort to investment arbitration under this clause, they would not need to base their claim on an investment treaty standard; they could bring a claim even if the wrongful act committed by the state does not meet the threshold of an investment treaty breach. Accordingly, a breach of a norm rooted in a non-investment treaty may as well give rise to an investment dispute. This infers that the investor may claim damages in investment treaty for the loss that it has incurred as a result of the misapplication of a rule or a violation of an obligation envisaged even in an international convention other than the applicable investment treaty. This line of reasoning suggests that a dispute settlement clause drafted in broad terms – which for instance refers to the submission of *any investment dispute* to investment arbitration – allows an investor to base its investment claim on any cause of action regardless of whether this cause of action is rooted in the investment treaty, contract, or another international conventional or customary rule.

7. The other two prototype dispute settlement clauses are used less frequently. One of them identifies the legal sources for the investor's causes of action referring not only to the investment treaty at hand but also other sources such as investment agreements between the investor and the state. The other prototype clause limits the subject matter of the dispute to one or more – but not to all – standards of treatment embodied in the investment treaty or even more restrictedly to the disputes about the quantum payable to the investor following an expropriation.
8. *Compania de Aguas del Aconquija SA and Vivendi Universal v. Argentine Republic*, ICSID Case No. ARB/97/3, Decision on Annulment, 3 July 2002, paragraph 55.
9. *See Salini Costruttori S.p.A. and Italstrade S.p.A. v. Kingdom of Morocco*, ICSID Case No. ARB/00/4, Decision on Jurisdiction, 16 July 2001, paragraph 59; *SGS Société Générale de Surveillance SA v. Republic of Philippines*, ICSID Case No. ARB/02/6, Decision on Jurisdiction, 29 January 2004, paragraph 131.
10. Zachary Douglas, 'The enforcement of environmental norms in investment treaty arbitration' in Pierre-Marie Dupuy & Jorge E Viñuales (eds), *Harnessing Foreign Investment to Promote Environmental Incentives and Safeguards* (Cambridge University Press, 2013) 415, 424.

Article II and Article III of the NYC constitute such causes of action rooted in another international convention than the investment treaty itself. The only qualification the investor needs to demonstrate for the purposes of establishing the jurisdiction of an investment tribunal under a broad dispute settlement clause is that the breach of the obligations under this other international convention leads to an *investment* dispute.

§5.03 THE BREACH OF THE NYC AND ESTABLISHING STATE RESPONSIBILITY

Articles II and III of the NYC set clear obligations. It is true that these provisions refer to domestic law (for instance in the determination of the law applicable to the arbitration agreement) and domestic concepts (such as public policy which constitutes a ground under Article V to oppose to the enforcement of a foreign arbitral award) in their application. These references to the domestic sphere do not however provide domestic courts with unlimited discretion in the interpretation and application of the NYC. An abuse of this discretion, an implausible interpretation of these concepts or a clear contradiction with settled case law clarifying the national understanding of these concepts would constitute breaches of the NYC.

Article 2 of the International Law Commission (ILC)'s Articles on Responsibility of States for Internationally Wrongful Acts (ARSIWA)[11] states that '[t]here is an internationally wrongful act of a State when conduct consisting of an action or omission: (a) is attributable to the State under international law; and (b) constitutes a breach of an international obligation of the State'. The misapplication of the NYC or the failure to apply its terms by the domestic courts of the host state satisfies both conditions.

With respect to attributability of conducts of state organs, Article 4 of the ARSIWA reads, '[t]he conduct of any State organ shall be considered an act of that State under international law whether the organ exercises legislative, executive, judicial or any other functions [...]'. Accordingly, the misapplication of the NYC by domestic courts is an act that is attributable to the state for the purposes of responsibility of the state under international law.

It is also clear that the misapplication of the NYC or the failure to apply its terms constitutes a breach of an international obligation of the state if that state is a Contracting State to the NYC.

Article 1 of the ARSIWA states that '[e]very internationally wrongful act of a State entails the international responsibility of that State'. One could thus conclude without any hesitation that a Contracting State to the NYC would be responsible under international law for the breach of the obligations set forth in the Convention when it misapplies or fails to apply any provision of the Convention.

What could be more controversial is the investor's standing to invoke this breach in investment treaty arbitration. Indeed, for a person to bring a claim before any

11. ILC, *Report of the Fifty-third Session* (2001), UN Doc. A/56/10, 2001/II(2) ILC Ybk 26.

dispute settlement mechanism, this person should be entitled to a legal interest over the substance of the benefit protected by this right. For instance, an investor may not invoke the breach of an interstate obligation to lower the gas emissions even if it proves that it has incurred some loss as a result of this breach. Such dispute could arise in the context of contamination of an ecotourism site.[12] The reason why the investor may not have standing to invoke the breach of this interstate obligation despite the adverse effect of this breach is that this very obligation does not refer any legal interest, substantial right, or benefit in favour of the investor. International responsibility of the state for the commitment of this purely interstate norm could only be invoked by another state towards which the obligation has been undertaken. The investor would not have standing to invoke a purely interstate cause of action, as it would not vindicate any interest of legal nature from that norm.[13] Such cases would not in general lead to an 'access to justice' debate, as the breach is not towards the investor and the investor does not have any legal interest to be protected under domestic or international law.

The question that should be addressed is whether the investor vindicates any interest of legal nature from the NYC so that it could have standing to invoke the breach of the Convention in an international dispute settlement mechanism. This question should be answered positively. Articles II and III of the NYC confer a direct interest of legal nature for the application of the provisions stipulated in the NYC on individuals (or legal persons). For instance, Article II requires Contracting States to recognize arbitration agreements and refer the parties to arbitration upon the request of one of the parties to the arbitration agreement. This could not be construed as a purely interstate norm. This norm creates a benefit, if not a right in favour of the individual. According to this rule, the individual is entitled to request from the domestic court to refer the parties to arbitration if the other party has already seized that court despite the arbitration agreement between the parties. If the domestic court does not refer the parties to arbitration upon the request of this party, it would directly infringe the individual's legal interest stipulated under the NYC. This conclusion is quite obvious considering that the legal consequences under Articles II and III become operative upon the request of individuals that are party to the arbitration agreement or creditor of arbitral awards rendered in a third country. An individual would also have legal entitlement to appeal a court judgment which has failed to apply or misapplied the NYC. Given this legal entitlement or interest, an investor, who is party to an arbitration agreement or creditor of an arbitral award, would have standing to invoke the breach of the NYC in investment treaty arbitration as a self-standing claim.

12. *See*, e.g. the dispute in *Peter A Allard v. The Government of Barbados*, PCA Case No. 2012-06, 1976 UNCITRAL Arbitration Rules, Award on Jurisdiction, 13 July 2014, paragraph 3.
13. Berk Demirkol, *Non-treaty Claims in Investment Treaty Arbitration*, 31 Leiden Journal of International Law 59, 85 (2018).

§5.04 ADMISSIBILITY OF THE SELF-STANDING CLAIM: IS THERE A REQUIREMENT TO EXHAUST LOCAL REMEDIES?

After having established that an investment treaty tribunal may have jurisdiction - under a dispute settlement clause recording host state's broad consent - to hear the breach of the NYC as a self-standing claim and that an investor has legal interest and thus standing to invoke such breach before an international dispute settlement mechanism, the final question that this chapter will address is whether the investor is required to exhaust local remedies before bringing an NYC claim in investment treaty arbitration.

Exhaustion of local remedies can be a procedural requirement. This procedural requirement is rooted in customary international law. The national state of an individual could espouse this individual's claim against the injuring state only once the individual has exhausted the effective local remedies available within the latter state.[14] Diplomatic protection cases aside, the local remedies rule finds application in human rights mechanisms (e.g. Article 35(1) of the European Convention on Human Rights,[15] Article 41(1)(c) of the International Covenant on Civil and Political Rights[16]) as well. Notwithstanding that, the procedural requirement to exhaust local remedies prior to submitting a claim before an international court or tribunal, does not usually find application in investment treaty arbitration unless it is specifically required in the applicable investment treaty. Article 26 of the Convention on the Settlement of Investment Disputes between States and Nationals of Other States (ICSID Convention)[17] confirms the reversal of the customary international law rule in the field of investment arbitration. It is generally accepted that the local remedies rule does not find application in non-ICSID investment treaty arbitration either unless otherwise provided in the relevant treaty.[18]

Exhaustion of local remedies can also be a substantive requirement to bring a claim asserting international responsibility of the state. That is to say, exhaustion of local remedies could constitute a component of the specific wrongful act committed by the host state. Unless the investor resorts to all available and effective remedies, state responsibility for a specific cause of action would not arise, as that specific wrongful act would not occur. This is because of the nature of this specific wrongful act and not because of the application of any procedural rule. The main example of the circumstances where exhaustion of local remedies becomes a substantive requirement for state responsibility is the case of denial of justice.[19] Only when the investor is denied

14. *Interhandel (Switzerland v. United States of America)*, ICJ Judgment, 21 March 1959 (1959) ICJ Rep 6, 27. *See also Elettronica Sicula S.p.A. (ELSI) (United States of America v. Italy)*, Chamber of the ICJ Judgment, 20 July 1989 (1989) ICJ Rep 15, paragraph 50.
15. Concluded on 4 November 1950, entered into force on 3 September 1953.
16. Concluded on 16 December 1966, entered into force on 23 March 1976.
17. Concluded on 18 March 1965, entered into force on 14 October 1966, 575 UNTS 159.
18. Douglas (*supra* n. 6), 98-99; Martins Paparinskis, *Investment Treaty Arbitration and the (New) Law of State Responsibility*, 24(2) European Journal of International Law 617, 642-643 (2013).
19. *See also Loewen Group, Inc and Raymond L Loewen v. United States of America*, ICSID Case No. ARB(AF)/98/3, Award, 30 March 2015, paragraph 156; *Franck Charles Arif v. Republic of*

justice by the whole judicial system,[20] a denial of justice could emerge. As opposed to the procedural requirement, which is a comity rule,[21] there is a substantive requirement to exhaust the local remedies in the specificity of some wrongful acts because otherwise the breach would not be complete.[22] Obviously, there is not such a substantive requirement for the emergence of each internationally wrongful act or each cause of action pleaded in investment treaty arbitration.

The obligations under Articles II and III of the NYC are not obligations to provide a treatment but specific obligations which require the Contracting States to act in certain way (recognize an arbitration agreement, refer the parties to arbitration, cease domestic court proceedings if there is a valid arbitration agreement, recognize and enforce an arbitral award if certain conditions are met). These obligations are not comparable to the obligation to provide an effective judicial protection to foreigners through the judicial system. This analysis infers that the violation of the NYC does not entail exhaustion of local remedies so that the breach would become complete. There will be a violation of an international obligation each time the state does not comply with the action required by the specific provisions of the NYC. The investor does not need to resort to other local remedies or exhaust them for the breach to be substantiated.

As a consequence, the state could be held responsible when a domestic court (even a court of first instance) fails to apply or misapplies the NYC. Accordingly, state responsibility would arise when the domestic court does not cease court proceedings and refer the parties to arbitration despite a valid arbitration agreement or when the domestic court refuses to recognize or enforce an arbitral award for another reason than the ones stipulated in the NYC or by misapplying one of the reasons listed in Article V of the NYC. In that context, rejecting a jurisdictional objection (or the enforcement of a foreign arbitral award) for the arbitration agreement not having been notarized or not having been drafted in a particular language would for instance amount to a breach of the NYC and might lead to an investment dispute. An investor does not need to exhaust local remedies so that this international wrongful act becomes complete and causes state responsibility to arise.

Moldova, ICSID Case No. ARB/11/23, Award, 8 April 2013, paragraph 442; *Apotex Inc v. United States of America*, UNCITRAL, Award on Jurisdiction and Admissibility, 14 June 2013, paragraph 281.

20. This could happen in different ways. The most typical cases of denial of justice are denial of access to justice, undue delay and manifest injustice. *See* Berk Demirkol, *Judicial Acts and Investment Treaty Arbitration* (Cambridge University Press, 2018), 171-191; Jan Paulsson, *Denial of Justice in International Law* (Cambridge University Press, 2005), 131-206.
21. *See* J.E.S. Fawcett, *The Exhaustion of Local Remedies: Substance or Procedure*, 31 British Yearbook of International Law 452, 457 (1954).
22. *See* Demirkol (*supra* n. 20), 75-86.

§5.05 IMPLICATIONS OF THE APPROACH SUGGESTED IN THIS CHAPTER

This chapter has discussed the question of whether the obligations in the NYC could serve as autonomous grounds for a self-standing claim in investment treaty arbitration. It is suggested that investors could invoke state responsibility for the breach of the provisions of the NYC without referring to any investment treaty standard. It finally attempts to explain why the approach suggested in this chapter is a preferable method rather than bringing an indirect investment treaty claim for the breach of one of the treaty standards as a consequence of the breach of the NYC.

[A] Completeness of the Breach

The first advantage of bringing a self-standing claim for the violation of the NYC instead of invoking the breach of an investment treaty standard is that whereas the breach of certain investment treaty standards involves a certain requirement for the completeness of the breach by way of resorting to further available remedies, the violation of the NYC does not.

An expropriation occurs 'when the effect of the measures taken by the state has been to deprive the owner of title, possession or access to the benefit and economic use of his property'.[23] Deprivation caused by a temporary measure does not however lead to an expropriation and remains incomplete. Similarly, an expropriatory measure entails an *irreversible* and *permanent* effect, which obstructs any form of exploitation of the asset or the right.[24] The tribunal in the *Glamis Gold v. USA* case required a 'final, definitive position' to find an expropriation.[25] Availability of an effective appeal would thus generally prevent an investor from claiming that the decision of the court of first instance has amounted to an unlawful expropriation. The same judgment, however, could breach the NYC and thus lead to a self-standing claim.

A similar requirement of completeness of the breach exists for the substantiation of the breach of the fair and equitable treatment and effective means standards. Unless the investor makes use of the local remedies in order to redress or correct an isolated decision in a reasonable way, the breach of these standards might not be complete. For instance, the tribunal in the *Frontier Petroleum v. Czech Republic* case stated in the context of an investment dispute concerning the state court's rejection to enforce an arbitral award, 'availability of full rights of appeal has satisfactorily eliminated any procedural imperfections in the process which occurred in the lower courts'.[26] The tribunal in *Stati v. Kazakhstan* also considered the availability and operation of the remedies and only then concluded that the host state committed a breach of the fair and

23. *Santa Elena v. Republic of Costa Rica*, Final Award, ICSID Case No. ARB/96/1, 17 February 2000, paragraph 77.
24. *Tecnicas Medioambientales Tecmed SA v. The United Mexican States*, ICSID Case No. ARB(AF)/00/2, Award, 29 May 2003, paragraph 116.
25. *Glamis Gold, Ltd v. United States of America*, UNCITRAL, Award, 8 June 2009, paragraph 332.
26. *Frontier Petroleum Services v. The Czech Republic*, UNCITRAL, Final Award, 12 November 2010, paragraph 410.

equitable treatment standard.[27] Although the completeness of a breach of the fair and equitable treatment standard does not require the exhaustion of the whole judicial remedies, the investor would still be expected to demonstrate that it has attempted to correct the initial wrongful decision. An investor would most of the time be expected to appeal a judgment of a court of first instance rejecting the enforcement of a foreign arbitral award before claiming that this rejection constitutes a breach of the fair and equitable treatment standard. This would not be the case if the investor brings a self-standing claim on the basis of the violations of the NYC.

In the context of the effective means standard, the tribunal in the *Chevron v. Ecuador* case stated that the investor is not required to satisfy a strict exhaustion of local remedies for a breach to emerge. The tribunal still required the investor 'to make use of all remedies that are available and might have rectified the wrong complained'.[28] This requirement to resort to further available remedies under an effective means standard claim makes a self-standing claim based on the violation of the NYC a more accessible and thus preferable method.

[B] Substantive Threshold of the Breach

The second advantage of bringing a self-standing claim for the violation of the NYC instead of an investment treaty claim is that the threshold of state responsibility for the former scenario may be lower than the latter. In other words, holding the host state directly responsible for the breach of the NYC is easier than attempting to demonstrate that the host state has breached its investment treaty obligations by omitting to give effect to the NYC.

Two examples may shed some light. Assume a domestic court finds that it does not enjoy jurisdiction to hear an enforcement claim based on Article III of the NYC for the reason that the dispute does not involve any territorial connection with the country of enforcement. The application of the NYC is not subject to any such jurisdictional requirement and the award creditor may attempt to enforce the award in any jurisdiction that is a Contracting State to the Convention. Indeed, the assets of the award debtor could be in countries that the dispute does not involve any territorial connection with. Therefore, the reasoning of the court, in this example, impedes the application of the NYC for a reason not stipulated in the Convention. Such restriction of the scope of the application of the NYC may be found in breach of the Convention. This violation of the NYC would raise state responsibility and the investor would be able to bring in investment arbitration a self-standing claim on the basis of this breach. In other words, it may hold the host state directly responsible for the breach of the Convention. This breach may not, however, amount to a breach of the fair and equitable treatment standard as the threshold to meet for the establishment of the breach is much higher.

27. *Anatolie Stati, Gabriel Stati, Ascom Group S.A. & Terra Raf Trans Trading v. Republic of Kazakhstan*, SCC Arbitration V (116/2010), Award, 19 December 2013, paragraph 1092.
28. *Chevron Corporation and Texaco Petroleum Company v. The Republic of Ecuador*, UNCITRAL, Partial Award on the Merits, 30 March 2010, paragraph 326.

The second example concerns a scenario where the domestic court rejects the enforcement of the foreign arbitral award for the reason that the award is against the public policy of the country of enforcement. An outrageous application of this ground in rejecting the enforcement of foreign arbitral awards may constitute a breach of the fair and equitable treatment standard. If, however, the reference to the public policy ground is not outrageous but is simply wrong, it would not be possible to hold the state responsible for an unfair treatment. In this scenario, an investment claim based on the investment treaty standards would fail. Although the tribunal's interpretation of the public policy ground is wrong (e.g., not supported by settled case law) and thus leads to international responsibility of the state for a wrongful application of Article V of the NYC, it might not be possible to establish that the judicial conduct has been unfair or inequitable or against the effective means standard. In this case, it would be preferable for the investor to bring an autonomous (self-standing) claim based on the NYC in investment treaty arbitration rather than claim the breach of an investment treaty standard.

Obviously, an investment tribunal cannot impose its public policy understanding or a certain public policy understanding that has found acceptance in comparative law. Indeed, Article V(II)(b) of the NYC refers to the public policy understanding in the country of enforcement. This suggests that each country interprets its own public policy. An investment tribunal could, however, examine whether the decision based on public policy considerations amounts to a breach of the treaty. This would require the tribunal to consider whether the domestic court has applied the public policy exception properly. In this case, the tribunal would control whether the domestic court's reference to this exception has been in compliance with the public policy understanding adopted in that jurisdiction, as well as in the framework allowed by Article V(II)(b) of the NYC. An implausible understanding or an understanding of public policy, which is in contradiction with a *jurisprudence constante* in that particular jurisdiction, would violate this provision. For example, if it had been confirmed many times by the highest court of the judiciary in the country of enforcement that an order of compound interest is compatible with the public policy understanding of the particular jurisdiction and if a domestic court of first instance refuses to enforce a foreign arbitral award because it grants compound interest, it would be clear that this latter court's application of the NYC would be wrongful.

Although such cases would not lead to a breach of the fair and equitable treatment, they still constitute a misapplication of the Convention and raise international state responsibility of the state. Notwithstanding with the discretion that Article V(II)(b) allows to the country of enforcement to interpret what is of public policy and what is not, a domestic court judgment that refuses the enforcement of a foreign arbitral award for a reason that is not considered of public policy under that country's domestic law would not be compatible with the NYC. This incompatibility constitutes a violation of the Convention – but not probably a breach of investment treaty standards. Only through a self-standing claim based on the NYC an investor may be successful in these circumstances in its investment treaty arbitration claim.

§5.06 CONCLUSION

This chapter suggests that investors may refer to the NYC and base their investment claim directly on the obligations set forth in the Convention when the host state has breached one of these obligations. An investment treaty tribunal may have jurisdiction to hear such claims under broad dispute settlement clauses.

The availability of this type of self-standing claim contributes to access to – international – justice by extending the procedural protection of the investment treaty arbitration mechanism to situations which do not involve an investment treaty breach. For the investor to bring such claim it would not be necessary to have a situation of unlawful expropriation or a breach of the fair and equitable treatment; the mere violation of the NYC would suffice to hold the host state responsible in investment arbitration.

Chapter 6

Access to Justice in Investment Arbitration and Non-disputing Party Participation

Crina Baltag

The past years have witnessed the beginning of a complex reform of investor-State dispute settlement (ISDS) system, with various developments taking place at various levels of the system. The purpose of this chapter is to instil a debate as to whether the real evolution in investment law and ISDS, based, in particular, on the discussions in the UNCITRAL Working Group III, is towards a regulation of investments, departing thus from the original purpose of the system, that of promotion and protection of investments. If we are witnessing such shift – or we incentivize it – then, the discussion regarding the access to justice in investment law and ISDS is timely. For the purpose of this chapter, the author will not explore the access to justice for investors and States, but it will focus on the issue of access to justice and non-disputing parties – amici curiae *– in investment law and arbitration.*

§6.01 INTRODUCTION

The past years have witnessed the beginning of a complex reform of ISDS system, with various developments taking place at different levels of the system. For instance, the implementation of a new generation of IIAs, and, in particular, of new FTAs signed by the EU[1] and the new models of BITs;[2] the amendment process of the ICSID Arbitration Rules – the most comprehensive one up to date;[3] the mandate of the UNCITRAL

1. *See* CETA, EU-Singapore FTA and Investment Protection Agreement, EU-Vietnam FTA and Investment Protection Agreement.
2. *See* the Dutch Model BIT approved on 19 October 2018.
3. *See* the comprehensive proposals for the amendment of the ICSID Rules, https://icsid.worldbank.org/en/amendments (Accessed 7 February2020).

Working Group III (Investor-State Dispute Settlement Reform) in assessing the concerns with the ISDS system and in finding possible solutions to address them;[4] and other initiatives dealing with particular issues, such as The Hague Rules on Business and Human Rights Arbitration.[5]

With over 900 investment arbitration cases at the end of 2018[6] and over 2,800 IIAs concluded by States up to date,[7] the reform process is not easy to grasp. Most of the initiatives mentioned above are meant to tackle various aspects of the legitimacy and efficiency of the ISDS system, including (in)consistency among arbitral awards, issues related to independence and impartiality of arbitrators and costs and duration of arbitral proceedings.

However, none of the avenues of reform mentioned above envisages a comprehensive substantive and procedural reform of investment law and ISDS. One could argue that a proper solution to any of the concerns raised with the system can only exist if such comprehensive approach is adopted. Further, challenges to the system appear to reveal dissatisfaction with the scope and purpose of investment law and ISDS. Voices advocating for reciprocity in the system tend to put the finger on the fact that investors have only rights, while States bear the obligations. In addition, the ISDS system originally considered as a two-way system: that investors and host States of investments must have adequate recourse when the obligations assumed in the investment context are breached, and so recorded under the ICSID Convention,[8] is now restricting the direct claims by investors against the host States. Jean Ho refers to the '[l]ack of investor accountability [that] is reinforced by asymmetrical dispute settlement provisions that allow investors to bring claims in arbitration directly against states for treaty violations, but not vice versa'.[9] Ho concludes that 'investment treaties

4. The mandate of the UNCITRAL Working Group III on ISDS will be further detailed below.
5. As explained by the initiators, the project is aimed at the creation of an international private judicial dispute resolution avenue available to parties involved in business and human rights issues as claimants and defendants and in filling the gap in the UN Guiding Principles on Business and Human Rights. *See* more details at https://www.cilc.nl/project/the-hague-rules-on-business-and-human-rights-arbitration/ (Accessed 31 August 2019).
6. *See* UNCTAD, *Fact Sheet on Investor–State Dispute Settlement Cases in 2018*, <https://unctad.org/en/PublicationsLibrary/diaepcbinf2019d4_en.pdf> (accessed 30 October 2019).
7. *See* https://investmentpolicy.unctad.org/international-investment-agreements (accessed 30 October 2019).
8. *See* Article 36(1) of the ICSID Convention: 'Any Contracting State or any national of a Contracting State wishing to institute arbitration proceedings shall address a request to that effect in writing to the Secretary-General who shall send a copy of the request to the other party'. *See also* Article 25(1) of the ICSID Convention: 'The jurisdiction of the Centre shall extend to any legal dispute arising directly out of an investment, between a Contracting State (or any constituent subdivision or agency of a Contracting State designated to the Centre by that State) and a national of another Contracting State, which the parties to the dispute consent in writing to submit to the Centre. When the parties have given their consent, no party may withdraw its consent unilaterally.'

   See also the cases submitted to ICSID by host States of investments: *Gabon v. Société Serete S.A.* (ICSID Case No. ARB/76/1); *Government of the Province of East Kalimantan v. PT Kaltim Prima Coal and others* (ICSID Case No. ARB/07/3); *Republic of Peru v. Caravelí Cotaruse Transmisora de Energía S.A.C.* (ICSID Case No. ARB/13/24).
9. Jean Ho, *The Creation of Elusive Investor Responsibility*, 113 AJIL Unbound 10, 11 (2018).

espouse the anomaly where investors can demand redress despite their own misconduct, while States appear conditioned to forego pursuit of investor responsibility'.[10] There is, indeed, a strong push towards investment regulation as opposed to investment promotion and protection, as seen in the new generation of IIAs, ensuring that investors, too, have obligations when it comes to their investments. However, this will require time until we reach that balance in the system. As suggested by Muchlinski, this new generation of IIAs should 'seek to balance investor rights and duties, preserve the State's right to regulate in the public interest and to acknowledge the importance of not only economic but also social and environmental goals in their design'.[11]

With this background, the question of access to justice, as such, in the context of investment law and arbitration, is legitimate, especially in the current circumstances. However, one must first clarify who the beneficiaries of this access to justice right are. Are we referring to investors, to States – host or home States – or other stakeholders? If the latter, who are these stakeholders? The purpose of this chapter is to instil a debate as to whether the real evolution in investment law and ISDS, based, in particular, on the discussions in the UNCITRAL Working Group III, is towards a regulation of investments, departing thus from the original purpose of the system, that of promotion and protection of investments. If we are witnessing such shift – or we incentivize it – then, the discussion regarding the access to justice in investment law and ISDS is timely. For the purpose of this chapter, the author will not explore the access to justice for investors and States, but it will focus on the issue of access to justice and non-disputing parties – *amici curiae* – in investment law and arbitration.

Since it is discussed elsewhere in this book, this chapter will not insist on clarifying, from a historical or legal perspective, the meaning of 'access to justice', or separately, of 'access' and 'justice'.[12] It suffices to state here that investment law and arbitration cemented the access of individuals to international arena, moving firmly from the espousal of claims through diplomatic protection to the right of individual investors to claim directly against States, with these States offering their unconditional consent for future disputes in this respect.

§6.02 INVESTMENT LAW AND ISDS

If we consider that the term 'access to justice' stands for the right to seek remedy before a court or other organ constituted under the law, then a quick look into the characteristics of investment law and ISDS is necessary.[13] While the disputes are between

10. *Ibid.*
11. Peter Muchlinski, *Negotiating New Generation International Investment Agreements. New Sustainable Development Oriented Initiatives*, in Steffen Hindelang and Markus Krajewski (eds), *Shifting Paradigms in International Investment Law: More Balanced, Less Isolated, Increasingly Diversified* (Oxford University Press, 2016) 41.
12. *See also*, Francesco Francioni, *The Right of Access to Justice under Customary International Law*, in Francesco Francioni (ed.), *Access to Justice as a Human Right* (Oxford University Press, 2007) 3 et seq.
13. *See*, Article 8 of the UDHR, Paris. 10 December 1948: 'Everyone has the right to an effective remedy by the competent national tribunals for acts violating the fundamental rights granted

investors and States, raising complex issues of public interest and State participation in arbitration, they are also brought under a procedure which is essentially built on the principle of party autonomy. The ISDS system is a system designed to provide corrective justice: disputes are submitted to arbitration by investors requesting arbitral tribunals to compensate them for breaches substantive standards of protection envisaged in the underlying IIA by the host State.

As to the access to justice, commentators highlighted the earthquake triggered by the 'recognition and consolidation of an indisputable right of access to international justice by private investors'.[14] As such it is seen that 'the "internationalization" of the right of access to justice of private actors tends to blur the traditional boundary between aliens' rights and human rights. [...] This focus on the individual as the title holder of rights is the hallmark of the international law of human rights'.[15]

ISDS, broadly speaking, but in particular arbitration, has its own peculiarities, as it bears State participation in the dispute, with all the consequences deriving from it. Further, the nature of the disputes has its specific fingerprint on the procedure as such. As mentioned before, the disputes are usually of great public interest as they profoundly impact public services offered to the local communities or they touch upon issues of environmental protection. Of course, the arbitration procedure, largely built on the arbitration rules for commercial disputes, had to be adapted, especially in the context of ICSID, to serve this unique setting. Precisely because of the characteristics of arbitration, including party autonomy, as mentioned, investment arbitration has guaranteed that disputes are de-politicized and arbitrators can render their awards free from any outside pressure.

However, this does not mean that the ISDS system as such is a closed one; to the contrary, there is, indeed, a shift from the traditional confidentiality of commercial arbitrations to the transparency of investment arbitration proceedings. Nowadays, most of the arbitral awards and a good number of proceedings in their entirety or most of them can be freely and easily accessed by anyone. As it will be further discussed below, while most of the recent IIAs provide for transparency of proceedings and hearings open to public,[16] this transparency is further ensured with the UNCITRAL Rules on Transparency in Treaty-based Investor-State Arbitration, effective 1 April 2014.

It is also submitted that investment arbitration, given the above-mentioned characteristics, 'fulfils a public function in influencing the behaviour of foreign

him by the constitution or by law. *Also*, Article 6(1) of the ECHR, Rome, 4 November 1950: 'In the determination of his civil rights and obligations or of any criminal charge against him, everyone is entitled to a fair and public hearing within a reasonable time by an independent and impartial tribunal established by law.' Further, Article 7.1 of the African Charter of Human and Peoples' Rights, Nairobi, 27 June 1981: 'Every individual shall have the right to have his cause heard. ...'.

14. Francesco Francioni, *Access to Justice, Denial of Justice and International Investment Law*, 20(3) European Journal of International Law 729, 731 (2009).
15. *Ibid.*, 731-732.
16. *See*, for example, Article 32 of Canada-Burkina Faso BIT, entered into force on 11 October 2017.

investors, states and civil society more generally by crafting and concretizing international standards of investment protection'.[17]

§6.03 NON-DISPUTING PARTIES AND ISDS

Foreign investments have a direct impact on the societal interests at large in the host State. This is the reason why investment law and ISDS have witnessed an unprecedented interest from other stakeholders, the non-disputing parties, also referred to as *amici curiae*.[18] The term 'non-disputing party' has been criticized as being misleading,[19] as, in reality, these *amici curiae* are not 'parties', but 'mere participants at most'.[20]

The arbitral tribunal in *Suez v. Argentina*, explained in 2005 that an *amicus curiae* is a friend of the court - and not a party to the dispute -, who helps the tribunal in reaching its decision by providing it with its novel arguments, expertise and perspectives:

> the *amicus curiae* role the petitioners seek to play in the present case is similar to that of a friend of the court recognized in certain legal systems and more recently in a number of international proceedings. In such cases, a non-party to the dispute, as 'a friend,' offers to provide the court or tribunal its special perspectives, arguments, or expertise on the dispute, usually in the form of a written amicus curiae brief or submission.[21]

While it is undisputed that *amici curiae* are not parties to the arbitral proceedings, they do have an interest in the dispute.[22] To be allowed in the proceedings, thus, *amici curiae* must fulfil certain conditions set forth in the applicable treaty provisions and arbitration rules.

The ICSID Arbitration Rules of 2006 included in Article 37(2) a new provision addressing the participation of non-disputing parties in the arbitration proceedings. Similar provision was included in Article 41(3) of the ICSID Additional Facility Arbitration Rules. Pursuant to Rule 37(2), the arbitral tribunal, after consulting both

17. Stephan W. Schill, *Crafting the International Economic Order: The Public Function of Investment Treaty Arbitration and its Significance for the Role of the Arbitrators*, 23 Leiden Journal of International Law 401, 401 (2010).
18. The chapter is not addressing the participation on non-disputing treaty parties in the proceedings.
19. Aurelia Antonietti, *The 2006 Amendments to the ICSID Rules and Regulations and the Additional Facility Rules*, 21 ICSID Rev. - FILJ 427, 435-436 (2006).
20. Eloise Obadia, *Extension of Proceedings Beyond the Original Parties: Non-Disputing Party Participation in Investment Arbitration*, 22 ICSID Rev. - FILJ 349, 366 (2007).
21. *Suez, Sociedad General de Aguas de Barcelona, S.A.and Vivendi Universal, S.A. v. Argentine Republic*, ICSID Case No. ARB/03/19 (formerly *Aguas Argentinas, S.A., Suez, Sociedad General de Aguas de Barcelona, S.A. and Vivendi Universal, S.A. v. Argentine Republic*), Order in Response to a Petition for Transparency and Participation as Amicus Curiae of 19 May 2005, paragraph 8.
22. *See also* Noah Rubins, *Opening the Investment Arbitration Process: At What Cost, for What Benefit?*, 3(3) Transnational Dispute Management 4 (2006), where the author submits that '*amicus* submissions are normally submitted in support of one of the parties (most frequently the respondent State)'.

parties, may allow a non-disputing party to file a written submission with the tribunal regarding a matter within the scope of the dispute. An ICSID arbitral tribunal, pursuant to Article 41(3), in determining whether to allow such a filing, shall consider, among other things, the extent to which:

> (a) the non-disputing party submission would assist the Tribunal in the determination of a factual or legal issue related to the proceeding by bringing a perspective, particular knowledge or insight that is different from that of the disputing parties;
> (b) the non-disputing party submission would address a matter within the scope of the dispute;
> (c) the non-disputing party has a significant interest in the proceeding.

In 2014, the UNCITRAL Rules on Transparency in Treaty-based Investor-State Arbitration came into force and provided for extensive provisions on the participation of *amici curiae* – referred to as 'third persons' – in investment arbitration proceedings.[23] Article 4(1) of the UNCITRAL Rules on Transparency provides that an arbitral tribunal, after consultation with the disputing parties, may allow third persons to file a written submission regarding a matter within the scope of the dispute. Article 4(3) includes the factors that arbitral tribunals shall take into consideration in allowing such submission, such as:

> [w]hether the third person has a significant interest in the arbitral proceedings; and ... [t]he extent to which the submission would assist the arbitral tribunal in the determination of a factual or legal issue related to the arbitral proceedings by bringing a perspective, particular knowledge or insight that is different from that of the disputing parties.

While Article 25(3) of the 2017 ICC Arbitration Rules only included a reference to the possibility of the arbitral tribunal to 'hear any other person', the ICC Note to the parties explains this provision as enabling the arbitral tribunal, after consulting the parties, to adopt measures allowing oral or written submissions by *amici curiae* and non-disputing parties.[24]

Article 3(1) of the Appendix III of the 2017 SCC Arbitration Rules provide that '[a]ny person that is neither a disputing party nor a non-disputing treaty Party ("Third Person") may apply to the Arbitral Tribunal for permission to make a written

23. Article 1(1) of the UNCITRAL Transparency Rules provide for the following with respect to their application: 'The UNCITRAL Rules on Transparency in Treaty-based Investor-State Arbitration ("Rules on Transparency") shall apply to investor-State arbitration initiated under the UNCITRAL Arbitration Rules pursuant to a treaty providing for the protection of investments or investors ("treaty") concluded on or after 1 April 2014 unless the parties to the treaty have agreed otherwise.' The discussions in UNCITRAL Working Group II on the Rules on Transparency mainly revolved around whether the tribunal should have full discretion or not in allowing non-disputing parties' participation.
24. Paragraph 143 of the *Note to Parties and Arbitral Tribunals on the Conduct of the Arbitration under the ICC Rules of Arbitration*, entered into force on 1 January 2019. Article 25(3) of the ICC Arbitration Rules, 2017, refers to the following: 'The arbitral tribunal may decide to hear witnesses, experts appointed by the parties or any other person, in the presence of the parties, or in their absence provided they have been duly summoned.'

submission in the arbitration'. In reaching a decision on the participation of *amici curiae*, after consulting the disputing parties, the tribunal:

> shall have regard to: (i) the nature and significance of the interest of the Third Person in the arbitration; (ii) whether the submission would assist the Arbitral Tribunal in determining a material factual or legal issue in the arbitration by bringing a perspective, particular knowledge or insight that is distinct from or broader than that of the disputing parties; and (iii) any other relevant circumstances.

New generation of IIAs strive to include provisions allowing for non-disputing party participation. For example, Article 31 of Canada-Mongolia BIT refers to the following:

> A Tribunal shall have the authority to consider and accept written submissions from a person or entity that is not a disputing party and that has a significant interest in the arbitration. The Tribunal shall ensure that any non-disputing party submission does not disrupt the proceedings and does not unduly burden or unfairly prejudice either disputing party.[25]

There is, however, a (desired) balance in the regulation of *amici curiae* participation in arbitration proceedings. This is justified by the fact that, as explained, *amici curiae* are not parties to the dispute and, as such, deference must be showed to the principle of party autonomy, the cornerstone of the arbitration proceedings. Consequently, arbitral tribunals must ensure that the participation of *amici curiae* is beneficial to the proceedings. This is translated in making sure that (i) no additional burden is placed on the parties; (ii) the efficiency of the proceedings is not affected; and that (iii) the parties are given the opportunity to be consulted with respect to the participation of *amici curiae* and respond to their submissions.

For this, Rule 37(2) of the ICSID Arbitration Rules included provisions concerning the manner in which the non-disputing parties would participate in the proceedings: 'the non-disputing party submission does not disrupt the proceeding or unduly burden or unfairly prejudice either party'. Further, the provision grants the parties to the dispute 'an opportunity to present their observations on the non-disputing party submission'. As explained by the ICSID Secretariat at the time of the adoption of Rule 37(2), '[t]he suggested changes would make clear that ICSID tribunals may accept and consider written submissions from a non-disputing person or a State, after consulting both parties as far as possible'.[26]

Pursuant to the UNCITRAL Rules on Transparency, the tribunal will 'ensure that any submission does not disrupt or unduly burden the arbitral proceedings, or unfairly

25. Agreement Between Canada and Mongolia for the Promotion and Protection of Investments, in force on 24 February 2017.
26. ICSID, *Suggested Changes to the ICSID Rules and Regulations. Working Paper of the ICSID Secretariat of 12 May 2005*, p. 11. Shortly after, on 1 January 2006, Morocco-US Free Trade Agreement entered into force and provided that the tribunal shall have the authority to accept and consider amicus curiae submissions from a person or entity that is not a disputing party. (Article 10.19), as well as the transparency of the documents of the case towards the non-disputing party and the public (Article 10.20(1)).

prejudice any disputing party' and that 'the disputing parties are given a reasonable opportunity to present their observations on any submission by the third person'.[27] Further, Article 4(2) of the UNCITRAL Transparency Rules refer to the information to be submitted by *amici* in making their application:

> (a) Describe the third person, including, where relevant, its membership and legal status (e.g., trade association or other non-governmental organization), its general objectives, the nature of its activities and any parent organization (including any organization that directly or indirectly controls the third person);
> (b) Disclose any connection, direct or indirect, which the third person has with any disputing party;
> (c) Provide information on any government, person or organization that has provided to the third person (i) any financial or other assistance in preparing the submission; or (ii) substantial assistance in either of the two years preceding the application by the third person under this article (e.g. funding around 20 per cent of its overall operations annually);
> (d) Describe the nature of the interest that the third person has in the arbitration; and
> (e) Identify the specific issues of fact or law in the arbitration that the third person wishes to address in its written submission.

Article 3(10) of Appendix III of the 2017 SCC Arbitration Rules takes these regulations a step further and allows the arbitral tribunal to condition the submission of *amicus curiae* on a security for reasonable legal or other costs expected to be incurred by the disputing parties as a result of the submission.[28]

While one can identify certain flexibility in the earlier cases, arbitral tribunals are cautious in allowing *amici curiae* participation, given the reasons referred to above. In *Methanex v. United States*, the first case to accept *amici curiae* participation, the claim was filed under the UNCITRAL Arbitration Rules, pursuant to NAFTA. On 25 August 2000, the International Institute for Sustainable Development (IISD) filed the request to submit an *amicus curiae* brief,[29] relying on the fact that its brief will be submitted 'on critical legal issues of public concern in the arbitration',[30] namely, on 'the definition of the concept of "expropriation" and its relationship to the regulatory function of governments, often referred to under international law as the government's "police powers."'[31] IISD further explained that it:

> seeks an opportunity to bring its international expertise to the assistance of the Tribunal to ensure that the joint goals of investment protection and environmental integrity can be achieved in the interpretation of Chapter 11, consistent with the

27. Article 4(5) and (6) of the UNCITRAL Rules on Transparency in Treaty-based Investor-State Arbitration.
28. *See also*, SIAC Investment Arbitration Rules, 2017, Rule 29.
29. *Methanex v. United States*, UNCITRAL, IISD's Application for *Amicus* Standing of 25 August 2000.
30. *Ibid*, paragraph 1.1.
31. *Ibid*, paragraph 3.1.

principles of sustainable development and the other closely related commitments in the Preamble of NAFTA.[32]

In submitting its request for *amicus* participation, IISD relied on the provisions of Article 15 of the UNCITRAL Arbitration Rules providing for the broad discretion of the arbitral tribunal in conducting the arbitration proceedings.[33] Three other NGOs further requested to join as amici: Communities for a Better Environment (CBE), the Bluewater Network of Earth Island Institute (Bluewater) and the Center for International Environmental Law (CIEL) by stating that their 'participation would be of significant assistance to the Tribunal', 'as a safeguard of democratic processes', and will 'ensure the legitimacy of the Tribunal's decision'.[34] NAFTA parties, Canada, Mexico and the US submitted their positions with respect to the participation of these *amici* in the proceedings and, except for Mexico's position, there was a considerable support for *amici curiae* participation in NAFTA proceedings. The *Methanex* tribunal accepted the participation of the *amici curiae*, by relying on the wording of the UNCITRAL Arbitration Rules 'intended to provide the broadest procedural flexibility within fundamental safeguards', and also considering that '[t]here is an undoubtedly public interest in this arbitration' which comes from the subject matter of the dispute.[35]. However, the tribunal held that the *amici* will neither have access to the oral hearings, nor be granted access to the documents of the case, although some information may be derived from the public domain or disclosed into the public domain within the terms of the agreement of the parties to the dispute.[36]

From the rather accommodating approach of the *Methanex* tribunal in 2001, arguing for *amici* participation in the interest of the arbitration process,[37] one can notice a more cautious attitude of the arbitral tribunals. In *Eco Oro v. Colombia*,[38] the latest investment arbitration case addressing a request for *amici curiae* participation, the arbitral tribunal rejected the request of the Comité para la Defensa del Agua y el Páramo de Santurbán, CIEL, the Asociación Interamericana para la Defensa del Ambiente (AIDA), MiningWatch Canada, Institute for Policy Studies (IPS) - Global Economy Project and the Centre for Research on Multinational Corporations (SOMO). The tribunal concluded that the petitioners have failed to meet this requirement that they would address a matter within the scope of the dispute, noting the 'generality of the assertion by the Petitioners and the total lack of any specificity from the Petitioners as to the relevance to the legal scope of the dispute'.[39] As to the assistance to the arbitral

32. *Ibid.*, paragraph 3.6.
33. *Ibid.*, paragraphs 4.1-4.3.
34. *Methanex v. United States*, Amended Petition of Communities for a Better Environment, The Bluewater Network of Earth Island Institute, and The Center for International Environmental Law to Appear Jointly as *Amici Curiae* of 13 October 2000, paragraph 2.
35. Decision of the Tribunal on Petitions from Third Persons to Intervene as "Amici Curiae" of 15 January 2001, paragraph 49.
36. *Methanex v. United States*, Decision of the Tribunal on Petitions from Third Persons, paragraph 47.
37. *Ibid.*, paragraph 49.
38. *Eco Oro Minerals Corp. v. Republic of Colombia*, ICSID Case No. ARB/16/41, Procedural Order No. 6 of 18 February 2019.
39. *Ibid.*, paragraph29.

tribunal offered by the *amici*, the tribunal noted that the petitioners have failed to explain the nature of their perspective, particular knowledge or insight to be brought in this dispute.[40] A similar conclusion was reach by the tribunal on the existence of a significant interest of the petitioners in the proceedings. While the tribunal noted that a point had been made by the petitioners that Colombian citizens have a 'lasting interest in the outcome of the dispute', the arbitral tribunal highlighted that the petitioners have failed to expand on 'why this gives them - or any of them - a significant interest'.[41]

A similar conservative approach as in *Eco Oro* was adopted by the arbitral tribunal in *Gabriel Resources v. Romania,* where the tribunal accepted in part the participation of Alburnus Maior, Greenpeace CEE, Romania and Independent Centre for the Development of Environmental Resources (ICDER) as *amici curiae* in the proceedings.[42] While the tribunal held that the *amici* have failed to show their 'particular expertise on the legal matters that they wish to address or that, more generally, they would offer expertise that is not already available to respondent on these issues',[43] it held that it is 'prepared to accept the possibility that the Applicants do have a particular knowledge of factual issues relevant to this dispute that may assist the Tribunal'.[44] Further, the arbitral tribunal raised doubts as to whether the applicants have a specific interest in the dispute. However, the arbitral tribunal did confirm that there is a public interest in the dispute, as '[t]he nature of the disputed Project, as well as the oppositions to it as far as they concern the people, the environment, the culture and the history, necessarily implicate a "public interest" and the outcome of these proceedings may impact upon it'.[45]

It is interesting to note that while the system has opened the door to the *amici curiae* participation, and, thus, arguably acknowledging that the consequences of investment disputes extend well beyond the claimant and respondent in the dispute, it did so with caution and, in any case, only sufficiently wide in order to respect the arbitration process, as it will be further discussed below. While with limited participation, authors highlight that '*amicus curiae* participation has become and will remain in the foreseeable future an important feature of the administration of justice in the field of foreign investments'.[46]

40. *Ibid.*, paragraph 32.
41. *Ibid.*, paragraph 34.
42. *Gabriel Resources Ltd. and Gabriel Resources (Jersey) Ltd. v. Romania*, ICSID Case No. ARB/15/31, Procedural Order No. 19 of 7 December 2018. The request of *amici* was received by the arbitral tribunal on 2 November 2018. *See also* the positions of the disputing parties of 28 February 2019.
43. *Ibid.*, paragraph 60.
44. *Ibid.*, paragraph 60.
45. *Ibid.*, paragraph 65.
46. Francioni (*supra* n. 14) 740.

§6.04 REBALANCING AND ACCESS TO JUSTICE IN INVESTMENT ARBITRATION: IS *AMICI CURIAE* PARTICIPATION THE SOLUTION?

International investment law and ISDS were built on the idea of promotion and protection of foreign investments. Naturally, if the focus is on the investments, the balance would be tipped at this end. With the new paradigm of investment regulation, one would argue that all stakeholders - whether in the process or as a consequence of the process - should have equal access to the system. This, of course, takes the ISDS reform to a different level: a reconfiguration of the system, without necessarily a revolution from within. As such, would an immediate solution lie in an enhanced participation of *amici curiae* in the ISDS proceedings?[47]

Arbitral tribunals have emphasized the role of *amici curiae* on the system as a whole, by referring to the 'support' given to the process by accepting *amici* submissions, as well as by opening it and making it more transparent:

> the Chapter 11 arbitral process [NAFTA] could benefit from being perceived as more open or transparent or conversely be harmed if seen as unduly secretive. In this regard, the Tribunal's willingness to receive *amicus* submissions might support the process in general and this arbitration in particular; whereas a blanket refusal could do positive harm.[48]

Similarly, the tribunal in *Biwater v. Tanzania*, stressed that the benefit of the written submission from *amici*, given their nature and expertise, is an 'important element in the overall discharge of the Arbitral Tribunal's mandate, and in securing wider confidence in the arbitral process itself'.[49]

To contrast with the 'support' to be given to arbitral tribunals by *amici* in investment arbitration proceedings, it is interesting to bring here the reason why *amici* intervention is allowed before the American courts. As one author explains, *amici* intervention is 'based on the public interest in the administration of justice and the recognition that a decision by a court might affect more people than just the parties to the proceedings'.[50] Similarly, before the ECtHR, the *amici* intervention is justified by the 'public interest in the decision-making of the Court', as such decisions have social, political and economic implications.[51]

However, as the system presents itself, the role of the *amici curiae* is limited. Arbitrators must fulfil a mandate and any concern with the system as a whole or with the societal interests should fit into this mandate. The decision of the tribunal in *Gabriel Resources v. Romania* shows this tension. Referring to the conclusion of the tribunal in

47. *See also* the proposal of a 'reversed' diplomatic protection, where the host States would espouse the claim of its own citizens against the investor. *See* Francioni (*supra* n. 14) 738.
48. *Methanex v. United States* (*supra* n. 36) paragraph 49.
49. *Biwater Gauff (Tanzania) Ltd. v. United Republic of Tanzania*, ICSID Case No. ARB/05/22, Procedural Order No. 5 of 2 February 2007, paragraph 50.
50. Nicole Bürli, *Third-Party Interventions Before the European Court of Human Rights* (Intersentia, 2017) 20.
51. *Ibid.*, 21. The author also explains that *amici curiae* also produce legal expertise or knowledge (pp. 46 et seq.).

Apotex v. USA, which concluded that there is public interest of the subject matter of an arbitration when 'the decisions to be issued in that arbitration are likely to affect individuals or entities beyond the Disputing Parties',[52] the *Gabriel Resources* tribunal further emphasized that the fact that the population will ultimately bear the costs of an adverse award is not sufficient to justify the existence of a public interest:

> public interest does not arise simply because an award of damages against the Respondent would be paid from the Romanian Government's reserves (as was suggested by the Applications). If this were the case then there would be a sufficient public interest for the admissibility of amici briefs in all investor state arbitrations. That is not, therefore, an acceptable criterion.[53]

The regulation of *amici curiae* participation in treaties and arbitration rules serves the purpose of ensuring the access of these non-disputing parties precisely in the light of the mandate grated to the arbitral tribunal. The assistance to the arbitral tribunal in determining a material factual or legal issue in the arbitration by bringing a perspective, particular knowledge or insight that is distinct from or broader than that of the disputing parties[54] should be assessed in this limitation on the powers of the tribunal. Such inherent characteristic of arbitration was highlighted by the tribunal in *UPS v. Canada*:

> it is about the procedure to be followed by an arbitral tribunal in exercising the jurisdiction which the parties have conferred on it. It does not itself confer power to adjust that jurisdiction to widen the matter before it by adding as parties persons additional to those which have mutually agreed to its jurisdiction or by including subject matter in its arbitration additional to what which the parties have agreed to confer.[55]

§6.05 CONCLUSION

The current reform process of ISDS might push certain adjustments in the system. Nevertheless, there is already a visible shift from investment promotion and protection to investment regulation, as shy as it may be at this stage. Some IIAs, such as CETA, are already anticipating an enhanced framework addressing both rights and obligations of investors and States. As to the representation of societal interests in ISDS, until the relevant stakeholders are granted full access to the ISDS system, participation of *amici curiae* is the half-way reasonable solution ensuring such participation.

52. *Apotex Holdings Inc. and Apotex Inc. v. United States of America*, ICSID Case No. ARB(AF)/12/1, Procedural Order on the Participation of the Applicant, Mr Barry Appleton, as a Non-Disputing Party of 4 March 2013, paragraph 42.
53. *Gabriel Resources Ltd. and Gabriel Resources (Jersey) Ltd. v. Romania* (*supra* n. 42) paragraph 65.
54. SCC Arbitration Rules, 2017, Appendix III, Article 3(2).
55. *United Parcel Service of America Inc. v. Government of Canada*, ICSID Case No. UNCT/02/1, Decision of the Tribunal on Petitions for Intervention and Participation as Amici Curiae of 17 October 2001, paragraph 39.

It can be validly argued that, indeed, access to justice means more than being invited to take a seat at the table but not being allowed to be involved in the preparation of the meal. For some, the submissions of *amici curiae* might 'merely present a façade intended by the tribunal to render the system more facially worthy of trust and to make potentially disgruntled groups happy'.[56] The current structure of the system restricts the access of *amici curiae* to the extent to which such participation would not disturb the process itself and, as such, it is far from ensuring full access to justice. However, as argued by some authors, while the function of *amici curiae* 'as instruments of access to justice is only indirect', 'to the extent that *amicus curiae* briefs bring into the arbitral proceedings factual and legal considerations concerning the safeguarding of public goods, such as human and environmental health or the preservation of local cultural heritage, they can become a powerful tool to widen the scope of investment arbitration'.[57]

56. Obadia (*supra* n. 20) 378.
57. Francioni (*supra* n. 14) 740.

Part III Access to Justice in Specific Disputes Submitted to Arbitration

CHAPTER 7

Access to Justice in Labour and Employment Arbitration in Light of the Brazilian and the USA Experiences

Carolina da Rocha Morandi

The arbitrability of labour and employment disputes is far from being a settled issue in international arbitration. There is a substantial diversity among jurisdictions with regard to whether or not such disputes may be arbitrable. Most jurisdictions, in fact, do not render arbitration agreements enforceable in labour law, mainly for two reasons: (i) the employee is seen as the weaker party in the relationship, which would require a special protection, and (ii) the amounts in dispute are often low, rendering the arbitration costs prohibitive to the employee and raising issues of access to justice. In spite of these concerns, a few jurisdictions have concluded that, subject to some safeguards, arbitration can be an advantageous mechanism to solve labour disputes both to the employer and the employee. In this chapter, the issue of access to justice in labour law will be analysed in light of the United States and the Brazilian experiences. The United States are the paramount example of a jurisdiction that enforces – and encourages – the arbitrability of labour and employment disputes. Brazil, in its turn, has recently approved a major reform in its labour system, allowing the arbitrability of employment disputes. Focusing on the access to justice issue, and on practical examples extracted from these two jurisdictions, this chapter will address the arbitrability of labour disputes and, when arbitrable, how to guarantee that the employees will have their rights of accessing justice enforced in arbitration.

§7.01 INTRODUCTION

It is known that the arbitrability of labour and employment disputes is a debatable topic in international arbitration.[1] Different states have taken different stands on the issue.[2] Most jurisdictions, in fact, do not render arbitration agreements enforceable in labour law, mainly for two reasons: (i) the employee is seen as the weaker party in the relationship, which would require a special legal protection, and (ii) the arbitration costs are often times high and could be prohibitive to the employee, raising issues of access to justice (i.e., breach of the parties' fundamental rights to have their claims heard by state courts). In spite of these concerns, a few jurisdictions have concluded that, subject to some safeguards, arbitration can be an advantageous mechanism to solve labour disputes to both the employer and the employee.

This chapter analyses the access to justice issues related to labour and employment arbitration in Brazil and in the USA. As it will be demonstrated, even in such jurisdictions where labour disputes are considered arbitrable, challenges in this respect are faced. Brazil and the USA have different obstacles to overcome, but most of them have their roots in the parties' rights of access to justice.

First the analysis will focus on Brazil. The arbitrability of labour disputes is still incipient in the country, especially when a dispute involves an individual employee. The legal background and the courts' approaches to the matter will be studied, followed by the analysis of the biggest challenges in light of the access to justice. The second part will focus on the USA stand on the issue. The USA is one of the main examples of jurisdiction which enforces labour agreements to arbitrate. A brief description of the legal background will be followed by the analysis of the current issues on the radar. Finally, a critical conclusion will be drawn based on these two case studies.

It should be noted that in both jurisdictions the main concerns are related to the context of individual disputes (employment arbitration), to which more attention will be dedicated in this chapter.

§7.02 THE BRAZILIAN EXPERIENCE

Arbitration in Brazil has been increasingly accepted since the Federal Supreme Court has decided in 2001 that the settlement of disputes through arbitration is in line with the Federal Constitution and, therefore, does not violate the parties' right of access to justice. The use of arbitration, however, had been mostly limited to commercial disputes. Lately, debates over the expansion of arbitrable issues have gained strength and reached the employment legal system.

1. Labour arbitration is understood as arbitration between employers and unions. Employment arbitration, in its turn, refers to the arbitration between employers and individual employees. Theodore J.St. Antoine, *Labor and Employment Arbitration Today: Mid-Life Crisis or New Golden Age?*, 32 Ohio St. J. Disp. Resol. 1, 3 (2017).
2. Gary Born. *International Commercial Arbitration* (Kluwer Law International 2014) 1008-1009.

[A] Legal Framework

[1] *Collective Labour Arbitration*

The Brazilian law allows labour arbitration of collective and individual disputes. Collective labour disputes are considered arbitrable in Brazil since the promulgation of the Federal Constitution in 1988, which states in Article 114, paragraph 1 that '[i]f collective negotiations are unsuccessful, the parties may elect arbitrators'. Paragraph 2 also refers to arbitration.[3] A few acts subsequently promulgated contained provisions in this respect. For example, the act which regulates the employees' right to strikes (Law no. 7.783/89) and the act which regulates profit sharing (Law No. 10.101/2000) provide for the possibility of arbitrating collective labour claims.

These provisions are in line with other Ibero-American countries, such as Portugal and Spain. In Spain, the Real Decreto-Ley 17/1977 provides for arbitration of collective labour disputes, as well as all matters related to strikes. In Portugal, the Novo Código do Trabalho (Law no. 7/2009 of 12 February 2009) also allows collective labour claims to be arbitrable. As noted by a Brazilian commentator, perhaps the majority of the countries allow labour arbitration only in the collective context.[4] This commentator pointed out that, as collective disputes have a bigger social impact than the individual ones, they could have received special attention of the legislators.[5]

Another reason for allowing collective labour arbitration disputes may be the fact that, traditionally, the labour justice system aims at protecting and safeguarding the interests of the weakest party in the relationship. The employee would be in a position of legal and technical inferiority, sometimes willing - or feeling compelled - to accept poor conditions to find or maintain a job. The role of the labour justice would be to avoid such situations and guarantee that the employees have their basic rights respected. Nevertheless, this protective approach is softened in the collective context. It is understood that the degree of submission in the collective environment is lower, as the negotiations are made by unions (the employers' and the employees') or by the employees' union and the companies. Thus, the bargaining power would be balanced and both sides would be on equal terms.

In this scenario, both doctrine and courts in Brazil seem to not have concerns with the arbitrability of collective labour claims. However, in spite of such provisions and acceptance, the perception in Brazil is that collective labour arbitration is rarely seen in practice.[6]

3. 'If any of the parties refuses collective negotiation or arbitration (...)'.
4. Walküre Lopes Ribeiro da Silva, *Arbitragem nos conflitos coletivos de trabalho*, 101 Revista de Direito do Trabalho 151, 155 (January/March 2001).
5. *Ibid.*
6. Estevão Mallet, *Arbitragem em litígios trabalhistas individuais*, 84 Revista do Tribunal Superior do Trabalho 43, 43 (April/June 2018); José Antonio Fitchner, Sergio Nelson Mannheimer and André Luís Monteiro, *Teoria Geral da Arbitragem* (Editora Forense 2018) 705.

[2] Individual Employment Arbitration

The scenario changes when it comes to disputes involving an individual employee, in which the assumption of balance and equal terms widely accepted in the collective field no longer exists. In fact, in that case, we see protective and more active legislators and courts. In this section, we will focus the analysis on the legislation and on interpreting the new provisions in the Brazilian law.

The Brazilian legal system was silent on the arbitrability of disputes involving individual employees until 2017. For some commentators, this silence meant that arbitrating such disputes was forbidden.[7] For others, after the end of the labour relationship, the employee would no longer be vulnerable and the disputes would be arbitrable.[8] Finally, others argued that, according to the legality principle provided for in the Brazilian Constitution, what is not expressly forbidden by law is allowed.[9] Therefore, in spite of the recent provision regarding the arbitrability of individual labour disputes, some commentators had, even prior to the promulgation of the law, expressed their opinion in favour of employment arbitration.[10]

As it will be discussed below[11], the debate was far from being settled. Thus, back in 2015, during the revision of the Brazilian Arbitration Act (BAA), there was a proposition to allow managers and directors appointed pursuant to the bylaws[12] to agree on inserting an arbitration clause in their labour contracts, which would only be enforceable if the employee initiated the proceedings or expressly agreed with its initiation.[13] By expressly stating the arbitrability of employment claims, the goal was to settle the debate. Although the project was approved by the legislative representatives (Congress and Senate), the referred provision was vetoed by the Executive Power (in that case, the then vice president). Among the veto's reasons, it was the fact that it created an undesirable distinction among employees.[14]

---

7. Maurício Gondinho Delgado, *Curso de direito do trabalho* (LTr 2006) pp. 1451-1452; Benedito Aparecido Tuponi Junior, *A (in)arbitrabilidade dos dissídios individuais trabalhistas*, 18 Revista Brasileira de Arbitragem, 58 (April-June 2008).
8. Francisco José Cahali, *Curso de Arbitragem* (RT 2011) 336.
9. Ana Lúcia Pereira, *Considerações sobre a utilização da arbitragem nos contratos individuais do trabalho*, 23 Revista Brasileira de Arbitragem e Mediação 89, 90 (October-December 2009); Fabiane Verçosa, *Arbitragem para a resolução de dissídios individuais trabalhistas em tempos de Reforma da CLT e de conjecturas sobre a extinção da Justiça do Trabalho: O Direito Trabalhista na encruzilhada*, 61 Revista Brasileira de Arbitragem 7, 11 (January/March 2019). Fitchner et al. (*supra* n. 6) at 706.
10. Carlos Alberto Carmona, *Arbitragem e Processo* (3d ed., Atlas 2009) 44.
11. *See* §7.02[B].
12. The Brazilian Corporate Law (Law no. 6.404/76) distinguishes Directors appointed pursuant to the bylaws from others hired by the company. The first, although not formally employed by the company, has to comply with the duties and responsibilities set forth in the company's bylaws.
13. Law no. 13.129/2015, Article 4, paragraph 4.
14. 'O dispositivo autorizaria a previsão de cláusula de compromisso em contrato individual de trabalho. Para tal, realizaria, ainda, restrições de sua eficácia nas relações envolvendo determinados empregados, a depender de sua ocupação. Dessa forma, acabaria por realizar uma distinção indesejada entre empregados, além de recorrer a termo não definido tecnicamente na legislação trabalhista. Com isso, colocaria em risco a generalidade de trabalhadores que poderiam se ver submetidos ao processo arbitral.' https://www2.camara.leg.br/legin/fed/lei/2015/lei-13129-26-maio-2015-780858-veto-147043-pl.html (accessed 20 July 2019).

After this first frustrated attempt, in 2017 the labour legal system in Brazil underwent a major reform, which became effective on 11 November 2017 and aimed at adding more flexibility to the labour justice system, reducing the state's intervention and increasing the parties' autonomy.[15] One of the changes was the insertion of Article 507-A in the Consolidated Labour Laws (CLT), according to which individuals may enter into an arbitration agreement when (i) they earn more than two times the sum established by the General Social Welfare Policy (RGPS), and (ii) as long as on the employee's own initiative or by means of his/her explicit consent.

The legislator added an arbitrability requirement connected to one of the parties to the labour contract, i.e. the amount of the employee's remuneration.[16] The choice of such criterion has been regarded as a way of balancing the inequalities between employers and employees, as it is based on the assumption that the higher the amount earned by the employee, the greater is his/her bargaining power or negotiating capacity.[17] It is known that the negotiating capacity of employees varies according to their financial situation, age, stage of the career, emotional situation, among other elements and that it has an impact on the relationship of subordination between employer and employee. By adopting the remuneration criterion to determine which employee is able to arbitrate his/her individual labour disputes, the legislator seems to have chosen the salary as the indicator of the employee's negotiating capacity. It was not done, however, without some criticism.

It was said that such decision was 'simplistic and shallow'.[18] Another commentator, based on his interpretation of the convention concerning discrimination in respect of employment and occupation (International Labour Organization Convention no. 111, of 1958), argued that classifying the employee according to his/her earnings is not advisable, as one's remuneration should not justify his/her condition of superiority.[19] Also, the sum established would not be large enough to justify one's true negotiating capacity.[20] Even if a small percentage of the Brazilian population earns more than such sum,[21] it would not be enough to allow the employee to freely negotiate his/her contractual terms and also not enough for him/her to bear the arbitration costs.[22] Would this then be a barrier to gaining access to justice?[23]

15. Joaquim de Paiva Muniz, *Arbitragem no direito do trabalho*, 56 Revista de Arbitragem e Mediação 179, 179 (January-March 2018).
16. It is perhaps needless, but it is always good to mention that the requirement set forth in the Brazilian Arbitration Act is also applicable to the labour disputes, thus the subject matter of the arbitration must be related to 'freely transferable property rights'.
17. Mallet (*supra* n. 6) 47.
18. Free translation. Verçosa (*supra* n. 9) at 23.
19. Georgenor de Sousa Franco Filho, *A arbitragem no moderno Direito brasileiro do trabalho*, 44 Revista de Direito do Trabalho 21, 27 (August 2018).
20. Mallet (*supra* n. 6) 50.
21. It is estimated that less than 2.5% of the Brazilian population earn more than five minimum wages. Márcio Yoshida, *A arbitragem e a reforma trabalhista*, 55 Revista de Arbitragem e Mediação 57, 58 (October-December 2017). Such sum is even smaller than the one established in Article 507-A of the Consolidated Labour Laws in Brazil. This means that less than 2.5% of the employees would not be able to arbitrate their employment disputes.
22. Verçosa (*supra* n. 9) 24.
23. *See* section §7.02[B][3] below.

The solution proposed by some authors would then be to assess the employees' negotiating capacity on a case-by-case analysis. On the one hand, it would allow the accurate investigation as to the employee's bargaining power.[24] On the other hand, such analysis might not be practicable. The legislator, thus, chose to substitute the wide concept of 'negotiating capacity' to a number, simplifying the application of the law. That is exactly what it is done, for example, when determining one's legal capacity: above certain age, one is able to perform civil rights and obligations. Not always will there be a perfect match between quantity and quality, but in the words of the Constitutional Court of South Africa: ' [t]he line has to be drawn somewhere, and there will always be people on one side of the line who do not benefit and whose positions are not significantly different to those of persons on the other side of line who do benefit'.[25]

Whether or not it was the adequate choice, it is clear the legislator's intent to safeguarding the interests of the employee, by drawing a financial income line. Comparing the criteria set forth in the CLT and the one vetoed from the Revised BAA, some authors considered this one to be more technical.[26] Such provision allowed only people trusted to make important decisions regarding the company's interests to refer their disputes to arbitration (managers or some directors). It was assumed that they would also be well informed about their rights and they would be in a position to choose how they want their disputes to be settled.[27] In such cases it could be considered that the employees' subordination to the employers is mitigated.[28] Moreover, as the proceedings had to be initiated by the employee or with their express consent, the provision would safeguard the employee's informed and conscious expression of will. This was not what prevailed, though. The legislator, followed by the approval of the Executive Power, chose a different criteria to safeguard the employees' rights.

For bad or good, a line was drawn. It is up to the practitioners to see whether or not this line is adequate in the concrete case. Entering into an arbitration agreement, whether it is a commercial or a labour one, requires a strategic analysis as to its cost-effectiveness. It should not be different in labour arbitration: the minimum amount provided in Article 507-A should be seen as a dotted line, to be fully drawn by the employers and employees in the concrete case, after a thorough and careful analysis. One could argue that it is naïve to think that this will happen in practice, as even in commercial arbitration we often see midnight clauses.[29] But the arbitration's

24. Mallet (*supra* n. 6) 25.
25. *President of the Republic of South Africa and other v. Hugo* (CCT 11/96), no. 31 in Mallet (*supra* n. 6) 51.
26. Verçosa (*supra* n. 9) 23.
27. *Ibid.*, 20.
28. *Ibid.*
29. Midnight clauses are defined as 'the last clauses to be considered in contract negotiations, sometimes late at night or in the early hours of the morning. Insufficient thought is given to how disputes are to be resolved (...), and an inappropriate and unwieldy compromise is often adopted (...)'. The authors also stress that 'Most international commercial arbitrations take place pursuant to an arbitration clause in a commercial contract. These are often "midnight

cornerstone is party autonomy, and the authority to draw a dotted or a full line belongs to the parties.

Finally, some additional considerations should be made regarding the Article 507-A. The first is that the provision only refers to arbitration clauses: '[i]n individual employment contracts (...) an *arbitration clause* may be agreed upon' (emphasis added). When choosing the term 'arbitration clause' instead of 'arbitration agreement', a door is left open to argue whether it would be allowed to arbitrate an individual labour dispute based on a submission agreement.[30] However, and apparently, this has not been seen as an obstacle to initiate arbitration proceedings.[31] The submission agreement would only be entered after the dispute has arisen, thus, after the labour contract is ended. It has been interpreted that with the termination of the contract, the relationship of subordination also ends, and the employee is free to express his/her consent.

The second consideration is that the clause must be inserted in the contract on the employee's own initiative or his/her express consent to it. At a first impression, it seems unnecessary to provide for such requirement, as the consent is the cornerstone of the arbitration, without which arbitration does not exist. The legislator probably wanted to emphasize the need for an *informed* consent of the parties, in line with the protective nature of the labour justice.[32] It should be added that the moment chosen to determine whether the parties consented to arbitration was the moment they agreed on inserting the clause in the contract. The insertion must be on the employees' own initiative or with his/her express agreement. However, proving such moment, that is, whose initiative it was, might be difficult in practice.

[B] The Brazilian Courts' Approach to Employment and Labour Arbitration

First of all, it should be noted that all the cases discussed in this section refer to contracts entered into before the Labour Reform, even though some were decided after November 2017. The Supreme Labour Court in Brazil (TST) has not yet had the opportunity to decide on a case whose arbitration agreement was signed after the Labour Reform. Even if the final outcome might remain open, there are some indications of how the TST will decide on the issue in the future.

As mentioned in section §7.02 [A] [1] above, issues against the arbitrability of collective rights disputes have not been raised.[33] The same might not be said about

clauses"'. Nigel Blackaby, Constantine Partasides, Alan Redfern and Martin Hunter. *Redfern and Hunter on International Arbitration* (6th ed., Oxford University Press 2015) 72-73.

30. Leonardo Paulo de Oliveira Andreotti, *Arbitragem para a resolução de controvérsias laborais no futebol brasileiro*, 1 Revista Brasileira de Alternative Dispute Resolution 125, 129 (January-June 2019).
31. Mallet (*supra* n. 6) 58.
32. Muniz (*supra* n. 15) 18.
33. Several cases cited in this section, which deny the possibility of arbitrating individual labour disputes, mention that if the dispute referred to collective rights, it would be arbitrable.

individual labour disputes,[34] even if the arbitration community in Brazil received the possibility of arbitrating these disputes with some enthusiasm. When Article 507-A was inserted in the CLT, the question raised was: will this be a breakthrough for the courts' dominant jurisprudence? From what we have seen so far, the horizon is not very hopeful. Due to the strong debate regarding the arbitrability of employment disputes, the section will focus on this issue.

When the first cases involving the arbitrability of individual labour rights emerged in 2005 and 2008, the TST expressed a favourable opinion towards arbitration. In fact, the first three decisions issued by the TST concluded in favour of the possibility of the employee to resort to arbitration when arguing his/her employment claims.[35] However, the scenario has changed as, in December 2008, the TST rejected the arbitrability of individual labour disputes.[36] Since then, oscillating decisions were awarded: sometimes the TST allowed the arbitrability of such disputes, sometimes it did not.[37] The inconsistency was such that, one day, on the same date, two decisions were published pointing at opposite directions: one in favour of the arbitration, another against it.[38]

Eventually, the TST consolidated the stand against the possibility of arbitrating employment disputes.[39] Among the reasons for not allowing arbitration, the TST highlighted (i) that labour rights are not waivable[40] (and the BAA only allows arbitration related to freely transferable rights), (ii) the employees are in a position of economic inferiority in individual disputes[41] and (iii) the violation of access to justice.

In one case decided on 19 September 2018, the TST rejected the arbitrability of the individual labour dispute and the Justice rapporteur not even mentioned that the

34. Luiz Augusto da Silva, *Arbitragem trabalhista e o problema da liberdade: reflexões à luz do ideal de não dominação, efetividade, e a reforma da lei de arbitragem (Lei nº 13.129/2015)*, 56 Revista de Arbitragem e Mediação 189, 191 (January-March 2018).
35. RR 1650/1999-003-15-00, 4th Chamber, Judge Rapporteur Maria Doralice Novaes, published in DJ on 30.09.2005; AIRR 2547/2002-077-02-40, 7th Chamber, Justice Rapporteur Ives Gandra Martins Filho, published in DEJT on 08.02.2008; and AIRR 1475/2000-193-05-00, 7th Chamber, Justice Rapporteur Pedro Paulo Manus, published in DEJT on 17.10.2008.
36. RR 955-2007/024-02-00, 8th Chamber, Justice Rapporteur Maria Cristina Irigoyen Peduzzi.
37. The TST is composed of eight chambers and specialized sections. The judicial proceedings are submitted to the full court, specialized sections or to one of its chambers (classes) – these randomly allocated. The competence to decide on a proceeding is set forth in the court's internal regulation. The cases mentioned in this section were decided by different chambers and that is the reason why they are not always harmonized.
38. RR 1799/2004-024-05-00, 4th Chamber, Justice Rapporteur Barros Levenhagen, published in DEJT on 19.06.2009; and AIRR 2823/2003-068-02-40, 2nd Chamber, Justice Rapporteur Renato de Lacerda Paiva, published in DEJT on 19.06.2009.
39. Several decisions against the arbitrability followed. All of them were awarded before the Labour Reform in 2017. Joaquim Muniz pointed out that out of the TST's eight chambers, six of them did not allow the arbitrability of employment disputes. Muniz (*supra* n. 15) 181.
40. Meaning: they cannot be derogated by agreement. The non-waiver principle of rights is provided in a few articles of the CLT, such as the 9th, 444 and 468. It is a restriction to party autonomy in labour relationships. By declaring that some rights are non-waivable, the legislator aimed at safeguarding the workers' fundamental rights, given the imbalance of powers inherent in the employment contract.
41. In Portuguese the term 'hipossuficiente' is used to describe such position. If someone is 'hipossuficiente', it means that he or she would not be able to afford the judicial costs without jeopardizing his/her or his/her family's livelihood.

Labour Reform had changed this scenario.[42] Grounding his decision on the argument that labour rights are not freely transferable, as they provide for the employees' livelihood, the minister also stated that arbitration is not compatible with the labour justice and, for such reason, the article providing for the arbitrability of labour disputes had been vetoed by the Executive Power from the Revised BAA in 2015. This, unfortunately, was not an isolated episode.[43] In another case, the respective Justice rapporteur stated that the constitutionality of the BAA was still under debate by the Supreme Federal Court (STF).[44] In fact, the STF declared the constitutionality of the Arbitration Act in 2001.[45]

The most recent case decided by the TST was not different. However, as the labour court of appeals had decided in favour of arbitration, the arbitral community was hopeful that the TST would ratify such position.[46] The ratification did not happen. The case was about a high executive of an investment bank in Brazil who filed a lawsuit claiming, among other things, the payment of extra working hours, damages for psychological harassment and loss of opportunity. It is worth noting that, during the course of the labour relationship, it was inserted in the contract an arbitration clause covering questions of restraint of trade. In its defence, the bank claimed the existence of an arbitration clause which ousted the courts' jurisdiction. In the first instance, the judge rejected the claim, emphasizing on Article 5, XXXV of the Federal Constitution, which states that 'the law shall not exclude any injury or threat to a right from the consideration of the Judicial Power', [47] and that labour rights are non-waivable. The Court of Appeal overturned the decision, affirming the validity of the arbitration clause. In sum, the appellate court declared that not all labour rights are non-waivable. Otherwise, parties would be prevented from negotiating them, which is not the case, as negotiation does happen in practice. The court stated that if this assumption were true, 'there would be a major impediment to the development of the legal and social system'.[48] It further clarified that 'it is in the concrete case that the judiciary will assess if that right is or is not available'.[49] Based upon these premises, the court concluded that there was no vulnerability of the employee, as the claimant was a high executive of an investment bank, possessing brainpower and financial expertise, and receiving substantial monthly payments. Claimant and respondent, in this case, were considered

42. AIRR nº 128300-94.2007.5.02.0020, 7th Chamber, Justice Rapporteur Cláudio Brandão, judged on 19.09.2018.
43. RR nº 1051-59-2012.5.09.0322, 1st Chamber, Justice Rapporteur Delaíde Miranda Dantas, judged on 14.12.2017.
44. AIRR nº 182200-18.2009.5.02.0021, 1st Chamber, Justice Rapporteur Lélio Bentes Corrêa, judged on 13.12.2017.
45. STF, SE-AgR 5206/EP, Justice Rapporteur Sepúlveda Pertence, Brasilia-DF, published in DJ on 30.04.2002.
46. Fabiane Verçosa, *Arbitragem para a Resolução de Dissídios Individuais Trabalhistas. Comentário ao Acórdão Prolatado pela 5ª Turma do TST no RR 11289-92.2013.5.01.0042. Rel. Min. Breno Medeiros, J. 06.02.2019*, 62 Revista Brasileira de Arbitragem 122, 158 (April-June 2019)
47. Article 5, XXXV of the Brazilian Constitution is the provision which guarantees the constitutional right of access to justice.
48. RO 0011289-92.2013.5.01.0042, TRT 1st Region, Rapporteur Judge Enoque Ribeiro dos Santos, published at DEJT on 21.04.2017, p. 14. Free translation.
49. *Ibid.* Free translation.

to be on equal footing and able to consciously choose arbitration. In addition, a non-compete clause is a freely transferable right and, therefore, disputes arising out of this specific matter are arbitrable.

However good such decision was, it was not maintained by the TST. It was overturned, once again, on the basis that the arbitrability of labour disputes is limited to collective rights, and arbitration is incompatible with individual labour rights.[50] Not a single line of the judgment addressed the Labour Reform and the fact that if the agreement was signed after the reform, the outcome could have been different.

The conclusion is that a few years after the Labour Reform, the TST seems to keep ignoring the modifications brought by it, in particular related to arbitration involving employment disputes. Commentators have expressed favourable opinions towards arbitration,[51] and arbitral institutions have taken actions to adapt their proceedings to labour disputes.[52] Yet, the TST has not – apparently – changed its view. The TST seems attached to the idea that labour rights cannot be derogated by agreement, and its interpretation of the Federal Constitution so far is that, as the law shall not exclude any injury or threat to a labour right from the consideration of the Judicial Power, referring such disputes to arbitration would mean denying access to justice to the parties.

[1] Challenges: Is Access to Justice at Risk?

The main barriers that individual labour arbitration is facing in Brazil could be summed up as follows: (i) labour rights are not waivable, and the parties have the constitutional right to have their claims heard by the judiciary, and (ii) even if the parties could arbitrate such disputes, arbitration costs may be prohibitive, restricting the parties' access to justice. The question we should analyse is: do such barriers represent a groundless resistance against arbitration or do they safeguard the employees' right of access to justice? All of them share a common ground: an interventionist and protective nature of the labour justice. Is this protection too excessive?

There are two ways of seeing the matter. The first is that another mechanism of solving labour disputes is offered to the parties and, with it, there is an extension of

50. RR 11289-92.2013.5.01.0042., Rapporteur Minister Breno Medeiros, 5th Chamber TST, j. 06.02.2019.

51. Several authors, both from arbitration and labour practices, have expressed their favourable opinions since the Labour Reform. For example: Fitchner et al. (*supra* n. 6), at 21-34; Muniz, (*supra* n. 15), at 180; Bruno Freire e Silva, *A Reforma Processual Trabalhista e o Acesso à Justiça*, 278 Revista de Processo 393, 399-400 (April 2018); Sergio Torres Teixeira, *Vias alternativas à jurisdição contenciosa da Justiça do Trabalho: superando mitos e apontado caminhos à luz da Lei nº 13.467/2017*, 187 Revista de Direito do Trabalho 51, 51-89 (March 2018).

52. Some Brazilian arbitral institutions noted that labour disputes require a special treatment when compared to commercial disputes and, in view of creating an adequate dispute resolution mechanism in this field, have issued specific rules for labour arbitration. Such institutions are the Arbitration and Mediation Center of the American Chamber of Commerce for Brazil (AMCHAM Brazil), which was the first one to launch a set of labour arbitration rules in May 2018, the Brazilian Center for Arbitration and Mediation (CBMA), which launched a Protocol for Labour Arbitration, Câmara de Mediação e Arbitragem Empresarial (CAMARB), and the Specialized Chamber of Mediation and Arbitration (Cames), which launched a set of rules.

their right to access to justice.[53] The second is that some matters cannot be decided in a private environment and that the costs related to a private dispute mechanism are too high, becoming an obstacle for the parties to pursue their rights.

[2] Waivable Rights

First, it must be made clear that the fact that the parties are waiving the rights to have the dispute heard by a state court does not mean that they are waiving the rights to obtain justice. Arbitral tribunals are composed of neutral third persons who decide the case based on and in accordance with the same material law as courts do. The arbitration proceedings, like the litigation of the dispute before a national court, is governed by due process of law principles. It cannot be assumed that just because a private person will decide the dispute, this person will not respect the rule of law. The arbitrator will judge the case based upon the same law, and will do so in a faster, sometimes confidential (if the parties choose so), and technical manner.

The impossibility to waive certain labour rights does not, and should not, forbid the use of arbitration to debate the monetary aspects of labour rights. Labour law seeks to avoid that arbitration turns into a ploy that imposes unilateral solutions to the employee with the purpose of defrauding labour rights. However, there is no impediment in the law to debate certain issues in arbitration.[54] For example: given the circumstances of the case, is the employee entitled to his/her right of holiday pay? To what extent? Has the employee fulfilled his/her duty to provide the company with a one-month notice before quitting?[55] These claims are related to monetary aspects of the employee's rights, which are perfectly negotiable; therefore, not classified as non-waivable. Depriving the parties to settle them in arbitration actually subtracts from them the right to choose which dispute resolution mechanism they think it is more adequate for them. The issue, then, reveals itself as a matter of contract freedom: to what extent the employee is free to choose arbitration considering the disparity of power between employer and employee. [56]

The freedom and the right to choose are key issues when debating access to justice. It must be guaranteed that the parties freely chose arbitration. Arbitration's cornerstone, whether it is commercial or labour, is the consent.[57] A defective choice removes the pillar on which arbitration lies. The employee must be aware of what

53. Silva (*supra* n. 51) 399-400.
54. As highlighted by a commentator, 'arbitration is allowed whenever the issue in discussion may be amicably settled by the parties, without the need of ratification by the Judiciary'. Free translation. Silva (*supra* n. 34) 191.
55. The CLT provides for a prior notice period in case of dismissal or resignation: the employee (when quitting) and the employer (when dismissing) are required to give a prior notice to the counterparty (Articles 487-491 CLT). If the employee fails to do so, the employer is entitled to deduct the proportionate amount of the employee's corresponding salary. If the employer fails to do so, the employee is entitled to compensation.
56. Silva (*supra* n. 34) 192.
57. 'This consent is essential: without it, there can be no valid arbitration.' Blackaby et al. (*supra* n. 29) 16. 'In order for an arbitration agreement to exist, the parties must have validly consented to that agreement.' Born (*supra* n. 2) 74.

arbitration means, how the proceedings work and the related costs, because once the parties agree to arbitrate, courts are no longer an option. As long as more options are available when they choose (arbitration and courts), one can argue that access to justice is being increased. But if the choice is not made freely and the courts are no longer an option, the parties would be deprived of justice.

[3] Arbitration Costs

The costs are perhaps the Achilles heel of arbitration. Surveys show that one of its most criticized aspects is its high costs.[58] Arbitration is a privately funded dispute resolution mechanism. Thus, parties to an arbitration agreement are expected to cover all the arbitration costs, which, unlike court proceedings, include administrative charges (in case of arbitral institutions), hearing costs, arbitrator's fees and other expenses incurred during the proceedings. When one of the parties is incapable of meeting these financial obligations, issues related to such party's access to arbitral justice – or any justice – may arise.

This debate, even in the commercial area, is unsettled. Different jurisdictions have taken different approaches. On the one hand, it stands the principle of access to justice: if a party cannot bear the arbitration costs and such party is bound by an arbitration agreement, it will not be able to pursue its rights in any tribunal or court.[59] On the other hand, stands the *pacta sunt servanda* principle, which implies that agreements and contracts must be respected.[60] The first approach may be classified as

58. (I) The 2015 International Arbitration Survey: Improvements and Innovations in International Arbitration, reported that cost (68%), lack of effective sanctions during the arbitral process (46%) and lack of insight into arbitrator's efficiency (39%) are the three worst characteristics of international arbitration. (II) The 2018 International Arbitration Survey: The Evolution of International Arbitration confirmed the 2015 survey's result: cost continues to be seen as arbitration's worst feature (67%), followed by lack of effective sanctions during the arbitral process (45%), lack of power in relation to third parties (39%) and lack of speed (34%). These results are available at: *The 2015 International Arbitration Survey: Improvements and Innovations in International Arbitration*, 7, https://www.whitecase.com/sites/whitecase/files/files/download/publications/qmul-international-arbitration-survey-2015_0.pdf (accessed 21 August 2019); *The 2018 International Arbitration Survey: The Evolution of International Arbitration*, 8, http://www.arbitration.qmul.ac.uk/media/arbitration/docs/2018-International-Arbitration-Survey---The-Evolution-of-International-Arbitration-(2).PDF (accessed 21 August 2019).
59. The analysis of different jurisdictions' case law and related doctrine might lead to the conclusion that this is not a sink or swim situation. The risks of disregarding the arbitration agreement from the get-go whenever a party claims impecuniosity are high, especially because the incapacity to meet the costs may involve subject interpretation or may be mispresented by one party. A wide interpretation in cases like this could lead to parties escaping from their obligations under the agreement to arbitrate, weakening the arbitration institute. A case-by-case analysis, then, is more adequate, as it will allow balancing those principles in the specific circumstances, instead of readily disregarding one of them. Would parties have consented to arbitration if they knew they would not be able to afford its costs? Are the parties unable to afford the costs or unwilling to? Are there options available to reduce the arbitration costs? *See* Carolina da Rocha Morandi, *Impecunious Claimant in Arbitration: An Exception to Arbitrate? Revisiting the Issue in Light of Tillman v. Tillman Case*, 26 Young Arbitration Review 40, 40-45 (Jul. 2017).
60. 'Once parties have validly given their consent to arbitration, that consent cannot be unilaterally withdrawn.' Blackaby et al. (*supra* n. 29) 16.

interventionist. As labour justice tends to lean towards a protective trait, we will focus the analysis on it.

In Germany, for example, known as a pro-arbitration country, whose Arbitration Act in based on the UNCITRAL Model law, the courts have decided that impecuniosity renders the arbitration agreement incapable of being performed and, as such, the impecunious claimant is entitled to pursue its rights before state courts.[61] In Portugal, the Supreme Court decided that, in case of a supervening fact that changed the financial capacity of the party, which could no longer afford the arbitration costs, the parties were released from their agreement to arbitrate.[62] These two examples bring the reflection: if some courts, even in pro-arbitration jurisdictions, are protective of the access to justice in case of impecuniosity, will labour courts in Brazil, which already have a protective trait, also interpret such situations as a denial of justice?

The courts in Brazil, and also legal doctrine, classify the nature of the employees' salaries as 'verba alimentar', which means that they are destined to their families' livelihood. As a consequence, it could be argued that there are situations in which the employees will not be able to bear the arbitration costs without jeopardizing their families' maintenance. This is the reason why it has been said that 'if a party does not have means to bear the related costs, it is inconceivable to deny him the possibility to pursue his rights'.[63] This would be equivalent to denying access to justice based on financial capacity, which would be incompatible to the constitutional right of access to justice.[64]

It should be noted, however, that there is a belief that arbitration is always very expensive, but, depending on the case, this is nothing more than a myth. For example, in Brazil, it is applied to labour disputes in court a simple interest rate of 1% a month on the total amount of the debt until the case is closed.[65] Analysing the latest Labour Courts statistics in Brazil, the average length of a lawsuit in the first instance courts is eight months; in the appeal courts, five months; in the TST, one year and four months.[66] From the filing of a lawsuit until the judgment is rendered, it takes on average twenty-seven months. This is at least three times longer than the length of a labour arbitration proceeding as provided for in the AMCHAM Brazil Labour Arbitration Rules, for example.[67] Considering the interest rates which apply on a monthly basis at the courts, the total amount spent with a labour dispute in the judiciary may be

61. CLOUT case 404, cited in Patricia Zivkovic, *Impecunious Parties in Arbitration: An Overview of European National Courts' Practice*, 23 Croat. Arbit. Yearb 33, 40-41 (2016).
62. Acórdao 311/2008, Rel. Aragão Seia, Diário da República, 2ª série, nº 148, 1 de Agosto de 2008, págs 34401-5.
63. Mallet (*supra* n. 6), at 45.
64. *Ibid.*
65. Under Brazilian law, the amount of damages should be adjusted to reflect the claimant's opportunity costs. This typically includes a monetary restatement plus accumulated interest rate.
66. https://www.cnj.jus.br/wp-content/uploads/2020/08/WEB-V3-Justi%C3%A7a-em-N%C3%BAmeros-2020-atualizado-em-25-08-2020.pdf (accessed 13 August 2019).
67. AMCHAM Brazil, after the Labour Reform, was the first institution in Brazil to launch a new set of rules destined to individual labour disputes. Among the innovations, there is a significant reduction of length and costs of the proceedings: https://estatico.amcham.com.br/arquivos/2018/arbitragem-trabalhista-regulamento.pdf (accessed 01 August 2019).

much higher than with arbitration.[68] The difference is that arbitration requires an advance on costs: the institutions will only administer the proceedings when the parties have paid the fees. Even if ad hoc, most likely the arbitrators will work only after there are some guarantees, or prepayments made. In courts, the value of the condemnation will only be paid in the end. Thus, the need to pay the fees in the beginning may constitute a barrier to initiate proceedings, which may be seen as a barrier to access justice.

Only the facts and circumstances of the given case will crystallize whether the arbitration costs are prohibitive to the parties, and if they truncate the employee's right of access to justice. For example, one may wonder whether the parties have taken alternative measures to safeguard their access to justice. The employer, being the defendant in the dispute, could pay the full advance on costs (although it is not obliged to). Also, the parties could choose a sole arbitrator instead of three; they could also choose an arbitration institution with low fee and costs schedules.[69] Even so, such measures could not have been enough to guarantee that the employee would be able to pay his/her share of the proceedings' costs. There is no general rule; only the particular case will tell.

Considering how labour courts in Brazil have already been reluctant to arbitration, it is likely that, even if they change their minds regarding arbitrability, they will probably not enforce arbitration clauses in situations like this, based on the denial of access to justice. What should be emphasized, though, is that courts should not simply deny the parties the possibility of going to arbitration just because the costs could be prohibitive. They might not be.

§7.03 THE USA EXPERIENCE: A BRIEF BACKGROUND

Among the jurisdictions which both enforce and encourage agreements to arbitrate in employment settings, the USA stands out. Initially, though, American courts were hostile to arbitration, considering it an intrusion on their jurisdiction. With the promulgation of The Federal Arbitration Act of 1925 (FAA) the approach of American courts towards arbitration changed.[70] The FAA requires both state and federal courts to enforce arbitration agreements, with limited exceptions.[71]

---

68. This example only took into account the interest rates. Should the monetary restatement also be added, the costs related to a lengthy labour court proceeding would be even higher when compared to a faster arbitration proceeding.
69. *See* (*supra* n. 52). There are institutions in Brazil which have created a special set of rules to labour arbitration proceedings, aiming at reducing their length and the related costs.
70. FAA section 2: Validity, irrevocability, and enforcement of agreements to arbitrate: A written provision in any maritime transaction or a contract evidencing a transaction involving commerce to settle by arbitration a controversy thereafter arising out of such contract or transaction, or the refusal to perform the whole or any part thereof, or an agreement in writing to submit to arbitration an existing controversy arising out of such a contract, transaction, or refusal, shall be valid, irrevocable, and enforceable, save upon such grounds as exist at law or in equity for the revocation of any contract.
71. Erin O'Hara O'Connor, Kenneth Martin and Randall Thomas, *Arbitration Clauses in CEO Employment Contracts: An Empirical and Theoretical Analysis*, 63 Vand. L. Rev. 957, 966 (2010).

However, for many years, the FAA was not deemed applicable to employment disputes, as it explicitly mentions to cover contracts 'evidencing a transaction involving commerce', and commerce in the same act excluded 'contracts of employment of seamen, railroad employees, or any other class of workers engaged in foreign or interstate commerce'.[72] As it has been pointed out by commentators, labour disputes were often arbitrated pursuant to collective bargaining agreements between employers and employee unions, and the proceedings occurred pursuant to the Labour Management Relations Act (LMRA) of 1947 (Taft-Hartley Act).[73] Later on, courts began to hold that employment contracts fell within the scope of the FAA and that the exclusion mentioned in section 1 of the FAA applied only to employees engaged in transportation industries.[74] Thus, the USA Supreme Court has repeatedly upheld the validity and enforceability of arbitration agreements in the domestic employment context.[75]

Court rulings on labour arbitration have served as the foundation of the American arbitration law. The *Steelworkers Trilogy* became a milestone in the USA regarding the arbitrability of labour disputes and the enforcement of labour arbitral awards.[76] The first two cases dealt with the enforcement of agreements to arbitrate. The third uphold the validity of an arbitral award. The holding was that doubts related to the coverage of an arbitration agreement were to be decided in favour of arbitration; also, in dealing with arbitral awards, the courts would be limited to analysing issues of due process, refraining from reviewing the merits of the case. Since then, labour arbitration has become increasingly popular. One study found that more than 90% of the employment contracts analysed contained arbitration provisions.[77]

Nancy A. Welsh, *Arbitration and Beyond: Avoiding Pitfalls in Drafting Dispute Resolution Clauses in Employment Contracts*, 1 J. Alternative Disp. Resol. Employment 35, 36 (1999).

72. FAA section 1: 'Maritime transactions' and 'commerce' defined; exceptions to operation of title 'Maritime transaction', as herein defined, means charter parties, bills of lading of water carriers, agreements relating to wharfage, supplies furnished vessels or repairs to vessels, collisions, or any other matters in foreign commerce which, if the subject of controversy, would be embraced within admiralty jurisdiction; 'commerce', as herein defined, means commerce among the several States or with foreign nations, or in any territory of the United States or in the District of Columbia, or between any such territory and another, or between any such territory and any state or foreign nation, or between the District of Columbia and any state or territory or foreign nation, but nothing herein contained shall apply to contracts of employment of seamen, railroad employees, or any other class of workers engaged in foreign or interstate commerce.
73. O'Hara et. al (n 71) 966. Thomas E. Carbonneau, 'Liberal Rules of Arbitrability and the Autonomy of Labor Arbitration in the United States', in Loukas A. Mistelis and Stavros Brekoulakis (eds), *Arbitrability: International and Comparative Perspectives*, International Arbitration Law Library, Volume 19 (Kluwer Law International 2009) 152. Welsh (*supra* n. 71), at Endnote 1.
74. *Circuit City Stores, Inc. v. Adams*, 532 U.S. 105 (2001). O'Hara et al. (*supra* n. 71) 966.
75. Born (*supra* n. 2) 1009-1011.
76. *United Steelworkers of Am. v. American Mfg. Co.*, 363 U.S. 564 (1960); *United Steelworkers of Am. v. Warrior & Gulf Nav. Co.*, 363 U.S. 574 (1960); *United Steelworkers of Am. v. Enterprise Wheel & Car Corp.*, 363 U.S. 593 (1960).
77. Such study analysed contracts in the EDGAR database. EDGAR (Electronic Data Gathering, Analysis, and Retrieval) is an online public database from the USA Securities and Exchange Commission (SEC). The SEC requires registered companies to file current and annual reports listing, among other things, contracts that materially affect the financial condition of the company. *See* Theodore Eisenberg, Geoffrey P. Miller & Emily Sherwin, *Arbitration's Summer*

Such percentage stands out, and it could actually be related to the increasing use of mandatory arbitration in employment contracts.[78] Mandatory arbitration in such context consists of a practice in which the employer requires employees to agree to arbitrate legal disputes rather than going to court. Although the choice of going to arbitration could seem voluntary, in practice signing the arbitration agreement is required if one wants to get or keep the job.

This trend splits opinions: while critics argue that these contracts are generally adhesion and arbitration could take away rights available from the employees, supporters argue that arbitration tends to be both faster and less expensive, being beneficial to both sides.[79] Even so, a Supreme Court decision in 1991, which authorized arbitration of claims under the Age Discrimination and Employment Act of 1967, upheld the enforceability of mandatory employment arbitration agreements.[80] This decision may have encouraged employers to include mandatory arbitration provisions in their contracts.

The debate about mandatory arbitration is a current challenge facing employment arbitration in the USA. For this reason, the chapter will focus on the use of mandatory arbitration in confronting the principle of access to justice.

[A] Is the USA Facing a Backlash Against Mandatory Employment Arbitration?

After the *Gilmer* decision in 1991, supported by subsequent decisions,[81] companies might have been encouraged to include mandatory arbitration provisions in their contracts with employees. Without debating the merits of arbitration and the advantages it could bring both to employers and employees, the focus of this section will be on the backlash that mandatory arbitration has received in the USA in light of the employee's right of access to justice.

The academic community and civil society organizations have heavily criticized the inclusion of mandatory arbitration provisions in employment contracts. Some argue that companies get the advantage of being *repeat players*, thus raising issues of impartiality in arbitral proceedings.[82] Others argue that it could represent a way of circumventing the courts and hindering people from joining forces in class-actions

Soldiers: An Empirical Study of Arbitration Clauses in Consumer and Nonconsumer Contracts, 41 U. Mich. J. L. Reform 871, 881-883 (2008).

78. Alexander J.S. Colvin, *The Growing Use of Mandatory Arbitration. Access to the Courts Is Now Barred for More Than 60 Million American Workers*. Economic Policy Institute, April 6, 2018, https://www.epi.org/publication/the-growing-use-of-mandatory-arbitration-access-to-the-courts-is-now-barred-for-more-than-60-million-american-workers/ (accessed 09 October 2019).
79. O'Hara et al. (n. 71) 967.
80. *Gilmer v. Interstate/Johnson Lane* 500 U.S. 20 (1991).
81. *AT&T Mobility LLC v. Concepcion* 563 U.S. 333 (2011); *American Express Co. v. Italian Colors Restaurant* 133 S. Ct. 594 (2013).
82. Roni Adil Radi Elias, *Assuring Fairness in Employment Arbitration: Do Employees Really Need the Arbitration Fairness Act?*, The Federal Lawyer, 12 (December 2015).

lawsuits[83]. Professor Alexander Colvin analysed how mandatory arbitration affects four key components of employment relations and individual rights in the workplace and concluded that 'mandatory arbitration exacerbates inequality in access to justice in the workplace'.[84] His conclusions were the following[85]:

(i) as in mandatory arbitration it is the employer's choice whether or not to adopt it and how the procedure will be structured, it turns out that the employer sets up arbitration unilaterally, often banning also class actions;
(ii) the risk of having a larger damage award in courts are higher than in arbitration, which reduces the employee's bargaining leverage;
(iii) assuming that the economic damages are lower, lawyers could be discouraged to represent clients on a contingency fee in arbitration, thus creating a barrier to representation in arbitration proceedings; and
(iv) mandatory arbitration could have adverse effects on the employer's internal conflict resolution proceedings (e.g., peer review panels, mediation using external third-party neutrals).

Three recent events heated the debate. The first was the Supreme Court decision in the *Epic Systems Corp. v. Lewis* case (Epic Systems).[86] The second was the *Gretchen Carlson* case, which became public and started a wave of criticism against mandatory arbitration in the context of sexual harassment claims. The third is the introduction of The Forced Arbitration Injustice Repeal Act (FAIR Act) in the House of Representatives in February 2019.[87]

The legal question in the *Epic Systems* case involved a conflict between two federal statutes: the FAA and the National Labour Relations Act (NLRA). While the Supreme Court has interpreted the FAA as to allow the enforcement of arbitration agreements for claims arising from federal statutes, section 7 of the NLRA provides that '[e]mployees shall have the right to self-organization (...) and to engage in other concerted activities for the purpose of collective bargaining or other mutual aid or protection'. The issue debated in the *Epic Systems* is whether section 7 of the NLRA gives workers a substantive right to collective litigation, rendering unenforceable the arbitration agreements that waive such right. In a 5-4 decision issued in May 2018, the court ruled that arbitration agreements requiring individual arbitration are enforceable under the FAA, prevailing over the employee's federal right to bring claims in class or collective actions as provided in the NLRA.

In the *Gretchen Carlson* case, Gretchen Carlson, a former anchor at Fox News, sued the Fox News CEO, Roger Ailes, for sexual harassment. Her employment contract had a mandatory arbitration clause. Despite such provision, she managed to circumvent the clause and have her claim heard by the American courts. Gretchen did not

83. Antoine (*supra* n. 1) 4.
84. Alexander J.S. Colvin, *Mandatory Arbitration and Inequality of Justice in Employment*, 35 Berkeley J. Emp. & Lab. L. 71 (2014).
85. *Ibid.*, 89-90.
86. *Epic Sys. Corp. v. Lewis*, 584 U.S. __, No. 16-285 (21 May 2018).
87. https://www.congress.gov/bill/116th-congress/house-bill/1423/text (accessed 18 August 2019).

reveal how her lawyers managed to get around the clause, but she is now committed to speak out and has focused her efforts on ending forced arbitration.

According to Gretchen, sixty million Americans have arbitration clauses in their employment contracts, and she argues that such clauses 'take away your Seventh Amendment constitutional right to an open jury process if you find yourself in any kind of a dispute with your employer'.[88] Gretchen states that it might be in the companies' interest to keep these matters confidential, but, for the victims, making the case public could deter perpetrators of harassments. If the cases are confidential, not only will harassment continue, but often times no one knows who the perpetrator is and if he or she will continue on the job.

She then supports a federal law introduced by a bipartisan group of lawmakers, including Senators Lindsey Graham of South Carolina and Kirsten Gillibrand of New York, that would prohibit mandatory arbitration clauses to solve claims of sexual harassment or other discrimination in employment agreements.[89] The bill was also publicly supported by Microsoft, which also stated that it had eliminated forced arbitration agreements with employees who make sexual harassment claims.[90]

The third event mentioned was the introduction of the FAIR Act in the House of the Representatives on 28 February 2019 by the USA Representative Hank Johnson and US Senator Richard Blumenthal. As set forth in the bill, the purposes of the act are to:

> prohibit pre-dispute arbitration agreements that force arbitration of future employment, consumer, antitrust, or civil rights disputes, and prohibit agreements and practices that interfere with the rights of individuals, workers, and small businesses to participate in a joint, class, or collective action related to an employment, consumer, antitrust, or civil rights dispute.

In order to urge the Congress to pass the FAIR Act, on 1 May 2019 Google employees organized a protest, requesting people to make three calls to lawmakers, two to the caller's senators and one to their representative. In such calls, people would request the lawmakers to end employers' forced arbitration practices.[91]

Whether or not such initiatives will prevail, they relaunch an important debate regarding mandatory arbitration and access to justice. The Supreme Court's rulings seem not to agree with the argument that access to justice is being suppressed. When deciding the *Gilmer case*, the court stressed that the employee had suffered no loss of substantive rights: it was a mere change of forum.[92] Also when the Supreme Court

---

88. https://www.vox.com/conversations/2018/4/30/17292482/gretchen-carlson-me-too-sexual-harassment-supreme-court (accessed 18 August 2019).
89. H.R.4734 – Ending Forced Arbitration of Sexual Harassment Act of 2017, available at https://www.congress.gov/bill/115th-congress/house-bill/4734 The bill was introduced in December 2017, but has not still been voted. The current status, accessed on 19 August 2019, is 'Referred to the Subcommittee on Regulatory Reform, Commercial and Antitrust Law'.
90. https://www.nytimes.com/2017/12/19/technology/microsoft-sexual-harassment-arbitration.html (accessed 15 August 2019).
91. http://m.globallegalpost.com/corporate-counsel/make-that-call-say-googlers-99369231/ (accessed 18 August 2019).
92. *Gilmer v. Interstate/Johnson Lane Corp.*, 500 U.S. 20 (1991) 26-28. The court reached such conclusion citing *Mitsubishi Motors Corp. v. Soler Chrysler-Plymouth, Inc.*, 473 U.S. 614 at 473 U.S. 628 (1985), in which it was stated: '[b]y agreeing to arbitrate a statutory claim, a party does

found that the waiver to a class action in the *Epic System case* did not violate the NLRA, it also did not agree that such waiver would violate the employees' right of access to justice.

Such rulings are controversial, especially in employment relationships, in which the employee (weaker party) is often times left with no alternative rather than signing the clause if he or she wants to get or keep the job. Even though the USA is a pro-arbitration country and the FAA has been long interpreted as favouring arbitration, there is a thin line between pro-arbitration policy and denying access to justice. By waiving the right to pursue rights through a class action, employees may often give up on pursuing their rights at all, as the costs for doing so would be much higher than the benefits. Not only would the employers be less accountable to employees, but the employees' concerns could end up being silenced. One may question: would not that be the goal of the companies (employers), as we see an increasing number of employment contracts containing mandatory arbitration provisions?[93]

As the debate has been relaunched and opposing views to the current Supreme Court rulings have been exposed in the media and protests, the (re)introduction of the referred bills in the House of Representatives adds a fresh impetus to the arguments against mandatory arbitration. The goal apparently is to change the current scenario through an executive move, as it seems that the judiciary will not change its stand very soon.

[1] *The Other Side of the Coin: Is Mandatory Arbitration Really an Obstacle to Access to Justice?*

Several articles have been written and arguments debated regarding this topic. The goal of this section, limited by its length, is not to debate them extensively, but only to point out some of the main arguments raised, hopefully creating some food for thought. Among the reasons in favour of mandatory arbitration, some can be highlighted: the courts costs can be much higher in the USA than arbitration costs; confidentiality of arbitration can safeguard both employers and employees' interest against reputational damage; and there is no empirical evidence that employers would be favoured by arbitration.

Apart from the well-known advantages of arbitration, which can benefit employers and employees alike, such as speed and the possibility of choosing an expert to decide the case,[94] it has been said that litigating in USA courts can be prohibitive (costs

not forgo the substantive rights afforded by the statute; it only submits to their resolution in an arbitral, rather than a judicial, forum.' It also cited stated that although all statutory claims may not be appropriate for arbitration, '[h]aving made the bargain to arbitrate, the party should be held to it unless Congress itself has evinced an intention to preclude a waiver of judicial remedies for the statutory rights at issue'.

93. *See* (*supra* n. 78).

94. An interesting statement was made by American commentators: 'if the parties care more about business expertise than they do about legal expertise, they might opt for arbitration'. O'Hara et al. (*supra* n. 71) 970.

wise) to employees.[95] A study based on American Arbitration Association cases indicated that employees whose income level is below USD 60,000 may not afford to go to court, but could afford arbitration.[96] Should that be the case, we may face this situation: on the one hand, a person that receives a job offer could be forced to waive sensitive statutory rights and procedures by signing a mandatory arbitration provision - even if not fully agreeing with it. On the other hand, if such employee is low-paid, he or she could not gain access to those statutory procedures if the court costs were prohibitive. Could any of these choices be interpreted as denying access to justice? What would be the alternative?

The second argument is related to confidentiality. As it has been said, 'we keep hearing it over and over again: for individuals and companies alike, reputation is everything'.[97] For the employer it might be obvious the interest in keeping the disputes confidential: the preservation of a positive public image, which directly impacts its potential to attract talented employees, and also the good relationship with clients, investors, etc. However, the employee may also benefit from the confidentiality. It is known that often times when a company is hiring, it runs a background check of the potential employee. Having a lawsuit against a previous employee may have a negative impact on future recruitment processes.[98] Therefore, by keeping disputes confidential, the employees also preserve their professional reputation.

Finally, some studies have shown that it is questionable whether the presumption of bias favouring employers in arbitration is true.[99] As reported by a commentator after reviewing a few studies comparing win rates in employment arbitration, 'it cannot be said that mandatory arbitration in actual practice is detrimental to the individual employee'.[100] Thus, it could not be assumed that the private forum would necessarily favour the companies.

There are always two sides of every coin. First, on the one hand, confidentiality preserves both companies' and employees' reputation. On the other hand, confidentiality conceals practices that could be detrimental to the employee, such as the claims regarding sexual harassment, as discussed above.[101] Second, even if empirical studies are not conclusive as to whether employers are favoured in arbitration, such results could mask two situations. First, fearing an unfavourable outcome in arbitration,

---

95. Alexander Colvin and Mark D. Gough, *Individual Employment Rights Arbitration in the United States: Actors and Outcomes*, 1020, https://digitalcommons.ilr.cornell.edu/cgi/viewcontent.cgi?article=2018&context=articles (accessed 29 August 2019); O'Hara et al. (*supra* n. 71) 962; Antoine (*supra* n. 1) 20, 25-26. Christopher R. Drahozal, *Arbitration Costs and Forum Accessibility: Empirical Evidence*, 41 University of Michigan Journal of Law Reform, 813, 826 (2008).
96. Elizabeth Hill, *AAA Employment Arbitration: A Fair Forum at Low Cost*, 58 (2) Dispute Resolution Journal, 8, 10-11 (2003).
97. Milos Novovic, *Loose Lips Sink Ships: Mandatory Confidential Arbitration of Employment Disputes as a Reputational Risk Management Tool*, 31 Journal of International Arbitration 541, 543 (2014).
98. *Ibid*.
99. David Sherwyn, Samuel Estreicher and Michael Heise, *Assessing the Case for Employment Arbitration: A New Path for Empirical Research*, 57 Stan. L. Rev. 1557, 1578 (2005).
100. Theodore J. St. Antoine, *Mandatory Employment Arbitration: Keeping It Fair, Keeping It Lawful*, 60 Case W. Res. L. Rev. 629, 640 (2010).
101. *See* §7.03[A].

employees could choose to not even initiate arbitration proceedings. Second, these results do not address the issue of the *repeat player*. Usually, companies participate in several arbitration proceedings throughout the years. The company, because of its previous experience with arbitration, would have a greater understanding of how the proceedings work, which could result in practical advantages. It could be argued that the employer's experience with arbitration against a one-timer could, in some way, increase the employer's leverage in the dispute.[102]

The reflection that should be made here is the following: is this backlash groundless? Even if mandatory arbitration may bring advantage to both employers and employees, from the access to justice perspective, it would not matter. What really matters is that it should be made available to the parties a mechanism through which they can solve future disputes. If such mechanism is found in state courts or in arbitration, it is a mere change of forum, as stressed in *Gilmer*. If the parties want to choose a better or a worse mechanism, it is up to them. When they choose, they are not waiving their right of access to justice; they are actually exercising it in a different forum.

However, in mandatory arbitration, the parties no longer have a choice to make, because they only have one option: to arbitrate their disputes. Let us illustrate with a roadway system metaphor. You can get to city A through routes 1 and 2. It does not matter which route you take; you will get there. You will choose your route based on the road conditions, the traffic, the length, tolls, etc. If route 1 is shut down, you will still get to city A, but only through route 2. Due to an imposition of the governmental authority who shut one road down, you will not be able to choose which one you think is faster or shorter or safer, but your destination will be reached. Replace route 1 for courts, route 2 for arbitration, city A for judicial remedy and the roadway system for access to justice. Even if you get your remedy anyhow, the potential ways of getting it were restricted. It is true that they were not denied; but they were restricted.

§7.04 THE USA AND THE BRAZILIAN EXPERIENCES: TWO CASE STUDIES

Brazil and the USA are two countries which allow the arbitrability of labour disputes, both collective and individual. In Brazil, such possibility is more recent: collective labour disputes are held arbitrable since the promulgation of the Federal Constitution in 1988, and individual labour disputes since the Labour Reform in 2017. The USA, in its turn, due to a wide interpretation of the FAA promulgated in 1925, has seen labour disputes go to arbitration for a longer time. Differences, however, are not only related to how long these disputes have been held arbitrable in these two jurisdictions. The legal systems' provisions, their acceptance by the judiciary and the challenges they face in each country are also different.

102. Antoine (*supra* n. 100) 635.

As to the first difference, in Brazil, the arbitrability of labour disputes is expressly set forth both in the Constitution and in the CLT. In the USA, it was construed through case law and the Supreme Court interpretation of the FAA. The second difference relates to the fact that employment arbitration in Brazil is still incipient and, as discussed, courts have been reluctant to accept its arbitrability in individual disputes. On the contrary, in the USA, courts tend to enforce arbitration agreements and uphold arbitral awards in this field. As mentioned above, it is estimated that sixty million Americans have arbitration clauses in their employment contracts.

Finally, the challenges faced by both jurisdictions are different. In Brazil, the challenges are mainly related to the objective arbitrability of employment disputes and prohibitive arbitration costs, which are signalled as obstacles to access to justice by a protective judiciary system. In the USA, the courts seem to have overcome those issues. Obviously, labour arbitration agreements are also subject to the same principles of validity that any other contract. This means that, should there be any defect in the formation of the contract, for example defect of consent, the agreement would not be held valid. However, the courts' approach is to enforce the agreements otherwise. The backlash has not yet come from the courts, but from the society instead, which has been very critical about mandatory arbitration.

One could see the American experience as a light in the end of the tunnel for the Brazilian courts. A study conducted in the USA about arbitration clauses in CEOs-employment contracts is very interesting to the Brazilian market.[103] As explained, the Brazilian legislator drew a line separating the employees who may have their claims arbitrable from the ones who cannot. Such line was drawn based on the employee's income. As also explained, the goal of the legislator was to only allow employees with certain bargaining power to go to arbitration. CEOs certainly have bargaining power within their companies and boards, and that is why some of its conclusions are useful to the Brazilian market.

First, only about half of the contracts analysed in the study sample contained arbitration clauses.[104] This is already the first lesson: it is not because the judicial system allows arbitration that all employment contracts should contain an arbitration agreement. Differently from mandatory arbitration in the USA, in which millions of contracts reproduce arbitration clauses, CEOs have bargaining power, and here they negotiate the terms of the employment contract, including the arbitration clause. The same should apply in Brazil: not only because the law authorizes employees who earn above a certain income level to arbitrate their employment disputes, that all such employees should go to arbitration. A case-by-case analysis should be made. As stressed by such author, 'the mixture of choices between courts and arbitration suggests that either categorical enforcement or non-enforcement of arbitration clauses in employment contracts would be unwise'.[105]

103. O'Hara et al. (*supra* n. 71).
104. *Ibid.*, 962.
105. *Ibid.*, 999.

Second, after testing empirically a few hypotheses, the author reached interesting conclusions. A few of them could shed some light on contracts in which arbitration would be advisable in Brazil. First, industries experiencing rapid changes (mergers, acquisitions, bankruptcies etc.), as the CEOs would be interested in a quicker solutions, have more employment contracts with arbitration clauses.[106] Second, CEOs who receive a greater percentage of their compensation in the form of incentive pay are more likely to prefer arbitration.[107] Calculating the compensation in the form of incentive pay, for example, restricted stock grants and stock options grants, may be very complicated. In this case, both companies and CEOs would rather have a specialist or technical expert to do so.

Nevertheless, if, on the one hand, the Americans can shed some light on the arbitrability of employment disputes in Brazil, on the other, it should be acknowledged that it is very difficult to see employment arbitration thrive in Brazil like it did in the USA. Brazilian law explicitly demands the need of express consent of the employee when the parties enter into the arbitration agreement. Should it be proven that the consent was not freely manifested, it is highly difficult that the courts would enforce such agreements. We may see room for growth in arbitration of employment disputes, but not for mandatory arbitration provisions.

§7.05 CONCLUSION

From what has been discussed throughout the chapter, the main concern about employment arbitration is related to whether or not employees have their rights of accessing justice jeopardized when they go to arbitration. In Brazil and in the USA this concern reveals itself in different ways. While in Brazil the issues are of arbitrability and prohibitive arbitration costs, in the USA they are of mandatory arbitration and the restrictions it imposes on the parties.

In Brazil, the arbitrability obstacle should have been overcome with the Labour Reform: now employment disputes are arbitrable and courts should accept it. The costs issue though is more complicated and it could, indeed, restrict parties' ways of having their judicial remedy granted. Only a case-by-case analysis will tell.

In the USA, the debate is about the use of mandatory arbitration. Even though it has been stated by the Supreme Court that there is no denial of justice in such cases, in practice we see that the choice is been removed from the parties – actually, from the employee. Such removal does not deny the parties the right of accessing justice, but it does restrict it.

If we think about dispute resolution mechanism as a system composed of many doors through which parties can get judicial assistance (courts, arbitration, mediation etc.), offering more doors means offering more ways of getting the judicial remedy. A larger variety of doors would, in theory, mean a wider way of accessing justice. If, however, the doors are not - at least easily - opened, such feeling may be delusional.

106. *Ibid.*, 998.
107. *Ibid.*, 984.

In conclusion, employment arbitration can be a tool used to either amplify or restrict parties' access to justice. What will determine if such right was restricted or not is the case-by-case analysis. If used right, that is, if it is chosen by both employer and employee to settle disputes which require a technical, fast and cost-effective resolution, it will be an important tool to amplify the access to justice in the employment field.

CHAPTER 8

Access to Justice in Sports Arbitration

Ian Blackshaw

In this chapter we will examine the access to justice from a sports arbitration point of view and will focus mainly on the role played by the Court of Arbitration for Sport (CAS). The CAS is based in Lausanne in Switzerland and has been operating for thirty-six years. During this time, the CAS has built up a body of jurisprudence, which has come to be known as a 'Lex Sportiva' – Sports Law. The CAS is now handling between 550 and 600 cases a year. The CAS handles almost all of the appeals from the International Sports Federations (ISFs) and, in fact, such appeals to CAS are mandatory under the respective Regulations of the ISFs. In other words, this is a case of 'forced arbitration' rather than voluntary arbitration. In fact, access to the ordinary courts for the settlement of sports disputes is restricted under these regulations. We will address the question whether such a system serves the needs of justice particularly in the light of the recent Decisions of the European Court of Human Rights in the Pechstein and Mutu cases, where claims that they had not received a fair trial by CAS under Article 6 of the European Convention of Human Rights were dismissed by the court. However, in the Pechstein case, the court awarded her moral damages of €8,000 on the grounds that 'she had requested a public Hearing of her case and this had been refused by CAS.'

§8.01 INTRODUCTION

ADR has developed in the last thirty years or so because traditional methods of settling disputes, especially business ones, through the courts and so-called heavy duty arbitration, through such bodies as the ICC based in Paris, have become too expensive, too inflexible and too dilatory. ADR particularly lends itself to the settlement of sports-related disputes because of the special characteristics and dynamics of sport[1] – not least where sporting deadlines are in play, which is often the case! Also, the world of sport prefers to settle sports disputes 'within the family of sport' and not to wash its dirty sports linen in public. Furthermore, sport is now big business[2] and, as such, sports disputes continue to be on the increase and need to be resolved fairly, effectively and swiftly. Mediation as a form of ADR is particularly useful in settling amicably sports disputes, because, primarily, it gets the parties in dispute talking and negotiating with one another and it facilitates the restoration and maintenance of personal and business relationships.[3] Med-Arb, which combines mediation and arbitration – mediation to identify the issues and, if not successful,[4] arbitration to settle them – is also proving an effective method of dispute resolution in the sporting field. But, by far the most important body offering various forms of ADR in Sport is the CAS, which is based in Lausanne, Switzerland;[5] and the CAS will be the principal focus of this chapter.[6] Also, several national sports arbitration bodies have been set up and modelled on the CAS, including The Sport Dispute Resolution Centre of Canada (SDRCC) and The Japan Sports Arbitration Agency (JSAA).[7] However, *en passant*, mention should be made of some other sports bodies offering extrajudicial settlement of sports-related disputes, such as the Fédération Internationale de Football Association (FIFA) Dispute Resolution Chamber in disputes arising under the FIFA Regulations on the Status and Transfer of Players; the AAA, which handles disputes involving the United States Olympic Committee (USOC); the FIBA Arbitration Tribunal (FAT), which deals with disputes relating to basketball; Sport Resolutions (UK), which offers arbitration and mediation in sports disputes; and the WIPO (World Intellectual Property Organization) Arbitration and Mediation Center, especially in relation to the settlement of sports domain name disputes.

We will also cover the recent Decisions of the European Court of Human Rights in the Mutu and Pechstein Cases in which the independence of CAS was challenged – unsuccessfully.

To return to the CAS and put the subject of the CAS, the focus of this chapter, into its overall context, we will begin with a brief history of this important sports disputes

1. These characteristics have been recognized by the European Union in the White Paper on Sport of 11 July 2007 and have been encapsulated in the expression 'specificity of sport'. *See* further Ian Blackshaw, *The 'Specificity of Sport' and the EU White Paper on Sport: Some Comments*, 3-4 International Sports Law Journal 87 (2007). The EU concept of the 'specificity of sport' (the special nature of sport) has been incorporated in the new so-called sport article of the Lisbon Treaty (Article 165), which came into force on 1 December 2009.
2. Sport is reputedly worth more than 3% of world trade; and in the European Union (EU), sports accounts for 3.7% of the combined GNP of the EU Member States.
3. *See* Ian Blackshaw, *Sports Mediations: Preserving Sporting and Business Relationships* by Association for International Arbitration (AIA), Brussels, Belgium, November 2010 Newsletter, at pp. 9 & 10.
4. Where Mediation is appropriate, it enjoys a general success rate of 85%.
5. *See* the CAS official website at 'www.tas-cas.org'.
6. On the subject of the settlement of sports-related disputes by Arbitration and Mediation generally, *see* Ian S. Blackshaw, *Sport, Mediation and Arbitration* (TMC Asser Press 2009).
7. *Ibid.*, 77-78.

resolution body, which was set up in 1983 and opened its doors for business in 1984. This means that the CAS has been operating for thirty-five years.

§8.02 BRIEF HISTORY OF THE CAS

[A] Origins

At the beginning of the 1980s, an increasing number of international sports disputes and the lack of any independent body to deal with them in a flexible, quick, inexpensive and binding manner prompted a number of international sports federations to look at this situation and see what could be done. Soon after assuming the Presidency of the International Olympic Committee (IOC) in 1981, the late Juan Antonio Samaranch had the idea of creating a sports court that would become 'the supreme court of world sport'. The following year at an IOC Meeting in Rome, the late Judge Keba Mbaye, from Senegal, an IOC member and at the time a Judge at the International Court of Justice in The Hague, was asked to chair a working party with the aim of preparing the Statutes of a sports dispute resolution body that, in time, would become known as the 'Court of Arbitration for Sport'.

In 1983, the IOC officially ratified the Statutes of the CAS, which came into force on 30 June 1984. On the same date, the CAS became operational under the late Judge Mbaye as its President, a position he has occupied with distinction until his death in 2007.

[B] The First Ten Years

The 1984 CAS Statutes were supplemented by a set of Procedural Regulations. Both were slightly modified in 1990. Under these regulations, the CAS was composed of sixty members appointed by the IOC, the International Federations (IFs), the National Olympic Committees (NOCs) and the IOC President – fifteen members each. The IOC President had to choose members outside the other three groups. All the operating costs of the CAS were borne by the IOC. In general, the proceedings were free of charge, except for financial disputes, in which the parties could be required to pay a share of the costs. The CAS Statutes could be modified only by the IOC meeting in General Session, on the proposal of the IOC Executive Board.

The CAS Statutes and Regulations provided for only one kind of contentious procedure, irrespective of the nature of the dispute. In addition, there was also a 'consultation procedure' open to sports bodies or individuals. Through this procedure, which no longer exists, the CAS could give a legal opinion on any sports-related issue.

In 1991, the CAS published a 'Guide to Arbitration', which included several model arbitration clauses, including one for incorporation in the statutes or regulations of international sports federations. This clause foresaw the creation of special rules to settle disputes arising out of a decision taken by a sports federation (the 'Appeals Procedure'). The first such body to adopt this clause was the International Equestrian Federation (FEI).

The next significant development was in February 1992, when a horse rider, named Elmar Gundel, lodged an appeal for arbitration by the CAS, based on an arbitration clause in the FEI statutes, in which he challenged a decision rendered by the FEI. This decision, which followed a horse doping case, disqualified the rider, suspending and also fining him. The award rendered by CAS on 15 October 1992 found partly in favour of the rider (the suspension was reduced from three months to one month). Dissatisfied with the CAS ruling, Gundel filed an appeal with the Swiss Federal Tribunal (Swiss Supreme Court). He disputed the validity of the award, on the grounds that it was rendered by a tribunal that did not meet the conditions of impartiality and independence needed to be considered as a proper arbitration court. In its judgement of 15 March 1993, the tribunal recognized the CAS as a true court of arbitration. And noted, *inter alia*, that the CAS was not an organ of the FEI; that it did not receive instructions from this federation; and that it retained sufficient autonomy with regard to it, in that it placed at the disposal of the CAS only three arbitrators out of the maximum of sixty members of which the CAS was composed. However, in its judgement, the tribunal drew attention to numerous links between the CAS and the IOC: the fact that the CAS was financed almost exclusively by the IOC; the fact that the IOC was competent to modify the CAS Statutes; and the considerable power given to the IOC and its President to appoint CAS members. In the tribunal's view, such links would be sufficiently serious to call into question the independence of the CAS if the IOC were a party to proceedings before it.[8]

As Matthieu Reeb, Secretary General of the CAS, has remarked: 'The Federal Tribunal's message was thus perfectly clear: the CAS had to be made more independent of the IOC both organizationally and financially.'[9] So this decision led to some major reforms of the CAS in 1994.

[C] The 1994 Reforms

First, the CAS Statutes and Regulations were completely revised to make them more efficient and to modify the structure of the institution to make it more independent of the IOC, which had sponsored it since its creation. The most important change resulting from these changes was the creation of an 'International Council of Arbitration for Sport' (ICAS) to deal with the running and financing of the CAS, thereby taking the place of the IOC (see below).

Another major change was the creation of two Arbitration Divisions of the CAS (the 'Ordinary Division' and the 'Appeals Division') in order to make a clear distinction between disputes of sole instance and those arising from a decision rendered by a sports body. And the CAS reforms were enshrined in a new Code of Sports-related Arbitration, which came into force on 22 November 1994.

8. *See* further comments on this landmark case in Ian Blackshaw, 'CAS 92/A/63 GUNDEL v FEI', in Jack Anderson (ed.), *Leading Cases in Sports Law* (TMC Asser Press 2013).
9. *See infra* n. 39.

All these reforms were approved in Paris on 22 June 1994 with the signing of the 'Agreement Concerning the Constitution of the International Council of Arbitration for Sport'- known as the 'Paris Agreement'.

[D] Later Developments

The ICAS was responsible for the creation of the decentralized offices of the CAS (referred to below) and also the 'Ad Hoc' Divisions (also referred to below); as well as the introduction of a 'Mediation Procedure' (see below).

More recently, the CAS has moved to new headquarters at the Chateau de Bethusy in Lausanne. This not only provides the CAS with the possibility to expand its personnel and facilities to cope with its ever-increasing workload, but also represents a further - physical - separation and independence of the CAS from the IOC. The CAS is also on the move again to larger premises at the Chateau de Beaulieu in Lausanne.

§8.03 THE INTERNATIONAL COUNCIL OF ARBITRATION FOR SPORT (ICAS)

The ICAS is the supreme organ of the CAS. Its main function is to safeguard the independence of the CAS and the rights of the parties appearing before it.[10] Thus, it is responsible for the administration and financing of the CAS. The ICAS has twenty members, who, on appointment, must sign a declaration in which they undertake to exercise their functions in a personal capacity, with total objectivity and independence. The members comprise five sports persons; five independent persons, who are outside the Olympic Movement and sport generally; five persons from the IOC; five persons from the Association of Summer Olympics International Sports Federations (ASOIF) and the Association of Winter Olympics International Sports Federations (AIWF); and five persons from the Association of National Olympic Committees (ANOC). ICAS members are appointed for four-year renewable terms. ICAS, like CAS itself, is a Swiss Foundation based in Lausanne, Switzerland. The ICAS appoints the CAS arbitrators and mediators and approves the budget and the accounts of the CAS.[11] The funding of CAS is shared between the constituents of CAS as follows: 4/12 by the IOC; 3/12 by the ASOIF; 1/12 by the AIWF; and 4/12 by the ANOC.

§8.04 THE ORGANIZATION OF CAS

The CAS, also known by its French acronym TAS (*Tribunal Arbitral du Sport*) - the official languages are French and English - is based in Lausanne, Switzerland, and has two permanent branches in Sydney, Australia, and New York, USA, facilitating access

10. For a complete list of the functions of ICAS, *see* Article S6 of the Code of Sports-related Arbitration (2016 Edition in force from 1 January 2016).
11. *Ibid.*, *see* generally on the ICAS Articles S4-S11.

to CAS for parties residing in Oceania and North America.[12] Because CAS is based in Switzerland, with its seat in Lausanne, the CAS is generally governed by Swiss Law.[13] It has its legal seat in Lausanne for all purposes, even when it hears cases outside Switzerland.[14] The CAS Court Office, headed by the Secretary General and assisted by several counsel and secretaries, supervises the arbitration and mediation procedures and acts as a registry; it also organizes the ad hoc divisions and deals with other administrative matters.

The CAS has a minimum of 150 arbitrators, who are specialists in arbitration and sports law.[15] They are appointed for four-year renewable terms and must sign a 'letter of independence' confirming that they will act impartially. The ICAS appoints the CAS Arbitrators in accordance with certain prescribed criteria.[16] In establishing the list of CAS arbitrators, the ICAS must 'consider continental representation and the different judicial cultures'.[17] The CAS also has a permanent president, who is an Australian Lawyer, John Coates, appointed in 2011 in succession to the previous President and Founder Member of CAS. Coates' mandate has recently been renewed for a further term of four years (see later on this subject).

CAS arbitrators, who sit on panels composed of one or three members, are not generally obliged to follow earlier decisions (*stare decisis*), but they usually do so in the interests of legal certainty.[18] Thus, a useful body of sports law (*lex sportiva*) is steadily being built up.[19] The extent to which this is happening continues to be the subject of academic debate.[20]

The CAS has recently introduced a new division: the Anti-Doping Division (ADD) to deal with anti-doping rule violations. The ADD has two instances: a first instance

12. *See* generally Matthieu Reeb, *The Role and Functions of the Court of Arbitration for Sport (CAS)*, 2 The International Sports Law Journal 21, 23-25 (2002).
13. For more information, log onto the CAS official website at 'www.tas-cas.org'.
14. For the legal and practical significance of this, *see* the Judgement of the New South Wales Court of Appeal of 1 September 2000 in the case of *Angela Raguz v. Rebecca Sullivan* [2000] NSWCA 240. In that case, a legal challenge against a CAS arbitral award was dismissed on the ground of lack of jurisdiction because the court upheld the choice of Lausanne, Switzerland as the seat (i.e., place) of arbitration under the CAS Code of Sports-related Arbitration.
15. At the time of writing, namely June 2019, there are some 350 CAS arbitrators, from 87 countries, and around 550–600 cases are now registered with the CAS each year.
16. These are laid down in Article S14 of the Code of Sports-related Arbitration.
17. *Ibid.*, Article S16.
18. *See* Case of *UCI v. J. 7 NCB*, CAS 97/176 Award of 28 August 1998, 14.
19. From time to time, the CAS publishes Digests of Cases, but respecting, as appropriate, the confidentiality of the parties. The latest Digest of CAS Awards Volume III covers the period the period 2001 – 2003 and was published in 2004 (Matthieu Reeb, Digest of Cas Awards II, 2001-2003 (Kluwer Law International 2004)). Previous Volumes I and II covered the periods 1986-1998 and 1998-2000 (Matthieu Reeb, Digest of Cas Awards II, 1998-2000 (Kluwer Law International 2002) and Matthieu Reeb, Digest of Cas Awards I, 1986-1998 (Kluwer Law International 2001)).
20. *See* Ken Foster, *Is There a Global Sports Law?* 2(1) Entertainment Law 1 (2003). Foster argues that the CAS as an institutional forum is not yet 'globally comprehensive'. And *see also* James A.R. Nafziger, *International Sports Law* (2d ed., Transnational Publishers, Inc. 2004) 48-61. Prof Nafziger characterises the CAS *lex sportiva* as 'still incipient'.

and an appeal instance.[21] The CAS has also introduced a 'pro bono' legal representation service for those athletes who would not ordinarily, on economic grounds, be able to afford to take their cases to CAS, operated by the Legal Aid Commission.[22]

CAS Arbitrations are conducted in accordance with the Code of Sports-related Arbitration, the latest version of which dates and is effective from 1 January 2019. The CAS is able to grant, subject to certain conditions, provisional and conservatory measures, such as orders to safeguard vital evidence, for example, in doping cases.[23] The CAS can also order expedited hearings in appropriate cases, a useful measure, where sporting deadlines apply, for example, in eligibility disputes where the sporting event concerned is due to take place imminently.[24] In general, CAS ordinary proceedings take between six and twelve months; whereas CAS appeal proceedings must be completed within three months from the transfer of the file to the Panel. CAS arbitration proceedings are generally confidential, although, as result of the ECtHR Decision in *Pechstein* (see later), public hearings of CAS cases are envisaged in future.

During the Olympic Games, the CAS operates an Ad Hoc Division (AHD), which was first set up on 28 September 1995, for the Centennial Atlanta Summer Games of the Modern Era in 1996, resolving disputes relating to the games within 24 hours and free of charge.[25] The AHD decides cases 'pursuant to the Olympic Charter, the applicable regulations, general principles of law and the rules of law, the application of which it deems appropriate'.[26] All athletes participating in the Summer and Winter Olympic Games have to submit their disputes to the CAS AHD. The actual submission forms part of the Athlete's Entry Form to participate in the Olympics. The standard Arbitration Clause for the AHD, which form part of the Code of Sports-related Arbitration, is as follows:

> I agree that any dispute, controversy or claim arising out of, in connection with, or on the occasion of, the Olympic Games, not resolved after exhaustion of the legal remedies established by my NOC, the International Federation governing my sport, ... and the IOC, shall be submitted exclusively to the Court of Arbitration for Sport (CAS) for final and binding arbitration in accordance with the 'Arbitration Rules for the ... Olympiad in ... [Host City].'

The CAS shall rule on its jurisdiction and has the exclusive power to order provisional and conservatory measures. The decisions of the CAS shall be final and binding. I shall not institute any claim, arbitration or litigation, or seek any other form of relief, in any other court or tribunal. The National Olympic Committee (NOC) confirms that all the relevant rules have been brought to the notice of the

21. For further information, *see* Ian Blackshaw, *Doping: CAS establishes an anti-doping division*, https://www.sportsandtaxation.com/2019/01/doping-cas-establishes-an-anti-doping-division/ (accessed 27 June 2019).
22. CAS Statutes, S6 10. & S7 2.b.
23. Article R37 of the CAS Code of Sports-related Arbitration; *see also* Ian Blackshaw & Tilo Pachmann, 'CAS Provisional and Conservatory Measures and Other Options to Be Granted Interim Legal Relief' in Antoine Duval & Antonio Rigozzi (eds.), *The Yearbook of International Sports Arbitration* (Asser Press 2015).
24. Article R 44.4 of the CAS Code of Sports-related Arbitration.
25. *See* Ian Blackshaw, *A sporting decision in just 24 hours*, The Times (23 July 2002).
26. Article 61.2 of the Olympic Charter in force as from 26 June 2019.

athlete/coach/trainer/official, and it has been authorized by the National Sports Federation concerned to sign this entry form on its behalf.

Of course, this mandatory submission to the CAS AHD raises questions of jurisdiction and, in particular, the possible 'ousting of the jurisdiction of the ordinary courts' for the settlement of sports disputes arising during the Olympics. This is an interesting and thorny issue; it is all a matter of consent and a real and genuine consent at that![27]

Athletes who fail to give this 'undertaking' will not be allowed to participate in the games, the pinnacle of their sporting achievements, even though they have qualified on sporting grounds to do so.

Quaere: is this a valid and legally binding consent to arbitration? Also, can the jurisdiction of the ordinary courts be ousted in this way?

As is well known, arbitration is a consensual process and relies on the agreement of the parties who submit to it. Thus, is the above undertaking the result of an exercise of freewill on the part of the athletes, who, in reality, are not given any choice in the matter if they wish to participate in the games and, if given the choice, would not sign it?

The juridical position seems to be clear and is as follows. The agreement to refer a dispute to arbitration is a contract in law; and like any other contract requires mutual consent ('consensus ad idem').

Such consent must be the result of the exercise of independent freewill. If a party is forced into a contract against his/her will, the lack of a real and genuine consent will vitiate the contract. In other words, there is no legally binding agreement and nothing, therefore, to enforce by law. These are the basic and widely accepted rules of contract law.

And what about the other matter of ousting the jurisdiction of the courts, which, generally speaking, is against public policy (not an easy concept to define in any jurisdiction!) and, as such, any attempt - even by agreement - to do so is void?

§8.05 CASTER SEMENYA CASE

It would be remiss, I think, not to include a brief mention of this case, which has been described by some commentators as perhaps the most important and influential case to be handled to date by the CAS in its thirty-five years' history and has been characterized by the CAS itself as 'pivotal'![28] The relevance of the Caster Semenya case is that it shows that the international sporting community relies on arbitration offered by CAS for settling international sporting disputes, especially those against the powerful international sports federations, such as the IAAF.

27. *See* Ian Blackshaw, *CAS at the London 2012 Olympics: a question of jurisdiction*, 3 Global Sports Law and Taxation Reports 11, 11-12 (2012).
28. For more detailed information on the CAS Decision in the Caster Semenya Case, *see* the CAS Media Release of 1 May 2019, which is reproduced on the GSLTR website at www.gsltr.com – access to which is free – on the same date.

The case involves a claim by the South African athlete, Caster Semenya and Athletics South Africa against the IAAF (International Association of Athletics Federations) regarding the 'IAAF Eligibility Regulations for Female Classification (Athletes with Differences of Sex Development' (DSD Regulations) on the grounds of discrimination.

A Hearing was held in Lausanne, Switzerland, at the CAS Headquarters on 18–22 February 2019, and subsequently the parties filed additional submissions and materials. At the hearings, a veritable array of witnesses and experts were heard, hence the length of the Hearing and the delay in the rendering of the CAS Award. Amongst the witnesses were the President of the International Association of Athletics Federation (IAAF), Lord Sebastian Coe, who gave evidence at the outset of the Hearing, and the appellant, Caster Semenya, who had the last word at the close of the Hearing.

On 30 April 2019, in a 165-page award, the three-member CAS Panel rejected, by a majority, the claim, holding that the appellants had not been able to establish that the Differences of Sexual Development (DSD) Regulations were 'invalid'. Furthermore, whilst the Panel found, on the basis of the evidence submitted by the parties, that the DSD Regulations were discriminatory, such discrimination is a necessary, reasonable and proportionate means of achieving the IAAF aim of preserving the integrity of female athletes in the events concerned – the female 400m – 1 mile. However, the Panel expressed some 'serious' concerns as to the future application, in practice, of the DSD Regulations.

It is reported that Semenya has appealed against the CAS Decision to the Swiss Federal Supreme Court. This case will, no doubt, be poured over and commented on by sports lawyers for some time to come and may lead to other similar DSD and transgender cases. Be that as it may, however, the case clearly demonstrates the importance of the CAS and the confidence that the worldwide sporting community places in this body for settling international sports disputes by arbitration!

§8.06 WILHELMSHAVEN FC CASE

Likewise, a brief mention also needs to be made of this case.[29] As in the Pechstein and Mutu cases (see below), justice was sought outside the normal sports arbitration system – that is, outside the CAS. The German football club, SV Wilhelmshaven (Wilhelmshaven), had been ordered by FIFA to pay training compensation, pursuant to the FIFA Regulations on the Status of Players and Transfers, to two Argentinian clubs in respect of a player, who had been trained by these clubs. Wilhelmshaven consistently refused to pay the compensation and appealed against the FIFA decision to the CAS, which upheld the FIFA ruling on both claims. However, Wilhelmshaven did not challenge the CAS ruling before the Swiss Federal Tribunal (Supreme Court). Eventually, a FIFA disciplinary committee imposed fines on Wilhelmshaven, and, following further fines, league points were also forfeited and the club was relegated to a lower league.

29. *SV Wilhelmshaven eV/Norddeutscher Fußball-Verband eV.* BGHZ 212, 70-89

After further unsuccessful proceedings before the CAS, Wilhelmshaven decided to refer the matter to the German national courts and to fight the forfeiture of the league points, as well as their relegation, through various instances, up to the German Federal Court (BGH).

This court, on 20 September 2016, dismissed the appeal by NFV (the North German Football Association), based on the principle that a parent association makes rules only for its members. Wilhelmshaven was a member of the NFV, but it was neither a member of the German Federal Football Association, Deutscher Fußball-Bund (DFB), nor of FIFA. The court explained that an association makes rules only for its members. The mere fact that the NFV was a member of the DFB and that the DFB was a member of FIFA, did not provide the legal basis on which the FIFA decision could be enforced against Wilhelmshaven.[30]

§8.07 THE LEGAL STATUS OF CAS AWARDS

Awards made by the CAS, like other international arbitral awards, are legally enforceable generally in accordance with the rules of International Private Law, and also specifically under the provisions of the NYC, signed by more than 125 countries. The CAS is also recognized under the European Convention on the Recognition of the Legal Personality of International Non-Governmental Organizations. Thus, the CAS decisions are legally effective and can be enforced internationally. This is particularly important in the case of disputes involving intellectual property rights, especially trademarks, which are generally of a territorial nature.

§8.08 LEGAL CHALLENGES TO CAS AWARDS

The CAS awards can be legally challenged in the Swiss Federal Court, also based in Lausanne, by a dissatisfied party, but only in very limited circumstances, in line with general arbitration legal principles, under the provisions of article 190(2) of the Swiss Federal Code on Private International Law of 18 December 1987. This article reads (in translation) as follows:

> [The Award] can be attacked only:
>
> (a) if a sole arbitrator was designated irregularly or the arbitral tribunal was constituted irregularly;
> (b) if the arbitral tribunal erroneously held that it had or did not have jurisdiction;
> (c) if the arbitral tribunal ruled on matters beyond the claims submitted to it or failed to rule on one of the claims;
> (d) if the equality of the parties or their right to be heard in an adversarial proceeding was not respected;
> (e) if the award is incompatible with Swiss public policy.

30. *See* further on this case *see* Ian Blackshaw, *International Sports Law: An Introductory Guide* (Asser Press 2017) 27-29.

In practice, perhaps ground (d) is the most important one, and the CAS bends over backwards, in each case, to ensure that the parties are properly heard and receive a fair Hearing.[31]

In practice, there have been few legal challenges to CAS awards. In 2003, in a challenge concerning the independence of the CAS, in view of its association with and partial funding by the IOC, the Swiss Federal Court held that the CAS offered all the guarantees of independence and impartiality to be regarded as a real court of arbitration, even where the IOC - as in that case - was a party in its proceedings[32].

In that case, two Russian cross-country skiers, Larissa Lazutina and Olga Danilova unsuccessfully questioned the independence of CAS in the Swiss Federal Tribunal (TFS) in 2003. These skiers were disqualified by the IOC after the 2002 Winter Olympic Games in Salt Lake City for doping offences. The International Ski Federation (FIS) suspended both of them for two years. Their appeal to CAS, calling for the IOC and FIS decisions to be overruled was dismissed. Their legal challenge to the TFS on the grounds that CAS, because it is a creature of and receives some funding from the IOC, is not a truly independent body, was also dismissed. The TFS held that CAS offered all the guarantees of independence and impartiality to be regarded as a real court of arbitration, even where the IOC - as in the Russian skiers' case - is a party to its proceedings. On the question of the partial financing of the CAS by the IOC, the court concluded as follows:

> To conclude our discussion of the financing of the CAS, it should be added that there is not necessarily any relationship of cause and effect between the way a judicial body is financed and its level of independence. This is illustrated, for example, by the fact that State courts in countries governed by the rule of law are often required to rule on disputes involving the State itself, without their judges' independence being questioned on the ground that they are financially linked to the State. Similarly, the CAS arbitrators should be presumed capable of treating the IOC on an equal footing with any other party, regardless of the fact that it partly finances the Court of which they are members and which pays their fees.[33]

However, the TFS made the following observation/recommendation to make the list of arbitrators more transparent for the benefit of the parties selecting them:

> It would be preferable, if the published list were to indicate, alongside the name of each arbitrator, which of the five categories mentioned in Article S14 they belonged to (arbitrators chosen from those proposed by the IOC, the Ifs and the NOCs; arbitrators chosen to safeguard the interests of the athletes; arbitrators chosen from among persons independent of the three aforementioned bodies) and, for those in two of these categories, by which IF or NOC they were proposed. The parties would then be able to appoint their arbitrator with full knowledge of the

31. *See* the Judgement of 22 March 2007 in the ATP Tour Appeal case brought before the Swiss Federal Court against a CAS Award of 23 May 2006; Reference: 4P 172/2006, which was brought under either paragraph (d) or paragraph (e) of article 190(2) of the Swiss Federal Code on Private International Law of 18 December 1987.
32. *See* Judgement of 27 May 2003 of the First Civil Division of the Swiss Federal Tribunal in the case of *A. & B. v. International Olympic Committee and International Ski Federation* (4P.267/2002; 4P.268/2002; 4P.269/2002; and 4P.270/2002).
33. *Ibid.*, paragraph 3.3.3.1.

> facts. For example, it would prevent a party in dispute with the IOC, in the belief that he was choosing an arbitrator completely unconnected to the latter, from actually appointing a person who was proposed by that organisation but who is not an IOC member (see Art. S14 of the Code, which advocates this practice).[34]

In the most recent legal challenge against the independence of the CAS, on 20 February 2018, the First Civil Chamber of the TFS unanimously confirmed the independence of CAS from the FIFA.[35]

Finally, mention should also be made briefly of a landmark decision of the TFS concerning the CAS. On 27 March 2012, the TFS overturned an Appeal decision by the CAS in the case of Matuzalem Francelino da Silva, a professional Brazilian footballer, who currently plays for SS Lazio Spa. This case has a long procedural history and the Swiss Court, for the very first time in the history of the Swiss Private International Law Statute, annulled the CAS decision for a violation of Swiss public policy, pursuant to the provisions of article 190 (2) (e) of this Statute. This particular ground for legally challenging arbitral awards in Switzerland, whether rendered by CAS or other Swiss arbitral bodies, is notoriously difficult to establish in practice, as 'public policy' ('*ordre public*') is a complex and vague concept and one that is restrictively assessed and interpreted.[36]

§8.09 THE ECtHR DECISIONS IN *PECHSTEIN* AND *MUTU*

The Decisions of the European Court of Human Rights in the *Pechstein* and *Mutu* cases concerned the access to justice of the sports persons concerned through the existing system of sports arbitration through the Court of Arbitration for Sport. As such, they are landmark decisions tending to uphold this legality and relevance of this system.[37] The key findings of the ECtHR in these Cases may be summarized as follows:

- 'Forced' arbitration clauses, such as those commonly used in Sports Governing Bodies' Regulations are not an effective waiver of rights under article 6.1 of the ECHR.
- CAS is a 'tribunal established by law' for the purposes of article 6.1 of the ECHR and must therefore comply with its requirements.
- The CAS system is sufficiently 'independent and impartial' to satisfy the requirements of article 6.1 of the ECHR.
- Neither Adrian Mutu nor Claudia Pechstein's rights to have their cases determined by an 'independent and impartial tribunal' under article 6.1 of the ECHR were violated.

34. *Ibid.*, paragraph 3.3.3.2.
35. For an analysis of this decision, please *see* the Arbitration Newsletter Switzerland of 3 April 2018 of the Swiss Law Firm of Thouvenin, https://thouvenin.com/wp-content/uploads/2018/04/20180403Arbitration-Newsletter-Switzerland-.pdf (accessed 27 June 2019).
36. For further information on this important TFS ruling, *see* Alara E. Yazicioglu, *Matuzalem case: red card to FIFA?* Global Sports Law and Taxation Reports 17, 17-21 (2012).
37. *Mutu & Pechstein v. Switzerland* (2 October 2018, nos 40575/10 et 67474/10; full judgment currently only available in French).

- Claudia Pechstein's right to a 'public Hearing' under article 6.1 of the ECHR was, however, violated.

The ECtHR Decisions were rendered with a 5-2 majority of the judges. The dissenting opinions from the Swiss and Cyprus Judges, Helen Keller and Georgios A. Serghides respectively, on the following substantive aspects of the majority judgement, may be summarized as follows:

[A] CAS Lack of Independence and Impartiality

The dissenting judges underline that the required level of proof of influence by the majority in the case of Pechstein, seems to indicate that the existence of the influence needs to be proven for each arbitrator on an individual basis. The judges argue that this exceeds what is normally required in cases of objective impartiality and independence.

The judges further state that, according to the settled case-law of the ECtHR, it is not sufficient for arbitrators to be impartial individually if the *structure* of the organization lacks the appearance of independence and impartiality. The court must have regard to 'the manner of appointment of its members and the duration of their term of office ... the existence of guarantees against external pressures ... and the question whether the body presents an appearance of independence' (citing *Campbell and Fell v. the United Kingdom*, 28 June 1984, nos 7819/77 and 7878/77, § 78).

When the court proceeds with such an analysis, it should not necessarily examine the lack of independence or impartiality of a certain judge. It should examine whether the organization concerned, as a whole, has a balanced composition. For instance, when examining the impartiality and the independence of an employment tribunal, the court would not have decided that the tribunal under examination needs to be deemed as being impartial on the sole basis that the judge who rendered the decision under examination was found to be impartial and independent. The court would have examined the structure of the tribunal and would have deemed the tribunal to be dependent and partial if, for instance, the tribunal concerned was exclusively formed from the representatives of employers. The same line of reasoning should have been applied, *mutatis mutandis*, to CAS.

In the same vein, the two judges underlined that the closed list of arbitrators, from which athletes must choose their arbitrator is problematic, since that list is administered by the ICAS. In particular, the two judges were not convinced by the Swiss Supreme Court's arguments in defence of a closed list, namely that non-specialized arbitrators would act as lawyers for the parties rather than impartial adjudicators and stated that 'in areas that are way more technical than sports – such as the pharmaceutical industry or aviation – the parties can freely choose their arbitrator without any problems'.

[B] The Court Should Have Analysed the Criterion of Being Established by Law in More Detail

The dissenting judges argue that the majority should have given some additional guidance as to how private entities, such as CAS, may fulfil the requirement of 'being established by law'. On this point, the judges recalled the Suda case (*Suda v. Tcheque Republic*, 28 October 2010, nos 1643/06, § 53), in which the ECtHR decided that the tribunal under examination was not established by law, given the fact that it was composed of arbitrators enumerated in a closed list established by a limited liability company and that the competence of the tribunal arose from the consent of Mr Suda. The judges stated that CAS, which is a part of ICAS, a private Swiss entity, is similar to the tribunal examined in the Suda case. It is not clear, therefore, why the tribunal in the Suda case was not considered to be established by law, whereas the CAS was. Hence, more explanation was needed on such an important issue.

[C] Mutu's 'voluntary' Waiver Was Used to His Detriment

The dissenting judges did not follow the majority in its reasoning according to which the claims advanced by Mutu, regarding the lack of impartiality of CAS, must be rejected on the ground that he voluntarily submitted his case to the jurisdiction of the CAS and not to that of an ordinary court. The dissenting judges found a contradiction in how, on the one hand, the waiver was not found to be unequivocal, when, on the other hand, the majority took Mutu's 'voluntary waiver' into account when ruling on his complaint about a lack of impartiality. The judges went on to state that, more generally, where a procedure does not offer the minimum guarantees of impartiality and independence, the ECtHR should more strictly analyse whether the applicant's waiver was indeed 'free, lawful and unequivocal'. According to the two judges, it seems difficult to conceive that an individual could waive his right to an independent and impartial tribunal and still be subject to a 'fair procedure' within the meaning of Article 6(1) of the ECHR.[38]

§8.10 OTHER REACTIONS TO THE ECtHR DECISIONS IN *PECHSTEIN* AND *MUTU*

The decisions have produced a number of mixed reactions as follows.

38. For an analytical review of these dissenting opinions, described as being 'powerful', *see* Andy Brown, *Mixed message from ECHR on CAS's independence,* The Sports Integrity Initiative, https://www.sportsintegrityinitiative.com/mixed-message-from-echr-on-cass-independence/ (accessed 27 June 2019).

[A] The CAS Reaction to the Pechstein and Mutu ECtHR Decisions

We publish below the Media Release of the CAS of 2 October 2018 on the ECtHR Decisions in the Pechstein and Mutu Cases and, as to be expected, the CAS stresses that the Decisions vindicate its independence and impartiality:

> **'MEDIA RELEASE**
>
> **STATEMENT OF THE COURT OF ARBITRATION FOR SPORT (CAS) ON THE DECISION MADE BY THE EUROPEAN COURT OF HUMAN RIGHTS (ECHR) IN THE CASE BETWEEN CLAUDIA PECHSTEIN / ADRIAN MUTU AND SWITZERLAND**
>
> **THE ECHR RECOGNIZES THAT CAS FULFILS THE REQUIREMENTS OF INDEPENDENCE AND IMPARTIALITY**
>
> *Lausanne, 2 October 2018* – The Court of Arbitration for Sport (CAS) has noted the ruling of the European Court of Human Rights (ECHR) in relation to the cases between Claudia Pechstein (speed skating / Germany), Adrian Mutu (football / Romania) and Switzerland. Both athletes filed appeals at the ECHR in 2010 against judgments of the Swiss Federal Tribunal (SFT) which confirmed the decisions rendered by CAS in these matters. The ECHR has dismissed all claims, except one concerning the right to a public Hearing. The ECHR judgment, published on its website, determines that:
>
> - The ECHR considers that there is an interest in allowing the disputes arising in professional sport, in particular those with an international dimension, to be submitted to a specialized jurisdiction, able to rule on such cases in a quick and inexpensive manner. (...) The recourse to an international arbitral tribunal, unique and specialized, facilitates a certain procedural uniformity and strengthens the legal certainty. That is all the more true when the awards of that arbitral tribunal may be appealed before the supreme court of a single country, i.e. the Swiss Federal Tribunal, which renders final judgments.
> - The ECHR recognizes that a non-State dispute resolution mechanism of first and/or second instance, with a possible appeal, even limited, before a State court, as a last instance, is appropriate in this area (of international sport).
> - Considering the particular nature of the CAS arbitration system, with mandatory arbitration clauses inserted in the regulations of sports federations, such arbitration shall offer the guarantees provided by Article 6 § 1 of the European Convention on Human Rights.
> - As far as the funding of CAS by sports entities is concerned, the ECHR emphasizes that State courts are always financed by governments and considers that this aspect is not sufficient to establish a lack of independence or impartiality of these jurisdictions in disputes between citizens and the State. By analogy, it is not possible to establish a lack of independence or impartiality of the CAS based on its funding system.
> - The ECHR does not see any relevant grounds to overturn the consistent jurisprudence of the Swiss Federal Tribunal stating that the system of a mandatory list of arbitrators complies with the constitutional requirements of independence and impartiality applicable to arbitral tribunals and that the CAS, when it acts as an appeals authority external to international federations, is similar to a judicial authority independent from the parties.
> - The public nature of the judicial procedures is a fundamental principle of Article 6 § 1 of the European Convention on Human Rights; such principle is also applicable to non-State courts ruling on disciplinary and/or ethics matters. In

> the case of Claudia Pechstein, the CAS should have allowed a public Hearing considering that the athlete had requested one and that there was no particular reason to deny it.

'The ECHR judgment is another confirmation, this time at a continental level, that CAS is a genuine arbitration tribunal and that such sports jurisdiction is necessary for uniformity in sport. The SFT already came to the same conclusion in 1993 and 2003; the German Federal Tribunal as well in 2016.While these procedures were pending before the ECHR (eight years), ICAS, the governing body of CAS, has regularly reviewed its own structures and rules in order to strengthen the independence and the efficiency of the CAS year after year. ICAS is now composed of a large majority of legal experts coming from outside the membership of sports organizations and has achieved an equal representation of men and women. The list of arbitrators has been increased and the privilege reserved to sports organizations to propose the nomination of arbitrators on the CAS list has been abolished. Furthermore, ICAS has already envisaged the possibility of having public hearings at its newer and much larger future premises at the Palais de Beaulieu in Lausanne.

CAS was created in 1984 to provide dispute resolution services to the sports world. For over thirty-five years, it has settled disputes involving athletes, coaches, federations, sponsors, agents, clubs, leagues and organizers of sports events from almost every country in the world through arbitration and mediation procedures. It handles over 550 cases each year.'

[B] Reactions from Some Leading Sports Lawyers

The ECtHR Decisions have drawn mixed reactions from sports lawyers and we would briefly mention some of the comments and views from some of them as follows. According to Dr Thilo Pachmann, a well-known Swiss Sports Lawyer:

> The ECHR came to the conclusion that every athlete has the right to a public hearing to have matters reviewed by the general public. Sports arbitration may not be held in secret as this has been the case until today. Any mandatory sports arbitration (such as the CAS system), which does not fulfil this standard was, thus, considered to violate art. 6 para. 1 of the European Convention on Human Rights and Switzerland was ordered to pay Claudia Pechstein, who had requested a public hearing but was denied one, compensation of €8,000 for 'moral damage' suffered.
>
> On the occasion of these two cases, the ECtHR further evaluated the independence and impartiality of the entire sports arbitration system. Notably, the ECtHR held unanimously that a certain link between the sports organizations and the ICAS exists as the ICAS, which is a Swiss foundation is governed by representatives of the sports organizations, elects the possible arbitrators and decides on the President of the panels. While the majority did not see any concrete problems in the cases presented – Claudia Pechstein 'only' had heard from hearsay that the president of her panel had a 'hard line on doping' and on Adrian Mutu's panel was 'only' an arbitrator who had previously been a partner in a law firm representing the opposing club – a very telling minority opinion was rendered.

The minority opinion – which was tellingly supported by the Swiss Judge Helen Keller – outlined in every detail the dominant position of the ICAS, which should have led to a different perception of the entire system. The minority opinion even challenged the question whether the CAS system may – due to its mandatory imposition on the athletes – be considered a 'court established by the law' or simply a legal body of the sports organizations. [39]

He concludes:

> Against this background, it is clear that the ECHR will carefully consider every future case in which an athlete claims the lack of the independence and impartiality of the CAS panels. This will pose a tremendous challenge to the entire sports law system under the rule of the ICAS.[40]

According to Nick de Marco, QC, a leading British Sports Lawyer:

> The Romanian former football player, Adrian Mutu, and the German professional speed skater, Claudia Pechstein, ... claimed that their ECHR Article 6 rights to a fair hearing had been violated in various ways. The two most significant challenges considered were (i) to the independence of CAS, and (ii) the failure to grant a public hearing. The Court dismissed the first challenge by a 5-2 majority with a powerful dissent, but upheld the second.
>
> An important starting point in the Court's determination of both aspects of the challenge was the recognition that the players' consent to CAS's jurisdiction was not unequivocal and could not be described as having been freely given (*'n'avait pas été libre et 'sans equivoque'.'* [147]). Like many players, they had to accept the arbitration clauses in the sports' governing bodies' rules if they wanted to earn their living by participating in the sport. I described this anomaly as *'compelled consent'* in an article discussing a previous decision in the Pechstein saga. Strasbourg jurisprudence provides that a person can waive some of their Article 6 rights to a fair hearing by agreeing to an arbitration clause, so long as such agreement is voluntary and not compulsory. The decision in *Mutu & Pechstein* reflects the practical reality in professional sport that such consent is not genuinely free. The player has not therefore waived their Article 6 rights and so the Court can intervene.
>
> The Court dismissed the challenge to CAS's independence. A person appearing before CAS can only nominate an arbitrator from a *'closed list'*. Who is on that list is determined by an executive that is weighted heavily in favour of sports governing bodies and not players. The majority of the Court, despite dismissing the challenge, found that Ms Pechstein did not have full freedom of choice over the selection of an arbitrator, unlike the norm in commercial arbitration [156] and that organisations opposed to athletes in CAS litigation exercised a *'real influence'* (*'une réelle influence'* [157]) in the mechanism for appointing arbitrators in force at the material time. However, the players had not established bias or lack of independence in respect to the *specific* arbitrators appointed in their cases, and so this limb of their challenge failed.
>
> The minority of the Court put forward a powerful (and in my respectful opinion, compelling) dissent on this point. They argued (at [13]) that according to the settled case-law of the Court, it is not sufficient for arbitrators to be impartial individually if the *structure* of the organisation lacks the appearance of independence and impartiality. The Court must have regard to 'the manner of appointment of its members and the duration of their term of office ... the

39. *See* the post on the 'Global Sports Law and Taxation Reports (GSLTR) website (www.gsltr), 4 October 2018, titled 'certain aspects of sports arbitration violates human rights'.
40. *Ibid.*

> existence of guarantees against outside pressures ... and the question whether the body presents an appearance of independence' (citing *Campbell and Fell v. the United Kingdom*, 28 June 1984, nos 7819/77 and 7878/77, § 78, Series A no. 80). The Court would expect the composition of employment tribunals, for example, to have a balanced composition.
>
> CAS has made some important institutional changes that begin to redress some of the alleged imbalance in its structure since the *Pechstein* case was before it, but this area of controversy is likely to continue and the majority decision in this case may not be the last word.[41]

According to Dr Alara Esfun, a Turkish Sports Lawyer, regarding the finding by the ECtHR that the CAS is an independent and impartial tribunal established by law as required by Article 6 § 1 of the ECHR:

> The ECtHR is yet to proceed to a detailed analysis of the criterion 'established by law' in relation to private law entities assuming a judicial function. As underlined by Judges Keller and Serghides in their dissenting opinion, more indications (by the ECtHR) on the relevant conditions for private law entities to constitute a 'tribunal established by law' would have been welcome, especially in the *Pecshtein* and *Mutu* decision since the Court concluded that the CAS is to be considered as a tribunal established by law under Article 6 ECHR.
>
> Regarding the independence and the impartiality of the CAS, the structural balance of the arbitral tribunal can indeed be ameliorated. This being stated, and as also argued by the dominant opinion on the matter, the CAS constitutes a very efficient and valuable institution to deal with the sports-related disputes. Its existence is extremely beneficial and needs to be safeguarded.
>
> It must also be noted that the CAS itself has already taken measures to make certain reforms to ensure an enhanced structural balance.[42]

See also the views of Dr Antoine Duval of the TMC Asser International Sports Law Centre.[43] Amongst other things, he questions the decisions by the ECtHR that the CAS is an independent and impartial tribunal and goes on to give his reasons for this view of the matter.

According to Dr Alexander Wild, a German Sports Lawyer and former intern at the TMC Asser International Sports Law Centre, he 'fully agrees with the dissenting opinions' and that 'there is a structural preponderance of sports federations within the CAS that put its independence fundamentally in question'. On the issue of the possibility of bias on the part of CAS Arbitrators, Wild points out that 'sportsmen have in fact no chance to check the arbitrator's independence since many of the awards are not published' and that 'professional sportsmen depend on the independence of the arbitrators, particularly if they do not voluntarily accept the jurisdiction of the CAS'. On the contrary, 'I too do appreciate the institution of the CAS. There is without doubts, as the ECHR states, 'an interest in allowing the disputes arising in professional sport, in

41. Nick de Marco, The *Right to a Fair Hearing in Sports' Cases*, Sports Law Bulletin, www.sportslawbulletin.org/right-fair-hearing-sports-cases/ (accessed 27 June 2019).
42. *See* Alara Esfun, *Sports Arbitration: The Pechstein Case – Neither a Tornado nor a Gentle Breeze*, Global Sports Law and Taxation Reports 8, 8-14 (2019).
43. *The 'Victory' of the Court of Arbitration for Sport at the European Court of Human Rights: The End of the Beginning for the CAS*, Asser International Sports Law Blog, https://www.asser.nl/SportsLaw/Blog/post/the-victory-of-the-court-of-arbitration-for-sport-at-the-european-court-of-human-rights-the-end-of-the-beginning-for-the-cas (accessed 27 June 2019).

particular those with an international dimension, to be submitted to a specialized jurisdiction, able to rule on such cases in a quick and inexpensive manner.''[44]

Finally, in the view of the author of this chapter, one can pick holes in a number of aspects of the *ratio decidendi* of the ECtHR Decisions in *Pecshtein* and *Mutu*. In particular, in my opinion, the court relied rather blindly, when deciding that the CAS was a fair and independent tribunal, on the Swiss Federal Supreme Court Ruling in the Larissa Lazutina and Olga Danilova Cases, mentioned above, without any detailed analysis of the application of this ruling to the particular facts and circumstances of the *Pecshtein* and *Mutu* Cases.

On the question of the independence of CAS from the IOC, it should be mentioned that the President of ICAS – the body introduced in the 1994 Paris Reforms and designed to increase the separation of the CAS from the IOC – John Coates is also Vice President of the IOC. This, to some extent, I would submit, throws into question the structural independence of the CAS.

The partial funding of the CAS by the IOC remains problematic, from an independence point of view, especially as the IOC is the supreme governing body of world sport.

I would add that I also agree that the two dissenting opinions are quite powerful and, in view of this, I am surprised that Pechstein's Appeal to the Grand Chamber of the ECtHR, for a review of the decisions and, in particular, a testing of these opinions, was dismissed.

§8.11 ECtHR DECISION IN *ALI RIZA AND OTHERS V. TURKEY*

Finally, a brief mention should also be made of this recent and important case of *Ali Riza and Others v. Turkey*[45] in which the ECtHR came to the conclusion that Turkey must reform its system for settling football disputes, in particular by the Arbitration Bodies of the Turkish Football Federation, in order to conform to Article 6 (1) of the ECHR (right to a fair hearing).

§8.12 CONCLUSION

There are a number of cogent arguments and reasons for settling sports disputes extrajudicially and, in particular, by arbitration and the CAS has certainly made a worthy contribution towards this end in its thirty-six years of operations.

The advantage of the CAS is that it operates internationally and provides a uniform jurisprudence and, in doing so, offers legal certainty to the sporting community throughout the world, especially as sport is a global phenomenon.

However, there is no room for complacency, as the dissenting opinions in the *Pechstein* and *Mutu* Cases demonstrate. To be fair to CAS, however, it recognizes that

44. Such views were presented to the author of this chapter in an e-mail from him to the author of 4 April 2019.
45. App nos. 30226/10, 17880/11, 17887/11, 1791/11 and 5506/16 (ECtHR, 28 January 2020).

improvements can be made to its organization and procedures. In fact, this is borne out by the recent changes to the CAS procedural rules allowing the holding of CAS hearings in public in certain circumstances.

The CAS is also ready to respond to the needs of world sport, which continues to be a significant global phenomenon, as demonstrated by the recent setting up of its Anti-Doping Division.

All of this, to a large extent, is proof that the CAS – as a leading if not *the* leading sports arbitral body – may be regarded as the 'Supreme Court of World Sport' as its founders intended, and that, access to justice through sports arbitration seems to be working well, in practice, and satisfying the various needs for alternative dispute resolution of the international sporting community.

CHAPTER 9

Access to Justice and Arbitrating EU Competition Disputes: Aye or Nay?

Johanna Hoekstra & Aysem Diker Vanberg

This chapter discusses access to justice in relation to competition law claims in the context of the EU legal framework and in this respect fills a gap in the literature. Most competition law enforcement systems in the world are based on two enforcement pillars: public enforcement and private enforcement. Public enforcement of competition law concerns the enforcement of competition law by the relevant government or the competition authority, whilst private enforcement entails litigation initiated by private parties, to have a court establish an antitrust infringement and to order the recovery of the damages suffered. Arguably, since the adoption of the 2014 Damages Directive, which aims to establish a level playing field among Member States, there has been an increase in private damages claims. Private enforcement claims are generally arbitrable. Advantages of arbitration comprise confidentiality, expertise, and flexibility of procedure. Disadvantages include potential costs, uncertainty over judicial review of arbitral awards, and difficulties in obtaining disclosure orders and other claims against third parties. Against this background, this chapter examines whether the use of arbitration in competition law claims lowers the procedural and substantive barriers to access to justice. In this regard, the chapter will first discuss the development of competition law in the EU. It will then analyse the arbitrability of competition law issues in the EU. The chapter then proceeds to analyse key issues that arise in relation to access to justice for competition law claims before concluding on whether arbitration plays a key role in solving these issues.

§9.01 INTRODUCTION

International commercial contracts often contain an arbitration clause to regulate any disputes that arise between the parties. Contracting parties prefer arbitration because of the perceived neutrality, confidentiality, and speediness of procedure.[1] This chapter analyses the role of arbitration in the private enforcement of competition law and examines whether arbitration can lower barriers to access to justice.

In competition law access to justice is mainly discussed in the context of access to procedure and the availability of remedies to affected parties, especially for follow-on claims.[2] Those are claims where a competition authority has found an infringement of the law and third parties affected by this infringement can claim remedies. Judicial procedures can be complex, uncertain, and costly and this represents a significant barrier for the parties to bring a claim.[3] Another barrier to bring a claim is the need of the parties for confidentiality as competition law claims often involve commercially sensitive information, which means parties could choose not to litigate because they do not wish for this information to become public.

This chapter focuses on access to justice with regards to competition law in the EU with a view to determine whether arbitration can lower these barriers. After this brief introduction, the second part of the chapter introduces the EU competition law framework. The third part discusses the difference between private enforcement and public enforcement of competition law and the current developments in the EU with regards to the private enforcement of competition law. The fourth part analyses the arbitrability of competition law disputes within the EU. The fifth part examines the key issues that arise in relation to access to justice in the context of competition law disputes. Finally, the chapter concludes on whether arbitration can lower procedural and substantive barriers and thereby enhance access to justice.

§9.02 THE EUROPEAN COMPETITION FRAMEWORK

It is now generally accepted that claims arising from violations of antitrust provisions in the US and in the EU are fully arbitrable.[4] Prior to delving into the submission of competition disputes to arbitration, it is worth explaining the EU competition law framework. The EU competition law provisions can be found in the TFEU and in

1. Emmanuel Gaillard & John Savage, *Fouchard, Gaillard, Goldman on International Commercial Arbitration* (Kluwer Law International 1999). *See also*: Cathleen Hopfe, *The Rise of International Commercial Arbitration and the Demise of Judicial Recourse: Whatever Happened to 'Public Policy'?* 9 World Arbitration. & Mediation Report 263 (1998).
2. Ariel Ezrachi & Maria Ioannidou, *Access to Justice in European Competition Law – Public Enforcement as a Supplementary Channel for 'Corrective Compensation* 19 Asia Pacific Law Review 195, 196 (2011).
3. *Ibid.*, 204.
4. *See* for instance: Renato Nazzini, *Concurrent Proceedings in Competition Law* (Oxford University Press 2014) Chapters 10 and 11; Gordon Blanke, 'EU Competition Arbitration', in L. Ortiz Blanco (ed.) *EU Competition Procedure* (3rd ed., Oxford University Press 2013) 1075-1112; Geradin Damien and Villano Emilio, *Arbitrability of EU Competition Law-Based Claims: Where Do We Stand after the CDC Hydrogen Peroxide Case?*, TILEC Discussion Chapter No. 2016-033 (2016); Renato Nazzini, *Are Claims for Tortious Damages for Breach of Antitrust Rules Arbitrable in the European Union? Some Reflections on the CDC Case in the Court of Justice*, 1 Italian Antitrust Review, 70 (2016).

Council Regulation 139/2004[5] (EU Merger Control Regulation) which concerns mergers and acquisitions. Claims under Article 101 TFEU and Article 102 TFEU for damages or for non-enforceability of a contract may be resolved by the way of arbitration. Also, it is worth noting that the EC is increasingly encouraging the use of arbitration clauses to monitor behavioural remedies in merger commitments.[6]

Article 101 TFEU prohibits restrictive agreements and practices between EU Member States that could restrict or distort competition in the internal market.[7] Pursuant to 101(2) TFEU such agreements or practices are null and void and can only be compatible with the internal market if they comply with Article 101(3) TFEU, which prescribes certain efficiency gains for the agreement to be exempt from Article 101 TFEU.

Article 102 TFEU concerns unilateral conduct. It is aimed at preventing undertakings that hold a dominant position in the internal market or a substantial part of it from abusing that position. It does not prohibit dominance, only the abuse of it.[8] Dominance is defined as a 'position of economic strength enjoyed by an undertaking which enables it to prevent effective competition being maintained on the relevant market by giving it the power to behave to an appreciable extent independent of its competitors, consumers, and customers'.[9] The text of Article 102 TFEU provides examples of abuse.[10] These are not exhaustive.

Finally, the EU Merger Control Regulation, applies to mergers, acquisitions, and joint ventures, which have an EU dimension and meet a certain turnover threshold.[11]

---

5. Council Regulation 139/2004 of 20 January 2004 on the control of concentrations between undertakings [2004] O.J. L24/1, which entered into force on 1 May 2004 and replaced the old Merger Regulation, Council Regulation 4064/89 of 21 December 1989 on the control of undertakings [1989] O.J l395/1.
6. *See* below heading §9.04 which discusses the arbitrability of competition law in more detail.
7. Article 101(1) TFEU states: 'The following shall be prohibited as incompatible with the internal market: all agreements between undertakings, decisions by associations of undertakings and concerted practices which may affect trade between Member States and which have as their object or effect the prevention, restriction or distortion of competition within the internal market, and in particular those which: (a) directly or indirectly fix purchase or selling prices or any other trading conditions; (b) limit or control production, markets, technical development, or investment; (c) share markets or sources of supply; (d) apply dissimilar conditions to equivalent transactions with other trading parties, thereby placing them at a competitive disadvantage; (e) make the conclusion of contracts subject to acceptance by the other parties of supplementary obligations which, by their nature or according to commercial usage, have no connection with the subject of such contracts.
8. In other words, having market power is not an issue as long as the undertaking does not abuse its market power.
9. *United Brands v. Commission* [1978] ECR 207, at paragraph 65.
10. Such abuse may, in particular, consist of: (a)directly or indirectly imposing unfair purchase or selling prices or other unfair trading conditions; (b)limiting production, markets or technical development to the prejudice of consumers; (c) applying dissimilar conditions to equivalent transactions with other trading parties, thereby placing them at a competitive disadvantage; (d)making the conclusion of contracts subject to acceptance by the other parties of supplementary obligations which, by their nature or according to commercial usage, have no connection with the subject of such contracts.
11. The Commission only examines larger mergers with an EU dimension, meaning that the merging firms need to meet certain turnover thresholds. There are two alternative ways to reach turnover thresholds for EU dimension. The first alternative requires: (i) a combined worldwide turnover of all the merging firms over €5000 million, and (ii) an EU-wide turnover for each of at least two

The EU Merger Control Regulation prohibits mergers and acquisitions, which might reduce competition in the internal market. As an example, if a merger is likely to reduce choice for consumers or is likely to raise prices, it may not be cleared by the EC. The EC must be notified of any merger with an EU dimension prior to its implementation. After the notification, the EC has twenty-five working days to analyse the deal, which is referred to as a Phase 1 investigation.[12] At the end of a Phase 1 investigation, either the merger is accepted unconditionally, or can be accepted conditionally, provided that the transacting parties are willing to undertake certain commitments (behavioural remedies[13] or structural remedies[14]) to alleviate competition concerns. Alternatively, if the EC requires an in-depth investigation, the case is referred to a Phase 2 investigation. Again, at Phase 2, the transacting parties may offer to undertake certain commitments. If these are accepted by the EC, then an independent trustee may be appointed to ensure compliance with the proposed commitments/behavioural remedies.

The EC can propose a package of remedies that the parties should undertake to allay the concerns of the EC with regards to anticompetitive behaviour. These types of remedies often concern behavioural remedies such as access to facilities/technologies or a commitment to terminate certain exclusive contracts. It is more likely that disputes arise as parties (including third parties upon which rights have been conferred) disagree on the interpretation of the remedies.[15] These remedies often use words like reasonable and fair, which are open for interpretation. Therefore, their implementation is difficult to monitor. Furthermore, the beneficiaries are not specifically identified in advance. The EC can in those cases require an arbitration commitment, which means that any third-party beneficiary can enforce its rights to the remedies through arbitration.[16] An example would be a dispute surrounding slots at airports. To encourage competition, airlines commit to transfer slots to new entrants to the market. If a dispute arises the arbitral tribunal or the court will interpret the access commitment with regards to the transfer of slots. The arbitrator is not a regulator and therefore cannot change the access commitments. He/she only interprets the commitments as they stand.

---

of the firms over €250 million. The second alternative requires: (i) a worldwide turnover of all the merging firms over €2500 million, and (ii) a combined turnover of all the merging firms over €100 million in each of at least three Member States, (iii) a turnover of over €25 million for each of at least two of the firms in each of the three Member States included under ii, and (iv) EU-wide turnover of each of at least two firms of more than €100 million. In both alternatives, an EU dimension is not met if each of the firms archives more than two-thirds of its EU-wide turnover within one and the same Member State.

12. EU Merger Control Regulation, Article 10.
13. A behavioural remedy is a remedy in which an undertaking agrees to do certain things and agrees to abstain from certain practices to alleviate competition concerns.
14. Structural remedies require some form of structural change on the part of the party or parties to whom the measures are directed, such as the divestment of assets. These are less common than behavioural remedies.
15. Gordon Blanke, *Actions under Articles 101 and 102 TFEU in International Arbitration*, 22 Singapore Academy of Law Journal 539, 544 (2010).
16. 2008 EU Notice on Remedies.

§9.03 PUBLIC ENFORCEMENT VERSUS PRIVATE ENFORCEMENT OF COMPETITION LAW

Most competition law enforcement systems in the EU are based on two enforcement pillars: public enforcement and private enforcement.[17]

Public enforcement of competition law encompasses the enforcement of competition law by the relevant competition authority such as the EC or the Federal Trade Commission or the Department of Justice in the United States. If the alleged antitrust infringement is confined to one Member State, the relevant authority is the National Competition Authority (NCA) in that Member State. Private enforcement concerns enforcement by private parties,[18] who incur damages as a result of breach of competition law provisions. Through private enforcement, claims for breaches of competition law can be brought, either on a follow-on[19]or stand-alone basis.[20]

As noted by Alexander Italianer, the former Secretary-General of the EC, public, and private enforcement of competition law are not mutually exclusive and they are indeed complementary tools.[21] Hence, there is a need for strong public enforcement, capable of detecting infringement and putting an end to anticompetitive practices, which also works hand in hand with an effective system of private enforcement allowing those harmed to obtain the compensation to which they are entitled.[22]

In 2001, in its *Courage* decision,[23] the CJEU confirmed that anyone who has been harmed by a violation of competition law provision/provisions must be able to recover damages, if there is a causal relationship between the competition law infringement and the loss incurred. This paved the way for private enforcement of competition law provisions.[24] Opposed to the US, the private enforcement of competition law has been underdeveloped in the EU, particularly due to lack of effective procedural tools that would support and secure the position of claimants in damages proceedings. In this respect, the adoption of the Directive 2004/104/EU on Antitrust Damages Actions[25]

17. Kai Hüschelrath and Heike Schweitzer, 'Public and Private Enforcement of Competition Law in Europe – Introduction and Overview' in Kai Hüschelrath and Heike Schweitzer (ed.) *Public and Private Enforcement of Competition Law in Europe* (Springer-Verlag Berlin Heidelberg 2014) 1-8.
18. The term 'private party' in this chapter is used to refer to an individual, a legal entity, an organisation, an undertaking or a public entity.
19. Follow-on claims are claims when there is an existing infringement decision on which a claimant can rely.
20. This is where there is no pre-existing infringement decision on which a claimant can rely. Stand-alone claims are quite rare due to inherent difficulties with evidence.
21. Alexander Italianer, *Public and Private Enforcement of Competition Law*, 5th International Competition Conference, 3 (2012), http://ec.europa.eu/competition/speeches/text/sp2012_02_en.pdf (accessed 15 July 2019).
22. *Ibid.*
23. Case C-453/99 Judgment of the Court of 20 September 2001, – *Courage Ltd v. Bernard Crehan and Bernard Crehan v. Courage Ltd and Others* – Reference for a preliminary ruling: Court of Appeal (England and Wales) (Civil Division) – United Kingdom.
24. This position was reaffirmed later in Manfredi. *See* C-298/04 *Vincenzo Manfredi v. Lloyd Adriatico Assicurazioni Sp*, EU: C: 2006, 6619.
25. Council and European Parliament Directive 2014/104/EU of 26 November 2014 on Certain Rules governing Actions for Damages under National law for infringements of the competition law provisions of the Member States and the European Union [2014] OJ L349/1.

(The Damages Directive), which aims to establish a level playing field among Member States, was a welcome step in tackling the underdevelopment of private enforcement of EU competition law. After a lengthy political discourse,[26] the Damages Directive was signed into Law on 26 November 2014.[27] The key contributions brought about by the Damages Directive include: the rules governing the disclosure of evidence,[28] limitation periods,[29] and ensuring that claimants have access to consensual dispute resolution mechanism,[30] including arbitration. In contrast to the Modernisation Regulation, the Directive explicitly references arbitration.[31] Albeit this development, the private enforcement of competition law is mostly centred in three claimant friendly jurisdictions namely, the United Kingdom, Germany, and the Netherlands and, the private enforcement of competition law, particularly in the form of damages actions, has not truly materialised in the remaining Member States.[32] This demonstrates that the Directive has not been entirely successful in encouraging private enforcement in all Member States and there is still some work to be undertaken to put in place procedural tools that will support victims of antitrust violations to make a claim. Arguably, the proposed new Directive, which enables groups of consumers harmed by illegal practices to seek compensation collectively,[33] will be instrumental to increasing the volume of private enforcement of EU competition law. On 11 April 2018, the EC published a proposal for a new Directive on representative actions for the protection of the collective interests of consumers (The Proposed Directive for Collective Redress).[34] The proposed Directive for Collective Redress sets out rules enabling qualified representative entities such as consumer organisations and independent bodies to seek representative actions aimed at the protection of the collective interests of consumers. When it becomes law, the proposed Directive would indeed be very useful for consumers who do not have the financial means to take their case to arbitration and litigation and would be an important instrument for access to justice. For instance, the proposed directive will enable consumers, who have paid significantly high insurance premiums as a result of

26. Sebastien Peyer, 'The Antitrust Damages Directive-Much Ado about Nothing?', in Mel Marquis and Roberto Cisotta (eds) *Litigation and Arbitration in EU Competition Law*, 33-46 (Edward Elgar 2015).
27. The deadline for transposing the Damages Directive expired on 27 December 2016. On 24 January 2017, letters of formal notice were sent to 21 Member States which failed to fully transpose the Directive to their national laws. As of early 2018, all Member States have transposed the Directive to their national laws. *See* The European Commission; Actions for Damages, Directive on Antitrust Damages Actions, http://ec.europa.eu/competition/antitrust/actionsdamages/directive_en.html (accessed 15 July 2019).
28. Damages Directive, Chapter 2.
29. Damages Directive, Article 10.
30. Damages Directive, Chapter VI, Articles 18 and 19.
31. Miriam Driessen-Reilly, *Private Damages in EU Competition Law and Arbitration: a Changing Landscape*, 31 Arbitration International 567, 571 (2015).
32. Jurgita Malinauskaite and Caroline Cauffman, The Transposition of the Antitrust Damages Directive in the Small Member States of the EU – A Comparative Perspective, 9 (8) Journal of European Competition Law & Practice 496 (2018).
33. This is referred to as collective redress in the EU and as class action in the US and in the UK.
34. Directive of The European Parliament and of The Council on Representative Actions For The Protection Of The Collective Interests Of Consumers, And Repealing Directive 2009/22/EC, COM(2018) 184 final 2018/0089 (COD).

a cartel agreement, to bring a follow-on claim against cartel members. As mentioned earlier, even if the consumers do not have the financial means to take their claim to arbitration or litigation, thanks to the proposed directive, this can be done by a consumer organisation on behalf of the consumers. The proposed Directive is strongly supported by consumer organisations including the European Consumer Organisation/Bureau Européen des Unions de Consommateurs (BEUC).[35] The European Parliament adopted its first-reading position on the Directive on 26 March 2019. At the time of the writing, the work on the proposal is ongoing in the Council.

§9.04 ARBITRATION AND COMPETITION LAW

Arbitration is a contractual arrangement based on the consensus of the parties. In the context of arbitration party autonomy can be defined as the freedom of the parties to determine the procedure to resolve any arising disputes between them.[36] This part discusses the arbitrability of competition law. It first examines whether competition law is arbitrable and then it proceeds to analyse the role of the arbitrator in relation to competition law.

[A] The Arbitrability of Competition Law

In the EU the relationship between arbitration and competition law started rather hesitantly. Initially, arbitrators preferred not to involve any issues related to competition law in their procedures because competition law is a matter of public policy and deciding on public policy issues might lead to the award being invalidated, this was coupled with the standpoint of the EC that competition law should not be dealt with in a private forum.[37] The EC was concerned that due to the lack of transparency and the private nature of arbitral proceedings competition law issues would not be properly taken into consideration by the arbitral tribunal.[38] This is coupled with the fact that private enforcement of competition law in the EU is not used frequently as discussed in part §9.03 of this chapter.[39] Over the past two decades the relationship between competition law and arbitration in the EU changed, and the EC now promulgates the use of arbitration as an additional dispute resolution mechanism in competition law

35. BEUC, The European Consumer Organisation, Proposal for a Directive on Representative Actions BEUC position paper, https://www.beuc.eu/publications/beuc-x-2018-094_representative_actions_beuc_position_paper.pdf (accessed 15 July 2019).
36. Alan Redfern & Martin Hunter, with Nigel Blackaby and Constantine Partasides, *Law and Practice of International Commercial Arbitration* (4th ed. OUP 2004) 315.
37. Assimakis P. Komninos, *Arbitration and EU Competition Law* 1, 6 (2009), http://arbitrationlaw.com/files/free_pdfs/arbitration_and_eu_competition_law.pdf (accessed 15 July 2019).
38. Celine Gauer & Johannes Lubking, *Arbitration and Competition: Between Conflict and Cooperations*, 3 Competition Law and Policy Debate 26 (2017).
39. Jan Dalhuisen, *The Arbitrability of Competition Issues*, 11 Arbitration International 151, 160 (1995).

and arbitrators are more confident dealing with competition law issues, given that they now have certainty as to their arbitrability.[40]

The CJEU concluded in its seminal *Eco Swiss* judgment that disputes arising from competition law can be submitted to arbitration. [41] Subsequent to *Eco Swiss*, national courts in the European Union have affirmed the arbitrability of EU competition law provisions as well as their corresponding national equivalents.[42] For instance, in England and Wales, in *ET Plus SA v. Welter*, Gross J stated that there is no convincing doubt that competition or antitrust claims are arbitrable.[43] In France, in the case of *Labinal v. Mors*, the Court of Appeal of Paris, held that competition issues arising from Article 101 TFEU can be subject to arbitration.[44] A similar approach was adopted by the Court of Appeal of Milan, confirming the arbitrability of competition claims.[45] More recently, albeit discreetly, in the Cartel Damages Claims,[46]the CJEU again provided support for the arbitrability of competition disputes. In this case, the CJEU clarified that national courts in a claim for competition law damages, could not rule out the application of a jurisdiction clause which would bring the dispute outside of that court.[47] This paved the way for jurisdiction clauses that stipulate arbitration.[48]

The Modernisation Regulation[49] was silent on the role of arbitration in the private enforcement of European Competition Law. Nevertheless, the abolition of the individual exemption regime under Article 101 (3) TFEU, laid the foundation for the direct application by arbitration tribunals of Article 101(3) TFEU.[50] Prior to the entry into force of the Modernisation Regulation in May 2003, national courts (and by extension arbitral tribunals) had no jurisdiction to rule on Article 101 (3) TFEU, which was the exclusive competence of the EC. Following the implementation of the Modernisation Regulation, national courts, and arbitral tribunals now have jurisdiction to apply Article 101 (3) TFEU. As noted above, this Regulation does not mention arbitration directly. However, it is accepted that the correct implementation of conditions and

40. Komninos (n 37) at 6.
41. *Case C-126/97, Eco Swiss China Ltd v. Benetton International NV*, Judgment of the European Court of Justice of 1 June 1999.
42. Renato Nazzini, *Litigating, arbitrating and mediating competition law disputes* 1, 9 (2009), https://www.cdr-news.com/categories/expert-views/litigating-arbitrating-and-mediating-competition-law-disputes#privatenational (accessed 15 July 2019).
43. *ET Plus SA v. Welter* [2006] 1 Lloyd's Rep 251, at [51].
44. *Labinal v. Mors* (1993) Rev Arb 645 (CA, Paris).
45. *Istituto Biochimico Italiano v. Madaus AG*, Milan Court of Appeal, 13 September 2002, (2003) 4 Dir Ind 346.
46. *Case C-352/13 Cartel Damages Claims (CDC) Hydrogen Peroxide S.A v. Evonik Degussa GmbH &Others*, European Court of Justice (Fourth Chamber) Judgment of 21 May 2015.
47. *Case C-352/13 Cartel Damages Claims (CDC)Hydrogen Peroxide S.A v. Evonik Degussa GmbH &Others*, European Court of Justice (Fourth Chamber) Judgment of 21 May 2015 paragraphs 63-72.
48. Lucian Ilie and Amy Seow, *International Arbitration and EU Competition Law Complement Rather than Contradict One Another*, 34 Journal of International Arbitration 1007, 1012 (2017).
49. Council Regulation (EC) No 1/2003 of 16 December 2002 on the implementation of the rules on competition laid down in Articles 81 and 82 of the Treaty (Text with EEA relevance).
50. Gordon Blanke, *The transformation of international arbitration and the emergence of the supranational arbitrator: lessons from EC Merger Control*, International Arbitration Review 211, 285 (2005).

obligations under decisions pursuant to Article 9 of the Modernisation Regulation, may be submitted to arbitration.[51]

Depending on the jurisdiction, courts often rely on arbitration laws to determine whether any specific legal issues are arbitrable.[52] As arbitrators already could apply Article 101 (1) and (2) TFEU and no express provision was included to exclude the application of Article 101 (3) TFEU the arbitrability of the article can be presumed.[53]

There are different situations in which competition law issues can arise in arbitration procedures. It is used both as a shield (defence) or a sword (cause for a claim). The first occurs more regularly as competition issues are frequently raised as a defence by one of the parties to have the contract declared void *ab initio*.[54] The defending party would argue that the agreement violates competition law and is therefore void. This would then prevent the party from having to pay damages for non-performance of the contract. It is also possible to bring competition law issues as part of a claim although this happens less frequently than the situation discussed above.[55] A contracting party could bring a claim that the other party has caused harm to the claimant by breaking competition regulations.[56] For instance, cartel members may bring a dispute to arbitration although this will of course raise questions as to what extent the contracts are part of the cartel which means the contracts might not be enforceable at all.[57]

As discussed in §9.02, if a public authority such as the EC finds there is a breach of competition law provisions, a party that has suffered damages because of the infringement can claim damages through arbitration (dependent upon agreement by the parties).[58] In the context of mergers, the EC uses arbitration clauses as a mechanism to monitor the correct implementation of merger commitments and it has developed an extensive practice of incorporating arbitration clauses into remedy packages as a condition to clear the merger.[59] Through arbitration, third parties can enforce any rights they have acquired following the agreed commitments between the companies

51. Blanke (*supra* n. 15), at 549. Dalhuisen (*supra* n. 39) at 151.
52. Komninos (*supra* n. 37) at 11. *See* for instance: France: Article 2060 of the Civil Code: One may not enter into arbitration agreements in matters of status and capacity of the persons, in those relating to divorce and judicial separation or on controversies concerning public bodies and institutions and more generally in all matters in which public policy is concerned. Netherlands: Article 1020 (3) of the Dutch Code of Civil Procedure: Arbitration Agreements in General .... 3. The arbitration agreement shall not serve to determine legal consequences of which the parties cannot freely dispose. Germany: Code of Civil Procedure – Section 1030 Arbitrability (1) Any claim involving an economic interest (vermögensrechtlicher Anspruch) can be the subject of an arbitration agreement. An arbitration agreement concerning claims not involving an economic interest shall have legal effect to the extent that the parties are entitled to conclude a settlement on the issue in dispute.
53. Blanke (*supra* n. 15) at 551.
54. Dalhuisen, (*supra* n. 39) at 161.
55. Blanke (*supra* n. 15) at 548.
56. Komninos (*supra* n. 37) at 7.
57. Blanke (*supra* n. 15) at 548.
58. Blanke (*supra* n. 15) at 549.
59. Gordon Blanke, *The transformation of international arbitration and the emergence of the supranational arbitrator: lessons from EC Merger Control*, International Arbitration Review 211 (2005).

and the competition authority and they can seek compensation for the damage that they suffer as a result of non-compliance from the merging parties with the agreed commitments.[60] The arbitrator is not a regulator and therefore cannot change these access commitments. The arbitral tribunal only interprets the commitments as they stand and through this enforce the rights of third parties.

The NYC has 165 signatories (including the EU Member States) and requires contracting states to enforce foreign arbitral awards. An award should not be enforced if it manifestly contradicts the public policy of the forum.[61] The CJEU held in its seminal *Eco Swiss* judgment[62] that Article 101 of the TFEU qualifies as public policy within the meaning of the New York Convention. A forum located in an EU Member State will thus need to take account of EU competition law when deciding on the enforcement of an award. Whilst the *Eco Swiss* case concerned the application of Article 101 TFEU the reasoning of the CJEU ('a system ensuring that competition in the internal market is not distorted') can be extracted to cover the other competition law provisions of the TFEU.[63]

Competition law cannot be contracted out, despite any agreement between the parties to exclude this.[64] They are mandatory rules of law (*lois de police*) which are defined as those laws that are 'deemed essential for the political, social, and economic organisation of the state'.[65] Mandatory laws are determined *a posteriori* by courts or legislative bodies.[66] In the context of the Rome I Legislation, mandatory laws of the *lex fori* should be applied regardless of the applicable law and regardless of whether the parties have excluded the specific laws from the contract.[67] The mandatory rules of the country where the contract is executed may be applied if otherwise (the execution of) the contract would be unlawful.[68]

[B] The Role of Arbitrators with Regards to Application of Competition Law

Whilst dealing with a dispute that concerns the application of Article 101 TFEU, the arbitrator can declare that a contract does not violate Article 101 (1), that a contract is void under Article 101 (2) and they can propose changes to make the contract compatible with Article 101 (3). Under Article 102 TFEU the arbitrator can find abuse of dominance, order specific performance (or ask the party to refrain from undertaking

60. *Ibid.*, at 212.
61. Brussels I Regulation 44/2001 (Recast) Article 34 (1).
62. Case C-126/97, *Eco Swiss China Ltd v. Benetton International NV*, Judgment of the European Court of Justice of 1 June 1999.
63. Damien Geradin, *Public Policy and Breach of Competition Law in International Arbitration: A Competition Law Practitioner's Viewpoint*, TILEC Discussion Paper DP 2016-029, 1, 12 (2016). http://ssrn.com/abstract=2786370 (accessed 15 July 2019).
64. *Eco Swiss* (*supra* n. 46). *See also*: Case C-393/92 *Almelo v. NV Energiebedrijf* [1994].
65. Phocion Francescakis, *Travaux du comité français de droit international privé*, 165 (1966-1969).
66. Catherine Kessedjian, *Mandatory Rules in International Arbitration: What Are Mandatory Rules?* 18 American Review of International Arbitration 147 (2007).
67. Rome I Legislation Article 9.2.
68. Rome I Legislation Article 9.3.

abusive behaviour), and award damages for loss suffered. Whilst dealing with a dispute that concerns the performance of a merger commitment, the arbitrators can ask the parties to undertake certain actions and/or to refrain from certain conduct.

Arbitrators do not have an express duty to apply competition law *ex officio* as this would be a violation of the principle of party autonomy.[69] It is up to the parties to decide the mandate of the arbitrator and this includes any substantive issues that may be treated during the proceedings. Therefore, if the parties do not include competition issues in the mandate the arbitrator should not address these. If the arbitrator would include these in the procedure, then it would make the award susceptible to being set aside under the NYC for exceeding the mandate of the tribunal.[70] As discussed above, an award that violates competition law can be set aside for public policy reasons. Hence, it is recommended that an arbitrator addresses these issues although he would then need to be mandated by the parties to include these issues in the procedure. The arbitrator has a duty of best effort to deliver an award that is enforceable and by deliberately exceeding the mandate he would be in disregard of that duty.[71] This is also recognised in the ICC rules on arbitration.[72]

As competition law is a matter of public policy the award would also not be enforced if it violates competition law.[73] This could lead to the case coming to public scrutiny.[74] As confidentiality is one of the key pillars of arbitration this risk should be pointed out by the arbitrator when dealing with competition law issues. Furthermore, by not applying competition law provisions, the arbitrator could be deemed liable for infringement of EU law, for instance if he enforces a cartel agreement he becomes liable for the continuation of the cartel.[75] The reason is that the award binds only the parties in their private dispute whilst underlying liability rising from a competition law violation could potentially make the arbitrator liable if he has rendered an award sanctioning the anticompetitive behaviour.[76] This possibility is more theoretical given that in practice institutional rules and national laws protect arbitrators from liability arising out of their work unless this work was conducted in bad faith.[77] There are no known examples in the EU and in the US of an arbitrator being prosecuted for criminal liability in a competition law case.[78]

If the parties do not allow the arbitrator to include relevant competition law issues in the procedure, the arbitrator could resign on grounds that he is not capable of exercising his mandate with respect to the arbitration rules or that the proceedings

69. Blanke (*supra* n. 15) at 556.
70. Article V (1) c.
71. William Schubert, *Reviewing Arbitration Awards for Competition Law Violations: A Playbook for Courts Implementing the New York Convention*, 52 (2015). http://works.bepress.com/william_schubert/1 (accessed 15 July 2019).
72. ICC Rules of Arbitration Article 41: 'In all matters not expressly provided for in the Rules, the Court and the arbitral tribunal shall act in the spirit of the Rules and shall make every effort to make sure that the award is enforceable at law.'
73. NYC Article V (2) b.
74. Blanke (*supra* n. 15) 564.
75. *Ibid.*
76. Schubert (*supra* n. 71) 58.
77. *Ibid.*, 60.
78. *Ibid.*, 61.

have an illegal purpose.[79] Arbitrators are not merely in service of the parties but are under a broader duty that encompasses a requirement for justice and this would entail a concern for public policy issues.[80] It would also be possible to separate the competition law issues from the other issues discussed and insert a caveat that the award will not be final until the competition law violations have been ruled on by a competent authority.[81]

Unlike courts, arbitrators do not fall under the cooperation and coordination mechanism as defined by Regulation 1/2003 given they are not an official organ of either the EU or any Member State. They are a private entity and are neither under an obligation to cooperate with the EC nor is the EC bound to provide them with any assistance.[82] The CJEU has confirmed that the arbitral tribunal is not 'bound by the duty of loyal cooperation' and they cannot refer any legal issues to the CJEU.[83]

In practice some form of voluntary cooperation is possible. Arbitrators can request relevant information from the EC or request that the EC makes a submission on the interpretation of competition law issues the case raises. Under the Damages Directive, National Courts can ask for the disclosure of certain evidence (albeit this is limited).[84] Whilst these are aimed at national courts given their intent, they are also relevant for arbitral tribunals. Although an arbitral tribunal is not a court, the arbitrator must take into account competition law where applicable and this includes the articles of the Damages Directive with regards to disclosure of evidence.[85]

The EC could act as an *amicus curiae (arbitri)* but should only be asked to do this if the EC is already aware of the proceedings, otherwise this might bring unwanted publicity to the parties.[86] Given the importance of confidentiality the arbitrator should only involve the EC if the parties have consented to this.

Arbitrators are not bound by Article 16 of Modernisation Regulation, which states that national courts cannot take decisions that run counter to a decision taken by the EC and that they should not take any decisions on cases which are currently before the EC. National courts may need to stay proceedings whilst awaiting a decision. This could take a long time. Arbitral tribunals neither need to follow decisions made by the EC (but would be wise to do so as otherwise the award could be unenforceable) nor do they need to stay proceedings when the issue is before the EC. It is only recommended that they do so if the issue is particularly complex or novel and only with full consent of the parties.[87] This does not mean that the arbitrator always needs to follow the

79. Blanke (*supra* n. 15) at 559.
80. Luca Radicati di Brozolo, *Arbitration and Competition Law: the Position of the Courts and Arbitrators*, OECD Hearings Arbitration and Competition DAF/COMP 40, 46 (2010) https://www.oecd.org/daf/competition/abuse/49294392.pdf (accessed 15 July 2019).
81. Maurits Dolmans & Jacob Grierson, *Arbitration and the Modernization of EC Antitrust Law: New Opportunities and New Responsibilities*, 14(2) ICC International Court of Arbitration Bulletin 37, 44 (2003).
82. Carl Baudenbacher & Imelda Higgins, *Decentralization of EC Competition Law Enforcement and Arbitration*, 8 Columbia Journal of European Law 1, 3 (2002).
83. Case 102/81 *Nordsee v. Reederei Mond* [1982] ECR 1095.
84. Damages Directive Articles 5 and 6.
85. Driessen-Reilly, (*supra* n. 31) 584-585.
86. Blanke (*supra* n. 15) 568.
87. Komninos (*supra* n. 37) 28.

decision made by the EC. If he finds the facts of the case different, he could issue a different ruling, and this would not contravene public policy.[88]

[C] The Application of EU Competition Law by Arbitrators

Under the principle of party autonomy, in the EU, parties are free to choose the law applicable to their contract.[89] In a case before an EU Member State the parties can only choose the law of a country.[90] In arbitral procedures the parties can also choose non-state rules as the applicable law, including the *lex mercatoria* and general principles of law or transnational commercial law rules such as the UNIDROIT Principles of International Commercial Contracts. [91]

If the parties to the contract have chosen the law of an EU Member State as the applicable law, then the arbitrator should apply EU competition law. Due to the supremacy principle, EU law is part of the law of the Member State and thus part of the applicable law. Regardless of the applicable law, an award that violates EU competition law risks being set aside if it is to be enforced in an EU Member State. Furthermore, the public policy of the seat of arbitration should be respected as the law applicable to the arbitral procedure is usually that of the Seat. If the contract could affect cross-border economic activity in the EU, the arbitrator would also need to consider whether EU competition law is applicable.[92]

The applicable law to non-contractual obligations in the EU is determined by the Rome II Regulation. Article 6 discusses competition claims and states that the applicable law shall be the 'the law of the country where competitive relations or the collective interests of consumers are, or are likely to be, affected'. If more than one state is affected, then the parties can ask for the application of the *lex fori* (provided the forum is one of the affected states). Whilst the Rome II Regulation does not apply in arbitration it is a strong indication that arbitrators should take into account competition law of states that will be affected by the breach. Therefore, if effects of the breach are likely to occur in EU Member States then the arbitrator should apply EU competition law.

If the arbitrator acts as amiable compositeur (that is he makes a decision *ex aqua et buono,* without reference to law) or if non-state rules (such as the *lex mercatoria*) are the applicable law, the tribunal would not be bound by the competition rules of the applicable law (given that there are none). The arbitrators would still need to apply EU

88. *Ibid.*, 29.
89. Rome I Regulation.
90. Rome I Regulation Article 3 (1) and Pre-Amble (15). *See also*: Olugbenga Bamodu, 'The Rome I Regulation and the Relevance of Non-State Law', in Peter Stone and Youseph Farah (eds) *Research Handbook in EU Private International Law* (Edward Elgar Publishing 2015) 221/222.
91. Symeon C Symeonides, *Contracts subject to Non-State Norms* 54 American Journal of Comparative Law 209, 214 (2006).
92. In Gencor, the General Court gave a clear definition of the concept of 'effect on competition within the Union' and identified three cumulative criteria to carry out the assessment: immediate, substantial, and foreseeable (case T-102/96, *Gencor Ltd v. Commission*, [1999] ECR II-753, paragraphs 90 and 92).

competition law in the other situations mentioned above given its status as public policy.

§9.05 ACCESS TO JUSTICE AND ARBITRATION

Access to justice means both procedural and substantive fairness and it represents a basic principle of rule of law.[93] At its core the notion ensures that a party has a fair hearing and has access to effective remedies. Access to justice issues in competition law arise mainly in the context of procedural fairness.[94] The competition law framework is only effective if the victims of an infringement (both businesses and consumers) can get compensated for any damages suffered.[95] Effective access to procedure also raises the costs of infringement which serves as a deterrent for businesses against violating competition law. [96] Therefore, ensuring access to procedure is necessary for the effectiveness of the competition law.

There are two categories where difficulties of access to procedure especially arise: cases where the injured parties are numerous and have a modest claim (such as consumers or Small and Medium Enterprises (SME)) or cases where the injured parties are customers or competitors of the infringing party.[97] In an Impact Assessment the UK government discussed how in most of the cases where the Office of Fair Trading (OFT) (now Competition and Markets Authority) found an infringement of competition law there were no follow-on cases and that the cost and complexity of procedure is one of the main reasons for the low number of cases filed.[98] The complexity of competition law also deters consumers because this has an impact on the potential success of their claim.[99] Consumers and SMEs benefit from more accessible and less costly procedures.[100] The second category, namely the competitors of the infringing parties, benefit especially from confidentiality given that these procedures often involve commercially sensitive data. A survey conducted by the OFT confirmed these reasons: lawyers most commonly suggested that removing barriers for private action would raise compliance of companies with competition law and companies suggested that reputation damage was a major reason for not bringing a claim.[101] This could also stop parties from raising competition law issues in an ongoing procedure or hinder a party from adequately

93. *See*, for instance, Article 6 and Article 13 of the ECHR. For the specific context of EU: Article 47 of the Charter of Fundamental Rights of the European Union which entails a 'right to a fair trial 'and a 'right to an effective remedy'.
94. Ezrachi (*supra* n. 2) 210.
95. Michael D. Hausfeld, *The Importance of Private Competition Enforcement in Europe*, 8 Competition Law International 65, 66 (2012).
96. *Ibid.*, 71.
97. Ezrachi (*supra* n. 2) 210.
98. Department for Business, Innovation, and Skills Impact Assessment, *Private actions in competition law: a consultation on options for reform* 7 (2012) https://assets.publishing.service.gov.uk/government/uploads/system/uploads/attachment_data/file/31529/12-743-private-actions-in-competition-law-impact-assessment.pdf (accessed 15 July 2019).
99. Maria Ioannidou, *Enhancing the Consumers' Role in EU Competition Law Enforcement: A Normative and Practical Approach*, The Competition Law Review 59, 70 (2011).
100. Ezrachi (*supra* n. 2) 211.
101. Ioannidou (*supra* n. 99) 9.

defending itself against a competition law issue claimed by the other party. The confidentiality of the arbitration is thus key in widening the access to procedure. For consumers and SMEs, the simplicity and informality of the arbitral procedure could lower barriers. However, the cost of arbitration (which can be significant) could be a deterrent. This is especially so given the low value of most consumer claims.[102]

This part explores whether arbitration successfully lowers the barriers to access to justice in competition law claims. It also analyses in the below four headings whether the expertise of arbitrators, the wide recognition and limited review of arbitral awards, the relatively predictable and confidential nature of arbitration can contribute to lowering these barriers by warranting substantive and procedural fairness as well as recourse to effective remedies for the victims of antitrust violations. It also discusses how the diverging standpoints on the reviews of arbitral awards can hinder access to justice in the context of arbitration.

[A] Expertise of Arbitrators

Arbitral tribunals are often regarded as a more suitable forum for competition law claims because of the subject expertise these cases require. In the English Court of Appeal, Mummery LJ held that arbitration is a suitable mechanism with regards to disputes on excessive pricing and blocking access because of the speediness, flexibility, and level of expertise that an arbitral tribunal can offer.[103] He held that courts often have a lack of expertise on these subjects.[104] The latter is discussed as a key advantage of arbitration in competition law cases.[105]

In an arbitration that involves the resolution of competition law disputes, subject experts that have an in-depth understanding of the issues can be chosen by the parties.[106] National courts may not have the same complete understanding of the economic and legal issues involved in competition law as a subject expert would. One of the key features of competition law is that it is very factual, it is almost impossible to establish a breach without in-depth research and use of extensive data.[107] As competition law issues are intrinsically rooted in the market they require an understanding of the facts that go beyond the law and that an expert arbitrator could be more suitable to render a decision on, and this could thus enhance substantive fairness in the judicial procedure. Whilst arbitrators are more likely to have an in-depth knowledge of the economic issues, they could have less expertise dealing with public policy issues than national courts do.[108] Regardless there seems to be some consensus that the expertise of arbitrators in matter of competition law can outweigh those of courts. A more in-depth expertise of competition law issues, including the economic aspects, would ensure a more balanced treatment of the claim which leads to an award that

102. *Ibid.*, 70-71.
103. *Attheraces Ltd v. British Horseracing Board* [2007] EWCA Civ 38.
104. *Ibid.*
105. Ilie and Seow (*supra* n. 48) 1007.
106. Blanke (*supra* n. 15) at 551.
107. Geradin (*supra* n. 63) at 7.
108. Baudenbacher (*supra* n. 82) 3.

takes into account all the relevant issues. On the contrary if a judicial decision is made without this in-depth understanding, violations of competition law might not be recognised or violations will be found where there are none. This will lead to unfair remedies for the victims of antitrust violations. In an arbitral procedure, the parties can choose the arbitrators and therefore they can ensure that the arbitral tribunal has the necessary expertise and that the parties feel confident the case will have a fair hearing that takes into account all relevant aspects. If the parties do not see the courts as having sufficient expertise this would form a barrier to bringing a claim and if the judges do not have a good understanding of the competition issues this might have a negative impact on victims of injustice. In other words, the expertise of arbitrators in competition law matters will lead to both substantive and procedural fairness thereby enhancing access to justice.

[B] The Recognition and Review of Arbitral Awards

Enforceability of court judgments is generally governed by bilateral conventions between states or by the Brussels Regulation between Member States for the purposes of the free movement of judgments throughout the EU. [109] This procedure can be complex, when this involves non-Member States. However, due to the NYC, arbitral awards can be enforced with minimum procedure. Hence, given the international nature of competition law infringements, the quasi-global enforceability of arbitral awards, has a real advantage over court litigation.[110]

Furthermore, arbitration may enable the enforcement of a legal principle not currently existing in the applicable law.[111] For example, if a competition law principle is not recognised in country A, use of nternational arbitration, may allow the extension of the competition principle into that jurisdiction.[112] In this regard, it may be argued that arbitration as opposed to litigation enhances parties' access to justice by wider enforcement and recognition.

The finality of the arbitral award is one of the key principles of arbitration. This means that the possibilities for an appeal are limited. It ensures certainty of procedure for the parties. The NYC has a strong bias in favour of recognition and enforcement of the arbitral award, subjecting these to only a minimum review.[113] The grounds on which the enforcement of an award can be challenged in the NYC are procedural and

---

109. Council Regulation (EC) No. 44/2011 of 22 December on jurisdiction and the recognition and enforcement of judgments in civil and commercial matters 0J 2001 L 12/1 16.01.2001. This might change with the new Hague Convention on the Recognition and Enforcement of Foreign Judgments in Civil or Commercial Matters of the 4 July 2019.
110. Renato Nazzini, 'Litigating, Arbitrating and Mediating Competition Law Disputes' 1, 10 (2009) https://www.cdr-news.com/categories/expert-views/litigating-arbitrating-and-mediating-competition-law-disputes#privatenational (accessed 15 July 2019).
111. *Arbitration and Competition Law: the Position of the Courts and Arbitrators*, OECD Hearings Arbitration and Competition DAF/COMP (2010) 40, 8 https://www.oecd.org/daf/competition/abuse/49294392.pdf (accessed 15 July 2019).
112. *Ibid.*
113. Schubert (*supra* n. 71) 20.

not substantive.[114] That is to say the award can only be successfully challenged for issues related to the arbitral procedure and not because of any substantive disagreement of one of the parties with the content of the award. The UNCITRAL Model Law on International Commercial Arbitration has similar rules.[115] Therefore, usually an international arbitration award cannot be challenged on anything else than procedural grounds. This gives the parties the certainty that the award will be enforced regardless of the forum where it is brought. This ensures confidence of the parties in the arbitration procedure and in the enforceability of the award.

A breach of public policy is one of the main grounds on which an arbitral award involving competition law issues might not be enforced. There are two issues that could arise: 1) the arbitrator did not apply the law correctly or 2) the violations of competition law have not been addressed.[116] The first issue is easier to discover given that the competition law violations are discussed and therefore the court would be aware of this when reviewing the award. The second issue is more difficult to discover given the confidential nature of arbitral awards and it would take a substantive effort from the court to uncover any hidden competition law violations.[117]

The lack of a substantive review on the merits gives the parties certainty which lowers barriers to access justice. In cases involving EU competition law there are conflicting views on how extensive an award should be reviewed. The existence of different approaches engenders uncertainty for the parties which can be a hindrance for the certainty of the procedure. The review of competition law violations can take a minimalist or maximalist approach in the EU context. The minimalist approach focuses on compatibility of the operative part of the award with competition law and advocates that the award should be enforced unless there are any substantive infringements of the law.[118] The maximalist approach requires that both the reasoning and operative part of the award should be compatible with competition law.[119] An example of the minimalist approach is the French case of *Thales*.[120] An arbitral award under which Thales had to pay damages for breaching an exclusive licensing agreement was challenged. Thales argued that the agreement breached Article 81 of the EC Treaty (now TFEU 101) although had not raised this argument during the arbitration. The court dismissed the appeal as the violation should be flagrant and the court would have to go into the merits of the case to judge whether there was an apparent violation of

114. Article V(1) NYC:((a) the agreement to arbitrate is invalid or the parties lacked capacity; (b) a party has not been given fair notice of the arbitration or opportunity to present its case; (c) the arbitrator has exceeded its authority; (d) the proceedings have been carried out inconsistently with the parties' agreement; and (e) the award is not yet binding or has been set aside) and Article V(2) (a) the subject matter of the award cannot be arbitrated under the law of that country and (b) the award goes against the public policy of the forum.
115. The UNCITRAL Model Law on International Commercial Arbitration of 1985 (with amendments as adopted in 2006) Article 34. This has been adopted by 72 states: http://www.uncitral.org/uncitral/en/uncitral_texts/arbitration/1985Model_arbitration_status.html (accessed 15 July 2019).
116. Schubert (*supra* n. 71) 20.
117. *Ibid.*, 23.
118. Blanke (*supra* n. 15) at 576.
119. *Ibid.*
120. *Thales v. Euromissile* [2006] E.C.C. 6 (Paris Court of Appeal, 18 November 2004).

competition law in the contract. The highest court in France (Cour de Cassation) confirmed the approach of the court of appeal in a later case by stating that the violation should be flagrant and concrete to qualify as a violation of public policy.[121]

An example of a maximalist review is from a court of appeal in the Netherlands which concerned an arbitration award under which one of the parties was ordered to pay damages and transfer information.[122] The other party challenged the enforcement of the award by stating that it violated Article EC 81 [now TFEU 101].[123] The court agreed and refused to enforce the award.

Proponents of the minimalist school focus on the importance of the enforceability of the award and certainty for the parties in how an award is reviewed. Their focus is therefore on the arbitration process. The existence of in-depth reviews of the merits of the case could become part of tactical play by the losing party. The losing party could then force a review on the merits with regards to competition law, which would lead to uncertainty, publicity, and the award possibly not being enforced.[124] This would lower the confidence the parties have in the arbitration process. The focus of the maximalist school is on the importance of the integrity of EU law and on advancing the coherence of the internal market. This requires a more thorough review of the issues to ensure that EU law stays coherent.[125]

Overall the minimalist approach has been the most successful and is followed by most national courts in the EU, but not by all.[126] The CJEU has not pronounced itself on this issue.[127] It can be questioned whether the approach of only flagrant violations of competition law constituting a breach of public policy is sufficient to ensure the effectiveness of EU competition law.[128] At the same time it should not be assumed that if courts review an award that they necessarily will arrive to a better conclusion than the tribunal on the interpretation of competition law.[129] The court might not have as much expertise as the arbitrator, may not have reviewed the data that led the tribunal to its conclusions in detail, or might have a different approach to issues which have not been settled with certainty.[130] This would mean that even a (maximalist) review on the merits of the award would not necessarily lead to a 'better' interpretation of the law.[131] Courts could use a certain amount of discretion when they determine whether or not an in-depth review of the award is necessary before allowing enforcement.[132] Whilst this

121. *SNF v. Sytec*, Pourvoi No. 06-15320 (Cour de Cassation, 4 June 2008).
122. *Marketing Displays Int'l v. VR*, 2 Cahiers d'arbitrage (Hauge Court of Appeal, 2005), as discussed in Alexis Mourre and Luca G. Radicati di Brozolo, *Towards Finality of Arbitral Awards: Two Steps Forward and One Step Back*, 23 Journal of International Arbitration 171, 179-184 (2006).
123. *Ibid.*
124. Radicati di Brozolo (*supra* n. 80) 46.
125. Blanke (*supra* n. 15) at 579.
126. Komninos (*supra* n. 37) at 43.
127. Opinion of AG Wathelet in Case C567/14, *Genentech Inc. v. Hoechst GmbH, formerly Hoechst AG, Sanofi-Aventis Deutschland GmbH*, [2016] ECR I-0000, at paragraph 66.
128. Geradin (*supra* n. 63) at 31.
129. Radicati di Brozolo (*supra* n. 80) 46.
130. *Ibid.*
131. *Ibid.*
132. Geradin (*supra* n. 63) at 31.

discretion could lead to a better application of competition law it adds an element of uncertainty to the arbitration procedure. This would be problematic for the parties to the dispute who can no longer rely on a transparent and certain enforcement procedure.

There is one example of the EC intervening with an arbitral award concerning competition law.[133] The award was confirmed by the national court and upon review the EC stated it did not agree with the interpretation of the law. As a response the parties complied with the view of the EC. If frequent use were made of this avenue by either the parties (through filing a complaint with the EC) or the EC (to which decisions of national courts are sent) this would engender uncertainty with regards to the finality of the award. Given that there is only one example of such a situation this is more a theoretical risk.

The two different approaches to the review of the award lead to procedural uncertainty as courts in different EU Member States may treat the same award differently when reviewing its compliance with public policy.[134] Until one approach is accepted the lack of a clear review process would represent a barrier for the parties because of the uncertainty of procedure they face. Uncertainty of procedure is a deterrent to bring a claim because the parties cannot anticipate the procedure and the outcome well. Furthermore, the maximalist approach adds to this uncertainty by imposing a more in-depth review of the award than is usually the case in arbitration. This means that parties cannot have the same reliance on enforceability of the award as they have under the minimalist review approach.

[C] The Relatively Predictable Nature of Arbitration Which Counters Procedural Uncertainties in Litigation

Certainty is a key element in international contracts and international disputes.[135] Arguably, compared to arbitration, court litigation brings more procedural uncertainties, as the parties have less control over the procedure. This therefore also represents a significant barrier to bringing a claim, especially in international cases where there is more of a (perceived) lack of certainty in procedure. The (perceived) neutrality of the arbitral tribunal is a significant reason why parties choose arbitration. If the parties make a choice for court litigation, they will need to include a choice of forum clause in their contract (or run the risk of the uncertainty of not knowing which forum will be seized). The choice of forum and law clauses are often determined by the party with the most bargaining power.[136] If the parties have equal bargaining power both would usually express a preference for their home jurisdiction. This has the advantage of

133. Preflex/Lipski available in Commission Xth Report on Competition Policy – 1980 (Brussels/Luxembourg, 1981), paragraph 126, 87-88.
134. Zia Akhtar, *Private Damages in EU Competition Law and Judicial Review of Commercial Arbitration*, 24(1) European Journal of Current Legal Issues 9 (2018).
135. Lord Justice Mustill, *Contemporary Problems in International Commercial Arbitration: A Response*, 17 International Business Lawyer 161,163 (1989).
136. Ingeborg Schwenzer, *Who Needs a Uniform Contract Law, and Why?*, 58 Villanova Law Review 723, 723-725, (2013).

familiarity in proceedings and legal interpretation. Even if the applicable law is not the *lex fori*, it is well-documented that the 'homeward trend' means that courts often apply the applicable law through the lens of the *lex fori*.[137] A choice for a neutral third forum is a potential solution as neither party has the advantage of a familiar legal system. However, the unfamiliarity of another legal system also creates uncertainty. Differences in legal procedure in the EU Member States affect for instance the discovery and use of evidence which is especially important in competition law cases.[138] The legal procedure for the private enforcement of competition law is left to the individual Member States and this creates uncertainty for the parties.[139] A choice for arbitration eliminates this uncertainty. It is perceived to be a neutral environment where the parties have strong control over the proceedings.

Under the NYC parties can choose the seat of arbitration and the winning party can enforce the award in a state where the losing parties has assets. This means that if a party has assets in multiple countries the winning party can strategically choose the forum where he wishes to have the award enforced. Thus, if the party wishes to avoid the award not being enforced for violation of competition law, they can go to the forum with the least stringent competition law. This would thus allow the party or parties to benefit from an anticompetitive agreement. This is especially the case as it is the national public policy of the forum which the New York Convention targets in article V. Whilst EU competition law would fall under the public policy of an EU Member State it would usually not fall under the public policy of a third state.[140] The parties could seek enforcement in a non-EU Member State to deliberately avoid the application of EU competition law. If the parties had used court litigation, they would not necessarily have this option as private international law has clear rules on when their domestic courts have jurisdiction. Arbitration could thus encourage forum shopping when seeking to enforce the award.

The advantages for the parties in choosing arbitration in (international) competition law cases thus lies in further control over the procedure as well as potentially more possibilities to make a strategic choice on where to seek enforcement. This additional control gives the parties further certainty which can encourage them to bring a claim and therefore lower procedural barriers for access to justice.

Whilst the above certainly holds for (larger) companies, SME and consumers face another issue in this regard. The costs of arbitration procedures are often higher than court proceedings, although there is conflicting data on the costs of arbitration versus litigation.[141] It is dependent on the forum as costs will differ per jurisdiction. ADR in the form of mediation or conciliation could be an alternative to lower access barriers for

137. Franco Ferrari, *Homeward Trend and Lex Forism in International Sales Law*, International Business Law Journal 333 (2009).
138. Ezrachi (*supra* n. 2) 204.
139. Christopher H. Bovis & Charles M. Clarke, *Private Enforcement of Competition Law*, 36 Liverpool Law Review 49, 54 (2015).
140. *See* for instance: Judgment of the Swiss Supreme Court, 8 March 2006, 4P.278/2005.
141. *See* for instance: Christopher R. Drahozal, *Arbitration Costs and Forum Accessibility: Empirical Evidence*, 41 University of Michigan Journal of Law Reform 813 (2008); Abraham L. Wickelgren, *An Economic Analysis of Arbitration versus Litigation for Contractual Disputes*, 59 The Journal of Law and Economics 393 (2016) and João Marçal Rodrigues Martins da Silva, *An*

SMEs and consumers because of low costs, speediness, and ease of procedure for especially consumers.[142] Furthermore, it can act as an elimination mechanism for those cases that have no merit or where the parties can agree relatively fast. At the same time the non-finality of any outcome could still lead to a claim if the parties cannot come to an agreement.

In addition, the cost issue can arguably be overcome by class actions. As noted under §9.03 The Proposed Directive for Collective Redress sets out rules enabling qualified representative entities, such as consumer organisations and independent bodies, to bring claims and seek compensation on behalf of consumers. When it becomes law, the Proposed Directive on Collective Redress, may tackle the cost issue and widen access to justice particularly for consumers.

The possibility to avoid the enforcement of an award in a Member State in a deliberate move to avoid the application of competition law could possibly endanger the fairness of procedure.

[D] Confidentiality

The confidentiality of arbitral proceedings is a considerable advantage for the parties in a competition law case. Court proceedings and investigations by competition authorities could require the disclosure of commercially sensitive information. This information could become (partly) public which might hurt the position of the parties. Thus, the confidential nature of arbitration may prompt parties to bring a claim, which they may not do so before courts. As a result, it may be said that arbitration widens access to justice particularly in competition disputes involving commercially sensitive information.

Whilst court litigation can advance the interpretation of the law arbitration does not do so because the arbitrator is not part of the legal order.[143] The confidentiality of the awards means that they are not publicly available although some institutions like the ICC do publish edited versions of their awards without identifying details. However, given that these are edited versions it can sometimes be difficult to understand the reasoning of the tribunal from reading the award. Arbitration does not further advance the interpretation of the law which means that future cases cannot build on this. This is especially important given the status of competition law as public policy and the involvement of multiple stakeholders (beyond the contractual relationship) which includes consumers and market competitors.

Answer to Criticisms Against the Lack of Efficiency in Arbitration: Measures to Reduce Time and Costs, 14 Revista Brasileira de Arbitragem 23 (2017).

142. Ioannidou (*supra* n. 101), at 70.

143. Guillaume Busseuil, *L'Avenir des Principes Unidroit Relatifs aux Contrats de Commerce International et des Principes Européens du Droit du Contrat: du Droit Mou ou Droit Dur?*, Centre de Droit Civil des Affaires et du Contentieux Economique 16 (2004).

§9.06 CONCLUSION

Several key issues arise in relation to access to justice in competition law disputes. These mostly concern access to procedure.

The first issue is confidentiality. Competition law cases are heavily fact reliant and are often lengthy. Competition law issues are of a commercially sensitive nature which parties might be apprehensive to disclose in a public forum and this could deter parties from starting a procedure. Arguably, the confidentiality of arbitration procedures can lower barriers for the parties to seek a resolution to their disputes as sensitive information would not be made public. The private nature of the arbitration procedure can keep competition law violations hidden and may arguably limit the progression of the interpretation of the law and the development of case law. This can have a negative effect on other stakeholders (including consumers) and on the understanding of the law in general

The second issue is uncertainty. The control the parties can exercise over the procedure in comparison with litigation is substantial. The parties can decide on the procedural rules, arbitrators, and the applicable law. This allows the parties greater certainty in the outcome of the procedure. At the same time uncertainty with regards to enforcement of arbitral awards may deter parties from resorting to arbitration. As stressed by Akhtar, the scope of judicial review of arbitral rewards in the EU is not a settled issue yet and there is conflicting case law on whether a maximalist or minimalist approach to the review should be taken.[144] The finality of the arbitral award and the relative certainty of enforcement are a corner stone for why parties entrust their disputes to arbitration. Therefore, any uncertainty as to the enforceability of the award would have a negative effect on the parties' decision on whether to arbitrate.

The issue of uncertainty also ties in with the need for subject expertise. Given the highly factual nature of competition law cases and the requirements on understanding not just the law but also the economics it is important that the tribunal deciding the case has the necessary knowledge. The expertise of arbitrators could lead to an award that reflects more truly the situation the company is in and therefore this could augment transparency and certainty, and lead to a fair outcome for the parties involved.

Furthermore, as discussed above, the wide enforcement and recognition of an arbitral award could enhance access to justice as it is easier to enforce a foreign arbitral award than a foreign court decision. As large companies often have assets in multiple states the enforcement of the award could be sought in different jurisdictions which allows the winning party a choice as to which state they seek enforcement, based on the assets of the company as well as the legislation. This also has adverse effects: it encourages forum shopping and could lead to parties actively choosing a non-EU member state to avoid EU competition law.

The final issue is the cost and complexity of procedure which could form a barrier for especially consumers and SMEs to bring any follow-on cases. As discussed under

144. Akhtar (*supra* n. 134) 9.

§9.05[C], ADR could tackle the issue of costs and complexity of procedure. Furthermore, the Proposed Directive on Collective Redress could also play an important role in lowering costs for consumers by enabling them to be represented by consumer organisations and independent bodies.

Arguably, with the increase in global commercial transactions, arbitration will be a predominant forum to resolve disputes arising from competition law. Overall, due to the flexibility, confidentiality, and speedy nature of procedure as well as the additional control the parties have over the procedure, arbitration could lower procedural barriers in competition law cases. Furthermore, the expertise of arbitrators in competition law and the extensive enforcement and recognition of arbitral awards could indeed enhance access to justice for victims of antitrust violations and lead to fair outcomes. Nevertheless, the costs associated with arbitration, coupled with the lack of clarity regarding the review of the award, may prompt parties to resort to litigation and other venues to access justice.

CHAPTER 10

Unpacking the Potential for Unilaterally Binding Arbitration: Improving Access to an Effective Remedy, and Business-Related Human Rights Violations

Youseph Farah

Access to justice is denied if victims of business-related human rights violation are unable to access a grievance mechanism, which is efficient, fair (fair trial), and one, which delivers outcomes that conform to internationally recognised obligations. At the heart of this debate is the comparative efficiencies between international court litigation on the one hand, and non-state grievance mechanisms on the other, the latter being identified by the UNGPs third pillar as being instrumental in completing the business and human rights agenda promoted by the UNGPs. Regrettably, the third pillar of the UNGPs remains under-theorised. Moreover, whilst there has been a surge in the use of operational non-binding grievance mechanisms by businesses in certain industries, the impression so far is that these operate outside a coherent system of access to justice. This article outlines the inefficiencies of international human rights litigation experienced in UK and US courts and advocates a rethink of the role of non-state grievance mechanisms in providing access to victims of business-related human rights violations.

§10.01 INTRODUCTION

While corporations can bring benefits for local communities by creating wealth and jobs, adding value and providing services, their corporate activity also can have negative consequences for people, impacting significantly on civil and political rights, on economic, social and cultural rights, on labour rights and the environment.[1] When this happens, victims of such adverse impact usually look to the 'state' to hold corporations to account for the harm they have caused, and to enable them to receive full and effective reparation. Unfortunately, there is overwhelming evidence showing that more often than not victims do not have an effective remedy against the unlawful conduct of corporations, and that 'there are clear gaps in the current human rights accountability system'.[2]

The 'Guiding Principles on Business and Human Rights' (UNGPs)[3] require a shift in approach, from where the state has exclusivity over human rights matters, including access to an effective remedy, to where the state occupies a central stage on human rights matters, with corporations having direct responsibilities, independent of national law.[4] The UNGPs recognise that alternative grievance mechanisms occupy an important space for the effective remediation of business-related human rights violations, and that a number of stakeholders play an important role in making this possible, such as states, independent statutory bodies (e.g., ombudsman), national human rights commissions, industry associations and most importantly for this research, corporations.[5]

UNGPs prescribe that corporations should 'participate in effective operational-level grievance mechanisms for individuals and communities who may be adversely impacted'.[6] The third pillar of the UNGPs which details access to an effective remedy does not offer specific solutions beyond containing abstractive principles, which leaves much room for interpretation.[7] Despite its potentially significant promises for victims' redress, the third pillar remains under-theorised,[8] and has received little implementation by businesses, to the extent that it has earned itself the title of the 'forgotten

---

1. It is increasingly evident that they may have as much as a government's impact on human rights. *See* United Nations – Human Rights Council, 'Guiding Principles on Business and Human Rights: Implementing the United Nations '"Protect, Respect and Remedy" Framework', UN New York and Geneva 2011, HR/PUB/11/04.
2. Report by Corporate Responsibility Coalition (CORE), 'Protecting Rights, Repairing Harm: How-State based non-judicial Mechanisms can help fill the gaps in existing frameworks for the Protection of Human Rights of People Affected by Corporate Activities', (2010), https://business-humanrights.org/sites/default/files/media/documents/ruggie/core-submission-to-ruggie-nov-2010.pdf (accessed 18 January 2017). *See* footnotes 33 and 34 for a fuller review.
3. United Nations – Human Rights Council (*supra* n. 1): The UNGPs rest on three pillars and are considered the most comprehensive contribution to the business and human rights discourse to date. Although the UNGPs are not legally binding, they have become an authoritative global standard on BHR. There is wide support for the UNGPs on the part of governments, intergovernmental organisations and corporations.
4. Florian Wettstein, *Normativity, Ethics, and the UN Guiding Principles on Business and Human Rights: A Critical Assessment*, 14(2) Journal of Human Rights 162, 163-165 (2015).
5. United Nations – Human Rights Council (*supra* n. 1): Explanatory notes on Principle 25.
6. United Nations – Human Rights Council (*supra* n. 1): Principle 28.
7. Maximilian J. L. Schormair & Lara M. Gerlach, *Corporate Remediation of Human Rights Violations: Restorative Justice Framework*, Journal of Business and Ethics, 1, 2 (2019) https://doi.org/10.1007/s10551-019-04147-2.
8. Juan José Álvarez Rubio and Katerina Yiannibas Globernance, 'Human Rights in Business: Removal of Barrier to Access to Justice in the European Union – Executive Summary', (2016) Institute for Democratic Governance. The full study due to be published in mid-2017 http://

pillar'.[9] Recognising this normative gap, in 2016 the UN High Commissioner for Human Rights (OHCHR) launched the 'Accountability and Remedy Project' which is entering its final stage.[10] Its emphasis is on the exploration of state and non-state-based grievance mechanisms.

This research concerns corporations' responsibility to improve victims' access to an effective remedy by engaging [in] various non-judicial grievance mechanisms, and focuses primarily on the 'legitimacy', and 'rights compatible' criteria envisaged under Principle 31 of the UNGPs. Unlike the other 'accessible', 'equitable' and 'predictable' constructs envisaged under Principle 31, which safeguard a victim's right to procedural justice, the former constructs include a 'public dimension' that safeguards the public's interest in the dispute, recognising that the resolution of business-related human rights violations engage multiple stakeholders and the wider public, which goes beyond the disputants.[11] These constructs are not fully distinct, but equally not entirely overlapping.

This research is distinctive because current practice, and policy thinking, do not give these constructs enough attention. This is a timely and original critical analysis of non-binding non-judicial grievance mechanisms such as mediation and operational level grievance processes, and binding non-judicial grievance mechanisms such as arbitration, in order to unpack their respective roles, individually and collaboratively, in strengthening the 'public dimension'. I demonstrate that non-binding non-judicial mechanisms exhibit significant weaknesses in the area of the above constructs, and therefore show why (and how) it is vital that arbitration should occupy a greater role in the resolution of business-related human rights violations. In relation to the latter I highlight that arbitration should adjust in order to provide meaningful access to justice for victims of business-related human rights violations.

Since 2016, there have been numerous calls to make more use of arbitration, such as the Hague Rules on Business and Human Rights Arbitration ['The Hague Rules'][12].

---

humanrightsinbusiness.eu/wp-content/uploads/2016/09/EXECUTIVE_SUMMARY_HRB_Research_Results.pdf [hereinafter 'Human Rights in Business: Removal of Barriers'] (accessed 05 October 2019).

9. Schormair & Gerlach (*supra* n. 7) 2.
10. United Nations Human Rights Office of the High Commissioner, OHCHR Accountability and Remedy Project, https://www.ohchr.org/EN/Issues/Business/Pages/OHCHRaccountabilityandremedyproject.aspx (accessed 05 October 2019). Mandate established by Human Rights Council Resolution adopted by the Human Rights Council on 30 June 2016 32/12. Business and human rights: improving accountability and access to remedy A/HRC/RES/32/10, https://documents-dds-ny.un.org/doc/UNDOC/GEN/G16/155/72/PDF/G1615572.pdf?OpenElement (accessed 05 October 2019).
11. Such claims, while often concerning financial reparation, can arise in the context of a violation of human rights, such as reparation claims concerning rape, child labour, slavery, discrimination, torture, right to life, right to self-determination and indigenous populations, and right to family life. *See* a useful list of how business conduct can affect human rights in https://www.ungpreporting.org/resources/how-businesses-impact-human-rights/ (accessed 05 October 2019).
12. For further information about The Hague Rules project *see* https://www.cilc.nl/project/the-hague-rules-on-business-and-human-rights-arbitration/ (accessed 20 February 2020) and Claes Cronstedt, Jan Eijsbouts and Robert C. Thompson, *International Business And Human Rights Arbitration*, http://www.l4bb.org/news/TribunalV6.pdf (accessed on 05 October 2019).

I share the view of the importance of arbitration; however, I envisage a different type of arbitration than has been discussed at that policy level. Unlike the arbitration model I propose in this article, the Hague Rules model which are modelled on the UNCITRAL Arbitration Rules (2013), a set of ad hoc rules that are almost never used where there is a clear disparity in the bargaining powers between the parties. These rules are therefore more suitable for situations where victims are able to join their claims in a collective redress claim against the corporation, which requires careful coordination and professional advice.

I show for the first time in academic writing that 'unilaterally binding arbitration' (UBA),[13] an adjudicative grievance process only binding on the business in relation to procedure and outcome, is well placed to safeguard the 'pubic dimension' and restore the power imbalance between corporations and victims.[14] Unlike the focus of the Hague Rules, the grievance design of UBA focuses more on victims' need for an affordable grievance mechanism which operates on the local level where the harm occurred, in relation to all sorts of harm caused by the violation of their human rights by corporations.[15] This is important because such a grievance mechanism offers an alternative debate away from a discourse which predominantly has focused on the 'private function' of offering efficient and procedurally fair grievance processes operating vis-à-vis the disputants, to one which reflects the 'pubic dimension' and recognises the 'public functions' that grievance mechanisms perform.

Part two of this chapter unpacks the concept of 'effective remedy' under various international documents and puts it within the context of the third pillar of the UNGPs. Part three, outlines in some detail the main types of non-binding non-judicial grievance mechanisms used by corporations. I provide critical analysis of the OECD NCP's experience in relation to the remediation of business-related human rights violations. This case study is useful in assessing the extent of conformity of non-binding non-judicial grievance mechanisms with the 'public dimension' embodied in each of the 'legitimacy', 'transparency' and 'rights compatible' criteria. This is then used in

---

13. There have been numerous calls by civil society lawyers and academics for the establishment of state-based non-judicial grievance mechanisms to have enforceable outcomes and a broad mandate over the types of human rights cases to be resolved by such processes. *See* Rubio and Globernance (*supra* n. 8). *See* the Hague Draft Rules (*supra* n. 12). Others have recommended the establishment of an international business and human rights arbitral tribunal; *See* Claes Cronstedt & Robert C. Thompson, *An International Tribunal of Business and Human Rights*, http://www.l4bb.org/news/TribunalV5.pdf (accessed 05 October 2019).
14. The UN working group on business and human rights have been considering the use of arbitration and their work does engage somewhat the 'public dimension', without explicitly identifying it as such. However, they have not considered 'UBA'. *See* Cronstedt, Eijsbouts & Thompson (*supra* n. 12).
15. *See* a study of assessing whether the PCA Optional Rules for Arbitration of Disputes Relating to the Environment and/or Natural Resources can be used for Business related human rights violations. PCA rules are available on https://pca-cpa.org/wp-content/uploads/sites/6/2016/01/Optional-Rules-for-Arbitration-of-Disputes-Relating-to-the-Environment-and_or-Natural-Resources.pdf (accessed 11 October 2019). *See also* Katharina Häusler, Karin Lukas and Julia Planitzer, 'Non-Judicial Remedies Company-Based Grievance Mechanisms And International Arbitration', in Juan José Álvarez Rubio and Katerina Yiannibas (eds), *Human Rights in Business: Removal of Barriers to Access to Justice in the European Union*, (Routledge 2017) 107 and 113.

part four of this chapter to show that 'UBA', when adjusted to take into account the above constructs, is a viable alternative grievance mechanism, which conforms to all the values envisaged under Principle 31, providing victims access to a grievance process which is procedurally and substantively fair, and one which fulfils important public functions.

§10.02 UNGPS AND ACCESS TO AN EFFECTIVE REMEDY FOR VICTIMS

It is firmly established under international law that it is the state's duty to ensure that victims of business-related human rights violations have access to an effective remedy.[16] According to international human rights law 'access to justice' is a basic principle of rule of law.[17] It is enshrined in Articles 2(3) and 14 of the United Nations International Covenant on Civil and Political Rights,[18] and Articles 8 and 10 of the United Nations Universal Declaration of Human rights.[19] In addition, Articles 6 and 13 of the European Convention on Human Rights (ECHR) contain similar stipulations; Article 47 of the EU Charter of Fundamental Rights guarantee the right to an effective remedy and the right to a fair trial (both being essential components of access to justice).[20] 'The notion of access to justice obliges states to guarantee each individual's right to go to court – or, in some circumstances, an alternative dispute resolution body – to obtain a remedy if it is found that the individual's rights have been violated.'[21] Access to justice enables victims to effectively enforce their right and remedy damage suffered, irrespective of the nature of the right.[22]

Neither the ECHR nor the Charter of Fundamental Rights define 'remedy'. The overriding requirement is for a remedy to be 'effective' in practice and in law.[23] There are no requirements regarding the form of the remedy, and states enjoy some discretion in this respect. This means that different types of remedies may redress different types of violations.[24] Remedy can take a variety of different forms, however corporations

16. Basic Principles and Guidelines on the Right to a Remedy and Reparation for Victims of Gross Violations of International Human Rights Law and Serious Violations of International Humanitarian Law. Adopted and proclaimed by General Assembly Resolution 60/147 of 16 December 2005.
17. Access to justice is safeguarded in a number of UN instruments, such as the 1998 Aarhus Convention on Access to Information, Public Participation in Decision-Making and Access to Justice in Environmental Matters and the 2006 Convention on the Rights of Persons with Disabilities. It is also part of United Nations Development Programme, https://www.unece.org/fileadmin/DAM/env/pp/documents/cep43e.pdf (accessed 05 October 2019).
18. General Assembly (1996), International Covenant on Civil and Political Rights, 16 December 1996.
19. United Nations General Assembly (1948), UDHR 10 December 1948.
20. European Union Agency for Fundamental Rights and Council of Europe, *Handbook On European Law Relating To Access To Justice* (Luxembourg: Publications Office of the European Union, 2016) 22.
21. *Ibid.*
22. *Ibid.*, 24-29. It is not confined to criminal charges and civil political as well as economic and social rights and obligations; the Charter, however, applies domestically only when Member States are implementing (or derogating from) EU law.
23. *Ibid.*, 92-95.
24. *Ibid.*, 101-107.

should as a minimum provide full and effective reparation, including 'apologies, restitution, rehabilitation, financial and non-financial compensation and punitive sanctions (whether criminal or administrative, such as fines), as well as the prevention of harm through, for example, injunctions or guarantees of non-repetition'.[25] Financial compensation should cover monetary awards proportionate to the gravity of the violation, which compensates for the 'physical or mental harm, lost opportunities, material or moral damages and costs for legal or other expert assistance'.[26]

The UNGPs have sought to clarify the respective roles and responsibilities of states, businesses and those affected by business-related human rights violations, through the UNGPs three-pillar structure.[27] From a normative perspective, they organise the relationship between corporations and individuals affected by their conduct without any legal constraints in place.[28] The victim's right to an effective remedy *vis-à-vis* the corporation under the third pillar, is framed in terms of voluntary responsibility. This is consistent with the general view that UNGPs have not resolved whether corporations are bearers of obligations under international law.[29] The third pillar of the UNGPs places the bulk of the responsibility on states to provide state-based judicial and non-judicial grievance mechanisms and/or to support effective non-state based non-judicial mechanisms.[30] However, the UNGPs establishes that corporations too have direct responsibilities.[31]

Unfortunately, victims' access to an effective remedy continues to face procedural and substantive challenges.[32] First, access to an effective remedy before courts in the host state has been too slow, at times lacking due process, affordable legal aid, or

25. United Nations - Human Rights Council (*supra* n. 1): Commentary to Principle 25. This wide scope of the meaning of effective remedy is very similar to the meaning given to it under Articles 19-23 of the Basic Principles and Guidelines on the Right to a Remedy and Reparation for Victims of Gross Violations of International Human Rights Law and Serious Violations of International Humanitarian Law Adopted and proclaimed by General Assembly Resolution 60/147 of 16 December 2005.
26. Columbia Law School Human Rights Clinic & Harvard Law School International Human Rights Clinic. *Righting wrongs?: Barrick Gold's remedy mechanism for sexual violence in Papua New Guinea: Key concerns and lessons learned* (2015) International Human Rights Clinic (IHRC) 70, http://hrp.law.harvard.edu/wp-content/ uploads/2015/11/FINALBARRICK.pdf (accessed 05 October 2019).
27. United Nation Human Right Council, *Promotion and Protection of All Human Rights, Civil, Political, Economic, Social and Cultural Rights, Including the Right of Development: Protect, Respect, and Remedy: A framework for Business and Human Rights: Report for the Special Representative of the Secretary-General on the issue of Human Rights and Transnational Corporations and other Business Enterprises, John Ruggie* A/HRC/8/5,7 April 2008, https://business-humanrights.org/sites/default/files/reports-and-materials/Ruggie-report-7-Apr-2008.pdf (accessed 05 October 2019).
28. Isabelle Duplessis, 'Soft international labour law: The preferred method of regulation in decentralized society', in *Governance, International Law and Corporate Social Responsibility* (International Institute for Labour Studies, International labour Organisation 2008).
29. *See* Andrew Clapham, *Human Rights Obligations of Non-State Actors*, (Oxford 2006) chapters 2 and 3.
30. United Nations - Human Rights Council (*supra* n. 1): Principles 25-27 of the UNGPs. As seen from the discussion above, this an obligation under international law.
31. Wettstein (*supra* n. 4) 163-165.
32. Cronstedt, Eijsbouts and Thompson (*supra* n. 12).

has been spoiled by political interference.[33] Second, the need to initiate international human rights litigation against a parent company alone or by joining the subsidiary to the proceedings, has not been as effective as one has hoped.[34] While there are some isolated success stories,[35] the experience has been disappointing.

Moreover, even if the procedural hurdles can successfully be overcome there is no guarantee that courts will apply substantive laws which enjoy the full support of internationally recognised human rights. The problem is that in the absence of a clear entry point to such human rights obligations or non-national system rules such as

33. For example, in the case of the Ogoni peoples' struggle for justice concerning the oil spill in Nigeria, a prominent Ogoni king remarked quite aptly that '[y]ou can never, never defeat Shell in a Nigerian Court. A case can go on for very many years. You can hardly get a judgment against an oil company in Nigeria. Shell is Nigeria and Nigeria is Shell' (John Vidal, *Ogoni king: Shell oil is killing my people*, The Guardian, https://www.theguardian.com/world/2016/dec/03/ogoni-king-shell-oil-is-killing-my-people (accessed 05 October 2019). Moreover, it took more than thirty years to get a judgment in Nigeria against Shell and it may take a significant period of time to enforce it. In January 2019, the Ogoni people represented by ten Ogoni Chiefs of Ejama Ebubu community of Ogoni in Rivers State, finally won a N134 billion case against Shell after the Supreme Court dismissed Shell's appeal following a litigation battle which started in 1991. *See* Davidson Iriekpen and Bayo Akinloye, *N134bn Ogoni Judgment Debt: Shell Loses Appeal at Supreme Court*, THISDAYLive, https://www.thisdaylive.com/index.php/2019/01/13/n134bn-ogoni-judgment-debt-shell-loses-appeal-at-supreme-court/ (accessed 05 October 2019). *See also* Amnesty International Ltd & Business and Human Rights Resource Centre, *Creating a Paradigm shift – Legal Solution to improve access to remedy for corporate human rights abuse*, p. 3 (2017), https://www.amnesty.org/download/Documents/POL3070372017ENGLISH.PDF (accessed 05 October 2019).
34. In the US for many years victims of business-related human rights violations brought claims under the Alien Tort Statue (ATS) [28 U.S.C. §1350] which gave the district court original jurisdiction 'of any civil action by an alien for a tort only, committed in violation of the law of nations or a treaty of the United States'. However, in the US Supreme Court Decision in *Kiobel v. Royal Dutch Petroleum* 133 U.S. 1659 (2013), the court confirmed, relying on *Sosa v. Alvarez-Machain* [542 U. S. 692], that the ATS is strictly jurisdictional and has no extraterritorial application. In order to displace this presumption against extraterritoriality, claimants must show that the claims touch and concern the territory of the United States with sufficient force. In *Jesner v. Arab Bank* 584 U. S. ____ (2018), the US Supreme Court further limited the scope of application of the ATS by ruling that it does not apply to foreign corporations. In the UK, in a recent decision, the UK Supreme Court, in *Vedanta resources v. Lungowe* [2019] UKSC 20, confirmed that the doctrine of *forum non conveniens* applies to the joinder of the non-EU subsidiary of a parent domiciled within the EU. The latter can however be considered as a success story for victims in the sense that the UK's Supreme Court refused to apply the doctrine because otherwise the victims would have been denied substantial justice for lack of access to justice in the appropriate forum (Zambia). In a previous decision by the English High Court the joinder of the subsidiary to the proceedings was denied because there was not enough evidence to show that there was a real issue between the victims and the EU domiciled parent company. The real issue was measured against the *Chandler v. Cape* [2012] EWCA Civ 525 test, which essentially enables a claim in tort to be brought directly against a parent company. *See Royal Highness Emere Godwin Bebe Okpabi And Others v. Royal Dutch Petroleum And Shell Development Company of Nigeria*, [2017] EWHC 89 (TCC).
35. One such success story is the claims made against a parent company under tort of negligence for a breach of health and safety provisions affecting the employees of the parent's subsidiary in South Africa (*Chandler v. Cape*). There were also numerous cases, which settled out of court. In the recent UK Supreme Court decision in *Vedanta resources v. Lungowe* the court found that there was a real issue between the UK parent company and the Zambian claimants, in the sense that a parent company could be held responsible for harm caused by its Zambia subsidiary. (Though the case was a setback in relation to the finding that England was *forum non conveniens*).

ethical codes or general principles of law, courts are not always able to provide rights compatible outcomes. Moreover, public policy gatekeeping under most conflict of law rules are insufficiently tested as to whether they can prevent the application of human rights incompatible laws.[36] The real issue is that even where the applicable law is human rights friendly, such obligations do not directly apply to a corporation, unless expressly made so under national law.[37].

The problem is that courts follow strict conflict of laws rules when determining the applicable law.[38] For example, under the EU Rome II Regulation on the law applicable to non-contractual obligations, including torts relating to human rights infringements,[39] the general rule is that the law applicable to the non-contractual obligation in a conflict of law situation is that of the country where the damage occurred (*lex loci damni*).[40] This rule applies irrespective of the country in which the event took place giving rise to that damage, and irrespective of the country (or countries) in which the indirect consequences of that event occur.[41] Moreover, certain conflict of laws rules such as Article 14(1) of Rome II Regulation do not allow the disputants to select non-state rules to govern the tort (*ex ante* choice), or an *ex post* choice of national law such as under Article 14(2) of the Rome II Regulation.[42] Despite the limits that certain conflicts of law rules place on the ability for parties to choose an applicable law,[43] an undertaking by a corporation to commit to internationally recognised human rights and standards is more likely to yield human rights compatible outcomes.[44] In part 4.3 of this Article, I show that the flexible nature of conflict of laws rules in arbitration are better placed to apply rules that lead to rights compatible outcomes.

In response to the obstacles facing business human rights litigation, the UN Human Rights Council set up a working group to proceed on advancing a binding treaty

36. Public policy and mandatory rules could apply instead of the applicable law, however exceptionally. For a fuller discussion *see* Lisbeth F.H. Enneking, 'Judicial Remedies, the Issue of Applicable Law', in Juan José Álvarez Rubio and Katerina Yiannibas, *Human Rights in Business: Removal of Barriers to Access to Justice in the European Union*, (Routledge 2017) 38-78 and 61-65.
37. *See* Rubio and Yiannibas (*supra* n. 36) for further discussion.
38. Regulation (EC) No 593/2008 of the European Parliament and of the Council of 17 June 2008 on the law applicable to contractual obligations (OJ L 177, Brussels 4.7.2008, p.6-16) (hereinafter Rome I Regulation).
39. Regulation (EC) No 864/2007 of the European Parliament and of the Council of 11 July 2007 on the law applicable to non-contractual obligations, (OJ L 199, Brussels 31.7.2007, p. 40-49) (hereinafter Rome II Regulation).
40. Enneking (*supra* n. 36) 50.
41. Rome II Regulation, Article 4(1).
42. *See* Article 14 of Rome II Regulation. *See also* Thomans Kadner Graziano, 'Freedom to Choose the Applicable Law in Tort, Articles 14 and 4(3) of the Rome II Regulation', in William Binchy & John Ahern (eds), *The Rome II Regulation and the Law Applicable to Non-Contractual Obligations: A new Tort Litigation Regime* (Leiden, 2009) section V.
43. It is not clear whether Article 14 of Rome II Regulation allows parties to agree on non-state law which is favourable to the victim. Moreover, under Article 14(1), with some exceptions, parties can only agree on a choice of law to govern non-contractual obligation after the dispute has arisen. *See* Graziano (*supra* n. 42).
44. *See* Häusler, Lukas and Planitzer (*supra* n. 15) 111.

on business and human rights in June 2014.[45] However, the current draft of the legally binding instrument to regulate international human rights law, the activities of transnational corporations and other business enterprises (zero draft), while it attempts to remove procedural obstacles experienced in international human rights litigation it does not give the much-needed attention to non-judicial grievance mechanism.[46]

The above shows that it is the state's duty under international law to provide access to an effective remedy. A corporation's incentive to engage in some non-judicial remediation processes are largely political or financial, but not legal. In the next part I clarify the normative framework under the UNGP, which places some responsibility, *albeit* an imperfect one, on corporations to establish or engage with viable grievance mechanisms that facilitate access to an effective remedy for victims.

§10.03 ACCESS TO REMEDY AND NON-BINDING NON-JUDICIAL GRIEVANCE MECHANISMS UNDER UNGPS THIRD PILLAR

Where a human rights grievance is concerned, the third pillar of the UNGPs articulates a right to remedy, the access to that remedy and enforcement mechanisms. Principle 25 of the UNGPs envisages a host of non-judicial grievance mechanisms that the state can establish or work with businesses to put in place.[47] It is well recognised that the UNGPs require corporations to engage with various types of grievance processes, such as operational level grievance mechanisms, mediation and binding non-judicial processes, and to provide 'a fair and independent process, being accountable, and producing outcomes that are consistent with human rights'.[48]

This access includes procedural as well as substantive safeguards, namely that access should be proportionate in terms of being expeditious, free to access and transparent (procedural safeguards), and that the quality of the outcome should be one which gives effect to the victim's human rights, redressing and repairing the harm

45. United Nations, Human Rights Council, Elaboration of an International Legally Binding Instrument on Transnational Corporations and other Business Enterprises with Respect to Human Rights, 25 June 2014, A/HRC/26/L.22/Rev.1. European Parliament, 'Towards a Binding International Treaty on Business and Human Rights', EPRS Briefing, April 2018.
46. Legally Binding Instrument to Regulate, in International Human Rights Law, the Activities of Transnational Corporations and Other Business Enterprises, Zero draft 16 July 2018, https://www.business-humanrights.org/sites/default/files/documents/DraftLBI.pdf (accessed on 05 October 2019).
47. United Nations - Human Rights Council (*supra* n. 1) Principle 25.
48. EU Commission Oil and Gas Sector Guide on Implementing the UN Guiding Principles on Business and Human Rights available at https://www.ihrb.org/pdf/eu-sector-guidance/EC-Guides/O&G/EC-Guide_O&G.pdf (accessed on 17 January 2020). *See also* Communication From The Commission To The European Parliament, The Council, The European Economic And Social Committee And The Committee Of The Regions 'A Global Partnership for Poverty Eradication and Sustainable Development after 2015' Com (2015) 44, Brussels 5 February 2015, p. 12.

caused (substantive).[49] Both procedural and substantive dimensions establish the core foundation of access to an effective remedy.[50]

There are two types of non-binding non-judicial grievance mechanisms. The first type is the operational level grievance mechanism which is a formal means enabled by the corporation for affected stakeholders to raise concerns about any impact they believe a company has had on them, and to seek redress. The assumption is that these mechanisms make it possible for grievances, once identified, 'to be addressed and for adverse impacts to be remediated early and directly by the business, thereby preventing harms from compounding and grievances from escalating'.[51] Moreover, by utilising communication channels with aggrieved victims and communities, corporations can then regularly identify adverse impact as part of their responsibility to conduct human rights due diligence, and identify systematic problems and adapt their practices in order to avoid or mitigate harm.[52]

The second type is mediation or conciliation, which is engaged externally by mapping and working with independent external remediation processes, such as national human rights commissions, collaborative initiatives developed by industry, initiatives linked to international certification bodies, or an OECD National Contact Point (NCP).[53]

The informal and autonomous nature of mediation make it less adversarial than arbitration or court litigation. Yet it is clear that mediation is more formalised than the operational level grievance mechanisms. These processes are not self-executory, in the sense that the participation in such external processes by businesses are not mandatory, and the third-party adjudicator has no power to deliver binding outcomes.[54]

The use of mediation assumes that the parties had failed to negotiate an acceptable solution, and that the corporation's internal system of remediation has either decided that no action should be taken, or that there is a gap between what the victim wants and what the corporation is willing to offer. Therefore, mediation is mostly effective at the early life of the dispute, and preferably should be limited to a short period of time.[55]

49. Directorate-General for External Policies – European Parliament, Access to Legal Remedies for Victims of Corporate Human Rights Abuses in Third Countries, PE 603.475 February 2019, p. 11.
50. United Nations – Human Rights Council (*supra* n. 1) Principle 31.
51. *Ibid.*, commentary to Principle 29.
52. *Ibid.*, commentary to Principle 29.
53. OECD Guidelines for Multinational Enterprises, OECD Publishing (2011). Section I part II, http://dx.doi.org/10.1787/9789264115415-en (accessed 05 October 2019). Adhering countries are required to establish NCPs responsible for 'undertaking promotional activities, handling enquiries and contributing to the resolution of issues that arise relating to the implementation of the Guidelines in specific instances'.
54. *See* Caroline Rees, 'Mediation in Business – Related Human Rights Disputes: Objections, Opportunities and Challenges', Harvard Kennedy Scholl, Working Paper No. 56, February 2010.
55. *See* for example: Rolf H. Weber, *Roundtable on Forty Years of the OECD Guidelines for Multinational Enterprises: Draft Background Paper Development of Coherent Procedural Rules for OECD Guidelines* Mediation, OECD Conference, Paris, Monday 19 December 2016. *See also* Rees (54) and Philip Bryden and William Black, *Mediation as a Tool For Resolving Human Rights Disputes: An Evaluation of the B.C. Human Rights Commission's Early Mediation Project*, 73(1) UBC Law Review 73 (2004).

In practice, corporations have mostly engaged with the non-binding types of grievance mechanisms. At least this is what transpires from grievance policies published by various corporations and industry associations.[56] These have undoubtedly improved the corporation's engagement with internationally recognised human rights, and may have mitigated or avoided harm all together.[57] However, there is little evidence to show that such non-binding processes have had much success in terms of the actual remediation of harm caused by their conduct.

[A] The Public Dimension of 'Access to an Effective Remedy'

In theory, non-binding non-judicial grievance mechanisms should conform to the values enshrined under Principle 31 of UNGPs.[58] Such grievance mechanisms should take place at no cost to the complainants; thus they can be deemed accessible, and where practicable they should resolve disputes quickly. The presumption is that addressing problems with individuals or communities, early and locally, are more likely to be resolved quickly, and efficiently.[59] There are therefore mutual incentives for victims and corporations to engage in such processes.

However, such processes do not fully cohere with the public dimension constructs that engage the interest of external stakeholders in the dispute resolution, including its outcome. It is this aspect of non-conformity, which is difficult to resolve.

56. Numerous grievance mechanisms issued by oil and gas corporations; a key document by The *International Petroleum Industry Environmental Conservation Association (IPIECA), Community Grievance Mechanisms in The Oil and Gas Industry. A Manual For Implementing Operational-Level Grievance Mechanisms and Designing Corporate Frameworks* (January 2015), http://www.ipieca.org/resources/good-practice/community-grievance-mechanisms-in-the-oil-and-gas-industry/ (accessed 05 October 2019). *See also* for example, the Dutch companies that publicly commit to the OECD Guidelines: Aalberts Industries, Aegon, Air France – KLM, Airbus Group, AkzoNobel, ASML, Ballast Nedam, Bam Groep, DSM, KPN, Rabobank, SBM Offshore, Shell, Telegraaf Media Group, Unilever, Vopak, Wessanen and Wolters Kluwer (Vicky Van Heck, 'VBDO Commitment to OECD Guidelines for Multinational Enterprises by Dutch Stock Listed Companies, Final Report, Dutch Association of Investors for Sustainable Development (VBDO), Ministry of Foreign Affairs of the Netherlands, October 2016, p. 3, https://www.vbdo.nl/wp-content/uploads/2018/07/VBDOReportOECDGuidelinesresearch-1.pdf (accessed on 14 October 2019)).
57. *See* Reporting Framework, http://www.ungpreporting.org/ (accessed 05 October 2019). *See also* the 'implementation hub' for key tools, guidance and examples of uses of the UN Guiding Principles by companies (ie human rights due diligence), governments, and others, https://www.business-humanrights.org/en/latest-news/un-working-group-issues-report-on-human-rights-due-diligence-with-recommendations-to-governments-companies-investors/ (accessed 05 October 2019).
58. United Nations – Human Rights Council (*supra* n. 1): Explanatory notes to Principles 27 and 29.
59. The office of the Compliance adviser/Ombudsman for the International finance Corporation, *A Guide to Designing and Implementing Grievance Mechanisms for Development Projects*, (2008) p. 2, http://www.cao-ombudsman.org/howwework/advisor/documents/implemgrieveng.pdf (accessed 05 October 2019).

[1] *The Role of 'Transparency' in the 'Public Dimension'*

It is important that grievance processes are visible, and that they support the development of the law and be a continuous source of learning. I find this prerequisite fundamental for the fulfilment of the public function of any dispute resolution mechanism. Principle 31 (e) of UNGPs requires that both the procedure and its outcome must operate with sufficient transparency concerning the receipt of complaints, and the key elements of their outcomes. On the one hand, the need for greater transparency is important to perform the public function of expressing important dialogue and enabling the public to ensure just procedures and rights compatible outcomes. On the other hand, confidentiality protects know-how, third parties and important trade secrets of the corporation, and at times victims too have an interest to keep the dispute resolution confidential. As the Harvard Corporate Social Responsibility Initiative put it, while the two main issues that come into play with respect to transparency include provision of information to aggrieved parties about how their case is being handled, and to stakeholders, at the same time confidentiality may be essential to protect the complaining or aggrieved individual from retaliation.[60] Moreover, confidentiality is equally 'important in enabling dialogue between the company and complainants in an atmosphere of sufficient mutual confidence for real interests to be raised and options for solutions discussed'.[61]

Thus, this tension between the mutually exclusive goals for transparency and confidentiality in non-judicial proceedings poses an important challenge. In arbitration for example, confidentiality usually gets a wide scope of application to cover all materials produced and exchanged, the deliberation of the tribunal and the arbitral award.[62] This had led some authors to cast doubt on the viability of arbitration in its traditional private form for resolution of human rights disputes.[63] Their justification is sound, in that disputes relating to human rights violations are of concern to the public

60. Caroline Rees, *Piloting Principles for Effective Company-Stakeholder Grievance Mechanisms: A Report of Lessons Learned*, (2011) Corporate Social Responsibility Initiative, Harvard Kennedy School, p. 24, https://www.business-humanrights.org/en/report-on-piloting-principles-for-effective-company-stakeholder-grievance-mechanisms-with-new-annexes-by-doug-cahn-stephan-sonnenberg-luc-zandvliet (accessed 05 October 2019).
61. *Ibid.*
62. Most national arbitration laws do not include a general obligation of confidentiality. The Model Law which represents best international practice does not spell out such a duty. Thus, the approach varies considerably depending on the applicable law to arbitration. Thus, parties' agreement and the institutional arbitration rules become decisive on the matter. Article 30 of the LCIA Arbitration Rules (2014) includes a wide obligation of confidentiality. The ICC rules only limit the duty to arbitrators and the institution itself (Article 1) and under Article 22(3).the arbitral tribunal has the discretion upon the request of any of the parties to the dispute to make orders 'concerning the confidentiality of the arbitration proceedings or of any other matters in connection with the arbitration and may take measures for protecting trade secrets and confidential information'.
63. Catherine Dunmore, *International Arbitration of Business and Human Rights Disputes: Part 2 – Advantages and challenges*, (December 2017), https://www.asser.nl/DoingBusinessRight/Blog/post/international-arbitration-of-business-and-human-rights-disputes-part-2-advantages-and-challenges-by-catherine-dunmore (accessed 05 October 2019).

and therefore there lies an interest in having them resolved by open and transparent proceedings.[64]

However, this might not be as big an obstacle as it may first seem. Most laws or institutional rules do not require a high degree of confidentiality. The duty of confidentiality is not absolute and may be waived and replaced by an open and visible process.[65] Moreover, in many instances during and post the arbitral proceedings parties may lawfully compromise the confidentiality of the proceedings or the award. This may occur in a number of situations, such as during a challenge made to the substantive jurisdiction of the tribunal brought before the national court at the seat of arbitration,[66] or during a request of the national court to compel the production of evidence,[67] or during a challenge to the validity of the arbitral award,[68] or during proceedings concerning its recognition and enforcement.[69]

For example, the Hague Rules on International Arbitration of Business and Human Rights Disputes[70] has offered such an approach, proposing to adjust the UNCITRAL Rules so to include a higher degree of transparency of proceedings.[71] With greater transparency one could then start introducing rules that increase public participation in the process.[72] Moreover, greater transparency enables the process to become a learning tool that informs corporations and policymakers of how best to respect, protect and fulfil human rights.[73]

Thus, insofar as this research focuses on the special role UBA can perform in providing resolutions to business-related human rights violations, there seem to be fewer obstacles to ensuring the transparency of the process. One can say therefore that the system of arbitration can be well suited for the adjudication of disputes between business enterprises and victims,[74] and thus as a matter of principle and practice should not pose an obstacle to the performance of the public dimension we have identified. This should allow numerous victims to aggregate their claims[75] and allow other legitimate stakeholders to engage in important dialogue concerning the implications of the dispute on public policy, and to ensure 'rights compatible outcomes'. Therefore, in the next section I will test the conformity of non-binding non-judicial processes to the 'legitimacy' and 'rights compatible outcomes' constructs.

64. *Ibid.*
65. *Ibid.*
66. Section 31(1) of the English Arbitration Act 1996.
67. Article 27 of the Model Law.
68. *Ibid.*, Article 34.
69. *See* Articles III, IV and V of the NYC.
70. *See* draft Rules from June 2019, https://www.cilc.nl/cms/wp-content/uploads/2019/06/Draft-BHR-Rules-Final-version-for-Public-consultation.pdf. (accessed 05 October 2019). Greg Fullelove & Daniel Harrison, *Business and Human Rights: Is International Arbitration the Future, and what does it mean for businesses?*, https://www.lexology.com/library/detail.aspx?g=e48288a8-6850-40ad-88da-920106439796 (accessed 05 October 2019).
71. Fullelove & Harrison (*supra* n. 70).
72. *Ibid.*
73. United Nations – Human Rights Council (*supra* n. 1) Principle 31(g).
74. Cronstedt, Eijsbouts and Thompson (*supra* n. 12).
75. *Ibid.*

[B] The 'Legitimacy' Construct

Non-binding grievance mechanisms in theory allow victims to be heard and understood which is an important part of the grievance resolution process.[76] Principle 31 (a) of UNGPs requires all grievance processes to be legitimate in the sense that they enable 'trust from the stakeholder groups for whose use they are intended and being accountable for the fair conduct of grievance processes'. Research has shown that users place more emphasis on procedural justice when deciding whether a grievance process is legitimate than they place on the outcome of the procedure.[77]

What does it mean to say that all grievance processes must be 'legitimate'? Legitimacy in the traditional sense is 'the property that a rule or an authority has when others feel obligated to defer voluntarily'.[78] In the context we are examining here, it correlates with a corporation's responsibility to comply with the decision of the mediator or with its own internal findings irrespective of whether there is an external authority with powers to compel it to conform. This is an important normative requirement under Principle 31(a) of the UNGPs, in the sense that it calls upon corporations to accede to legitimate grievance mechanisms and to voluntarily comply with the processes and outcome.

There is also a public dimension enshrined in Principle 31(a) of UNGPs which is not explicit in its text. One of the main functions of the court once a dispute has arisen is to restore the natural harmony[79] that had existed before the harm occurred and to express values important to the public. Although the majority of domestic and international human rights litigation are essentially concerned with private law claims between victims and corporations, such as civil claims under the tort of negligence,[80] these concern matters arising out of severe human rights violations. These violations often concern sovereign and extraterritorial regulatory matters,[81] and reflect 'a set of principles and assumptions, conscious or unconscious, about the appropriate distribution of risk, reward and responsibilities between the different actors involved'.[82] This helps better understand a corporation's responsibility to respect human rights,[83] an area of law which needs to develop. Moreover, this much-needed open debate is

76. *See* the importance of being heard in administrative disputes involving human rights breaches (David Cowan, Simon Halliday, *The Appeal on Internal Review Law, Administrative Justice and the (non-) Emergence of Disputes* (Hart 2003) 153 and 156). *See also* David Cowan and Caroline Hunter, *Internal Review in Homelessness Cases: A Mixed Blessing?*, 1(3) Journal of Housing Law 43 (1997).
77. Tom R. Tyler, *Procedural Justice, Legitimacy, and the Effective Rule of Law*, 30 Crime and Justice 283 (2003).
78. *Ibid.*
79. *See* Owen Fiss in the context of court litigation on the role of the court of restoring Natural Harmony (Owen Fiss, *The Social and Political Foundations of Adjudication*, 6(2) Law and Human Behaviour, 124 (1982).
80. *See* footnotes 33 and 34 including a survey of most important examples.
81. Enneking (*supra* n. 36) 47.
82. Jennifer A. Zerk, *Multinationals and Corporate Social Responsibility* (Cambridge University Press 2006) 104-142.
83. On this issue *see* Enneking (*supra* n. 36) 47.

intrinsic to the whole notion of open justice which enables the public to become active in ensuring just procedures and just outcomes.[84]

The impartiality and independence of the adjudicator, grievance handler, or mediator (for ease of use 'adjudicator') is an important constitutional due process value essential for safeguarding procedural justice, and is an important metric used when measuring the legitimacy of the grievance mechanism. The test usually used when assessing the impartiality of the adjudicator is that there should not arise justifiable doubts about their impartiality or the institution managing it.[85] Impartiality is measured from subjective and objective standpoints.[86] The subjective enquiry is about determining the personal conviction of the adjudicator where the test is that the adjudicator should not favour (or disfavour) a party for any reason other than what is required under the law. Under the jurisprudence of the ECtHR the adjudicator's subjective impartiality is presumed.[87]

The objective enquiry protects against the appearance of bias, which reassures observers and those who are involved in the dispute proceedings that justice is not only done but that it is 'manifestly and undoubtedly be seen to be done', a matter which increases the confidence in the integrity of the administration of justice[88] and in turn the perception of its legitimacy. The enquiry is to assess whether there exist objectively ascertainable facts which would raise justifiable doubts about the impartiality of the adjudicator.[89]

Operational level grievance mechanisms struggle to meet the above definition because there are strong ascertainable links between the adjudicator and the corporation.[90] This lack of neutrality adversely affects the perception of fairness[91] in the eyes of those stakeholders for whom its use is intended, which in turn reduces the

84. Emma Rowden, *Distributed Courts and Legitimacy: What Do We Lose when We Lose the Courthouse*, 14(2) Law, Culture and the Humanities 263, 266 (2018).
85. United Nations - Human Rights Council (*supra* n. 1), the legitimacy criterion under Principle 31 is understood to demand the impartiality of the tribunal. It states '... that the parties to a grievance process cannot interfere with its fair conduct ...'.
86. *See* the Section 6 of the ECHR, and *Micallef v. Malta* (2010) 50 E.H.R.R. 37.
87. *Ibid.*, *Micallef v. Malta* at 94.
88. *See* English Jurisprudence on this issue in *Lanes Group Plc v. Galliford Try Infrastructure Ltd* (t/a Galliford Try Rail) [2012] 13 EG 92, paragraph 46; *R v. Gough* p. 673. *see also*, per Devlin L.J. in *Reg. v. Barnsley Licensing Justices, Ex parte Barnsley and District Licensed Victuallers' Association* [1960] 2 Q.B. 167; Lord Hewart C.J. in *Rex v. Sussex Justices, Ex parte McCarthy* [1924] 1 K.B. 256, 259.
89. *Fey v. Austria* (Application no. 14396/88) ECHR 1993. The test is applied for impartiality differs among jurisdictions. The English court for example uses the test of whether the ascertainable facts lead the fair minded and well-informed observer to conclude that there is real possibility that the tribunal was bias *Magill v. Porter* [2002] 2 AC 357 . In other jurisdictions though the court usually will use the reasonable person in measuring impartiality. *See SA Auto Guadeloupe Investissements v. Columbus Acquisitions Inc et al (2015)* (in France), and IBA rules on the conflict of interest which adopts a test of reasonable likelihood. IBA Rules on the Conflicts of Interest in International Arbitration 2014, file://ueahome/eresssf1/fpb16tdu/data/Downloads/IBAGuidelinesonConflictofInterest2014%20(2).pdf (accessed 05 October 2019).
90. In the context of internal appeals and administrative ADR, *see* SH. Jones B. Bailey and AR. Mowbray, *Cases Materials and Commentary on Administrative Law* (Sweet & Maxwell, 2005) 92.
91. Tyler (*supra* n. 77) 298.

perception of legitimacy of the process due to a reduced trust in the mechanism's ability to exercise its authority in a fair and an impartial way.[92] Making important institutional adjustments should mitigate this apparent bias, for example by enabling an appeal procedure[93] or by avoiding an overlap of competences between the alleged wrongdoer and the adjudicator reviewing the alleged violation.[94] While this is unlikely to remove justifiable doubts about the impartiality of the grievance process,[95] it should nonetheless provide more confidence in the impartiality of the adjudicator and increase the trust in the grievance process.

[C] The 'Rights Compatible Outcomes' Construct

Principle 31(f) of UNGPs states that all types of grievance mechanisms should be 'rights compatible ... ensuring that outcomes and remedies accord with internationally recognised human rights'. This means that victims should be entitled to full and effective reparation. There is though a tension between the conciliatory nature of non-binding non-judicial dispute resolution grievances and the observation of human rights, because there may exist compelling incentives for the disputants to compromise and settle the matter driven by a 'right interest' approach at the expense of full enjoyment of human rights.[96]

For example, the global oil and gas industry association (IPIECA) Community Grievance Mechanisms toolbox, which is based on the IPIECA operational experiences of its members and which supports oil and gas companies to create and implement community grievance mechanisms, instructs the appeal body available under the toolbox to reach a 'satisfactory resolution for the company and the complainant'.[97] The toolbox does not require that the resolution should be rights compatible. Such grievance mechanisms are tailored for situations where clashing interests between those of the victim and those of the company are proactively removed by a system of dialogue. However, it may fall short where the clash concerns interests and/or values that cannot be reconciled other than through a binding resolution built on the respect of internationally recognised human rights.

Similarly, mediation has been criticised as delivering outcomes which are not about 'just settlement', but rather 'just about settlement'.[98] The argument is that mediation may place too much emphasis on the interests of parties at the expense of evaluation of the law,[99] and that its use could diminish *the quality of justice* – a means test for the constitutional perspective of the 'delivery of justice' (including the quality

92. Tyler (*supra* n. 77) 299.
93. *See* IPIECA (*supra* n. 56).
94. Columbia Law School Human Rights Clinic & Harvard Law School International Human Rights Clinic (*supra* n. 26) 10.
95. *Magill v. Porter* (*supra* n. 89) for the Supreme Court's approach to impartiality.
96. Rees (*supra* n. 54).
97. *See* IPIECA Community Grievance Mechanism Toolbox, Step 6, http://www.ipieca.org/resources/good-practice/community-grievance-mechanisms-toolbox/ (accessed 05 October 2019).
98. Hazel Glenn, *Judging Civil Justice* (Cambridge University Press 2010) 117.
99. Rees (*supra* n. 54).

of 'fairness'). If the main mandate given to the mediator is to facilitate a resolution of the dispute, then the interests of the parties may trump justice considerations[100] and the outcome may then risk not being human rights compatible. This is again an important matter because according to Sourdin, 'fairness (or justice) (is) a core element in the effective resolution of disputes'.[101] Non-consideration of justice might mean that the underlying issues in the dispute remain unresolved even where the parties reach a settlement.

The few case studies concerning non-judicial remediation processes have found serious shortcomings, among other things in relation to fulfilling the rights compatible legal construct.[102] For example, in an important study of Barrick Gold's remedy mechanism for sexual violence in Papua New Guinea, it was found that many of the rights holders did not consider the offered remedies by Barrick Gold as proportionate to the alleged harm as required under international law.[103]

Much however depends on the powers and functions of such non-binding mechanisms which can differ based on their design. Some for example may have investigatory powers which they can implement on their own initiative.[104] Mediation can be either facilitative or evaluative. In its basic nature, facilitative mediation is about the facilitation of a settlement. Evaluative mediation requires the mediator to help the parties assess the legal merits of their case in accordance to the applicable law and make recommendations to the parties as to the strength of their case. The use of latter is more likely to yield human rights compatible outcomes.

[D] National Contact Points under the OECD Guidelines on Multinational Corporations

There is little evidence about the practice of non-judicial grievance mechanisms used for the resolution of business-related human rights violations.[105] I do not intend here to provide a full survey of all available initiatives. Instead I will provide a concrete analysis of the Organisation for Economic Cooperation and Development National Contact Points (NCP) which serve as a good practical example of mediation used for business-related human rights violations. I will demonstrate the design and theoretical weaknesses that have had a clear adverse impact on the effectiveness of such processes.

---

100. Glenn (*supra* n. 98).
101. Tania Sourdin, *Alternative Dispute Resolution*, (3rd ed. Pyrmont, NSW: Lawbook Co., 2008) 12-15. *Also*, Akin Ojelabi, *Mediation and justice: An Australian perspective using Rawls' categories of procedural justice*, 31(3) Civil Justice Quarterly Journal 318, 320 (2012).
102. Schormair & Gerlach (*supra* n. 7) 4.
103. Columbia Law School Human Rights Clinic & Harvard Law School International Human Rights Clinic (*supra* n. 26).
104. Report of the United Nations High Commissioner for Human Rights, *Improving accountability and access to remedy for victims of business-related human rights abuse through State-based non-judicial mechanisms*, Human Rights Council Thirty-eighth session 18 June–6 July 2018, paragraph 9, https://documents-dds-ny.un.org/doc/UNDOC/GEN/G18/132/70/PDF/G18132 70.pdf?OpenElement, (accessed 05 October 2019).
105. Schormair & Gerlach (*supra* n. 7).

The OECD Guidelines for multinational enterprises are recommendations directed by governments at multinational enterprises operating in or from adhering OECD countries. They provide, *inter alia*, non-binding principles and standards for responsible business conduct in accordance with internationally recognised human rights and labour rights.[106] The OECD Guidelines include procedural guidance setting broad principles relevant for the implementation of the NCPs established by adhering states.[107] Their main mandate is to maintain a non-judicial state-based dispute resolution mechanism for handling complaints related to the business conduct of multinational enterprises operating in these countries.[108] NCPs operate in accordance with core criteria of 'visibility, accessibility, transparency and accountability to further the objective of functional equivalence'.[109]

The NCPs' grievance mechanism has no uniform structure. Adhering states have considerable discretion in organising their NCPs and the grievance procedural rules.[110] Consequently, according to a careful study by the OECD Watch, the NCPs and their procedures vary among OECD adhering states.[111] In the context of our analysis of the public dimension of Principle 31, the design and practice of the NCPs raises a challenge in relation to the 'rights compatible' construct. As a matter of design, it is not clear whether the NCPs role is an adjudicative one, in the sense that whether as a matter of principle an NCP should evaluate and determine whether the conduct of the corporation was in breach of the OECD Guidelines,[112] or whether the NCPs should limit their role to facilitating a resolution.

The practice drawn from various NCPs in their handling of complaints concerning human rights violations demonstrate that such processes exhibit weak accountability features failing to resolve complaints in most cases. For example, in 2018 only 9% of complaints reached an agreement by mediation in all NCPs.[113] Moreover, 'meaningful' remedies for victims are very difficult to achieve.[114] The voluntary nature of the Guidelines mean that businesses are under no obligation to take part in the

106. The Foreword of OECD Guidelines for Multinational Enterprises 2011, p. 3.
107. *Ibid.*
108. Decision of the Council on the OECD Guidelines for Multinational Enterprises – I, https://www.oecd.org/corporate/mne/theoecdguidelinesformultinationalenterprisesdecisionofthecouncil.htm (accessed 05 October 2019).
109. OECD Guidelines (*supra* n. 53).
110. *Ibid.*, Procedural Guidance I(A).
111. OECD Watch, *Guide to the OECD Guidelines for Multinational Enterprises' Complaint Procedure: Lessons from Past NGO Complaints* (2006) p. 19, https://www.oecdwatch.org/wp-content/uploads/sites/8/2006/11/Guide-to-the-OECD-guidelines-for-multinationals-enterprises-complaint-procedure.pdf (accessed 05 October 2019).
112. *See* Bernadette Maheandiran, *Calling for Clarity: How Uncertainty Undermines the Legitimacy of the Dispute Resolution System Under the OECD Guidelines for Multinational Enterprises*, 20 Harvard Negotiation Law Review 205, 219 (2015).
113. *See The State of Remedy Under OECD Guidelines: Understanding Cases concluded in 2018 through the lens of remedy*, OECD Watch, June 2019 p. 1, https://www.oecdwatch.org/wp-content/uploads/sites/8/2019/06/State-of-Remedy-2018-2019-06-08.pdf (accessed 05 October 2019). *See also* a condemning report by the OECD Watch a decade earlier (*The OECD Guidelines for MNEs: Are they 'fit for the job'?* (2009), p. 5, https://www.oecdwatch.org/wp-content/uploads/sites/8/2009/09/Are-they-%E2%80%98fit-for-the-job%E2%80%99-1.pdf (accessed 05 October 2019).
114. OECD Watch 2019 (*supra* n. 113) p. 2.

proceedings. The most they can do is issue a recommendation under Article 3 of the procedural guidance. While in some instances NCPs undertake an evaluative approach and issue a determination whether or not the Guidelines were breached, such as seen from the practice of the UK NCP, they lack the power to compel a party (or for the same matter a foreign government) to produce evidence or share vital information.[115]

Moreover, the procedural guidance itself is brief, and does not provide the NCPs with enough muscle to force businesses to engage with the process, other than through the loose language of Article 3(c), to conduct a proper investigation, deliver a recommendation based on the application of the Guidelines and monitor compliance. According to OECD Watch, most NCPs, except for those in the UK and the Netherlands, refrain from recommending a remedy when mediation fails and do not resort to their investigatory powers in order to assess whether the OECD Guidelines have been breached.[116] The risk with this approach is that in addition to not having a remedy at all there seems to be an expectation that victims and enterprises should endeavour to reach a settlement during the mediation phase.[117] This cannot always produce outcomes which fully protect human rights.

[E] Assessment of Non-binding Non-judicial Grievance Mechanisms

There are three important conclusions to be drawn from the operational level grievance mechanisms and from the OECD NCPs example as outlined above. First, non-binding non-judicial mechanisms exhibit serious weaknesses in terms of legitimacy and their ability to provide human rights compatible outcomes. Their use should therefore be contingent on improvement on those values. Victims who have commenced a non-binding non-judicial process should be able to access an external binding process as soon as it becomes apparent to the case handler or to the victim that the internal process is unlikely to yield a quick, cheap, transparent and a rights compatible outcome.

Second, in regard to mediation I propose that its use should be confined to situations where the mediator assumes an active investigatory role which could lead to a recommendation based on the full enjoyment of international human rights free from considerations of efficiencies.[118]

Third, national human rights commissions,[119] NGOs, government institutions and industry bodies should have a greater role in administering such processes which

115. Crude Accountability & KPO consortium: Final Statement after examination of Complaint, UK NCP for OECD Guidelines for Multinational Enterprises, November 2017, paragraph 25.
116. OECD Watch 2019 (*supra* n. 113) p. 2.
117. *Ibid.*, p. 3.
118. *See* Ojelabi (*supra* n. 101) relating to the fundamental goal of the courts to deliver justice.
119. The National Human Rights Commission (the Commission) which should ordinarily function as a non-judicial grievance mechanism in line with Resolution 48/134 of the United Nations General Assembly. Unfortunately, there appears to be no evidence of any noteworthy action or pronouncement regarding the Ogoni human rights situation and some other cases of human rights violations. the Commission has failed to live up to its expectations in terms of promotion and protection of human rights, due to under-performance by the Commission as including poor funding, lack of autonomy and accessibility among others *See* O.V.C Okene, *National*

strengthen the effectiveness of the remediation process, and increase transparency due to their institutional capacity to monitor compliance with Principle 31 of UNGPs. This involvement would enhance dialogue among all stakeholders and ensure that all actors of the civil justice system have a role in ensuring just procedures and just outcomes.

§10.04 CAN UBA CONFORM TO THE 'LEGITIMACY' AND 'RIGHT COMPATIBLE OUTCOMES' CONSTRUCTS?

I start by emphasising that traditional model(s) of commercial arbitration are not suitable for the resolution of disputes arising out of business-related human rights violations. In the traditional model when grievances arise there is an assumption of parity and an assumption that disputants are experienced and well-informed actors who are able to participate in complex arbitral proceedings. This is usually not the case in relation to victims of business-related human rights violations. These disputes require adjustment of key features of the traditional model in order for arbitration to fulfil its potential and conform to the values envisaged under Principle 31 of UNGPs.

The use of binding non-judicial grievance mechanisms I envisage in this part may not be suited for all claims and all types of victims. In particular, such processes may only be suitable where it is possible to satisfy the consensual nature of binding arbitration and therefore are most likely to occur in certain types of projects which have noticeable long-term presence such as the extractive industry, Build Operate and Transfer Projects, and project finance.[120]

[A] Unilaterally Binding Arbitration and the Requirement of Consent

Due to the disparity in the powers of the parties in relation to their legal expertise and their financial ability to fund the dispute resolution, unlike in ordinary arbitration where the procedure as well as the outcome (award) are binding on all parties, arbitrating business-related human rights violations and their outcomes should be binding on the corporation alone. I refer to this as 'unilaterally binding arbitration'. UBA is not a new concept and it can be found for example under domestic consumer protection schemes such as the Financial Ombudsman which is a grievance mechanism established by UK Parliament in 2001 with a mandate to resolve disputes between financial businesses and their customers.[121]

Human Rights Commission And The Promotion And Protection Of Human Rights In Nigeria – Reflections, Emerging Challenges And Suggestions For Effectiveness, https://works.bepress.com/ovunda_v_c_okene/33/ (accessed 05 October 2019).

120. *See* figure 3 of the IPIECA Human Rights Due Diligence Process, a practical guide to implementation for oil and gas companies, p. 7, http://www.ipieca.org/resources/good-practice/human-rights-due-diligence-process-a-practical-guide-to-implementation-for-oil-and-gas-companies/ (accessed 05 October 2019).

121. Part XVI of The Financial Services and Markets Act 2000, sections 226 and 227 which establish compulsory jurisdiction over regulated activities brought by a qualifying complainant, and that the outcome is binding on the financial business once accepted by the complainant, respectively.

UBA is only possible where the parties have agreed to arbitrate existing or future disputes.[122] In direct actions for civil wrong most victims would not have entered into an arbitration agreement before the dispute has arisen. Moreover, victims are in a weak bargaining position to convince a corporation to submit to arbitration. In the absence of a valid agreement no court will sanction the process and this may result in challenges to the validity of an award or its recognition and enforcement.[123]

However, corporations may find themselves bound to arbitrate in the following situations. The first opportunity for arbitration arises during the negotiation of an investment contract between corporations and states concerning projects that present large-scale or significant social or economic risk or opportunity, such as in the extractive industry, or renewable energy projects.[124] The Principles for Responsible Contracts recommend that:

> [t]he business investors should enter the negotiation with a clear idea of how the project's objectives, opportunities and risks relate to their responsibility to respect human rights' and that the state and the corporation 'should enter the negotiation aiming to ensure that any adverse human rights impact is prevented, mitigated or remedied throughout the project's life cycle.[125]

It does not go as far as to claim that this should be binding yet it is submitted that this should be factored into the contractual negotiations as a tool to help integrate the management of human rights risk of the business.[126]

This is particularly applicable to business operations or transactions that require licensing by the host state. For example, before it is possible for oil and gas companies to explore, produce and refine crude oil, or to transport carbohydrate, a company must seek first the permission to do so from the host state.[127] Companies usually obtain this permission by the grant of a licence by the State or else they operate under contractual terms included in a Production-Sharing Agreement (PSA).[128] Such licensing requirements are common in Private Public Partnership projects involving the construction or operation (or both) of essential facilities, of land leasing (agriculture), in the extractive

122. Jan Paulson, *Arbitration unbound: Award Detached from the law of its Country of Origin*, 30(2) International Comparative Law Quarterly 358, 367 (1981).
123. *See* Articles 8 of the Model Law and Article II and V of the NYC, which deals with challenges to recognition and enforcement, and Article 34 of the Model Law which deals with challenges to the validity of the arbitral award.
124. *See* pp. 4-6 of The Principles for Responsible Contracting: Integrating the Management of Human Rights Risks into State-Investor Contract Negotiations UNHR Office of the High Commission (2015), https://www.ohchr.org/Documents/Publications/Principles_ResponsibleContracts_HR_PUB_15_1_EN.pdf (accessed 05 October 2019). The Responsible Contracts document identifies ten key principles to help integrate the management of human rights risks into contract negotiations on investment projects between host state entities and foreign business investors. *See* p. 3.
125. *Ibid.*
126. *Ibid.*
127. Greg Gordon, John Paterson, Emre Üsenmez and James Cowie, 'Oil and Gas Law on the United Kingdom Continental Shelf: Current Practice and Emerging Trends in Public and Regulatory Law', in Greg Gordon, John Paterson, Emre Üşenmez (eds), *UK Oil and Gas Law: Current Practice and Emerging Trends Volume I: Resource Management and Regulatory Law* (Edinburgh University Press 2018) 5.
128. *Ibid.*, 66.

sector and generally in relation to the building and maintaining and operating of public infrastructure.[129] Some of these projects are transformational and impact millions of people.[130] Businesses and governments should consider the use of UBA if it becomes apparent during the negotiation of the terms of the licence or contract that its use will serve as a viable grievance mechanism for local communities and individuals adversely affected by the business conduct. This should be required as part of the preselection criteria.[131] Equally lawyers and legal advisors acting for the parties should consider the viability of the use of UBA and other forms of grievance mechanisms as part of their responsibility to respect the UNGPs and conduct due diligence.[132]

Moreover, a corporation can consent to arbitrate existing or future disputes under industry association rules or under rules accompanied to the financing of a project such as the Equator Principles.[133] For example, IPIECA and other similar organisations should consider developing and offering a grievance policy for their members that make compulsory the use of UBA in addition to the non-binding processes, perhaps in the form of an escalation clause.[134] In supply contracts companies should use their leverage to include a UBA arbitration clause with their immediate suppliers and should persuade their business partners to include a similar commitment through the supply chain.[135]

In the next sections I assess whether UBA can satisfy the requirement of impartiality and independence and assess whether it is able to improve this dialogue of public values among all stakeholders in the civil justice system.

[B] 'Legitimacy' in Arbitration

Arbitration operates within the civil justice system as opposed to being an alternative to it. It coheres and communicates with the different bodies that make up the civil justice system and which can address business-related human rights abuse.[136] An arbitral tribunal, for example seated in Nigeria or Chile, derives its powers and legitimacy from that jurisdiction (the seat of arbitration), and from the agreement to

129. *See* the National Academic Press, p. 103, https://www.nap.edu/read/24744/chapter/8#103 (accessed 05 October 2019). Bent Flyvbjerg, in *What you should know about megaprojects and why: An overview*, 45(2) Project Management Journal 6 (2014), states at that 'Major infrastructure PPPs, might include everything from transportation, water, and energy, to information and communications technology, industrial processing plants, and mining'.
130. Flyvbjerg (*supra* n. 129) 6.
131. *See* part III UNCITRAL Guide on Privately Financed Infrastructure Projects, United Nation, New York 2001, https://www.uncitral.org/pdf/english/texts/procurem/pfip/guide/pfip-e.pdf (accessed 05 October 2019).
132. Stefanie Lemke, *The UN Guiding Principles and the Legal Profession: Quo Vadis?*, 2(2) Business and Human Rights Journal, 351 (2017).
133. *See* the Equator Principles, Principle 6, https://equator-principles.com/ (accessed 20 October 2019).
134. Escalation clauses expects parties to mediate first or negotiate in view of reaching a friendly settlement, failing that parties agree to arbitrate.
135. Cronstedt, Eijsbouts and Thompson (*supra* n. 12).
136. Paragraph 22 of Report of the United Nations High Commissioner for Human Rights, *Improving accountability* (*supra* n. 104).

arbitrate. Thus, individuals, usually with the consent of the arbitral tribunal, can approach the court at the seat to compel the corporation to disclose evidence,[137] or to issue an interlocutory measure ordering the company to remove a threat to the community.[138]

In particular, arbitrating the claim at the place where the harm occurred is more likely to establish much-needed dialogue with all parts of the community affected by the harm, directly or indirectly, and engage all stakeholders in the outcome of the dispute. The main value of such a system is that controversies, which take place (for example in Nigeria, concerning an oil spill adversely affecting local communities, such as the struggle of the Ogoni people)[139] are adjudicated by local adjudicators, if need be utilising effectively the entirety of the civil justice system.[140] Most importantly, it helps achieve policy coherence between non-judicial mechanisms, and court litigation, and enables states to 'work towards developing a legal and regulatory environment that enables these various mechanisms to make a positive collective contribution to accountability and remedy in business and human rights cases'.[141]

This is particularly important where the adjudication of such disputes influence an important national dialogue. Such a dialogue took place during the South African Apartheid reparation claims brought before US courts.[142] In those proceedings the government of South Africa initially objected to bring the suits in US courts claiming that this would interfere in the Truth and Reconciliation process and undermine South Africa's 'sovereign right to determine, according to internal political and constitutional order, how best to address apartheid's legacy'.[143]

Institutional arbitration can record such instances and provide regular analysis, detect patterns and causes of grievances, contributing to important national debates, influencing policies, procedures or practices in order to prevent future harm.[144] Thus, arbitration in the host state positions the dispute resolution within the civil justice system and allows the national court to perform its oversight in respect to its function as a guarantor of procedural justice, whilst delivering human rights compatible outcomes. Whilst non-binding non-judicial processes can achieve this vital dialogue they usually do so at a much lower scale. In any case they lack the necessary linkages

137. Article 27 of the Model Law.
138. *Ibid.*, Article 17.
139. *See* the *Ogoni case* (*supra* n. 33).
140. *See Lungowe v. Vedanta* where the court of Appeal stated during *forum non conveniens* analysis the Court cautioned that: 'there must come a time when access to justice in this type of case will not be achieved by exporting cases, but by the availability of local lawyers, experts and sufficient funding to enable the cases to be tried locally'.
141. *Improving Accountability* (*supra* n. 104) paragraph 22.
142. *In re S. African Apartheid Litigation*, 238 F. Supp. 2d 1379 (J.P.M.L. 2002).
143. *See* Lindwini Kuntson, *Aliens, Apartheid and US courts: Is the Right of Apartheid Victims to claim Reparations from Multinational corporations at last Recognized?* 7(12) Journal of International Human Rights, 173, 177 (2010). In 2009, SA withdrew its objection that the proceedings to be brought in the US. *See Apartheid Reparation Lawsuits*, https://www.business-humanrights.org/en/apartheid-reparations-lawsuits-re-so-africa?page=4 (accessed 20 October 2019). *See also* Youseph Farah, 'Toward a Multi-Directional Approach to Corporate Accountability', in Sabine Michalowski, *Corporate Accountability in the Context of Transitional Justice* (Routledge 2014).
144. United Nations – Human Rights Council (*supra* n. 1) Principle 31(g).

with the other actors in the civil justice system, something the OECD example above demonstrates, as does the fact that there is little evidence in practice of successful non-binding non-judicial grievance mechanisms.

As to the issue of impartiality, it is widely recognised under international law and practice that the arbitrator must remain independent and impartial throughout the dispute process.[145] Despite the test of impartiality varying from one system to another, most systems, including the test under the IBA Rules on Conflicts of Interest, converge on the idea that the test is an objective one and should strive to remove the appearance of bias as much as it should remove the threat of actual bias.[146] Given our preference for local adjudication, using local lawyers and practitioners, special care should be given to the appointment of qualified and unbiased arbitrators who also do not appear to be skewed in either the interest of victims or a corporation.

[C] 'Rights Compatible Outcomes' in Arbitration

Judges are required to apply the law and reach a final and binding judgment. However, judges do occasionally engage in facilitating settlements between litigants under many civil procedure rules and increasingly under common law.[147] Moreover, judges may encourage parties to mediate as part of court-sanctioned mediation depending on the applicable jurisdiction.[148] Thus, the outcome of court litigation should in principle be rights based, in the sense that courts apply to governing law, with the potential for it also being 'interest based'. However, it is difficult to see how a court will sanction a settlement that does not allow the full enjoyment of human rights.

Similarly, arbitrators occupy an important semi-judicial role where they act like judges, weighing the facts and evidence, applying the law and reason and reaching a final decision on the merits of the dispute. The main mandate of the arbitrator is to deliver a binding arbitral award.[149] Thus, similar to court litigation, arbitration as a matter of principle and practice should deliver rights compatible outcomes. Whilst arbitrators under most jurisdictions, particularly those with a civil law tradition, play a

---

145. Model law Article 12. In England and Wales the duty of the arbitrator to remain impartial was drawn from the cases relating to the impartiality of the judge and a civil servant. *See R v. Gough* [1993] AC 646 at 670; *Porter v. Magill* [2002] 2 AC 357. The latter adjusted the test of impartiality in order for it to conform to Article 6 of the Human Rights Act 1998. *See also* IBA Rules (*supra* n. 89).
146. *See* Principle 2(b) and (c) of the IBA Rules (*supra* n. 89). *See also* the debate we make in heading [1] of this chapter. Article 11 of the Hague Rules (*supra* n. 12) stipulates that the chairperson of the arbitral tribunal should have a different nationality for the disputants.
147. This has been the practice in Austria under Section 204(1) of Code of Civil Procedure, in Germany under Section 278(1) of the Code of Civil Procedure, in Switzerland under Article 197 of the Civil Code, in Belgium under article 731 of the Civil Code, in France under Article 21 of the Civil Code, in Italy under Article 185 of the Civil Code and in the Netherlands under Article 87(1) of the Code of Civil Procedure. Also, increasingly in common law jurisdictions such as the Section 1.4 (1) and (2)(f) of the UK Civil Procedure Rules (CPR). *See also* Klaus Peter Berger and J. Ole Jensen, *The Arbitrator's Mandate to Facilitate Settlement*, 40(3) Fordham International Law Journal, 887, 902-903 (2017).
148. CPR PD: Pre-Action Conduct and Protocols, paragraph 8.
149. Berger & Jensen (*supra* n. 147) 902.

role in assisting parties to conciliate and reach a settlement, they usually perform this function without recourse to caucusing, and only perform such a role when all parties have agreed to entrust them with such a power.[150] This dynamic nature of arbitration allows arbitrators to evaluate whether a settlement would best serve the interests of the victim.

Under most institutional arbitration rules such as those of the ICC, AAA, or LCIA, or the UNCITRAL Rules which can be used in *ad hoc* arbitration, the arbitrator must apply the applicable law agreed by the parties or in the absence of such a choice the 'rules she considers to be most appropriate'.[151] Thus, parties can agree on an applicable law, including in relation to claims brought in tort. The main challenge though is whether arbitration can deliver *human* rights compatible outcomes.

Parties could subject a dispute to internationally recognised human rights law[152] or other industry or lending standards[153] designed to safeguard human rights.[154] These rules should have as a minimum a complementary or a corrective function[155] and help to inform the tribunal when evaluating the applicable national law. Equally, where parties agree to apply principles of international human rights the tribunal should be able to resort to such principles directly as the proper substantive law without having first to identify a lacuna under domestic law, or a clash with international law (complementary and corrective functions of international law).[156] In the unlikely event that domestic law provides a more favourable remedy to the victim than available under international law, the tribunal should prefer that because ultimately the parties

150. *See* Bernd Ehle, *The Arbitrator as Settlement Facilitator*, in *Walking A Thin Line: What An Arbitrator Can Do, Must Do Or Must Not Do* (Bruylant 2010). This practice is less common in common law jurisdictions. However, in recent years there has been movement in common law jurisdictions towards adopting the civil law tradition where arbitrators can act as settlement facilitators, such as in Hong Kong, Singapore, Australia and certain provinces in Canada, and India the practice is allowed by law.
151. *See* Article 21 of the ICC Rules of Arbitration.
152. *See* Häusler, Lukas and Planitzerv (*supra* n. 15) 111.
153. Such as the Equator Principles (*supra* n. 133). It is a risk management framework, adopted by financial institutions.
154. Principles for Responsible Contracting (*supra* n. 124) Principle 3, which expect businesses and states to supplement investment contracts with international standards where there are gaps in domestic law which prevents the safeguarding of human rights. *See* IPIECA Business and Human Rights Project, http://www.ipieca.org/news/human-rights-day-and-the-oil-and-gas-industry/ (accessed 20 October 2019).
155. Similar to Article 42 of ICSID – Washington Convention 1965. In *Klockner v. Cameroon*, Ad Hoc Committee Decision, May 3, 1985, the ad hoc committee found that international law under Article 42 of ICSID, in the absence of an agreement between the parties, has a gap-filling and a corrective function. Though, it is important to note that it would be too simplistic to capture the debate concerning the role of international law under Article 42 of ICSID in this footnote; Equally, the debate concerning the role of international law under Article 42 of ICISD, arises in relation to the interpretation of an international treaty. Whereas in our context, the arbitral tribunal gives effect to parties' intention. Therefore, the analogy with Article 42 is merely a useful example.
156. *See* annulment decision in *Wena Hotels Limited v. Arab Republic of Egypt* (ICSID Case No. ARB/98/4). *See also* Emmanuel Gaillard, and Yas Banifatemi, *The Meaning of "and" in Article 42(1), Second Sentence, of the Washington Convention: The Role of International Law in the ICSID Choice of Law Process*, 18(2) ICSID Review-Foreign Investment Journal 375 (2003), pp 403-404.

had intended a role to international law the enhances that right rather than takes away from it. Equally, industry codes may have legal effects in arbitration.[157] For example, a parent oil and gas company could establish an obligatory code of conduct for its subsidiaries, suppliers, and business partners[158] which could then form part of the applicable law if relevant to the dispute.

§10.05 CONCLUSIONS

This chapter has explored the limits of non-binding alternative grievance mechanisms in providing an effective remedy for victims, traced primarily along Principle 31 of the UNGPs legal constructs that include a public dimension, namely those of 'legitimacy', 'transparency' and 'rights compatible outcomes'. A grievance mechanism can only serve its purpose if it can perform these important public functions. Therefore, alternative grievance mechanisms should be viewed as complementary to all the other important actors that form the civil justice system in order to allow the remediation of business-related human rights violations.

I have presented a unique approach to arbitration that actively promotes and delivers effective access to justice, and that fills the gap left by weak court remediation avenues and weak non-binding non-judicial grievance mechanisms. I advocate that unilateral arbitration provides a more flexible, cost-effective, rights-based, transparent and legitimate grievance process for victims. In particular, UBA performs strongly in terms of performing the public functions identified above, in the sense that it is able to communicate important public values that often arise in the context of business-related human rights violations, and it is able to form important linkages with other actors in the civil justice system. To that end, it would go beyond existing principles and Guidelines that rely on the goodwill of the parties involved.

In order, however, for it to yield its full potential, more needs to be done in order to make UBA more transparent and more able to engage further with non-binding grievance mechanisms. Further work should investigate how arbitral procedures should be adjusted in order to ensure that public interests are met, in particular, '*amicus curiae* participation, collective redress, specialised arbitrators, financial assistance and oversight of the implementation of the award'.[159] This latter is very

157. For a literature survey focusing on the relationship between codes and national laws, *see* R. Jülich & H. Falk, *The Integration Of Voluntary Approaches Into Existing Legal Systems: Literature Survey* (Centre for Industrial Economics, WP-99/09/4 1999). *See also* Halina Ward, *Legal Issues in Corporate Citizenship,* (2003) International Institute for Environment and Development (IIED), prepared for Swedish Partnership for global responsibility, pp. 5-24 focusing on enforcement through litigation, https://pubs.iied.org/pdfs/16000IIED.pdf (accessed 05 October 2019).
158. For general discussion *see* S. Prakash Sethi, *Setting Global Standards and Guidelines for creating Codes of Conduct in Multinational Corporation* (John Wiley & Son 2003. *See also* IPIECA, *Oil and Gas Industry Association for Environment and Social Issues*, http://www.ipieca.org/about-us/ (accessed 05 October 2019).
159. Rubio and Globernance (*supra* n. 8) 19.

important in order to bridge the inequality of the power gap between the victim and a corporation and was pointed out to be one of the main challenges for the successful use of arbitration in business-related human rights violations.[160]

160. Cronstedt, Eijsbouts and Thompson (*supra* n. 12).

Part IV Access to Justice and Technology: Arbitration and ODR

CHAPTER 11

Access to Justice Through Online Dispute Resolution Is Not Science Fiction: A Practitioner's Perspective on the Good, the Bad and the Future

*Mirèze Philippe**

Are people waking up to online dispute resolution (ODR) was a question that the author asked and commented in a blog on Global Pound Conference. The hot topic of the role of technology in dispute resolution was high on the agenda in the recent years and the topic is being increasingly at the centre of discussions. Although innovation and technological advancements are occurring at a constantly rapid pace, services to resolve disputes online remain extremely limited or almost non-existent. The absence of such services providing access to justice can potentially end up in a denial of justice. The use of technology in the legal process and in any redress system is inevitable. Regrettably, countless practitioners take cognisance of ODR's unique potential but are incapable of investing the relevant time and resources to fatten the 'golden goose'. Ironically, we walked on the moon, justice is not yet online! Many platforms and initiatives failed because it is not money generating. But who deals then with complaints? Why cannot justice be rendered and on time? Why do small claims have to be dropped because it is not worth wasting time and money? Millions of disputes remain without remedy because people are not aware of mechanisms which can offer remedy without going to courts. What are the reasons for which online justice is lagging behind? What has gone wrong and what lessons can we learn from past experiences to avoid repeating the same mistakes? Is now not the time to bring ODR where it is missing and fully implement the benefits that ODR has to offer to settle

* The views expressed are those of the author and do not reflect those of ICC, ICC Court or its Secretariat.

disputes out-of-court or in courts but online? The author shares in this article her strong belief that online justice is possible. The article will address in turns the undeniable advantages of ODR, the lessons to learn from past mistakes, and recommendations for the future.

§11.01 INTRODUCTION

Access to justice is a human right and impeding such access equates to denial of justice. Providing access to justice through online dispute resolution (ODR) is an effective way to contribute to cure denials of justice for many. ODR can enhance access to justice for individuals who may have little or no access to adequate legal remedies such as individuals with low income, in remote locations or with disabilities. It is time to make ODR available where it is missing and fully implement the benefits that ODR has to offer to settle disputes out-of-court or in courts. Providing remedy is not only a matter of justice, it also impacts business and generates trust which is a crucial element of success. For example, marketplaces which offer remedies to their clients ensure that their clients are satisfied with the goods and services purchased online and invest in long-term relationships. Likewise, resolving disputes out-of-court, through simple, swift, and inexpensive channels impact the entire society and the economy in general. There is a dire need for out-of-court redress mechanisms in civil small claims and consumer disputes, whether domestic or cross-border, which may be resolved online and contribute to reducing the courts' backlogs. Court systems are indeed sometimes 'unintelligible for the great majority of non-lawyers' as observed by Richard Susskind,[1] and parties should not be compelled to be assisted by lawyers in small claims. Furthermore, it is unrealistic to continue progress without including justice in the revolution that technology has operated.[2]

Scholarly and practitioner discussions have propelled ODR to where it currently stands as the solution to many of the disputes that are arising in this digitised millennium. The role of technology in dispute resolution has become high on the agenda as the topic is increasingly occupying the centre of discussions. 'Are people waking up to online dispute resolution?' was a question discussed in a blog post in which it was observed that there has been a surge of interest in the legal community to discuss ODR.[3] The use of technology in the legal process and in any redress system is inevitable. The service expected by the users is long overdue. In a world that is rapidly

1. Foreword by Richard Susskind in Ethan Katsh & Orna Rabinovich-Einy, in M. Ethan Katsh, Orna Rabinovich-Einy, *Digital Justice: Technology and the Internet of Disputes* (Oxford University Press 2017).
2. Globally the number of Internet users increased from 413 million in 2000 to over 3.4 billion in 2016, https://ourworldindata.org/internet#growth-of-the-internet (accessed 28 August 2019) & https://ourworldindata.org/how-many-internet-users-does-each-country-have (accessed 28 August 2019). The one-billion barrier was crossed in 2005. Every day over the past five years an average of 640,000 people went online for the first time, which increases the potential number of disputes, https://ourworldindata.org/internet-history-just-begun (accessed 28 August 2019).
3. Mirèze Philippe, *Are People Waking Up To Online Dispute Resolution*, https://www.imimediation.org/2017/05/22/people-waking-online-dispute-resolution/ (accessed 28 August 2019).

developing it is surprising to observe that ODR is lagging behind. Regrettably, thus far, ODR has suffered the treatment of the 'golden goose'. Countless practitioners take cognisance of ODR's unique potential but are incapable of investing the relevant time and resources to fatten the goose. Instantaneous access to information and services has become normal and a must. Everything is online, and yet, justice cannot be accessed online like any service. Ironically, we have walked on the moon, but justice is not yet online.[4]

Over the past two decades many authors and ODR experts have highlighted the advantages of settling disputes online. Two ODR pioneers, Ethan Katsh and Janet Rifkin, published in 2001 the first book about conflict resolution in cyberspace and showed how ODR can be used as a supplement to dispute resolution.[5] Another ODR pioneer, Colin Rule, published the result of studies showing the value of investment in dispute resolution tools and systems, which evidences the economic benefits of effective redress processes and how satisfaction as a metric of success counts.[6] Ethan Katsh and Colin Rule have amply published about ODR, and Colin Rule has built several dispute resolution systems; both are considered the 'fathers' of ODR.

Graham Ross, a mediation practitioner and ODR advocate, has observed that the current main development is 'the growing interest in courts around the world in creating online court facilities and integrating ODR tools into their justice system'.[7] Undeniably, this is progress because the digitalisation of the courts will increase users' confidence in justice provided online and remove distrust in ODR out-of-court mechanisms. A number of countries have been at the forefront of applying ODR in courts, like Lithuania or Singapore. Efforts are undertaken in various countries by public and private initiatives, but they are only a handful. Dispute resolution, whether public and private, remains severely missing online. This gap affects litigants as they should have the freedom to select the mechanism they consider best appropriate to their type and value of dispute.

Indisputably, courts cannot absorb a massive number of complaints ever growing and justice is not rendered on time. Users hesitate to file claims with state courts because procedures are extremely long, they can be costly especially if users are represented by professionals, and the value of the claims may not be worth going through such a process. Millions of disputes remain without remedy as most people are not aware of out-of-court mechanisms. Although many platforms and initiatives failed

4. Mirèze Philippe, *We Walked On The Moon, Justice Is Not Yet Online*, Revue Pratique de la Prospective et de l'Innovation 48 (2017).
5. Ethan Katsh and Janet Rifkin, *Online Dispute Resolution – Resolving Conflicts in Cyberspace* (Jossey-Bass 2001); the authors have founded in 1998 the National Center for Technology and Dispute Resolution (NCDR) linked to the University of Massachusetts (*see* odr.info (accessed 28 August 2019)).
6. Colin Rule, *Quantifying the Economic Benefits of Effective Redress: Large E-Commerce Data Sets and the Cost-Benefit Case for Investing in Dispute Resolution*, 34(4) University of Arkansas at Little Rock Law Review 767 (2012).
7. Graham Ross, *Online Dispute Resolution Moves to the Courts*, 17 December 2018, https://www.themediationroom.com/single-post/2018/12/17/Online-Dispute-Resolution-Moves-to-the-Courts?utm_campaign=b445c545-f262-4d11-a483-46ab7dbfe1fc&utm_source=so (accessed 28 August 2019).

for the reasons that will be discussed in this chapter, we can learn lessons from past experiences and avoid repeating the same mistakes.

Technology is critical to enhance the efficiency of justice, provided standards and ethics are applied.[8] The advantages of ODR are undeniable and it is worth reminding the most significant benefits to convince professionals and users that investing in ODR is indispensable for the short, medium, and long-term. Consumer to consumer (C2C), business to consumer (B2C), and business to business (B2B) disputes, including in domestic and cross-border disputes, can be settled using online resolution mechanisms, and so can civil claims and certain criminal claims like cybercrimes claims handled by the Malaysian cyber court. ODR is mostly used for the settlement of disputes which have arisen out of online transactions but is also used for offline transactions.

ODR is an indispensable redress mechanism and is no longer science fiction. Although several ODR providers were successful, it is however still considerably under-explored. The keys to ODR's success are available. Models exist as discussed in this chapter and can serve to inspire other initiatives. It is not rocket science. It requires pragmatism and perseverance.

In 2010, Colin Rule, Vikki Rogers and Louis Del Duca observed that:

> Ever since the field of online dispute resolution (ODR) started in the late 1990s, there has been talk about creating a global system for resolving cross-border consumer issues. Significant progress has been made over the years with some impressive attempts, but none of the efforts have truly taken root. [9]

Over two decades have passed since building platforms, holding annual ODR Forums in addition to all conferences discussing potentials of ODR, publishing about the benefits and the need for online justice, discussing standards and best practices. One would think that given the time spent by thought leaders on discussing theoretical and practical issues, justice would already be available online. What are the reasons for which online justice is lagging behind and what does it take to make it available? Should we not start by going back to the basics to be aware of the benefits of ODR?

To understand how ODR can enhance access to justice, this chapter will first address the undeniable advantages of ODR, the 'good' (§11.02). It will then explain why access to justice through ODR has so far not been successful and what mistakes we need to learn from, the 'bad'. Once the advantages highlighted and the mistakes discussed, the chapter advances proposed recommendations for the 'future' of ODR (§11.03).

---

8. Daniel Rainey, *Third-Party Ethics in the Age of the Fourth Party*, 1(1) International Journal of Online Dispute Resolution 37, 42 (2014). *See also* ICODR Standards https://icodr.org/standards/ (accessed 28 August 2019).
9. Colin Rule, Vikki Rogers & Louis Del Duca, *Designing a Global Consumer Online Dispute Resolution (ODR) System for Cross-border Small Value – High Volume Claims – OAS Developments*, 42(3) Uniform Commercial Code Law Journal 221 (2010).

§11.02 UNDENIABLE ADVANTAGES OF ONLINE DISPUTE RESOLUTION

Raising awareness about the numerous benefits of ODR remains topical. No doubt that underlining the benefits and usefulness of online redress mechanisms will convince all stakeholders that ODR services are long overdue.

[A] Out-of-Court Dispute Settlement

In 2000, reports and guidelines were issued by organisations recommending online mechanisms to resolve disputes. Merchants were encouraged to participate in 'reputable, independent third-party dispute resolution programmes, including online dispute resolution processes', as provided by Guidelines for Merchant-to-Consumer Transactions drafted by a group of leading technology companies which created the Electronic Commerce and Consumer Protection Group (E-Commerce Group).[10] The dispute resolution clause in such Guidelines stated that the 'merchants should provide consumers with fair, timely, and affordable means to settle disputes and obtain redress'. The International Chamber of Commerce (ICC) published a policy statement on Jurisdiction and applicable law in electronic commerce, dealing with B2C transactions and consumer protection, in which it was recommended a systematic approach for resolving consumer disputes by utilising a company's internal customer satisfaction mechanism, or utilising an online alternative dispute resolution, and only if a dispute persists, to resort to legal action.[11] The Organisation for Economic Co-operation and Development (OECD) Guidelines for consumer protection in the context of electronic commerce[12] was designed to protect consumers in their online shopping, the same way they are protected in other forms of commerce, recommended among others, to provide consumers with the option of alternative dispute resolution mechanisms that offer effective resolution in a fair, timely manner and without undue cost or burden to the consumer. Thus, international organisations, businesses as well as consumers' representatives agreed and recognised the need for out-of-court disputes settlement.

A report on Access to Justice and the Internet, Potential and Challenges, stated that:

> The Assembly reiterates that access to justice is a cornerstone of any democratic State based on the rule of law, and a prerequisite for people's effective enjoyment of their human rights. However, it notes that accessing the justice system often entails high costs in terms of time and money and may be impeded by the courts' limited resources.[13]

---

10. Electronic Commerce and Consumer Protection Group, www.ecommercegroupageorg/guidelines.htlm (accessed 28 August 2019); the Guidelines were available in 2001 but no longer exists on the Internet.
11. Policy statement on Jurisdiction and applicable law in electronic commerce, published by ICC on 6 June 2001, but no longer exists on the Internet.
12. OECD Guidelines for consumer protection in the context of electronic commerce, 9 December 1999: http://www.oecd.org/internet/consumer/34023235.pdf (accessed 28 August 2019).
13. Jordi Xuclà, *Access to Justice and the Internet: Potential and Challenges*, published by the Committee on Legal Affairs and Human Rights of the Council of Europe, 2015, https://pace.coe

It further encouraged:

> member States to promote and further develop ODR mechanisms, acknowledging the potential of ODR procedures for settling disputes more speedily, cheaply and less conflictually than through litigation. ODR mechanisms may provide more flexibility in terms of procedures employed and remedies prescribed.[14]

These examples prove that ODR mechanisms recommended since 2000 are still relevant although change is extremely slow. Online mechanisms have the potential to significantly increase access to justice across all jurisdictions, including resolving cross-border disputes. We can witness successful applications of ODR which confirm that online mechanisms are an answer to offer remedy and can thus draw inspiration from successful processes to offer similar services.

Internal mechanisms used by marketplaces such as eBay,[15] Amazon,[16] Alibaba,[17] enable the online settlement of millions of low-value disputes every year and have proved that settling disputes online through automated and non-automated systems is possible. No similar service exists for disputes arising on platforms that do not have integrated resolution systems, and no platform for resolving cross-border consumer disputes online currently exists.

Big firms such as Cisco and COFCO benefit from in-house online amicable settlement mechanisms avoiding that any problem escalates to litigation or arbitration. Businesses often observe that they are in the business of doing business, not litigating.

Using the Matterhorn platform to settle family and traffic disputes online has been successful.[18] Judges interviewed by Matterhorn explained the benefit of resolving many family disputes online, as they save hundreds of people to show up in person in courts for disputes which may be swiftly settled from home or any place, and they save time for judges to concentrate on more pressing cases.[19] The Civil Resolution Tribunal in British Columbia (Canada)[20] resolves thousands of disputes as demonstrated in their statistical reports.[21] The message displayed on Ombudsman Services platform summarises clearly the double benefit of resolving disputes online, it states '[w]e're here to support consumers and empower businesses'.[22]

.int/pdf/f0ea4673550f14e5a517db5c09bc47d06cd8ec193326667a8259ffe25682ae848428feba12 /doc.%2013918.pdf (accessed 28 August 2019).

14. *Ibid.*
15. https://resolutioncenter.ebay.com/ (accessed 28 August 2019) and https://resolutioncentre.ebay.co.uk/ (accessed 28 August 2019).
16. https://pay.amazon.com/uk/help/201754740 (accessed 28 August 2019).
17. https://service.alibaba.com/ensupplier/faq_detail/20435717.htm (accessed 28 August 2019).
18. https://getmatterhorn.com/ (accessed 28 August 2019); *see also* other ODR providers dealing with family and divorce disputes https://www.itsovereasy.com/; http://resolvedivorce.co.uk/ (accessed 28 August 2019).
19. Judges interviewed by Matterhorn, *see* https://getmatterhorn.com/get-results/family-court/ (accessed 28 August 2019).
20. https://civilresolutionbc.ca/ (accessed 28 August 2019).
21. *See* March 2019 statistics: https://civilresolutionbc.ca/crt-statistics-snapshot-march-2019/ (accessed 28 August 2019).
22. https://www.ombudsman-services.org/about-us (accessed 28 August 2019).

[B] Levelling the Playing Field

ODR helps level the playing field in many ways:

(1) Communication: ODR facilitates communication between people from different countries and cultures and enhances worldwide understanding by assisting disputants in reaching settlement of their disputes easily and swiftly.[23] The objective is to get disputants to participate and feel that they can communicate in a user-friendly environment and on an equal footing.
(2) Neutral place: ODR helps resolving disputes in a user-friendly, non-aggressive digital space, to negotiate, mediate or arbitrate where necessary, and avoiding that complaints escalate to serious conflicts. It allows reducing any discomfort of being present in the same room with the other party, the lawyers, the neutrals or the judges, if the meeting had to take place in person. This is particularly true for unrepresented parties. Disputants can take the time to think and write and avoid being intimidated in court. Moreover, it enables the parties to reach an amicable solution and not being imposed a decision they have not reached together. Although settlements proposed cannot affect the parties' liberty to file a claim with a competent court, a wise party will not risk incurring additional costs and wasting more time if the solution proposed is acceptable.
(3) Self-representation: ODR offers access to justice and redress mechanisms to any person entitled to obtain remedy and to use ODR without being a professional of dispute resolution. This is particularly meaningful in consumer disputes and in civil and commercial small claims where users cannot afford paying the services of professionals to represent them.
(4) Equal access: parties have equal opportunities to access simultaneously the same information, in a standard environment, and this prevents parties from being advantaged or disadvantaged by their temporal proximity to a court.
(5) No forum selection: ODR avoids the complications of forum selection and jurisdictional issues mainly in cross-border disputes. Wherever ODR providers and their servers are physically located, they are neutral and can offer their services worldwide unless they exclude certain countries. In the past, some providers had excluded countries where human rights were not respected and where breach of confidentiality was recurrent. ODR used in consumer or small disputes is much simpler and consists in a streamlined process adapted to low-value disputes that should not require more time than

23. Some aspects of ODR advantages were discussed in Mirèze Philippe, *NetCase: Keep going where progress leads you*, 38(1) University of Toledo Law Review 417 (2007); Mirèze Philippe, *ODR Redress System for Consumer Disputes: Clarifications, UNCITRAL Works & EU Regulation on ODR*, 1(1) International Journal of Online Dispute Resolution 57 (2014); Mirèze Philippe, *Equal Access to Information & Justice: A report on the Online Dispute Resolution (ODR) Forum 2017 - The Huge Potential of ODR Greatly Underexplored*, 4(1) International Journal of Online Dispute Resolution 53 (2018), articles available on https://www.arbitralwomen.org/author/mireze-philippe/ (accessed 28 August 2019).

a few hours or days. Usually, the complainant completes an online form stating his/her version of the facts and any proposed solutions to resolve the dispute.[24] The respondent is notified and given a few days to respond; it can respond and propose different solutions; the parties can continue to negotiate or decide to escalate the dispute to another dispute resolution mechanism or to terminate the process. If the opponent does not respond it may receive a message reminding it of the benefit of the streamlined online process and possible consequences for refusing to participate in the process, such as having the claim submitted to courts. They may be reminded of the economic benefit and the benefit of preserving a relationship, be it commercial or a family or a neighbourhood relationship. Disputants who experience a fair process would be more willing to participate and to accept the solution proposed.

There seems to be confusion between settling consumer and small disputes online through automated or assisted systems or through negotiation or mediation without any reference to any applicable law, and settling disputes through arbitration. Unlike arbitration, there is no need for a forum which will determine the applicable law to the procedure. The settlement is not a jurisdictional decision and does not end with an award that may require enforcement. Where the ODR procedure is arbitration, conducting the arbitration online makes no difference for the place of arbitration. The applicable law to the procedure will be the law of the place determined as being the seat of arbitration, whether the procedure is taking place online or offline. Hearings may be held anywhere, including virtually. The only difference resides in conducting a procedure using web platforms which allow users to benefit, among other advantages, from swift communications and instantaneous access to information.

(6) Predictability: the outcome of disputes resolved online and displayed by ODR providers on their platforms offer predictability as to how disputes may be settled.
(7) Limited costs: ODR providers usually charge low fees, knowing that the low-value but high-volume disputes likely to be submitted to them will compensate the low charges.
(8) Access for disadvantaged people: ODR gives access to justice to people with lower incomes or living in remote places far from the courts. Likewise, it offers equal access to justice to persons with disabilities. Access to the Internet is an affirmative human right, as established in the United Nations International Declaration of Human Rights (UDHR).[25] A report on persons with disabilities was presented at the Annual Conference of the International

24. Rule et al. (*supra* n. 9) 13.
25. Paul T. Jaeger, *Disability, human rights, and social justice: The ongoing struggle for online accessibility and equality*, 20 (9) First Monday (2015), https://firstmonday.org/ojs/index.php/fm/article/view/6164/4898 (accessed 28 August 2019).

Bar Association[26], indicating that around one billion people which represents 15% of the global population 'have some form of disability and experience discrimination in many areas of life, exacerbated by the barriers they face in accessing justice'. The report specifies that:

> Technology can support efforts to help persons with disabilities overcome marginalisation in society and by the justice system. ODR offers a good example of the potential for increasing access to justice for persons with disabilities, including in rural or remote areas, by using technology-facilitated platforms. It is important that the legal community be open and alert to effective uses of such solutions where they can enhance inclusion of persons with disabilities, even if these may be at an early stage of evolution and may not be specifically aimed at persons with disabilities.

Recognising that ODR can help cure unfair situations where persons with disabilities have no or little access to justice is remarkable. Persons with physical disabilities need more than anyone else to purchase goods and services online and may be more exposed to lack of satisfaction which may require remedy.

[C] Additional Key Advantages of ODR

In addition to the usefulness discussed above, ODR presents further benefits:

(1) Permanent access: one of the noteworthy advantages of ODR is the capability of accessing the platform to file a claim, negotiate, and follow-up a procedure anytime, any day, and from anywhere. Needless to wait for office hours or to line up at the doors of tribunals to file a complaint, users can continue their activities without wasting time and follow-up their case from home or while travelling.
(2) Secure environment: ODR offers access to information and documents in a secure environment. Messages and documents are posted on a platform rather than sent through unprotected emails. It removes the risk of sending emails inadvertently to wrong recipients.
(3) Satisfaction and trust: the key to growing business is providing satisfaction to customers and generating trust through accessible online redress systems. Similarly, while the process may be confidential, publishing the outcome of the disputes eliminates uncertainties and demonstrates that sellers apply a transparency policy and are willing to compensate buyers when justified. Additionally, conducting surveys enable customers to share their positive or negative experience, which may lead to new business as 'there's no better

26. Julinda Beqiraj, Lawrence McNamara and Victoria Wicks, *Access to justice for persons with disabilities: From international principles to practice*, International Bar Association, October 2017, https://www.ibanet.org/Document/Default.aspx?DocumentUid=9D5D0EAF-690B-4DAE-8D21-50F40C143A88 (accessed 28 August 2019).

way to collect direct feedback from (your) customers and improve (your) product or service'.[27]

Likewise, if providers are part of a certification programme this will contribute to generating trust. ODR providers must adhere to such a programme meant to confirm that they comply with certain standards of good practices[28] and are trustworthy. The certification seal must be displayed on the providers' platforms, and must be removed if the certification is not renewed after an annual evaluation.

Furthermore, publishing annual statistics about the type of disputes, their outcome, and the number of disputes settled through online mechanisms also contributes to generating trust and enabling users to assess the providers' activity.

(4) ODR for online and offline transactions: disputes arising from transactions either conducted online or offline may be resolved through ODR.

(5) ODR adaptable to nearly all types of disputes: although most ODR programmes focus on consumer and commercial disputes, ODR expanded to employment, family, real estate, insurance, and even certain criminal disputes. Malaysia started its first cyber court in 2016 specialising in hearing cybercrime cases, such as bank fraud, hacking, falsification of documents, defamation, and online gambling.[29] It was reported that in 2015 alone, CyberSecurity Malaysia received 3,752 cases of online fraud and hacking independently from the cases that may have gone unreported or unnoticed by the victims.[30] Malaysia hopes to settle such disputes swiftly online.

(6) ODR mechanisms: they encompass the flexibility of resolving disputes through a variety of mechanisms, such as automated settlement, assisted settlement, negotiation, mediation, arbitration, or a combination of one or several mechanisms. It can start with a negotiation phase through automated settlement or technology enabled negotiation where parties negotiate directly with one another online. Should this phase fail, it can be submitted to a facilitated online settlement through mediation. Failing settlement, it can escalate to arbitration or litigation.

(7) Courts' decongestion: consumers and businesses are equally concerned by resolving disputes without the need for physical presence at a meeting or hearing. Typically, in online negotiation and mediation the meeting room is replaced by a virtual space. It brings people together without requiring them to appear in person at court or travel for a hearing in arbitration. In general,

27. Steven MacDonald, *Why Customer Complaints are Good for your Business*, 5 March 2019, https://www.superoffice.com/blog/customer-complaints-good-for-business/ (accessed 28 August 2019).
28. *See* Cortés (*supra* n. 68) 62.
29. https://www.nst.com.my/news/2016/09/169883/malaysias-first-cyber-court-begins-operations-today (accessed 28 August 2019).
30. https://gltlaw.my/2018/05/24/special-cyber-court-and-e-court/ (accessed 28 August 2019); according to a UK-based market research firm Juniper Research, global cybercrime losses were projected to reach USD 2 Trillion by 2019.

consumers and small businesses either do not file complaints for small disputes, or they do but rarely obtain judgements before several months or years. All jurisdictions around the world suffer from significant backlogs, due to budgetary constraints, lack of tools, and understaffing. Consumer, civil, and commercial small claims represent nearly half of the disputes submitted to courts. If such claims are settled through online mechanisms, they would considerably reduce the courts' congestion, which can then concentrate on disputes less likely to be settled online, at least for the moment, and users will obtain decisions in a few days or weeks if the parties participate efficiently in the procedure.

(8) Economy and environment: going paperless avoids the trouble of printing, photocopying, and dispatching documents by normal postal mail, and thus, spares time and money, respect the environment and saves space for filing mounds of documents. Noam Ebner wrote that ODR also contributes to saving the environment because parties and professionals need not travel to meet.[31]

[D] Scenarios of Typical Disputes and Examples of Out-of-Court Online Settlement Mechanisms

A few scenarios will illustrate typical simple and small disputes which may be resolved out-of-court and where ODR's assistance may be the solution.

[1] Scenarios of Typical Simple and Small Disputes

In a case where an online purchase of a dysfunctional device for the value of 100€ was delivered, can a buyer obtain remedy without submitting its claim to courts? The merchant may have an integrated settlement mechanism, and if this is not the case, the buyer may use an ODR platform dedicated for resolving disputes online. Can a claim following an online purchase of a travel package deal for the value of 1000€ which was not in conformity with the advertisement on the seller's platform be resolved online? A claim for refund may indeed be resolved through an automated settlement mechanism, for example by using the SmartSettle platform[32]. Likewise, how about a claim arising out of a cancelled booking of an event venue, can it be resolved online? In this scenario, the venue owner retained 80% of the deposit instead of 5% as per the contract on the ground that the cancellation was made allegedly out-of-time. The parties may use an assisted online negotiation or mediation to resolve their dispute out-of-court.

Offline transactions may similarly be settled using online settlement services. In a scenario where, following a presentation made by a seller, a small enterprise

31. Noam Ebner and Colleen Getz *ODR: The next green giant* 29(3), 283-307 (Conflict Resolution Quarterly, 2012).
32. https://smartsettle.com.

purchased equipment for 30.000€ but issues arose as to whether the equipment was fit for the purpose. The enterprise sought to return the equipment and be refunded. In this case, the parties can use an assisted online negotiation or mediation or submit the claim for example to iCourthouse, which is a streamlined version of a courthouse.[33] The enterprise has indeed no time and money to waste on seeking remedy in courts and needs a swift solution to enable it to run its business and reinvest the 30.000€. What happens in a scenario where the renovation of a classroom was scheduled during Christmas holidays, and where the service provider failed to do the work? The school in this scenario was compelled to find another provider and had to pay an extra 5.000€. Can the school claim compensation and use an online settlement service to resolve the dispute? The school may indeed, as in the previous scenario, use an assisted online system or an online courthouse system.

How about family disputes, can they be settled online? In a scenario where the husband and wife cannot agree on the terms of the divorce, or after the divorce where the husband does not pay the alimony dues, do they need to go to courts to resolve their disagreement? An online mediation may be conducted for example through SIËSDE Dispute Resolution Technologies[34] or iMEDIATE.[35] Online resolution of this type of disputes has proven in many instances to be effective. Can neighbourhood disputes be a type of disputes submitted to ODR? As in all scenarios presented, they can likewise be resolved online. If a property owner decides to trim the overhanging branches of a tree leaning on his property but the neighbour refuses to bear the costs, an online mediation may be the solution. ODR services dedicated to neighbours' disputes exist, for example, on the Community Disputes Resolution Tribunals (CDRT) platform.[36]

[2] Examples of Out-of-Court Online Settlement Mechanisms

A few ODR platforms will be mentioned to demonstrate through which mechanisms such scenarios may be resolved.

[a] Automated Settlement

Hundreds of thousands of transactions occur every day in marketplaces which are opportunities for conflicts that need to be resolved swiftly. Issues are in general simple and need no human involvement to offer remedies. Algorithms permit resolving recurrent and similar complaints. For a list of typical complaints, a list of available remedies is offered. Typically, a buyer complains about the non-conformity of the product with the description provided, the non-delivery or the late delivery of the

33. http://www.i-courthouse.com/main.taf (accessed 28 August 2019).
34. https://siesde.com/.
35. http://www.ichatmediation.com/ (accessed 28 August 2019).
36. Singapore announced in February 2018 that CDRT will provide an affordable forum to resolve online conflicts between neighbours: https://www.straitstimes.com/singapore/neighbours-can-now-settle-disputes-through-online-mediation (accessed 28 August 2019).

product, a broken or dysfunctional product. The algorithm proposes potential remedies such as the refund of the product, or its replacement, or a different product.

[b] Blind-Bidding

A recent case demonstrated that disputes may be resolved using algorithms in blind-bidding systems which are different from automated settlement systems. In reporting about this case, it was observed that 'ODR history was made this week when a court case, issued in the new Online Civil Money Claims Court for England and Wales, was resolved by use of an online tool that enabled the parties to participate in an advanced version of blind-bidding'.[37] The article further reported that 'after three months in the court process, including an unsuccessful telephone mediation, the parties were able to settle the dispute within an hour of first use of the blind-bidding tool', using SmartsettleONE, developed by ICan Systems Inc. of British Columbia, and provided through the website of The Resolver.

SmartsettleONE enables the parties to make offers and counter-offers by each moving up or down a flag along a slider any number of times until a resolution is reached. Such processes demonstrate that ODR might be the forum for dispute settlement in the near future.

[c] Online Mediation, Ombudspersons

Some types of disputes may be submitted to negotiation or mediation mechanisms, which have also proven to be successful, a few examples are hereafter provided. Graham Ross indicated that online mechanisms 'should not be looked at as a threat to the work of mediators, but as a great opportunity to improve the service they provide'.[38]

RisolviOnline.com,[39] is a mediation platform administered by the Milan Chamber of Commerce. Once the online complaint form is completed, RisolviOnline contacts the other party to invite it to take part in a negotiation. If the other party agrees to participate, a mediator will assist in finding a reciprocal satisfying solution.

AnOliveBranch,[40] based in Ireland, offers a novel, quick, economic, and simple form of mediation process. Individuals, enterprises and dispute resolution professionals can use it to settle civil, personal, and commercial disputes. Its three-stage approach delivers early effective intervention for swift resolution. A user of the platform stated:

---

37. Graham Ross, *First Case in the Online Court to be Resolved by Algorithm*, 15 February 2019, https://www.themediationroom.com/single-post/2019/02/15/First-Case-in-The-Online-Court-To-Be-Resolved-by-Algorithm?utm_campaign=0432c51a-641a-4703-95d1-d0fe0c5663c5&utm_source=so (accessed 28 August 2019).
38. *Ibid.*
39. https://www.risolvionline.com (accessed 28 August 2019).
40. www.anolivebranch.com (accessed 28 August 2019).

'I was not ready to get formal, so AnOliveBranch provided a discreet and confidential way to address the situation'.[41]

Immediation,[42] is a new ODR platform offering services to users in Australia. It intends to expand its services to other jurisdictions once it moves into international arbitration in addition to mediation. Businesses and consumers can file claims to be resolved through this platform. A claimant uploads a claim and then the platform sends an invitation to the respondent to participate. If the respondent participates, the claimant either decides to bear the costs or request the respondent to pay, or also ask the respondent to pay half. If the respondent does not wish to participate, the process stops here.

On a mediation platform called The Resolver,[43] users can select TheMediation-Room for mediation generally or BoardroomResolve for shareholder mediation.[44] Videos demonstrate mediation procedures conducted online and how efficient they can be.

Ombudsman Services,[45] based in the UK, indicates on its website that its job is to resolve complaints so that consumers are put back into the position they were in before the issue occurred, and to help businesses understand their customers so they can serve them better and resolve problems faster.

[d] Hybrid Mechanisms

Resolver Group, a very successful provider founded in 2012 and based in the UK, has received by the end of 2018 over 3 million cases and resolved over two billion pounds of issues.[46] The service was until recently offered in the UK but has expanded to Canada and India. Resolver occupies a unique place in the market as stated by its founder James Walker,[47] 'offering a free service to consumers that helps businesses built an insight into the behaviour of their consumers'. The reasons that motivated his founder to create Resolver, are similar to those for which the author has been militating for the past two decades: to offer remedy through ODR. Walker found it inexplicably hard to resolve an issue, find information about his rights and find templates. He stated: '[w]hy was there not somewhere that had all of these together? Why was there no single site that helped me record my case, told me what to do (and when to do it) and, if my issue remained unresolved, knew when and where to go to get independent resolution'.

Resolver helps consumers and small businesses to resolve issues through an automated process by asking what happened, what was the impact and what is the

41. A client in the UK mentioned this to the mediator Nancy Radford, who reported it on AnOliveBranch platform: http://www.anolivebranch.com/testimonials/2017/6/11/client.
42. www.immediation.com (accessed 28 August 2019).
43. www.theresolver.com (accessed 28 August 2019).
44. www.themediationroom.com (accessed 28 August 2019); www.BoardroomResolve.com (accessed 28 August 2019).
45. https://www.ombudsman-services.org/about-us (accessed 28 August 2019).
46. https://www.resolvergroup.com/ (accessed 28 August 2019).
47. James Walker, *Building Better Markets*, 4(1) 48 International Journal of Online Dispute Resolution (2017).

most appropriate way to resolve the issue in the opinion of the person filing a complaint. It then presents the information in the best way to help the business understand, address, and resolve the issue. If the issue is not resolved, the consumer can then escalate its case; there exists a number of escalations within the company level, and a possible escalation to Ombudsman or ADR. If neither of these possibilities exists, Resolver provides consumers with three choices: a consumer support service provided by the government; a legal advice provided by the UK consumer association or raising a case with the courts. Resolver provides consumers with their rights, what they should know and key outcomes before they file a complaint to help them know if they should be raising an issue and if they do, to have a better set of expectations. In addition to being facilitators, it will soon provide mediation and arbitration services in energy, banking, and telecoms disputes.

[e] Private Court System

iCourthouse[48] defines itself as the web's destination for justice and as being a streamlined version of courthouse. According to the information on iCourthouse, justice moves swiftly and surely. iCourthouse serves the community of Internet users in many of the ways that a brick-and-mortar courthouse serves its community. It is an online courthouse where disputes can be presented for trial before a jury of peers, any time, for any reason.

[f] Arbitration

The Cyberjustice Laboratory in Montreal, Canada, created by Karim Benyekhlef and Fabien Gélinas has been active since 2010 and is a hub for thought and creativity.[49] It created open source applications, some of which served for the foundation of the Condominium Authority Tribunal of Ontario platform meant to resolve condominium disputes.[50] If the negotiation phase does not end amicably, parties may ask for an online hearing with a tribunal member who would render a decision through the platform.[51]

Online arbitration is a mechanism which may be chosen by parties who wish to obtain an enforceable award. Some providers offer the possibility to conduct arbitrations exclusively online, such as FastArbitre.[52] This allows businesses to remain focused on their business while having a dispute conducted exclusively online and an award rendered within two months. The procedure starts with an amicable phase that is free of charge. If the parties fail to reach a settlement agreement, the platform moves

48. http://www.i-courthouse.com/ (accessed 28 August 2019).
49. https://www.cyberjustice.ca/en/laboratoire/presentation/ (accessed 28 August 2019).
50. https://www.condoauthorityontario.ca/en-US/tribunal/the-cat-process/stage-3-tribunal-decision/ (accessed 28 August 2019).
51. Amy J. Schmitz, *Expanding Access to Remedies through E-Court Initiatives*, 67(1) Buffalo Law Review 89 (2019).
52. https://fast-arbitre.com/en/ (accessed 28 August 2019).

the parties to the arbitral phase if parties so wish. The cost for this phase varies between 750€ and 2,250€, depending on whether it is a small commercial dispute such as claims for unpaid bills, a dispute related to contracts or to intellectual property or to disputes between associates and/or investors.

Finally, a few dispute resolution organisations built their own platforms to offer their arbitration users the opportunity to conduct their proceedings exclusively or partially online. ICC, AAA-ICDR, and WIPO were among the first organisations to build platforms.

ICC built the NetCase platform to enable parties and arbitrators to conduct their procedures in a dedicated secure environment and access files from anywhere without having to carry mounds of documents.[53] NetCase facilitated communications between all stakeholders in a case in a user-friendly setting. It offered instantaneous and round-the-clock information. The speed of posting was equal to an email with the important difference that documents and messages were encrypted and did not travel unprotected like emails, but within a secured system to which access was restricted. Documents were stored in a chronological order and assigned to a specific section depending on whether they were correspondence, memoranda, exhibits, procedural orders, Terms of Reference or awards. It was easy to identify the documents and their origin. A powerful search engine enabled searches no matter the format and language of documents.

The platform comprised different sections with different kinds of information namely: an address book, the stage of progress of the proceedings, information on the constitution of the tribunal, details about the financial aspect, a calendar of the proceedings. Stakeholders could communicate among themselves in dedicated spaces only accessible to the group, for example only between arbitrators. A uniform system of organisation enabled all players to see the same material, in the same presentation, in the same environment, and at the same time. Upgrades were regularly undertaken. They followed evaluations issued by users at the end of each case whereby they shared their comments and recommended improvements.

In a big majority of cases conducted on NetCase over the years of its life, users were very satisfied and therefore very disappointed when the service was interrupted. In one important case involving a state party, several lawyers and paralegals on each side, thousands of documents posted on NetCase, the entire case was administered through NetCase, and the parties were immensely satisfied. NetCase was an opt-in service and if one party or one arbitrator refused to use the platform no party and no arbitrator could benefit from the advantages of the platform. Despite the success of NetCase and the overall satisfaction of users who found it practical and useful, the ICC decided to suspend this service awaiting the construction of a more modern platform.

53. The NetCase platform was built by the author, for further information *see* Mirèze Philippe, *NetCase: a new ICC Arbitration Facility*, Bulletin of ICC International Court of Arbitration, Special Supplement of the ICC Bulletin, Using technology to resolve business disputes 53 (2004); Mirèze Philippe, *New upgrades to ICC NetCase*, 19(1) ICC International Court of Arbitration Bulletin, 23 (2008); Philippe (*supra* n. 22).

[E] Examples of Online State Courts

Some countries wisely invested in digitalising courts. Some of them are inspiring models. A few examples are provided to illustrate the variety of initiatives.

The Abu Dhabi Global Market Courts (ADGM Courts)[54] launched in 2018 the digital courtroom which will have the authority to handle civil and commercial disputes.

The Provincial Court of British Columbia in Canada launched in 2017 the nation's first online Civil Resolution Tribunal (CRT)[55] for civil claims up to $5,000, allowing to resolve debt or damages, and to recover personal property. It offers services in three phases: a negotiation phase by which the complainant is encouraged to communicate online with the other party and try to quickly settle the dispute; a facilitation phase if the negotiation fails and by which trained CRT staff will try to help parties settle their dispute; and an adjudication phase by which, failure to settle, a tribunal member may make a decision that can be enforced like a court order in Provincial Court, unless any of the parties files an objection.

China is the country where going electronic for private and public justice is happening fast. In addition to private initiatives for ODR platforms to settle consumer disputes, the country intends to move justice online. The Litigation Platform of Hangzhou Internet Court[56] launched its first cyber court in 2017 to handle cases such as online trade disputes, copyright lawsuits, and product liability claims for online purchases.

Estonia which started building the information society two decades ago became one of the world's most developed digital societies. On the e-Estonia platform, a sentence on the homepage resonates particularly with the message this chapter tries to convey: '[w]e have built a digital society, so can you'.[57] In 2006, Estonia launched the Court Information System (KIS)[58] offering a single information system for all types of court cases.[59]

Hawaii Judiciary's Electronic Filing and Service System (JEFS)[60] allows eligible and registered attorneys and registered unrepresented parties to electronically file documents for all cases in the Hawaii courts.

In India, operating e-courts in some states has been very successful, including using videoconferencing, and the model was replicated in other states.[61]

In Lithuania, any person can file a claim online by simply using an identity card number to identify oneself in the online court system. Lithuanian Court e-Services e.teismas.lt[62] enables any citizen or company to file a claim, upload documents, and

54. https://www.adjd.gov.ae/EN/Pages/Courts.aspx (accessed 28 August 2019).
55. https://civilresolutionbc.ca/ (accessed 28 August 2019).
56. https://www.netcourt.gov.cn/portal/main/en/index.htm (accessed 28 August 2019).
57. https://e-estonia.com/ (accessed 28 August 2019).
58. https://www.rik.ee/en/international/court-information-system (accessed 28 August 2019).
59. https://e-estonia.com/solutions/security-and-safety/e-justice (accessed 28 August 2019).
60. https://jimspss1.courts.state.hi.us/JIMSExternal/login.iface (accessed 28 August 2019).
61. https://services.ecourts.gov.in/ecourtindia_v6/ (accessed 28 August 2019).
62. https://www.teismai.lt/en/news/news-of-the-judicial-system/the-start-of-operation-of-the-lithuanian-court-e-services-portal-e.teismas.lt/1404 (accessed 28 August 2019).

pay the stamp-duty online. People who use the platform save one-quarter of the stamp-duty. Ninety standard forms are available to assist users in preparing their case.

In the state of Nuevo Leon, Mexico, the Virtual Tribunal[63] which started with civil claims in 2002, has now reached a situation where 90 % of all files are authorised in the virtual environment. The system is accessible anywhere in the world providing real-time information, with possibility for searches, videoconferencing, thus significantly reducing costs and time. A dashboard was developed to follow the workload of courts and give advance notification of possible delays or bottlenecks. This has permitted for a more strategic deployment of resources.

Rwanda has an Electronic Case Management System (IECMS)[64] in all courts countrywide which started operating in 2017. Anyone filing a case with the courts, except in some primary courts, must use it and will automatically receive feedback through email or SMS.

In September 2016, the UK launched an ambitious programme to reform the justice system and bring technology and modern ways of working.[65] Online services have already been launched to apply for divorce, making a money claim, and appealing to the tax tribunal. Her Majesty's Online Court's 'turns the concept of a court away from being a building with all the cost and inconvenience such involves, into a service'.[66]

In USA many state courts are on their way to become paperless with an obligation for lawyers to electronically file documents that judges can access via devices. A few states have implemented pilot projects to settle a variety of types of disputes. Some projects are successful; the city of Columbus for example seems to have saved on costs of negotiating and mediating income tax small claims and has increased its collection of recovered unpaid taxes[67].

§11.03 LESSONS TO LEARN FROM THE PAST AND RECOMMENDATIONS FOR THE FUTURE

The ODR advantages are undeniable as discussed above and ODR is the perfect tool which can offer access to justice to millions of people deprived from remedy. Levelling the playing field should be a convincing argument to make such a service available online in all regions of the world. However, ODR is not taking off as expected.

When online trade and services were a booming industry since the mid-1990s, around 200 ODR providers had built platforms to offer an online mechanism for resolving disputes arising from online transactions (the estimation results from a

63. http://www.tcanl.gob.mx/uniscripts/mgrqispi.dll?APPNAME = sitcav&PRGNAME = CapturaRecupContrasena (accessed 28 August 2019).
64. https://iecms.gov.rw/en/ (accessed 28 August 2019).
65. https://www.gov.uk/guidance/the-hmcts-reform-programme (accessed 28 August 2019).
66. Graham Ross *Her Majesty's Online Court*, 16 February 2015, https://www.themediationroom.com/single-post/2015/02/16/Her-Majestys-Online-Court (accessed 28 August 2019).
67. Schmitz (*supra* n. 46); pilot projects were for example implemented in the States of Michigan, Ohio, New York, Texas, Utah.

research conducted around 2000).[68] Providers were mostly in Canada and USA, and a few in Europe and Asia. A large number has since fallen along the way[69] for many reasons discussed below.

The downside of ODR is that it presupposes that participants have access to technology which is not true for everyone. Access is however likely to exist in public places, such as libraries, town halls, cybercafés. It may not be available in remote places and broadband connection may be slower in some areas, although the network coverage is constantly growing.

Also, some lawyers fear that ODR will take away clients and will make them lose business which is utterly wrong, because people do not hire lawyers for small disputes.

Undoubtedly readers will wonder why ODR is still lacking two decades after having started building platforms and reflecting on such service. What have the pitfalls been and why are we not there yet? The reasons will be discussed in this second part which will address the mistakes to avoid and the lessons to learn from past experiences, while sharing some recommendations for the future which may contribute to the success of online projects.

[A] First Key to Success: Do Not Be a Bystander, Be an Innovator

Offering remedy through online mechanisms to people who cannot afford going to courts and using the services of lawyers in small disputes is a human right and does not support controversy. State courts' congestions in all jurisdictions should convince governments, judges, and lawyers that other methods should be made available. Questioning whether access to justice online is possible is groundless - many ODR providers have proven that it is not science fiction - and is no longer a sustainable business strategy, no matter the challenges for building platforms to settle disputes online. We must stop being bystanders; we must dare to take initiatives and be innovators. We must offer online justice like any other online service and make it a priority. Successful online services demonstrate that transition to online justice can be faster than anyone could anticipate. The success of ODR is everyone's business including public and private justice. Any investment made now will benefit the users, the professionals and the courts in the short, medium, and long-term. Solutions and mechanisms exist, and if they do not exist, they can be built by learning from existing models or by building mechanisms from the ground up. It is not rocket science. It requires expertise in the field for which the platform is built, common sense and to be convinced by the project.

---

68. Mirèze Philippe, *Where is everyone going with online dispute resolution (ODR)*, 2 Revue de Droit des Affaires Internationales 167 (2002). For information about ODR providers and mechanisms, although not up to date, *see* Gabrielle Kaufmann-Kohler & Thomas Schultz, *Online Dispute Resolution Challenges for Contemporary Justice* (Wolters Kluwer Law 2004); and also Pablo Cortés, *Online Dispute Resolution for Consumers in the European Union* (Routledge Research in IT and E-Commerce Law 2011).
69. Lists of ODR providers are available on http://odr.info/provider-list/ and http://www.odreurope.com/odr-services/odr-platforms-apps (accessed 28 August 2019) (not exhaustive and not up to date).

[B] Second Key to Success: Continuity

One of the major mistakes to deplore is building platforms and abandoning them. Lack of continuity has contributed to users' scepticism about the feasibility of online justice. A platform may have satisfied the users or not entirely satisfied them, but the minute a service is available in the market users have expectations; interrupting such service without offering a service in replacement – pretending it needs improvement – is an appalling mistake. Platforms must be regularly upgraded as technology is constantly developing; any plan for upgrading should consider which aspects of the features may be maintained, modified or upgraded, but getting rid of all the coding and the functionalities is unnecessary. No one wins from stopping a web project on the ground of some malfunctions; it is a bad business plan because a provider loses its image and the funds invested. For every problem there is a solution, we can learn from our mistakes. Therefore, the rule of the day is perseverance.

Two platforms illustrate such lack of continuity. They were funded by the Commission of the European Communities and launched in 2001. They offered valuable services which were shortly thereafter interrupted.

The first is the European Extra-Judicial Network (EEJ-NET). In 1998, the Commission considered that most consumer disputes were characterised by a disproportion between the economic value and the cost of the judicial settlement and decided to create a database of out-of-court dispute resolution bodies. It addressed a recommendation to such bodies[70] emphasising 'the need to boost consumer confidence' by settling disputes out-of-court. In 2001, the Commission issued a recommendation setting principles to be respected by existing and future bodies. EEJ-NET's role was to act as a one stop contact point where consumers could seek information about out-of-court bodies existing in their jurisdiction, and to which they could address their complaint.

The second is Electronic Consumer Dispute Resolution (ECODIR). The same consideration of access to justice, a key element for consumers, motivated the Commission to create this project. The Universities of Namur (Belgium) and Dublin (Ireland) developed the platform and benefited from the expertise of eResolution, a Canadian ODR (which no longer exists). The ECODIR process was voluntary and dealt exclusively with disputes arising out of online transactions involving at least one consumer. The process included three phases: a negotiation phase of eighteen days at the expiry of which and failing a settlement a mediation which could not exceed fifteen days would start; if such second phase failed, the mediator would send to the parties within two days a motivated recommendation; if the parties did not approve the recommendation within seven days the case would terminate.

In addition to the investment wasted, over fifteen years passed during which no service existed. ECODIR and EEJ-NET were complementary and offered exactly the type of services that consumers need. EEJ-NET was a contact point and ECODIR an ODR provider.

70. http://europa.eu.int/comm/consumers/policy/developments/acce_just/index_en.html, the page is no longer active.

EEJ-NET was replaced by the European Consumer Centres Network (ECC-Net),[71] launched in February 2016. ECC-Net provides information on consumer rights and who to contact. When a consumer clicks on 'Resolve your consumer complaint' and selects 'Online Dispute Resolution', then 'File a complaint', he or she must answer three questions: if the consumer resides in the European Union, Norway, Iceland or Lichtenstein; if the complaint concerns a product or service bought online; and if both previous answers are positive the consumer can then complete a form to file a complaint. A report dated 6 December 2018 provided information about the traffic on the platform and the number of complaints. [72] It indicated that complaints lodged on the platform in its second year of operation amounted to 36,000 cases; 37% of consumers would have been successfully contacted directly by the trader to try and settle the dispute rapidly.

It is to be hoped that this service will continue developing and will not be suspended like its predecessor. However, ECC-Net is not an ODR provider meant to resolve disputes. Such a platform does not exist in Europe.

[C] Third Key to Success: Business Planning and Adequate Budgeting

Another significant mistake is the lack of long-term business planning and thus lack of adequate budgeting. Unless a platform is an information webpage with no other features, the investment required for building a platform cannot realistically be for a short term or for a temporary marketing action. It is a business and strategy matter having an impact on a firm and the project must be given all the attention it requires. Budgeting for building a house is different from budgeting for building a platform. A house may be considered old after a decade or two, whereas a platform will be outdated in a very short period. Budgeting for building a platform can be compared to budgeting for bringing up and educating a child who requires constant care.

Budgeting for building a platform must cover every phase from drafting specifications to conducting several tests phases, maintenance of the website, 24/7 support, dissemination of information to familiarise users with the features offered, rapid fixing of any malfunction, and regular upgrading as part of a marketing plan. This includes the team to put in place for a project comprised mainly of in-house experts who know the needs of the firm and how it works on a daily basis, and of a project manager to liaise between the end users and the computer engineers.

Alleging that building a platform is costly without weighing the pros and cons does not constitute an accurate analysis. Long-term business development must be seriously considered rather than immediate costs. An online service for administering dispute resolution procedures carries with it advantages for dispute resolution organisations, ODR providers, courts, and not only users. The return on investment can be relatively fast depending on the efforts invested.

71. https://ec.europa.eu/info/live-work-travel-eu/consumers/resolve-your-consumer-complaint/european-consumer-centres-network_en (accessed 28 August 2019).
72. https://ec.europa.eu/info/alternative-dispute-resolution-reports_en (accessed 28 August 2019).

One of the difficulties lies in the fact that some projects are funded by external funders who may be less interested by long-term benefits than by the revenue generated on the short or medium term.

[D] Fourth Key to Success: Clear Specifications and Realistic Projects

Another repeated mistake is neglecting the time and effort for drafting detailed and understandable specifications. Determining the needs and drafting every step of the processes, the results expected, how each process interacts with another one, is a long and an essential investment. Every time this sequence was neglected, it resulted in malfunctions and incorrect processes or missing processes. The 2016 Queen Mary International Dispute Resolution Survey about Pre-empting and Resolving Technology Media and Telecoms Disputes identified requirements as a very common reason for dispute.[73]

The key to success for well-thought specifications is to include people with expertise and experience. If such people are not involved, models of specifications serve no purpose. In-house experts, project managers, and computer engineers must work permanently together to draft clear and detailed specifications and to ensure a close follow-up and understanding of the needs and expectations of end users. The latter needs a user-friendly system that any person can use whether IT literate or not, a permanent and instantaneous access to their files, to retrieve information easily among several documents, and to have online assistance where necessary.

Moreover, projects must be realistic. Being ambitious is in general positive, but it would be wise to step back and analyse how best to proceed further than to stop a project. If the budget, time, drafting of specifications, building, and testing the platform cannot encompass all phases envisaged from the outset, splitting into several phases may be a solution. The benefit would be to consolidate each phase before developing the next one. It also helps learning about how users appreciate the services offered and implement improvements progressively.

Online projects rarely progress as initially envisaged, it is difficult to anticipate all situations and problems likely to occur, but many problems may be avoided if all necessary phases are properly planned as opposed to skipping phases considered not important for the sake of gaining time. A company may spend more money fixing mistakes than investing appropriate efforts from the inception.

[E] Fifth Key to Success: Think Tank and Proper Market Survey

For competition reasons, businesses in general do not share their knowledge and experience as much as academics do. Technology however requires such sharing with all stakeholders, especially in the young field of ODR.

73. *See* page 12, www.arbitration.qmul.ac.uk/media/arbitration/docs/Fixing_Tech_report_online_singles.pdf (accessed 28 August 2019).

In addition, one of the mistakes in this field is the improper or insufficient market survey before building and launching platforms. It could have assisted in estimating the number of disputes in a market at a certain point in time and the likely evolution of that number over a certain period. Market research companies can assist providers in planning potential evolutions.

In 2001, Gabrielle Kaufmann-Kohler has invited to a colloquium in Geneva various stakeholders from the legal and technology fields. She gathered various profiles including academics, professionals who built ODR platforms, and computer engineers, with the objective of starting a dialogue aimed at finding solutions to conduct dispute resolution online. Since then a group was constituted and meets annually in ODR Forums to share experience with peers, information about research conducted, new technologies, standards, and projects.[74] It is essential to remain informed about advancements made and to take inspiration from existing solutions instead of reinventing the wheel.

On 4 April 2019, FastArbitre[75] published a free licence of its online dispute resolution platform developed by Seraphin.legal.[76] The source code of the technology is available online.[77] This constitutes an essential contribution by Consortium eJustice[78] to the development of public digital justice. It is also a major participation of the French community to the ODR bricks already available on Cyberjustice,[79] and anticipates an international community of Open Justice.

[F] Sixth Key to Success: Involvement of End Users and Intensive Testing

As mentioned above, budgeting to build a house or to build a platform is entirely different, but one thing is common: delivery delays. They are inevitable and must be foreseen in the planning. Regrettably, testing is often neglected when delivery cannot be postponed.

Platforms must not be built on assumptions; expectations of end users and clients count. They need to see that their feedback was considered and potential improvements made accordingly. Each phase of the project must be intensively tested with them to ensure that all aspects of a service were duly examined. They are allies and their feedback forms part of the marketing plan and ultimately of the success of a project.

It is also essential to involve magistrates, dispute resolution organisations, and law firms to test ODR platforms. Who else is better positioned to share insights about the functionalities? Start-ups are taking initiatives to build ODR platforms and to fill the

74. Mirèze Philippe, *Equal Access to Information & Justice: A report on the Online Dispute Resolution (ODR) Forum 2017 - The Huge Potential of ODR Greatly Underexplored*, 4(1) International Journal of Online Dispute Resolution 55 (2018).
75. https://fast-arbitre.com/en/ (accessed 28 August 2019).
76. https://www.seraphin.legal/ (accessed 28 August 2019).
77. https://github.com/Open-Justice/ODR (accessed 28 August 2019).
78. http://consortium-ejustice.org/ (accessed 28 August 2019).
79. https://www.cyberjustice.ca/en/ (accessed 28 August 2019).

gap of dispute resolution needs, but co-operation with legal services is vital to ensure the success of mechanisms to put in place.

[G] Seventh Key to Success: Proper Communication and Marketing

Another dominant mistake is the lack of regular promotion of ODR services and of education of users to learn about their benefits. As part of the marketing campaign, before delivering a phase of a project, tests and results may be reported to start disseminating the information and educating future users. Users are eager to discover out-of-court dispute resolution services and to test them until they become familiar with such services and trust them. Online trade gained success over time until users discovered how useful it can be, before shifting from offline to online. Likewise, trust may be gained with visible, measurable, efficient dispute resolution services provided online. Presentations are indispensable in public meetings, companies, consumers' associations, universities, town halls, cybercafés, and any forum where users may gather and learn about these features. Videos must be available on ODR platforms, on the Internet and blogs, to contribute to promoting ODR services. Thanks to technology and available media, marketing means are accessible to anyone who needs to spread the word.

The European Commission organised an ADR Assembly in June 2018[80] to discuss how the EU framework for alternative dispute resolution (ADR) for consumers is currently applied in practice and how it can be made fully effective for consumers and traders. The summary report states that 'by promoting accessible, high quality, and cost-effective dispute resolution, the European Commission aims to protect consumers, increase consumer confidence, and foster prosperity and growth in the Single Market'.[81] It further notes that:

> promoting success stories, having ambassadors, publishing decisions, and using social and traditional media were suggested ways in which awareness, understanding and support for ADR could be promoted. Communication was also identified to be a vital part of quality case-handling, educating and empowering consumers and ensuring transparency in the dispute resolution process.[82]

[H] Eighth Key to Success: Hard Data Records

The lack of reporting about a service was one of the reasons for which many ODR providers failed. The usefulness of settling disputes online cannot be measured if no statistics demonstrate the efficiency of the system and whether an ODR provider is trustworthy. Only a few ODR providers publish annual statistics. Gaining users'

---

80. European Commission ADR Assembly 11-12 June 2018, Brussels, Summary Report: https://ec.europa.eu/info/sites/info/files/com_2019_425_f1_report_from_commission_en_v3_p1_1045545_0.pdf (accessed 28 August 2019).
81. *Ibid.*
82. *Ibid.*

confidence is crucial, especially when they have no direct contact with the people in charge of the resolution of their dispute, irrespective of the mechanism used.

Evaluating the efficiency of a service can be assessed through hard data reporting about proven results, such as the number of claims filed on an ODR platform, their nature, how many were resolved, the time needed to resolve them, if the settlement reached was satisfactory, what the value of the claim was and the remedy obtained, what mechanisms are mostly used.

A report on Joint Technology Committee ODR for Courts,[83] indicates that courts have implemented ODR for low-dollar personal injury claims, landlord-tenant, small claims, and minor traffic and code enforcement violations. The report goes on indicating that ODR 'is a proven tool with a documentable record of success over a sustained period of time: billions of disputes have been resolved outside of court using ODR' and that ODR 'is becoming central to the discussion of the future of courts'. The statement about the record of success of disputes resolved out-of-court through ODR is remarkable especially coming from state courts.

[I] Ninth Key to Success: Appropriate Choice of Computer Engineers

Despite the huge number of technology suppliers, engineers, and developers building platforms around the world in a century where technology is embedded in every minute of our lives, it is difficult to find appropriate professionals who are ready to invest time in understanding a project and contributing to the drafting of specifications adapted to the needs of the clients. The time-efficiency requirements may lead to investing less time in certain phases, but efficiency requires time. When technology suppliers are not selected properly, this is the beginning of a long and painful journey with lots of time, energy, and money wasted.

The agreement between the client and the supplier should include among others two important clauses: one dealing with the planning of delivery and what is expected to be delivered at each phase, and a dispute resolution clause that clearly defines how potential conflicts may be resolved. Suppliers often request a first down payment of forty to fifty per cent of the contract price. It is recommended to ensure that they were able to understand the project and implement correctly the first phase for which a down payment was made. If such phase was not properly understood and tests were not satisfactory, it might sometimes be wise to terminate the agreement before investing too much time and funds. It happened that clients were not satisfied with the first phase but were compelled to continue with the selected provider because an agreement was signed, a substantial payment made and work invested. It is worth terminating an agreement when it is possible to mitigate damages than to have to live with a platform which does not meet the expectations reflected in the specifications.

83. *Joint Technology Committee Resource Bulletin – ODR for Courts*, version 2.0 updated and adopted on 29 November 2017, https://www.ncsc.org/__data/assets/pdf_file/0031/18499/2017-12-18-odr-for-courts-v2-final.pdf (accessed 28 August 2019).

[J] Tenth Key to Success: Centralisation and Standardisation of Information – Procedural Rules

The cornerstone to successfully motivate consumers and professionals to use ODR is, first to centralise and standardise information about available services and make them easily accessible, and second to propose model procedural rules.

[1] Centralisation and Standardisation of Information

One of the main reasons for the failure of many ODR providers is the lack of centralisation and standardisation of information about ODR providers. Many ODR providers existed and others still exist but users do not know about them, how to choose a provider for a given type of dispute and how reliable they are. Information is often found incidentally.

Therefore, the first recommendation is to centralise information to grow awareness about ODR services, enhance ease of access to information, and enable potential users to make an informed choice. There is a dire need for such service that is currently lacking.

In 2000, OECD and ICC had issued lists of ODR providers. However, keeping lists up to date required an investment that no organisation considered worth pursuing considering the frequent changes. The odr.info platform hosted by the National Center for Technology & Dispute Resolution (NCTDR) lists a few providers although the list needs updating as some providers are no longer operational. It was recommended that an international organisation should centralise information on ODR providers and potentially evaluating them,[84] but no organisation has so far been interested in such a mission that requires a dedicated service to follow-up on providers and update an online database. Listing information could comprise: their business address and weblink to the platform, type of disputes they handle, for which amounts in dispute, in which countries, in which languages, and if they are members of a certification programme. The organisation could be a contact point and could also assist complainants in selecting the most appropriate ODR provider for a given dispute.

The second recommendation is to adopt general standards for any ODR mechanism and to display standard information on ODR platforms, which is indispensable to offer users predictability and avoid striking differences.

The main information to provide concern the following aspects:

- contact details with business address, telephone, and email;
- names and roles of people operating the platform;
- when the provider started operating;
- if the provider is a member of a certification programme;
- the types of disputes it handles, for example family disputes;
- cap amounts above which the provider will not handle disputes;

84. The author recommended centralising information about ODR providers, *see* Philippe (*supra* nn. 23 and 68).

- languages that it can handle;
- if the services offered are limited to a certain number of countries, for example only China;
- rules used for the administration of the disputes;
- a chart of the procedural steps with time limits and an average duration to resolve a dispute;
- the dispute mechanisms proposed, such as blind-bidding, assisted negotiation, mediation, arbitration, hybrid mechanisms;
- how to file a complaint and what should it contain, for example the required solution by the claimant;
- the time limit for the answer and what should it contain;
- if the dispute settlement is not made through an automated system, the method of selecting the third party or neutral or professional designated to assist in resolving the dispute, and his/her role;
- the time limit for the provider to propose a solution or submit a decision depending on the mechanism used;
- what happens in case of delays;
- what happens if a party does not participate and what are the other available remedies;
- whether the decision is binding or non-binding, and if the losing party does not carry out the decision, what are the other available remedies;
- whether the provider will publish on its website the list of disputes and the settlements reached;
- what are the reasons for terminating a procedure, for example when either or both parties stop participating, or when they do not pay the fees requested by the provider;
- whether the procedure is confidential;
- the costs to be expected and how they will be allocated;
- finally, annual statistics are very informative.

[2] UNCITRAL Technical Notes on Online Dispute Resolution

Furthermore, model rules are needed. The UNCITRAL Technical Notes on Online Dispute Resolution provide practical guidance but they are not procedural rules like the UNCITRAL Arbitration Rules or the ICANN Rules for Uniform Domain Name Dispute Resolution Policy.

The UNCITRAL has put in place in 2010 a Working Group III on ODR, entrusted with the drafting of a set of rules for a global ODR system to handle cross-border, low-value, high-volume claims.[85] The various reports of the Working Group available on UNCITRAL[86] show that the discussions have departed from the initial mandate of

85. Rule et al. (*supra* n. 9).
86. www.uncitral.org/uncitral/en/commission/working_groups/3Online_Dispute_Resolution.html (accessed 28 August 2019).

creating a simple redress system for low-value, high-volume B2C disputes arising from Internet transactions. Delegates ended up including B2B disputes and discussing arbitration and enforceable awards. This was utterly wrong considering that the system envisaged concerned small disputes resolved online without the complications of arbitration which is better adapted to high-value disputes. Moreover, arbitration mechanisms in B2B disputes already existed and needed not be created within the framework of this Working Group meant to deal with an inexistent system. Delegates having participated in the Working Group were from different cultures;[87] the variety of backgrounds could have been an enriching factor. Regrettably, differences emerged, and consensus remained out-of-reach on many aspects.

Finally, the Working Group delivered in February 2016 UNCITRAL Technical Notes on Online Dispute Resolution,[88] aimed at assisting providers and users with certain aspects. They are non-binding and take the form of a descriptive document reflecting elements of an ODR process. They are neither best practices, nor exhaustive or exclusive. They do not impose legal requirements binding on parties and other entities. They do not imply modification to any ODR rules that parties may have selected. Although, they are not standard ODR procedural rules, they are useful and provide guidance, such as definitions of ODR, ODR providers, ODR platforms, techniques of settlement of disputes, transparency and independence, stages of an ODR proceeding, scope of an ODR process, roles and responsibilities, steps for the commencement of an ODR proceeding, explanations on a negotiation phase, facilitated settlement and the final stage, appointments, powers, and functions of neutrals. There exists so far no feedback about whether and how the UNCITRAL Technical Notes have been used, by which type of population and for which purposes. An interesting report presents the different ways such Notes can be used to assist in the implementation of ODR systems.[89]

§11.04 CONCLUSION

To conclude, moving public and private justice to the digital world in all jurisdictions is possible. Public and private online justice in the twenty-first century should be a priority. The advantages of access to justice through ODR demonstrate that investment in online justice made now will benefit the users, the legal professionals and the courts in the short, medium, and long-term. Progress is in our hands, we must contribute to give any litigant access to justice online. Creating a global ODR system for resolving cross-border, low-value, high-volume disputes, in B2C, B2B, C2C disputes, and civil

87. *See* interesting discussion by Daniel Rainey, 'ODR and Culture', *in* Mohamed Abdel Wahab, Ethan Katsh & Daniel Rainey (eds.), *Online Dispute Resolution Theory and Practice* (Eleven International Publishing 2012) 197.
88. UNCITRAL Technical Notes on Online Dispute Resolution, April 2017: http://www.uncitral.org/pdf/english/texts/odr/V1700382_English_Technical_Notes_on_ODR.pdf. (accessed 28 August 2019).
89. Report of Workshop for Developing an APEC Collaborative Framework for Online Dispute Resolution, 2019/SOM1/EC/009, 4-5 March 2019, http://mddb.apec.org/Documents/2019/EC/EC1/19_ec1_009.pdf.

claims is essential. Building platforms may be a challenge but is perfectly feasible. We can learn from existing mechanisms. A redress mechanism through ODR is certainly not science fiction. It is neither rocket science. It requires pragmatism and perseverance.

CHAPTER 12

The Resolution of B2B Disputes in Blockchain-Based Arbitration: A Solution for Improving the Parties' Right of Access to Justice in the Digital Age?

Sara Hourani

Blockchain technology was first introduced at the end of the 2000s when Satoshi Nakomoto released his whitepaper on the Bitcoin cryptocurrency. The specificity of this technology is that it functions on a decentralised basis as there is no use of a trusted intermediary or central authority. Smart contracts are software codes including the terms and conditions that run on a network leading to a partial or full automated self-execution and self-enforcement of the transaction. In essence, a smart contract is a software programme that is stored on the blockchain. Smart contracts can be used in supply chain management, trade finance and energy trade. In the context of these different transactions, it would be relevant to include an arbitration clause in the smart contract to prompt the parties to resolve their differences with regards to the performance of the contract. This type of dispute resolution has received widespread attention for the resolution of specific low-value claims. In light of these technological innovations, this chapter focuses on an examination of the extent to which the blockchain-based arbitration procedure guarantees the parties' right of access to justice in B2B disputes as an alternative to traditional face-to-face arbitration. This chapter effectuates in the first instance an explanation of blockchain and smart contract technology and the role that arbitration plays in this context. Then the chapter explores the reasons behind the adoption of blockchain-based arbitration, and whether this ameliorates the parties' possibility of access to justice in contrast to traditional arbitration. The chapter finally analyses in the third section the extent that the parties' rights are protected by the current international and national legal framework for providing adequate access to justice to resolve their disputes.

§12.01 INTRODUCTION

Technological innovation is increasingly impacting the different ways in which commercial parties can have access to justice for the resolution of their disputes.[1] For example, the SCC has recently launched the SCC Platform which is an online platform that facilitates the management of each arbitral case by the parties, the SCC and the arbitral tribunal.[2] The platform was designed to administer all documents related to the case, evidence submission, procedural orders and communication with the SCC. This launch follows a series of case management platforms that were created such as the AAA WebFile Platform. However, technological innovation is not only stopping at the adoption of cloud-based solutions for improving the parties' experience of the arbitration process.

New technologies are bringing new tools to the table that businesses can use in order to increase efficiency in dispute resolution. As such, the past few years have witnessed the emergence of legal programming that is spreading with the springing of various Lawtech start-ups that are coming up with different technological solutions in the dispute resolution field.[3] Blockchain technology in particular has been at the centre of the dispute resolution industry's interest. To illustrate the spreading use of such new technologies in dispute resolution, Chinese Internet courts have already started using blockchain technology-backed evidence in order to increase the time efficacy of its proceedings.[4] Following in these footsteps, the State of Vermont passed a bill in 2016 that establishes that blockchain data is valid evidence before the courts.[5] Technology is impacting arbitration as the main contribution is an increased efficiency and the reduction of costs.[6] In this context, there have recently been several suggestions for developing blockchain-based arbitration in order to benefit from an improved efficacy of the process.[7]

1. *See* a wider discussion of this in Tibor Tajti (Thaythy), *The Impact of Technology on Access to Law and the Concomitant Repercussions: Past, Present, and the Future (From the 1980s to Present Time)*, 24(2) Uniform Law Review 396 (June 2019).
2. *See* the announcement of the SCC, https://sccinstitute.com/scc-platform/ (accessed 30 June 2019).
3. Riikka Koulu., *Blockchains and Online Dispute Resolution: Smart Contracts as an Alternative to Enforcement*, 13 (1) Scripted, 41-69, 66 (May 2016). *See* Mattereum, CodeLegit, SeedLegals, Luminance and CrowdJustice as a few examples of LegalTech start-ups.
4. Marie Huillet, *China's Supreme Court Rules That Blockchain Can Legally Authenticate Evidence*, https://cointelegraph.com/news/chinas-supreme-court-rules-that-blockchain-can-legally-authenticate-evidence (accessed 30 June 2019).
5. Act No. 157 (H.868).
6. Gauthier Vannieuwenhyse, *Arbitration and New Technologies: Mutual Benefits*, 35 (1) Journal of International Arbitration 119, 119.
7. The EOS Alliance is posing the question regarding the need and feasibility of blockchain-based arbitration, *see* https://eosalliance.io/dispute-resolution-arbitration/ (accessed 30 June 2019). *See* the Telos Blockchain Network Arbitration Rules and Procedures in https://resources.telosfoundation.io/governance_documents/TBNARP_Adopted_2018-10-26.pdf (accessed 30 June 2019). *See* Garrick Hileman & Michel Rauchs, *Global Blockchain Benchmarking Study*, Report for the Cambridge Centre for Alternative Finance and EY (2017), https://www.ey.com/Publication/vwLUAssets/ey-global-blockchain-benchmarking-study-2017/$FILE/ey-global-blockchain-benchmarking-study-2017.pdf (accessed 30 June 2019). *See* Norton Rose Fulbright,

Blockchain technology was first introduced at the end of the 2000s when someone using the pseudonym of Satoshi Nakomoto released a whitepaper on the Bitcoin cryptocurrency.[8] Bitcoin brought a number of revolutionary novelties to payment methods that has led to the spread of other cryptocurrencies. However, the impact of Bitcoin did not stop at cryptocurrencies as the technology that it utilises has been receiving widespread interest for uses going beyond payment methods.[9] There is a growing interest in the use of blockchain technology in business and international trade for example; more particularly in the context of supply chain management.[10] Therefore, the importance of Bitcoin and cryptocurrency lies in the technology that these use. Blockchain technology, as with other types of digital technologies, is bound to have an impact over traditional methods of dispute resolution.[11] Namely, this type of Distributed Ledger Technology (DLT) is impacting arbitration and it is raising questions regarding the legality of its application in this type of dispute resolution.

In light of these technological innovations, this chapter focuses on an examination of the extent to which the blockchain-based arbitration procedure is needed to improve the parties' right of access to justice in business-to-business (hereinafter 'B2B') disputes as an alternative to traditional face-to-face arbitration. The chapter's focus is on commercial disputes of an international character that involve cross-border transactions. To approach this question, the chapter effectuates in the first instance an explanation of blockchain and smart contract technology. Then it discusses the role that arbitration plays in this context. Afterwards the chapter explores the reasons behind the adoption of blockchain-based arbitration, and whether this ameliorates the parties' possibility of access to justice in contrast to traditional arbitration. The chapter finally analyses in the last section the extent that the parties' rights are protected by the current international and national legal frameworks for providing adequate access to justice to resolve their disputes.

International Arbitration Report, Issue 9 (October 2017), https://www.nortonrosefulbright.com/-/media/files/nrf/nrfweb/imported/20170925---international-arbitration-report---issue-9.pdf?la=en-gb&revision=cbb8b5c6-72fc-460c-8a30-e6ca10caea06 (accessed 30 June 2019).

8. Satoshi Nakamoto, *Bitcoin: A Peer-to-Peer Electronic Cash System*, https://bitcointalk.org/bitcoin.pdf (accessed 30 June 2019).
9. IEEE Future Directions Blockchain Initiative White Paper: Reinforcing the Links of the Blockchain (November 2017), https://blockchain.ieee.org/images/files/pdf/ieee-future-directions-blockchain-white-paper.pdf (accessed 30 June 2019).
10. Saveen A. Abeyratne & Radmehr P. Monfared, *Blockchain Ready Manufacturing Supply Chain Using Distributed Ledger*, 05(09) International Journal of Research in Engineering and Technology 1, 3 (2016). Also *see*, Jeffrey Neuburger & Wai Choy, *Supply Chain Innovation: Implementing Blockchain Technology*, Practical Law Journal, 26 (June/July 2019).
11. *See* Riikka Koulu, *Law, Technology and Dispute Resolution: The Privatisation of Coercion* (Routledge 2018).

§12.02 AN OVERVIEW OF BLOCKCHAIN TECHNOLOGY AND SMART CONTRACTS

[A] An Overview of Blockchain Technology

One of the main ideas behind the creation of blockchain technology was to bypass central authorities such as the State or a managing authority in authenticating payments.[12] As such, instead of placing trust in one authority the technology is based on a decentralised technological infrastructure that consists of a peer-to-peer system to manage data.[13] Therefore, one of the main novelties brought by blockchain technology is the elimination of a central authority to manage the processing of online transactions. The introduction of this 'trustless' network to process transactions is the main disruptive feature that made this technology attract the attention of various business stakeholders.[14]

Blockchain technology can thus be defined as being a decentralised digital database that consists of secure transactions that are copied and shared amongst the members of the network.[15] Each transaction on the blockchain is found in a block that contains the information on the transaction and the reference to the encryption code of the previous transaction block.[16] The encryption code of each transaction block is represented by its own hash reference number that identifies the block and its content. Also, each transaction block needs to be signed by a private key that is given to the initiator of the transaction.[17] This means that only those who have a private key can make a request on the blockchain system for the transaction to be processed and that each transaction is then encrypted once it passes the validation and consensus process.

The blockchain system runs by having an initial request for a transaction to be processed and this request will then be broadcast to all members on the network referred to as nodes.[18] Once each node on the network receives the request, it has to carry out a 'proof-of-work' which is the resolution of a difficult mathematical problem through computation.[19] At this stage of the process the individual nodes check the validity of the transaction before relaying it any further onto the network.[20] When each node finds a proof-of-work for the new transaction block, it adds the transaction block

12. Paolo De Filippi & Samer Hassan, *Blockchain Technology as a Regulatory Technology: From Code is Law to Law is Code*, 21 (12) First Monday, 6 (5 December 2016).
13. *See* Joshua A.T. Fairfield, *Smart Contracts, Bitcoin Bots, and Consumer Protection*, 71 Washington & Lee Law Review Online Edition 35 (2014).
14. *See* Philip Boucher, *How Blockchain Technology Could Change Our Lives*. Brussels, Belgium: European Parliamentary Research Service (February 2017). *See* Frank Pasquale & Glyn Cashwell, *Four Futures of Legal Automation*, 63 UCLA Law Review Discourse 26 (2015). Also *see* Michael Casey & Paul Vigna, *The Age of Cryptocurrencies: How Bitcoin and Digital Money Are Challenging the Global Economic Order*, 9-10 (New York: St Martin's Press, 2015).
15. Konstantinos Christidis & Michael Devetsikiotis, *Blockchains and Smart Contracts for the Internet of Things*, 4 IEEE Access, 2292, 2293 (2016).
16. *Ibid.*
17. *Ibid.*
18. Nakamoto (*supra* n. 8) at 3.
19. *Ibid.*
20. Christidis and Devetsikiotis (*supra* n. 15) at 2293.

to its existing chain of blocks and it communicates the block to all nodes on the network.[21] If all nodes on the network have found that the transaction is valid, then they reach a consensus on the authenticity of the block.[22] When the transaction block is accepted by all nodes on the network as being authentic and validated, it is added to the chain of blocks which constitute a ledger. The ledger is then copied amongst the members of the network so that these can reach a consensus on how to organise the data and validate it.[23] Once consensus is reached amongst the members of the network the blocks are timestamped and validated, and then are added to the existing ledger or chain of blocks.[24] If the transaction is rejected through consensus on the network, the rejected block is logged on the blockchain system (and discarded) thus showing that the transaction is potentially fraudulent or the result of malicious conduct on the network.[25] The nodes are thereafter notified of the potential attack on the security of the network and can subsequently trace the fraudulent transaction.[26]

It should be noted that not all networks are the same as there are different types of blockchain systems. The main distinction is between public permissionless networks and private permissioned networks. Public permissionless networks are blockchain systems that are open to the public whereby all participants can make requests for transactions and be able to read the data.[27] At the other end of the spectrum is the private permissioned network where only participants with a known identity can join the network and have access to the data.[28] This distinction is important as not all blockchain networks have the same level of access to the initiation of transactions and to participation in the validation process of the data.

To sum up, blockchain is a digital storage mechanism that allows for the recording, tracking and verification of data.[29] Transactions are processed on a distributed and decentralised basis as all members of the network are involved in the authentication and validation process. This makes the system become highly secure and it minimises the risk of hacking or tampering with the data as there is more than one source of verification of the data and traceability of changes on the system.[30]

21. Nakamoto (*supra* n. 8) at 3.
22. Christidis and Devetsikiotis (*supra* n. 15) at 2293.
23. *Ibid.*
24. *See ibid.*
25. Abeyratne and Monfared (*supra* n. 10) at 3.
26. *Ibid.* Also *see*, Andreas Antonopoulos, *Mastering Bitcoin: Unlocking Digital Cryptocurrencies* (1st ed., O'Reilly Media Inc. 2014).
27. Xiwei Xu, Ingo Weber, Mark Staples, Liming Zhu, Jan Bosch, Len Bass, Cesare Pautasso & Paul Rimba, *A Taxonomy of Blockchain-Based Systems for Architecture Design*, IEEE International Conference on Software Architecture 243, 245 (2017).
28. *Ibid.*, 245 and 248.
29. Ali Hadi Mohsin, A. A. Zaidan, Bilal Bahaa, O. s. Albahri, A.s. Albahri, M.A. Alsalem & K.I. Mohammed, *Blockchain Authentication of Network Applications: Taxonomy, Classification, Capabilities, Open Challenges, Motivations, Recommendations and Future Directions*, 64 Computer Standards and Interfaces 41, 43 (2019).
30. Abeyratne S.A. and Monfared R.P. (*supra* n. 10) at 2.

[B] An Overview of Smart Contracts

[1] Explanation of Smart Contracts

Smart contracts are a more advanced application of blockchain technology, and they are the product of the proliferation of cryptocurrencies and distributed ledger technologies.[31] This innovation allows for the processing of multiple and complex transactions by using the blockchain system as a platform.[32] To shed more light on the role that arbitration plays as a dispute resolution mechanism within smart contracts for the purposes of this chapter, it is important to carry out an explanation of what smart contracts are and the function that they occupy in this subsection.

Smart contracts were first referred to by Nick Szabo in the 1990s as 'a set of promises, specified in digital form, including protocols within which the parties perform on these promises'.[33] This definition refers to the idea that smart contracts are software codes that include the terms and conditions of a contract and that run on a network leading to a partial or full automated self-execution and self-enforcement of the contract.[34] At the time that Szabo came up with the idea of smart contracts he did base it on blockchain technology. However, with the emergence of Bitcoin the idea of an automated contract that runs as a computer code became intertwined with blockchain technology.

In essence, a smart contract can be identified as being a software programme that is stored and that runs on the blockchain system.[35] A smart contract utilises the blockchain as a platform for the automated self-execution of the terms and conditions of a transaction. An example of how this would work in practice is that if there is failure to deliver goods by one party under a sale of goods agreement then a fine or damages will be automatically drawn from the breaching party's account.[36]

[2] Uses of Smart Contracts

There are several reports that have suggested that smart contracts can be used by different industry stakeholders for transactions in different fields.[37] According to these reports, smart contracts can be used for rendering a more efficient performance of

31. Koulu R. (*supra* n. 3) at 53.
32. *See* De Filippi & Hassan (*supra* n. 12), and Christidis and Devetsikiotis (*supra* n. 15) at 2301.
33. Nick Szabo, *Smart Contracts: Building Blocks for Digital Markets*, 1996, https://www.fon.hum.uva.nl/rob/Courses/InformationInSpeech/CDROM/Literature/LOTwinterschool2006/szabo.best.vwh.net/smart_contracts_2.html (accessed 28 June 2020).
34. Sara Hourani, *Cross-Border Smart Contracts: Boosting International Digital Trade through Trust and Adequate Remedies*, UNCITRAL special volume 'Modernizing International Trade Law to Support Innovation and Sustainable Development (2017).
35. Christidis and Devetsikiotis (*supra* n. 15).
36. *See* Koulu (*supra* n. 3) at 54.
37. *See* IEEE Future Directions Blockchain Initiative White Paper: Reinforcing the Links of the Blockchain and Smart Contracts Alliance in collaboration with Deloitte Report, Smart Contracts: 12 Use Cases for Business & Beyond: A Technology, Legal & Regulatory Introduction-Foreword by Nick Szabo (December 2016).

transactions that are complex in nature.[38] For example, smart contracts can be used in supply chain management.[39]

The global supply chain management industry is estimated to be worth around 16 trillion USD.[40] A vast number of manufacturers, distributors, suppliers, retailers, transporters and logistics companies operate in this complex web of transactions. The scale of this web of transactions and the complex nature of the systems involved often leads to issues such as high transactional costs, problems arising from mistakes and errors made in the manual handling of paperwork and issues relating to fraud and theft amongst others.[41] It has been suggested that the introduction of supply chain visibility that could be accessed by all members involved on the chain would help enhance and minimise these issues, which would help reduce overhead costs.[42] This enhanced visibility can be introduced by the use of smart contract technology which would process all transactions and data on the system in an automated manner without the need of having a managing authority on the system.[43] The supply chain system would therefore be integrated into one platform in order to allow for the automated processing and verification of transactions and documentation. Automated flows of information within the system would eliminate the requirement for manual entry of data which would reduce human error and render the system to be more efficient.[44]

In order to have this global B2B integration within the supply chain, it has been widely suggested that combining the smart contract platform with machines connected to the Internet-of-Things devices would result in this real time streaming of information and data processing.[45] This means that the software blockchain-based system would be connected to the machines that would manufacture, transport and handle the goods which would update the system and streamline the information on it at each stage of the process. A number of companies have already started developing such record-tracking smart contracts to be used in supply chain management.[46]

As observed, smart contracts enable for the automated execution of multiple transactions without the need to make new requests into the system every time a transaction needs to be processed. This automation characteristic brings a number of

38. Hourani (*supra* n. 34).
39. IEEE Future Directions Blockchain Initiative White Paper (*supra* n. 37).
40. *See* Boucher (*supra* n. 14).
41. *Ibid.*, at 16.
42. Alex Hughes, Andrew Park, Jan Kietzmann & Chris Archer-Brown, *Beyond Bitcoin: What Blockchain and Distributed Ledger Technologies Mean for Firms*, 62 Business Horizons 273, 277 (2019).
43. *See* Smart Contracts Alliance in collaboration with Deloitte Report, Smart Contracts (*supra* n. 37).
44. *See* Bernard J La Londe & James M Masters, *Emerging Logistics Strategies: Blueprints for the Next Century*, 24 (7) International Journal of Physical Distribution and Logistics Management 35 (1994).
45. *See* Kari Korpela, Jukka Hallikas & Tomi Dahlberg, *Digital Supply Chain Transformation toward Blockchain Integration*, Proceedings of the 50th Hawaii International Conference on System Sciences 4182 (2017), Abeyratne & Monfared (*supra* n. 10), Christidis & Devetsikiotis (*supra* n. 15) and Roberto Michel, *Your Path to the Digital Supply Chain*, Logistics Management 29-32 (May 2018), https://www.logisticsmgmt.com/article/your_path_to_the_digital_supply_chain (accessed 28 June 2020).
46. *See* Boucher (*supra* n. 14) at 17 and Abeyratne & Monfared (*supra* n. 10) at 2.

advantages to the efficient processing of different trade operations like those required in supply chain management. Consequently, these business uses of smart contracts open up the need for incorporating a dispute resolution mechanism such as arbitration within the smart contract platform to resolve ensuing disputes. An explanation of smart contract arbitration will thus be discussed in the next section.

§12.03 WHAT IS SMART CONTRACT ARBITRATION?

Problems are bound to arise from the execution of the smart contract whether this concerns a breach by one of the parties or an issue that occurs on the blockchain system. In light of this, it would be relevant to include an arbitration clause in the smart contract to prompt the parties to resolve their differences with regards to the performance of the contract.[47] Arbitration is currently the most popular private method of dispute resolution for B2B disputes.[48] Opting for an arbitration clause to be embedded within the smart contract presents a number of advantages including the avoidance of determining private international law issues such as the relevant national jurisdiction for hearing the case.[49] Other benefits for incorporating an arbitration clause rather than choosing other methods for dispute resolution within the smart contract would be that the dispute is settled by a third party and this settlement has force of law. This would present the parties with the advantage of having an outcome which has a final and binding legal value. Namely, arbitration could facilitate the recognition of the legal validity of the automated enforcement of the outcome of the smart contract arbitration procedure due to the final and binding legal value of the award.[50] This would save time and further the cost resulting from the dispute.[51]

There is currently no uniform standard arbitration procedure for smart contract arbitration. The concept is based on dispute resolution taking place electronically on the blockchain. The smart contract arbitration process has several characteristics that differ from those of traditional arbitration procedures. These characteristics mainly relate to the coding of the arbitration agreement and the automation of parts of the procedure.

Several procedural designs have been created for the smart arbitration procedure. These designs vary the levels of automation that are adopted in the process. The design in essence depends on what the parties would require and opt for. There are systems that propose for the procedure to be entirely automated in that there are no human

47. *See* Vannieuwenhuyse (*supra* n. 6). Also *see* Amy Schmitz and Colin Rule, *Online Dispute Resolution for Smart Contracts*, 2019 (2) Journal of Dispute Resolution 103, 122 (2019).
48. Queen Mary University of London and White & Case 2018 International Arbitration Survey: The Evolution of International Arbitration, http://www.arbitration.qmul.ac.uk/media/arbitration/docs/2018-International-Arbitration-Survey-report.pdf (accessed 18 May 2019), 7.
49. *See* Vannieuwenhuyse G. (*supra* n. 6).
50. Except where the law has restrictions on this point, then the automated enforcement of the award would not be legal.
51. *See* Winston Maxwell & Gauthier Vannieuwenhuyse, *Robots Replacing Arbitrators: Smart Contract Arbitration*, (1) ICC Dispute Resolution Bulletin 24, 28-29 (2018) for more reasons on why arbitration should be adopted as the dispute resolution mechanism in smart contract disputes that have a commercial nature.

intermediaries or arbitrators throughout the entire process.[52] Under these designs, the arbitration process would be managed by the blockchain system and the arbitrator would be an algorithm. There are however smart contract arbitration systems that have incorporated the option of a partial automation to be incorporated in the arbitral procedure. These systems offer the possibility of having human intervention for certain parts of processing the claim and for rendering the arbitral award. One of the most well-known smart contract arbitration procedures that has adopted this mixed stance is the CodeLegit arbitration.[53]

A brief explanation of the CodeLegit procedure will be effected here as an example of a smart contract arbitration procedure to show how it would be carried out in practice. The CodeLegit arbitration procedure is based on the Arbitration Library which is the arbitration protocol on the smart contract equivalent to the arbitration agreement. Before the protocol is entered into the smart contract, the parties would have to have an off-chain traditional arbitration agreement. If there is an issue concerning the performance of the smart contract or if the smart contract fails to perform adequately due to a bug in the system, the CodeLegit arbitration procedure is triggered by one of the parties. Once the procedure is triggered, the smart contract is paused. The Arbitration Library then sends the notice of arbitration to the appointing authority who is the managing body of the procedure. The appointing authority asks the parties to appoint an arbitrator and once the choice is made, the arbitrator is contacted by the authority. The necessary procedural documents are then communicated by the parties to the arbitrator via email then are processed by the smart contract for verification and proofing. If the parties and arbitrator consider it necessary, the hearing can take place via the use of ICT. Once the arbitrator issues the arbitral award, he would send it to the appointing authority who then enters it in the system in the form of code that is automatically enforced. Additionally, the arbitrator has the choice to also send the award in writing if necessary.

As an explanation of what smart contract arbitration has now been made clearer, the question of how smart arbitration improves access to justice ensues.

§12.04 SMART CONTRACT ARBITRATION: BETTER FORUM FOR ACCESS TO JUSTICE IN B2B DISPUTES?

This section focuses on a discussion of the need to adopt smart arbitration as a procedure to resolve disputes arising from international commercial contracts. It provides a practical assessment of the need for smart contract arbitration and whether this would enhance the business parties' access to justice.

52. *See* Jun Zou, Yan Wang & Mehmet A Orgun, *A Dispute Arbitration Protocol Based on a Peer-to-Peer Service Contract Management Scheme*, IEEE International Conference on Web Services 41, 45 regarding the proposal that the computer note can act as an arbiter in case there is a dispute on the smart contract. Also *see* Maxwell & Vannieuwenhuyse (*supra* n. 51) on how the machine would act as the arbitrator.

53. *See* CodeLegit White Paper on Blockchain Arbitration, https://docs.google.com/document/d/1v_AdWbMuc2Ei70ghlTC1mYX4_5VQsF_28O4PsLckNM4/edit (accessed 18 May 2019).

[A] Smart Contract Arbitration: A Forum that Enhances the Parties' Access to Justice

[1] Efficiency

Arbitration proceedings are currently facing the issue of becoming less efficient than they were initially designed to be. Traditional face-to-face arbitration is becoming increasingly 'judicialised' which means that arbitration is turning into a procedure that is very similar to that of litigation from the standpoint of the time that it takes to process cases.[54] Thus, the time length that current arbitration proceedings take has become a much debated issue in the arbitration community.[55] This issue is quite problematic as arbitration law encourages the efficiency and expedition of procedures.[56] Moreover, the cost of going to arbitration is another issue affecting the efficiency of proceedings as the cost of arbitral proceedings is very high.[57] These costs have been increasing in the past few years.[58] These concerns are thereafter contributing to the creation of impediments for adequate access to justice in arbitration.

One of the main advantages that smart contract arbitration offers is efficiency in terms of time and cost.[59] First, smart contract arbitration is an online procedure. This consists of having the proceedings in electronic form, and administering and conducting the proceedings on the blockchain platform. This helps the parties avoid incurring travel and venue costs for these proceedings. Also, using smart contract arbitration gives more accessibility to the parties as they would be able to access all information relating to the case via the smart contract platform.[60] The smart contract platform is an efficient document repository as it verifies the authenticity of all submitted documents as a result of the blockchain verification and encryption mechanism.[61]

Second, the smart contract arbitration procedure benefits from automation functioning on the basis of the decentralised structure of the network. This means that there is no need to resort to outside help to enforce the arbitration agreement and consequently the arbitral award.[62] However, this also means that since the procedure

---

54. *See* for example Leona Trakman & Hugo Montgomery, *The 'Judicialization' of International Arbitration: Pitfall or Virtue?*, 30(2) Leiden Journal of International Law 405 (2017).
55. *Ibid.*
56. *See* Vannieuwenhyse (*supra* n. 6) at 120.
57. Nigel Blackaby, Constantine Partasides QC, Alan Redfern, & Martin Hunter (eds), *Redfern and Hunter on International Arbitration*, chapter 1 (6th ed. 2015). Also *see*, Steven Seidenberg, *International Arbitration Loses Its Grip*, ABA Journal (1st April, 2010), https://www.abajournal.com/magazine/article/international_arbitration_loses_its_grip (accessed 29 June 2020).
58. *Ibid.*
59. *See* Francisco Uribarri Soares, *New Technologies and Arbitration*, 7 Indian Journal of Arbitration Law 84, 84 (2018).
60. Mark Giancaspro, *Is A 'Smart Contract' Really A Smart Idea? Insights From A Legal Perspective*, 33 Computer Law & Security Review 825, 827 (2017).
61. Jeremy Barnett & Philip Treleaven, *Algorithmic Dispute Resolution-The Automation of Professional Dispute Resolution Using AI and Blockchain Technologies*, 61 (3) The Computer Journal 399, 406 (2018).
62. Maxime Hanriot, *Online Dispute Resolution (ODR) As A Solution To Cross Border Consumer Disputes: The Enforcement of Outcomes*, 2 McGill Journal of Dispute Resolution 1, 20 (2015-2016). Also *see*, Maxwell and Vannieuwenhuyse (*supra* n. 51) at 28. *See* Alexander

documents are automatically authenticated and verified the procedure has the potential to be administered automatically without any human intervention.[63] This leads to having more certainty in the processing of all necessary documents needed for the process and to having no human error involved. This reduces administrative processing time and overheads related to this. The decentralised and distributed structure of the network means that the platform is transparent where there is real time visibility and streamlining of the procedure and any issues arising in an automated manner. As a result of the enhanced transparency of the process, there is easier access to documents and for proof of events, actions or omissions amounting to conflict.[64] The smart contract arbitration procedure is additionally self-sufficient due to the automated execution of the different parts of the procedure.

Third, the flexibility of the smart contract arbitration is also a factor amounting to the efficiency of the procedure. The flexibility in the design of the arbitration procedure could be a potential aspect that would reduce time and cost issues.[65] This is as the parties could agree to a bespoke procedure that is modelled around the needs of the substantive contract. This would include agreeing on the automation levels to be adopted for the procedure. Also, private permissioned blockchain networks[66] provide for more flexibility in the process as data could be reversible on these if the parties, the administrator or the arbitrator wish to change any of the inputted data on the smart contract.[67]

Savings on the time and cost of the procedure are the two main features of this promised efficiency of smart contract arbitration. The increase in efficiency would be an important factor to enhance the parties' experience of resolving their disputes. Smart contract arbitration offers an additional main advantage as will be discussed in the next subsection.

[2] Confidentiality and Security

When it comes to traditional arbitration, there have been problems of security of the systems used for storage of case documentation.[68] For example, in *Libnanco v. Republic of Turkey*[69] the defendant admitted to obtaining information illegally by hacking the claimant's correspondence. Moreover, in *Caratube International Oil Co. and Devincci Salah Hourani v. Republic of Kazakhstan*[70] the arbitral tribunal admitted in an

Savelyev, *Contract Law 2.0: 'Smart' Contracts as the Beginning of the End of Classic Contract Law*, National Research University Higher School of Economics, Basic Research Program Working Paper, Series: Law WP BRP 71/LAW/2016, 15.

63. Giancaspro M (*supra* n. 60) at 827.
64. *Ibid.*, at 827.
65. Maxwell and Vannieuwenhuyse (*supra* n. 51) at 28.
66. *See* §18.02 [A] of this chapter.
67. Ibrahim Shehata, *Three Potential Imminent Benefits of Blockchain for International Arbitration: Cybersecurity, Confidentiality and Efficiency*, Young Arbitration Review, 3 (2018).
68. *Ibid.*, at 5.
69. ICSID ARB/06/8.
70. ICSID ARB/13/13.

unpublished order that evidence that was obtained via a hack and that became part of the public domain was valid.

The decentralised and distributed architecture of the smart contract arbitration process makes the system more resilient to hacking compared to traditional methods of using cloud storage.[71] This is due to the proof-of-work that happens on the system.[72] This is the verification of valid transactions by all members on the network. There is no single point of failure on the blockchain as the data is stored on the ledgers of all members of the network, so if one node is hacked data can still be retrieved from the other nodes and they can verify the authenticity of the transactions as a result. Therefore, the security of the smart contract system is provided by encryption and timestamping each transaction block on the system. Consequently, the smart arbitration procedure benefits from higher security levels than using clouds especially in private permissioned networks.

The increase in efficiency and security of smart contract arbitration proceedings enhances the parties' access to justice in cases of commercial disputes. This comes under Garth and Capellati's definition of access to justice as their findings place an emphasis on cost and time as important features of access to justice.[73] Based on the results of this section, it can be concluded that smart contract arbitration is an adequate tool for low-value disputes as well as emergency proceedings.[74] It can be said that Article 4(2) of Appendix V of the ICC Arbitration Rules can corroborate this stance as it states that ICT-based meetings can take place for emergency arbitrations. It can also be concluded that smart contract arbitration is the most adequate method for resolving disputes or problems that lead to conflict from the performance of the smart contract.[75] Nevertheless, there are many areas of uncertainty in the implementation of smart contract arbitration in practice. These limitations have an effect over the parties' access to justice as this could eventually hamper the efficiency of the blockchain-based procedure.

[B] The Practical Limitations of Smart Contract Arbitration as a Forum for Resolving Disputes

[1] Limited Flexibility

The main issue that affects smart contracts in general is the fact that they are composed of computer code. This raises a number of questions such as whether code is considered to be legally equivalent to a contract or contract term. This is a question that

71. Mohsin et al. (*supra* n. 29) at 43, and Koulu (*supra* n. 3) at 50.
72. *See* §18.02 [A] of this chapter and Eliza Mik, *Smart Contracts: Terminology, Technical Limitations and Real World Complexity*, 9 (2) Law, Innovation and Technology 269, 275 (2017).
73. Bryan Garth & Mauro Capelleti, *Access to Justice: The Newest Wave in the Worldwide Movement to Make Rights Effective*, Articles by Maurer Faculty, 1142, 1186-1190 (1978).
74. *See* Vannieuwenhyse (*supra* n. 47) at 120.
75. *See* Koulu (*supra* n. 3) at 65-66.

remains unclear in the law as it stands today.[76] Building on this, the concern regarding the interpretation of the smart contract, or of the smart contract arbitration agreement in this case, ensues. Namely, a discrepancy between the meaning of the contract in words and in code can very well happen.[77] In addition to this, if there are vitiating circumstances such as mistakes that have affected the agreement, then it would be difficult for the concerned party to detect this prior to the execution of the proceedings. If that occurs, this can be quite problematic as the smart contract will be automatically executed with no way of stopping the execution. It has been argued that moving towards electronic-based communication without having a 'human' touch or intervention can lead to a whole deal of misinterpretation.[78] The potential misunderstanding or vitiating factor that has affected the conclusion of the contract and its legal validity will be overlooked in the process due to the automated enforcement.[79] This reflects the limited flexibility of the smart contract arbitration procedure.

[2] Security Issues

Blockchain technology is not entirely immutable from a security point of view as different blockchain-based systems have been the victims of different hacks and security breaches.[80] These hacks can take place by recovering the user's private key that is used to sign the transaction request on the blockchain.[81] Hacks on the system can also take place by taking advantage of the majority consensus system on the blockchain network.[82] The majority consensus system is used to reach consensus amongst the nodes of the blockchain network to verify and authenticate transactions. If the hackers get hold of the majority of the nodes on the network this result in a security breach as they can then control the network and authenticate fraudulent transactions on the system. It must be noted though that this is less likely to occur on a private permissioned blockchain network, which is what would be used for running a smart contract arbitration procedure.

76. *See* for example the UK Government's Public Consultation that addressed this question, https://www.lawsociety.org.uk/news/stories/cryptoassets-dlt-and-smart-contracts-ukjt-consultation/ (accessed 07 July 2019)
77. Maxwell & Vannieuwenhuyse (*supra* n. 51) at 27.
78. Mohamed Abdel Wahab & Ethan Katsh, 'Revolutionizing Technologies and the Use of Technology in International Arbitration: Innovation, Legitimacy, Prospects and Challenges', in *Arbitration in the Digital Age: The Brave New World of Arbitration*, Maud Piers & Christian Aschauer (eds) 37 (Cambridge University Press 2018).
79. Giancaspro (*supra* n. 60), at 829, Gabriel Jaccard, *Smart Contracts and the Role of Law*, 23 Justletter IT, 22 (November 2017), and Mik (*supra* n. 72) at 280-281 and 287.
80. *See* Mike Orcutt, *Once Hailed as Unhackable, Blockchains are Now Getting Hacked*, MIT Technology Review (Feb 19, 2019), https://www.technologyreview.com/s/612974/once-hailed-as-unhackable-blockchains-are-now-getting-hacked/ (accessed 30 June 2019).
81. Xiaoqi Li, Peng Jiang, Ting Chen, Xiapu Luo & Qiaoyan Wen, *A Survey on the Security of Blockchain Systems*, Future General Computer Systems, 5 (2017).
82. *Ibid.*, at 4.

[3] *Data Privacy Issues*

It is not yet clear what happens to the data that is stored on the blockchain system. This raises questions of compliance with the General Data Protection Regulation, for example, for cases where this EU legislation applies.[83] This can be problematic from the stance of the confidentiality of the arbitration proceedings as the data protection situation remains unclear.

[4] *Lack of Efficiency*

It has been argued that it might not be possible to implement smart contract systems on a large scale.[84] This is due to problems with system responsiveness which would essentially mean that that system would function at a very slow pace. Notwithstanding, this is not an issue in private permissioned blockchain networks.

Smart contract arbitration seems to offer a number of practical solutions to some of the issues that are encountered in traditional face-to-face arbitration. These solutions could help enhance the parties' access to justice in certain contexts such as blockchain-based platforms for supply chain document handling and logistics. It has also been observed that access to justice via blockchain-based arbitration is not immune from technical and legal barriers. From a practical perspective therefore, smart contract arbitration enhances access to justice in some ways and can hinder it too.

In order to have a complete understanding of the full extent to which smart contract arbitration currently enhances access to justice for B2B disputes, it is important to discuss how the current legal framework applies to such procedures. The next section is thus going to examine the degree to which the blockchain-based arbitration procedure is recognised and enforced by the law to ensure commercial certainty and adequate access to justice for the disputing parties.

§12.05 A LEGAL ASSESSMENT OF THE CURRENT ARBITRATION LEGAL FRAMEWORK APPLICABLE TO SMART CONTRACT ARBITRATION

This section examines the legality of the blockchain-based arbitration procedure. The section covers some of the main procedural areas that would be disrupted by smart contract arbitration in the arbitration process. This section aims to provide a brief overview of how different aspects of this type of procedure are enforceable under the applicable law and analyses whether this method of dispute resolution can be considered as having business viability to enable adequate access to justice from a legal perspective.

83. *See* Eliza Mik, *Electronic Platforms: Openness, Transparency & Privacy Issues*, 26 (6) European Review of Private Law, 853 (2018).
84. Giancaspro (*supra* n. 60) at 834.

[A] Smart Contract Arbitration Agreements

[1] The Form of the Arbitration Agreement

The special characteristic of a smart contract arbitration agreement with regards to its form is that the agreement is authenticated in code. If the agreement is purely concluded in digital form without referring to a natural language contract, this raises the question of whether the signatures of the arbitration agreement by the parties can be validated and recognised by the legal framework if they are in the form of code.

Article II(2) of the NYC states that the term agreement in 'writing' shall include an arbitral clause in a contract, or an agreement signed by the parties or that is contained in an exchange of letters or telegrams. Article II(2)'s scope of application became more extensive in application as a result of the adoption of the UNCITRAL Recommendation for Article II(2) of the NYC in 2006.[85] According to this recommendation, consideration must be given to the wide use of electronic commerce. It can be concluded that a wider interpretation can be given to the 'in writing' requirement of the NYC.[86] By applying these provisions to an arbitration agreement that is in the form of code, it can be said that the NYC recognises that such an agreement is in writing. Article 7 of the UNCITRAL Model Law confirms this as an arbitration agreement in writing has a wide meaning under this text. Article 7 states that an arbitration agreement is considered to be in writing if it is met by electronic communication. Communication is defined in the text as any communication that the parties make by means of data messages.

There are nevertheless limitations under the NYC regarding the acceptance of an arbitration agreement in code as fulfilling the 'in writing' requirement. Articles II(3), V(1)(a) and IV(1)(b) NYC all refer the courts back to the applicable national law.[87] This means that if the national law in question does not recognise a wide understanding of the 'in writing' requirement of the NYC, then the agreement in code might not be recognised under the Convention. The CodeLegit arbitration procedure for example currently imposes the need to have a natural language arbitration agreement before it can be embedded in the smart contract code.[88] This perhaps shows the careful approach that some blockchain-based arbitration platforms are adopting to avoid falling into the limitations of the applicable domestic law. Another limitation towards the wider interpretation of the 'in writing' requirement under Art II(2) NYC is found in the non-binding nature of the UNCITRAL Model Law. Article 7 of the Model Law has

85. Recommendation regarding the interpretation of Article II, paragraph 2, and Article VII, paragraph 1, of the Convention on the Recognition and Enforcement of Foreign Arbitral Awards, done in New York, 10 June 1958, adopted by the United Nations Commission on International Trade Law on 7 July 2006 at its thirty-ninth session, https://uncitral.un.org/sites/uncitral.un.org/files/media-documents/uncitral/en/a2e.pdf (accessed 28 June 2020).
86. Reinmar Wolff, 'E-Arbitration Agreements and E-Awards', in Piers & Aschauer (*supra* n. 78) 171-172.
87. *See* Ihab Amro, *Enforcement of Cross-Border Online Arbitral Awards and Online Arbitration Agreements in National Courts,* 5 (2) Slovenska arbitrážna praska, 17 (2016).
88. CodeLegit White Paper (*supra* n. 53) at 2.

no legally binding value as it operates as a guidance that domestic courts can ignore and simply not apply.[89]

These limitations posed by the domestic legal systems towards recognising the signature in code can however be potentially tempered. Article VII(1) NYC disposes that if the jurisdiction has adopted other international treaties that have a more favourable approach towards the recognition and enforcement of foreign arbitral awards then this would supersede what is provided under the NYC. The UNCITRAL Recommendation for Article VII(1) of the NYC added the clarification that this also applies to the recognition and enforcement of arbitration agreements.[90] This means that the limitations imposed under Articles II(3), V(1)(a) and IV(1)(b) NYC might not apply, unless the jurisdiction in question did not adhere to any treaty or adopted any law favouring a wider application of the 'in writing' requirement. For example, for states that have adopted the United Nations Convention on the Use of Electronic Communications in International Contracts, the signature in code could fall under the remit of the Convention and be accepted by their courts.[91] The limitation to this recognition is nevertheless if the jurisdiction in question has not adopted this Convention.

[2] Submission for Recognition (and Enforcement) to National Courts

In smart contract arbitration, the parties may choose to trigger the arbitral proceedings on their own without necessarily contacting the arbitration administrator to ask them to commence proceedings. In order to do so they are prompted by the blockchain system if there is an issue with or affecting the execution of the original smart contract. Once the parties choose to go through arbitration on the smart contract, the arbitration agreement and thus procedure is automatically triggered. This is the approach that has been adopted by the CodeLegit procedure for example.[92] An examination of whether the automated trigger of the enforcement of the arbitration agreement via the relevant protocol (code) is compliant with the current law will be analysed in this subsection.

Article II(3) NYC provides that national courts shall refer to the arbitration agreement if a claim was made before them by one of the parties. It is uncertain to conclude whether the automated enforcement of the arbitration agreement is contrary to Article II(3) as the national court would still be able to be seized before the parties choose to go through arbitration in a smart contract procedure. However, a potential conflict between the automated trigger of the arbitration agreement and this provision could occur if the agreement had already been triggered and it was null and void, inoperative or incapable of being performed. This situation can lead to a breach of

89. *See* Wolff (*supra* n. 86) at 172.
90. UNCITRAL Recommendation regarding the interpretation of Article II, paragraph 2, and Article VII, paragraph 1 (*supra* n. 85).
91. *See* Article 9 of the United Nations Convention on the Use of Electronic Communications in International Contracts deals extensively with the requirements of form. *See* Wolff (*supra* n. 86) at 167-170 for a more detailed discussion on the scope of application of the Electronic Communications Convention to electronic signatures in arbitration agreements.
92. *See* CodeLegit White Paper (*supra* n. 53) at 2 and 5.

Article II(3) NYC as the smart contract proceedings would automatically start executing, unless the programmer intervenes and modifies the code to stop the proceedings from continuing.

Articles V(1)(a) and IV(1)(b) NYC refer the national courts to the applicable law of the arbitration agreement and to the validity of the arbitration agreement in the concerned domestic law.[93] These provisions require for the parties to submit the arbitration agreement to the relevant national court to assess its validity. The application of these NYC provisions may mean that the automated enforcement of the arbitration agreement in the smart contract arbitration procedure might not be valid under the NYC due to its potential invalidity under the domestic legal system in question.[94] This is due to the differing requirements imposed by the domestic civil procedure rules with regards to how they should be submitted to start the arbitral proceedings.

Moreover, problems in relation to the automated enforcement of the arbitration agreement could arise due to the problem of the interpretation of consent that is recorded in code. Also, writing code might not reflect the terms that the parties agreed upon for the arbitration agreement as it is written by the programmer.[95] Again, these limitations can be potentially reduced subject to the application and existence of a treaty, as per Article VII(1) NYC, that would recognise arbitration agreements found in code and that would be automatically enforced. It can be noted that the automated enforcement of the arbitration agreement is not that different in its effects to the commencement of arbitral proceedings on the basis of a traditional arbitration agreement, so this might not necessarily be an issue from a legal standpoint.

[B] The Arbitral Proceedings

[1] Conduct of the Proceedings

Depending on the design of the smart contract arbitration procedure, there might be systems that are based on an entirely automated procedure. This could mean that the proceedings would be processed completely automatically without giving the parties the chance to present their arguments in the arbitration case.

Conducting proceedings on such a basis can potentially lead to a breach of due process depending on the *lex arbitri* that is applicable to the arbitral proceedings. This is for example in breach of Article 6 of the ECHR regarding the right to a fair trial.[96] According to this provision, the right to a fair trial entails the right to have a fair hearing. Not having a hearing in a case would therefore leads to the result of not having a fair trial. Article 47 of the EU Charter of Fundamental Rights on the right to an effective remedy and to a fair trial also imposes the need to have a hearing.

93. *See* Wolff (*supra* n. 86) at 173-174 for a discussion on the limitations facing the submission of electronic arbitration agreements to national courts.
94. *See* Giancaspro (*supra* n. 60), at 829 and Mik (*supra* n. 72) at 275-276.
95. Koulu (*supra* n. 3) at 65-66.
96. *See* Maxwell & Vannieuwenhuyse (*supra* n. 51) at 30.

In a recent case,[97] the Amsterdam Court of Appeal held that proceedings that did not give the chance to the parties to have their case heard were not legally valid. This case involved a borrowing agreement for Bitcoins which was concluded through an online platform. The agreement contained an arbitration clause which stated that if the borrower defaulted on the payment ninety days past the due date, the loan default would be sent as a claim to arbitration. The clause also stated that if the borrower wanted to be part of the arbitration proceedings, before the award was issued, he had to send a written request to the arbitration firm and pay a 99 USD fee. The arbitral proceedings took place in electronic form by email. Three different arbitral awards were subsequently issued which decided that the borrower had to pay back the loan to the creditor. The Court refused the recognition and enforcement of the arbitral awards. The Court held that the arbitration proceedings denied the party a reasonable opportunity to defend their claim which violated the principle of hearing both sides of the argument in the case. According to the Court, such a violation which was embedded in the arbitration agreement itself is contrary to public policy under Dutch Law. This also fell under the remit of Article V(2)(b) NYC which allows a national court to deny recognition and enforcement of an arbitral award on the basis of being contrary to the public policy of that jurisdiction.

It is thus important that the smart contract arbitration proceedings and their design ensure that the right to a fair trial is respected, as this would otherwise hamper the parties to have adequate access to justice through this type of dispute resolution. Under CodeLegit arbitration for example, the parties first get the opportunity to have a paper-based arbitration procedure, unless the arbitrator finds it necessary to have oral hearings take place.[98] This seems to be in line with due process and the right to a fair trial.

[2] Composition of the Arbitral Tribunal

There is no set standard on the composition of the arbitral tribunal in a smart contract arbitration procedure. Certain procedures such as CodeLegit arbitration have designed to have a human arbitrator in the process. However, there have been suggestions to automate the procedure as a whole and to thereby have the process and award made by Artificial Intelligence.[99] If there was to be such an arbitrator, then to what extent does the current law recognise this?

The NYC does not specify what the composition of the arbitral tribunal should be. From this first reading, it might be deduced that an AI arbitrator might be accepted under the NYC. Nevertheless, there are several limitations that apply starting with the form of the award which deals with signatures and authentication of the award. This can be a potential limitation under Article V (1)(e) of the Convention as it depends on the domestic law to accept the signature of the award by the machine. Moreover, Article V(1)(d) of the Convention imposes another limitation on this as it states that if

97. ECLI:NL:GHAMS:2019:192.
98. CodeLegit White Paper (*supra* n. 53) at 5.
99. *See* Maxwell & Vannieuwenhuyse (*supra* n. 51) at 29-30.

the composition of the arbitral tribunal is not accordance with the *lex arbitri* then this is not recognisable under the Convention. Notably, certain domestic legal systems like France for example only allow for a human being to act as an arbitrator, which acts as a limitation to the recognition of AI as an arbitrator.[100] Article 1450 of the French Code of Civil Proceedings strictly states that an arbitrator needs to be a physical person.

[C] The Arbitral Award

[1] The Form of the Arbitral Award

The special characteristic of a smart contract arbitral award with regards to its form is that the arbitral award is authenticated in code.[101] This raises the question of whether the arbitrator or arbitrators can include their reasoning and signatures in code and whether this could be potentially considered to be a digital signature. To reduce any risks, for example the CodeLegit arbitration system was designed to include an arbitral award in writing if necessary due to legal requirements leading to its recognition and enforcement.[102] However, an examination of whether the applicable law recognises the arbitrators' signatures in code in a smart contract arbitration award will be carried out here.

The New York Convention does not impose a specific form of arbitral awards.[103] Article I(1) omits to provide any information with regards to the valid forms of an arbitral award that would be compliant with the Convention. Article VII(1) of the Convention, as mentioned above in § 12.05 (A) of this chapter, however states that the provisions of the Convention shall not affect the validity of preferential rules on the recognition and enforcement of arbitral awards that are imposed in national jurisdictions. This provision together with Article I(1) of the NYC seem to have an accepting stance of awards that are in code form.

Further, the UNCITRAL Recommendation for Art II(2) NYC has clarified the stance of the NYC on the meaning of arbitral agreements 'in writing' and parties' signatures by recommending to take into account the context of electronic commerce. This can be argued to have an incidental application for arbitral awards with regards to the form that they can have to comply with the Convention.

Although the NYC seems to have a favourable stance towards the recognition and enforcement of an arbitral award in code, it does bring limitations to this recognition. This limitation is found under Article V(1)(e) of the Convention which provides that the recognition and enforcement of the arbitral award may be refused if the award has not yet become binding, or has been set aside or suspended in accordance with the applicable national law. This means that if the national law in question does not

100. Mohamed Abdel Wahab, *Online Arbitration: Traditional Conceptions and Innovative Trends*, ICCA Congress Book 5 (2013).
101. CodeLegit White Paper on Blockchain Arbitration (*supra* n. 53).
102. *Ibid.*
103. *See* Wolff (*supra* n. 86) at 178-179 for a more detailed discussion on this.

recognise for arbitral awards to be in code form, then such arbitral awards would not be recognised and enforced under the Convention.

[2] The Communication of the Arbitral Award to the Parties

The special characteristic of a smart contract arbitral award with regards to the procedure in which it is communicated to the parties is that it would be communicated to them directly by code on the smart contract. Again, as a matter of reducing any potential risks for recognition and enforcement certain systems like CodeLegit include the possibility of sending the arbitral award to the parties in writing by post if necessary, and by email.[104] However, an examination of whether the applicable law recognises complete communication of the award in code is observed in this subsection.

There is no provision in the New York Convention that imposes any specific manner in which the arbitral award shall be communicated to the parties.[105] Thus, it can be deduced that the NYC is favourable towards the communication of the arbitral award in code in smart arbitration proceedings.

The limitation though can still fall under Article V(1)(e) of the Convention as the *lex arbitri* or the law at the jurisdiction of enforcement may not recognise and enforce arbitral awards that were communicated through code. In this case, the arbitral award would not be considered to be valid under the NYC and would be refused recognition and enforcement.

[3] Submission of the Arbitral Award to the National Courts for Recognition and Enforcement

The special characteristic of a smart contract arbitral award with regards to its submission to the national courts for recognition and enforcement lies in its automated enforcement via the relevant protocol or code on the smart contract. This means that there would be no need for any court intervention to recognise and/or enforce the arbitral award. This subsection is going to examine the legality of this characteristic of automated enforcement of the arbitral award.

Article III of the NYC states that each Contracting State to the Convention shall recognise arbitral awards as binding. However, it also states that the enforcement of arbitral awards by national courts should be made in accordance with domestic laws. Article IV of the Convention refers to providing an original award or authenticated copy of the award for domestic courts to recognise and enforce an arbitral award. As both provisions refer back to the laws of national jurisdictions, it can be concluded that the

104. CodeLegit White Paper on Blockchain Arbitration (*supra* n. 53).
105. Wolff (*supra* n. 86), at 179.

recognition of the automated enforcement of the arbitral award under the Convention depends on the national law in question.

In this context, the questions whether the outcome is legally binding and then whether the enforced outcome can be reversed arise. The automated enforcement of the award can create issues of due process and this can be eventually considered to be an unfair contract term.[106] The automated enforcement of the award might not be valid from a legal standpoint due to procedural issues or problems with remedies.[107] Moreover, based on the analysis above of the application of Articles III and IV of the NYC, the automated enforcement of the arbitral award may be in conflict with national laws regarding the recognition of the award.[108]

§12.06 CONCLUSION

Moving towards technologically enhanced procedures for resolving disputes such as smart contract arbitration is becoming increasingly accepted and likely. Arbitration has been increasingly becoming dependent on technology in the past few years.[109] The COVID-19 era has also contributed to the acceleration of the need to use technology for the resolution of arbitration disputes.[110]

It has been observed in this chapter that smart contract arbitration has a number of advantages that could enhance the commercial parties' access to justice in specific circumstances such as high volume-low value disputes and emergency disputes. This type of process would be particularly appealing to be used in the context where there is already a functioning smart contract between the parties like in the example of supply chain management. Smart contract arbitration also has the potential to widen access to justice to micro, small and medium enterprises as a result of the advantages that it carries.[111] Smart contract arbitration does however come with its limitations, the main one being the rigidity of the procedure.

With regards to the legal analysis of the recognition of the international and national legal framework of the smart contract arbitration procedure, it has been observed that although the NYC is quite favourable towards many aspects of the process there are still a number of limitations that this poses. The result of the legal analysis is that the parties' rights are not guaranteed by choosing this type of forum.

---

106. Koulu (*supra* n. 3) at 67.
107. Giancaspro (*supra* n. 60) at 832.
108. *See* Pietro Ortolani, *The Impact of Blockchain Technologies and Smart Contracts on Dispute Resolution: Arbitration and Court Litigation at the Crossroads*, 24(2) Uniform Law Review, 430 (June 2019) for a more detailed discussion on the issues created by self-enforcement of arbitral awards.
109. Abdel Wahab & Katsh (*supra* n. 78) at 52.
110. *See* Baker McKenzie report, *COVID-19: Implications for the future of Dispute Resolution*, https://www.bakermckenzie.com/-/media/files/insight/publications/2020/04/covid19-implications-for-the-future-of-dispute-resolution_v5.pdf (accessed 30 June 2020), at 3.
111. Schmitz & Rule (*supra* n. 47) at 124.

Perhaps the current solutions to these issues lie in the design of the smart contract arbitration procedure to guarantee better access to justice for the parties. It is very important to build a dispute resolution system that is efficient and that can generate the trust of its users.[112] The system and procedure design for example might be part of these solutions which can be modelled in a way to help in the efficiency of the process.

112. Orna Rabinovich-Einy & Ethan Katsh, *Blockchain and the Inevitability of Disputes: The Role for Online Dispute Resolution*, 2019(2) Journal of Dispute Resolution, 47-76 (2019), at 72.

Part V Access to Justice and Arbitral Institutions

CHAPTER 13

Access to Justice Through WIPO's Arbitration Rules

Aislinn O'Connell

WIPO, a UN special agency, supports arbitration through its specialised Arbitration and Mediation Center, using a set of rules designed with intellectual property disputes in mind. This chapter considers the WIPO Arbitration Rules, from inception to the latest (2020) iteration, and whether these rules enable access to justice. Through a careful examination of specific provisions of the WIPO Arbitration Rules, and contrast and comparison with both the WIPO Expedited Arbitration Rules and alternative Arbitration Rules, the chapter concludes that the WIPO Arbitration Rules embed access to justice in all aspects of the arbitration process. The chapter examines in detail three aspects of the Arbitration Rules, and how these may impact access to justice. First it looks at costs, followed by the selection and appointment of the arbitral Tribunal and lastly, it examines operational issues with particular emphasis on the possibility of electing to use the WIPO Expedited Arbitration Rules. The chapter concludes in bringing together these elements that, although access to justice is not specifically mentioned in the rules, its principles are firmly embedded throughout its Arbitration Rules.

§13.01 INTRODUCTION

WIPO is a UN specialised agency.[1] Established in 1967 with the purpose 'to encourage creative activity, to promote the protection of intellectual property throughout the

1. *See* https://www.un.org/en/sections/about-un/funds-programmes-specialized-agencies-and-others/ (accessed 24 January 2020).

world',[2] WIPO now defines its mission as follows: '[WIPO] promotes innovation and creativity for the economic, social and cultural development of all countries, through a balanced and effective international intellectual property system'.[3] Its origins date back much farther than 1967, finding its antecedent bureaux established to support the Paris and Berne Conventions. After their merger in 1893 to create the United International Bureaux for the Protection of Intellectual Property (BIRPI, from the French *Bureaux Internationaux Réunis pour la Protection de la Propriété Intellectuelle*), the combined Bureaux administered several more treaties, until the Convention Establishing the World Intellectual Property Organization (the WIPO Convention) was enacted in 1967, and WIPO formally replaced BIRPI in 1970.[4]

As of 2019, WIPO has 192 Member States, and administers 26 international treaties.[5] Headquartered in Geneva, Switzerland, it provides a range of services in intellectual property administration and enforcement. It also administers ADR processes through the WIPO Arbitration and Mediation Center (AMC).[6] Established in 1994 in Geneva, and with an additional office in Singapore, the WIPO AMC administers disputes through mediation, arbitration and expert determination. The WIPO AMC also administers domain name disputes, and has covered 'some 43,000 cases under the Uniform Domain Name Dispute Resolution Policy (UDRP) and related policies'.[7]

This chapter focuses on the WIPO Arbitration Rules,[8] as revised and updated in 2020,[9] and considers whether these rules enable access to justice. The chapter also considers the WIPO Expedited Arbitration Rules[10] and how they differ from the Arbitration Rules where appropriate. While the term 'access to justice' does not make an appearance in either set of rules, the concept of access to justice is embedded throughout both documents, leading to an arbitration system which embeds throughout it the flexibility which is needed to ensure that justice is accessible to all parties to a dispute. This flexibility is reflected in the variety of disputants who have been party to WIPO ADR processes. From their Caseload analysis,[11] WIPO states that disputing parties have been 'large-sized companies, SMEs and start-ups across industries and sectors, artists and investors, R&D centers, universities, producers and collecting societies'.[12] Furthermore, the range in remedies, venue, and language also serve to augment the declaration that justice is accessible through WIPO ADR – although the

2. Convention Establishing the World Intellectual Property Organization (Signed at Stockholm on 14 July 1967 and as amended on 28 September 1979), paragraph 2 of Preamble.
3. https://www.wipo.int/portal/en/ (accessed 24 January 2020).
4. Carolyn Deere Birkbeck, *The World Intellectual Property Organization (WIPO): A Reference Guide* (2016 Edward Elgar) 7.
5. https://www.wipo.int/about-wipo/en/ (accessed 24 January 2020).
6. https://www.wipo.int/amc/en/center/background.html (accessed 24 January 2020).
7. https://www.wipo.int/amc/en/center/caseload.html (accessed 24 January 2020).
8. WIPO Arbitration Rules (2014).
9. The WIPO Arbitration Rules 2020 are almost identical to the 2014 Rules, with the sole difference in Article 67, which does not change the substantive meaning. Thus, for the purposes of this chapter, references to the 2014 Rules, unless specifically differentiated, can be taken to be applicable to the 2020 Rules also.
10. WIPO Expedited Arbitration Rules (2014).
11. https://www.wipo.int/amc/en/center/caseload.html (accessed 24 January 2020).
12. *Ibid.*

AMC has offices only in Switzerland and Singapore, locations for ADR proceedings have included 'France, Germany, Ireland, Italy, Netherlands, Singapore, Spain, Switzerland, United Kingdom and United States of America'.[13] The AMC also makes available a number of anonymised arbitration case examples, which serve to demonstrate the breadth of subject matters which are covered by the AMC – from patent arbitration in medical devices to arbitration in an artist promotion dispute, from trademark coexistence to software copyright[14] – the variety of issues which the AMC is competent to administer over is demonstrative of the wide range of areas in which justice is accessible.

This chapter begins with a discussion of the 2020 WIPO Arbitration Rules. It then considers in greater detail three aspects of the Arbitration Rules, and how these may impact access to justice. Looking first at costs, which can be a barrier to participation, and thus access to justice, the chapter considers the fees payable for AMC proceedings, as well as the process of deposits, and the potential for hearings for emergency relief. Moving on to the constitution of the arbitral Tribunal, the chapter considers the potential for access to justice issues in appointing arbitrators. Operational issues, including location, and timescales are considered in the following section, with particular emphasis on the possibility of electing to use the WIPO Expedited Arbitration Rules. The chapter concludes by bringing together the elements discussed, and asserting that, although access to justice is not specifically mentioned in the Rules, the principles are thoroughly embedded throughout the principles.

§13.02 AN OVERVIEW OF WIPO ARBITRATION AND EXPEDITED ARBITRATION

WIPO administers two separate but related sets of Arbitration Rules. This section introduces the AMC, its function and the two sets of rules under which the AMC administers arbitrations, commenting throughout on the promotion of access to justice through the Rules. It begins by discussing why arbitration is a suitable ADR method for IP disputes, how this subject matter focus may impact access to justice, then moves on to discuss how disputes are referred to the AMC for arbitration.

[A] Why Arbitration for IP Disputes?

WIPO established the AMC in 1994, to offer specialised IP alternative dispute resolution. It is particularly focused on providing solutions for cross-border disputes in IP-related contracts (patent licensing, trademark coexistence, etc.), and in non-contractual disputes (patent infringement, copyright infringement, etc.).[15] The AMC's focus on cross-border disputes promotes certainty in applicable law and dispute

---

13. *Ibid.*
14. https://www.wipo.int/amc/en/arbitration/case-example.html (accessed 24 January 2020).
15. https://www.wipo.int/amc/en/center/background.html (accessed 24 January 2020).

resolution, in contrast to litigating in national courts. It also provides for the appointment of neutral arbitrators, to eliminate any 'home court' advantage, or perception thereof.[16] ADR is a particularly attractive solution for IP holders, due to the nature of the disputes. Confidentiality, trade secrets, and the fear of information becoming available in the public domain can contribute to a reluctance to engage with litigation. WIPO's Arbitration Rules include specific provisions about confidentiality and trade secrets, creating a system whereby confidential information can be withheld even from the Tribunal itself.[17] This focus on particular concerns of intellectual property disputes is of clear assistance in access to justice – while issues of confidentiality may deter IP holders from seeking to resolve a dispute, the WIPO Rules provide clear and certain solutions to this difficulty.

A further difficulty with litigation in intellectual property disputes is the potential for difficulty regarding the technical nature of the dispute. This can be alleviated by selecting qualified arbitrators who have the relevant technical knowledge. In this interest, WIPO maintains a list of some 1,500 qualified persons,[18] and can assist parties to the arbitration in selecting their arbitrators.

Finally, arbitration can reduce the timescales required to litigate an intellectual property dispute. Both the WIPO Arbitration Rules and the WIPO Expedited Arbitration Rules provide clear timescales for the completion of the arbitration process, although these can be extended with the consent of all parties.[19]

In sum, the flexibility and customisability of WIPO's Arbitration Rules, combined with the neutrality of an independent adjudicator, as well as the possibility of arbitrating without a physical hearing, make this an attractive and viable option for parties to an IP dispute. This flexibility also embeds within it access to justice principles, by allowing the parties to determine what best suits the individual dispute, while still giving overall control to the AMC, in case of one party being obstructive.

[B] How Is a Dispute Submitted to the WIPO AMC?

There are two main routes by which a dispute can be submitted to the WIPO AMC. The first is a dispute which arises from a contractual agreement which contained within it an arbitration clause (in drafting arbitration clauses, these are referred to as 'future disputes'), and the second is where the parties currently engaged in a dispute have requested that their dispute be referred to the AMC for arbitration (in clause drafting, this is referred to as an 'existing dispute'). The WIPO AMC provides assistance in drafting clauses for both of these possibilities, by giving guidance and model clauses for specific situations.

The WIPO AMC provides online a number of model clauses for inclusion in the agreement or for submission of an existing dispute to the WIPO AMC. The arbitration

16. WIPO Arbitration Rules (2020) Article 20.
17. WIPO Arbitration Rules (2020) Article 54.
18. WIPO Arbitration Rules (2020) Article 19.
19. WIPO Arbitration Rules (2020) Article 4(f); WIPO Expedited Arbitration Rules (2014) Article 4(f).

model clause allows for the preselection of the location, number of arbitrators, language and applicable law.[20] The WIPO AMC also provides model clauses for expedited arbitration,[21] mediation followed by [expedited] arbitration,[22] and expert determination followed by [expedited] arbitration.[23] These model clauses are available in English, Chinese,[24] French,[25] German,[26] Greek,[27] Japanese,[28] Korean,[29] Portuguese[30] and Spanish.[31] To further assist in the creation and inclusion of arbitration clauses, the AMC provides an online clause generator which not only allows for the selection of the elements listed above, but also contains the possibility to include specifications about appointment procedure, qualifications of arbitrators, electronic case management, evidence and time periods for delivery of the final award.[32]

Two particular strengths of the model clauses with regard to access to justice bear further discussion. First, the model clause covers both contractual and non-contractual disputes, and second, the model clause (and indeed the WIPO Arbitration Rules) do not limit their subject matter to intellectual property contracts or disputes. All versions of model arbitration clauses promulgated by WIPO include the following wording:

> Any dispute, controversy or claim arising under, out of or relating to this contract and any subsequent amendments of this contract, including, without limitation, its formation, validity, binding effect, interpretation, performance, breach or termination, as well as non-contractual claims shall be [referred/submitted to ...]

Given the nature of intellectual property contracts and disputes, it is a clear strength of the model clause that it refers explicitly to non-contractual claims as being part of the subject matter of the arbitration agreement. This promotes access to justice by eliminating the possibility of a party challenging the authority of the Tribunal to rule on a matter which does not specifically relate to the contract at hand – for example intellectual property infringement. The explicit inclusion of non-contractual claims within the ambit of the clause protects the position of Claimant and Respondent, and prevents a vexatious disputant from unnecessarily delaying proceedings with a challenge to authority. The explicit inclusion, therefore, of all disputes which relate to the contract, even if not a contractual dispute, embeds principles of access to justice within the WIPO arbitration process from even before the dispute arises.

20. https://www.wipo.int/amc/en/clauses/arbitration/ (accessed 24 January 2020).
21. https://www.wipo.int/amc/en/clauses/expedited_arbitration/ (accessed 24 January 2020).
22. https://www.wipo.int/amc/en/clauses/med_arb/ (accessed 24 January 2020).
23. https://www.wipo.int/amc/en/clauses/exp_det_arb/ (accessed 24 January 2020).
24. https://www.wipo.int/amc/zh/clauses/index.html (accessed 24 January 2020).
25. https://www.wipo.int/amc/fr/arbitration/contract-clauses/clauses.html (accessed 24 January 2020).
26. https://www.wipo.int/amc/de/clauses/index.html (accessed 24 January 2020).
27. https://www.wipo.int/amc/el/clauses/index.html (accessed 24 January 2020).
28. https://www.wipo.int/amc/ja/clauses/index.html (accessed 24 January 2020).
29. https://www.wipo.int/amc/ko/clauses/index.html (accessed 24 January 2020).
30. https://www.wipo.int/amc/pt/clauses/index.html (accessed 24 January 2020).
31. https://www.wipo.int/amc/es/arbitration/contract-clauses/clauses.html (accessed 24 January 2020).
32. https://www.wipo.int/amc-apps/clause-generator/ (accessed 24 January 2020).

The second strength of the model clauses, and indeed of the Rules more generally, is that they do not limit the authority of the AMC (and consequently the Tribunal) to intellectual property disputes or contracts. This embeds principles of access to justice within the process of arbitration as a method of dispute resolution as it also prevents vexatious disputants from introducing delays to the process with unnecessary challenges to the authority of the Tribunal or the AMC. Although the WIPO rules are designed with intellectual property disputes in mind, they are not limited solely to this subject matter. Thus, in preventing the delaying or obstruction of arbitration proceedings via a challenge to the suitability of the Arbitration Rules or authority of the Tribunal to administer the dispute, the WIPO Rules further protect access to justice for disputants.

The clear availability of information regarding arbitration as a method of dispute resolution, combined with the level of assistance provided by the AMC in drafting clauses leads to a strong presumption that the WIPO Arbitration Rules are accessible to all parties to an IP dispute. In particular, the clause generator tool, which enables the creation of arbitration clauses with little prior knowledge, makes robust and certain arbitration agreements a possibility without cost, making dispute resolution in commercially sensitive areas a possibility for all, and embedding access to justice from the very beginning of the process of engaging in WIPO Arbitration. It further protects access to justice by removing the impact of inequalities of bargaining power on negotiations.

It is worth noting at this point that the WIPO Expedited Arbitration Rules prioritise time at the expense of flexibility – expedited arbitration is completed by a single arbitrator,[33] and thus reduces the availability of options as compared to the standard Arbitration Rules, which allow the appointment of a number of arbitrators agreed by the parties.[34] However, the choice of expedited arbitration over standard arbitration would indicate that the priority of the parties is the speed of proceedings, and thus this does not present a concerning barrier to access to justice. The choice to prioritise certain aspects of the arbitration of others is rather a function of access to justice. The expedited Arbitration Rules are still subject to the same oversight of the AMC, and selection of an arbitrator is covered by the same procedures, embedding access to justice in this method of arbitration also.

Once the parties have selected arbitration as a method of dispute resolution, the Arbitration Rules set out the method of requesting a dispute be submitted to the AMC for arbitration. This requires the claimant to submit their request for arbitration to the AMC containing the documentation applicable to the dispute, including a description of the circumstances.[35]

33. WIPO Expedited Arbitration Rules (2020) Article 14(a).
34. WIPO Arbitration Rules (2020) Article 14(a).
35. Specifically, Article 9 of the Rules requires: (i) a demand that the dispute be referred to arbitration under the WIPO Arbitration Rules; (ii) the names, addresses and telephone, e-mail or other communication references of the parties and of the representative of the Claimant; (iii) a copy of the arbitration agreement and, if applicable, any separate choice-of-law clause; (iv) a brief description of the nature and circumstances of the dispute, including an indication of the rights and property involved and the nature of any technology involved; (v) a statement of the

The request for arbitration may also contain the Statement of Claim, but this is not required. Under the Expedited Arbitration Rules,[36] as the Claimant is required to also provide a Statement of Claim, they are not required to provide duplicated information.

An advantage of the WIPO Arbitration Rules and Expedited Arbitration Rules is the ability to serve documents digitally. Parties may use e-mail or other method of delivery which is recorded.[37] Parties can also use the WIPO eADR online case management system, which provides for secure transmission of documents and e-mail alerts to all parties.[38] This service, as well as WIPO videoconferencing facilities, are made available to interested parties free of cost. This greatly improves access to justice as it eliminates the need for costly registered delivery of documents to multiple locations, and enables the possibility of online ADR, or eADR, as WIPO refers to it.

The next sections will consider specific elements of WIPO Arbitration which can present issues for access to justice, considering in detail the provisions of the WIPO Arbitration Rules and Expedited Arbitration Rules. First among these is the issue of costs.

§13.03 COSTS OF WIPO ARBITRATION

Like all arbitral institutions and arbitration processes, including ad hoc arbitration, there are substantial costs to be paid in order to obtain an arbitral decision. The AMC fixes costs for the arbitrations with a regularly updated schedule of fees. It specifies what can come within these costs, as follows:

(i) the arbitrators' fees;
(ii) the properly incurred travel, communication and other expenses of the arbitrators;
(iii) the costs of expert advice and such other assistance required by the Tribunal pursuant to these Rules; and
(iv) such other expenses as are necessary for the conduct of the arbitration proceedings, such as the cost of meeting and hearing facilities.[39]

[A] Fees Payable in WIPO Arbitrations

As mentioned above, the WIPO Arbitration Rules set out the costs which it can administer as part of the arbitration process. All claims submitted to the WIPO AMC are

relief sought and an indication, to the extent possible, of any amount claimed; and (vi) any nomination that is required by, or observations that the Claimant considers useful in connection with, Articles 14 to 20. WIPO Arbitration Rules (2020) Article 9.

36. WIPO Expedited Arbitration Rules (2020) Article 9.
37. WIPO Arbitration Rules (2020) Article 4; WIPO Expedited Arbitration Rules (2014) Article 4.
38. https://www.wipo.int/amc/en/eadr/index.html (accessed 24 January 2020).
39. WIPO Arbitration Rules (2020) Article 73(a).

required to pay a non-refundable registration fee,[40] the amount of which is fixed in the schedule of fees, which is regularly updated.[41] Counterclaims are required to pay an additional registration fee. As well as this, there are administration fees payable for arbitrations and expedited arbitrations. The maximum administration fees payable are fixed at USD 25,000 for arbitration and USD15,000 for expedited arbitration.[42] In practice, however, fees can be much lower than this, with a fixed fee (USD 1,000 for expedited arbitration, USD 2,000 for arbitration) for disputes of up to USD 2.5 million, an increased fixed fee (USD 5,000 for expedited arbitration, USD 10,000 for arbitration) for disputes between USD 2.5 million and USD 10 million, and proportionately increasing fees of up to the amounts mentioned above for disputes of over USD 10 million. Nonetheless, the fees payable are substantial amounts of money – an arbitration with both a claim and counterclaim, of any value less than USD 2.5 million would have administration fees of USD 6,000. However, for higher value claims, given that the AMC operates on a non-profit basis,[43] WIPO's Arbitration Rules or Expedited Arbitration Rules can be a reasonably affordable choice of institutional arbitration. The ICC, for example, requires a non-refundable deposit of USD 5,000, substantially more than that required by the AMC.[44] On top of this, their administrative fees expenses are calculated on a percentage basis of the total claim value, with administrative fees of up to USD 150,000 for the highest value disputes. The non-profit operation of the AMC removes some potential barriers of access to justice for disputing parties, in reducing the amount immediately payable. However, the fees involved are still substantial, and can represent a barrier to access to justice for those parties in a weak financial position or those with lower value disputes. Given that the lowest banding of fees is 'up to' USD 2.5million, this presents a potential barrier for lower value disputes where one party is in a precarious financial position. Where this weak financial position is as a result of the dispute to be arbitrated, the impact is increased, as the costs of the dispute are made more difficult to pay by the existence of the dispute itself.

Arbitrators' fees are a cost separate to administration costs, and these are also set out in the schedule of fees and costs made available by WIPO. For expedited arbitration of up to USD 10 million, fixed arbitrators' fees are in place. For expedited arbitration claims of more than USD 10 million and claims under the Arbitration Rules, arbitrators' fees are 'as agreed by the Center in consultation with the parties and the arbitrator(s)',[45] with an indicative rate of USD 300 to USD 600 per hour. This is not out of line with other arbitral institutions,[46] although given the large boundaries of the lowest

40. WIPO Arbitration Rules (2020) Article 69.
41. https://www.wipo.int/amc/en/arbitration/fees/ (accessed 24 January 2020).
42. *Ibid*, although these apply only to claims of over USD 10 million.
43. https://www.wipo.int/amc/en/center/faq/index.html (accessed 24 January 2020).
44. https://iccwbo.org/dispute-resolution-services/arbitration/rules-of-arbitration/#article_c1 (accessed 24 January 2020).
45. https://www.wipo.int/amc/en/arbitration/fees/ (accessed 24 January 2020).
46. Louis Flannery, Gautham Chandrakumar, Krystal Lee and Alastair Kwan, 'Arbitration Costs Compared' (2 January 2019, *Global Arbitration Review*) https://globalarbitrationreview.com/editorial/1178433/arbitration-costs-compared (accessed 13 December 2019). Although the AMC is not discussed in this article, it allows for a comparison of costs across a range of arbitral institutions.

bandings of WIPO disputes (up to USD 2.5 million), costs can be disproportionate in low-value disputes, making access to justice more difficult for those with relatively low-value disputes.

Several policies, however, embed the principle of access to justice within the WIPO fees and costs schedule. WIPO reserves the ability to offset administration fees from mediation or expert determination against combined med-arb or expert determination followed by arbitration cases, removing the possibility of undue financial hardship for parties which attempt to reach a solution by mutual agreement.[47] The AMC also fixes the fees for a sole arbitrator or for a three-arbitrator panel in consultation with the parties to a dispute and the Tribunal, taking into account daily or hourly fees, maximum rates and also issues such as the subject matter of the dispute and arbitration, diligence and rapidity of the arbitral Tribunal, and the total time spent by the arbitrator(s).[48] The empowering of parties to a dispute to be consulted in the fees to be paid for the resolution of their dispute embodies the participatory nature of access to justice.[49]

[B] Deposits Required

Article 72 of the WIPO Arbitration Rules makes provision for deposit by the parties to an arbitration of an amount determined by the AMC of an advance to cover the costs of arbitration. The general rule is that parties shall each deposit an equal amount to cover the costs of the arbitration, and the AMC may require supplementary deposits.[50] This is not an unusual procedure for arbitration, and indeed the process of deposits is discussed from an access to justice perspective with reference to the SIAC in this book.[51]

The WIPO Arbitration Rules make provision for circumstances where the claim and counterclaim are of substantially different amounts, allowing the AMC to order payment of deposits on the part of each party for their respective claims.[52] This prevents a situation whereby an obstructive party can prevent access to justice by submitting an inflated claim, and then requiring the other party to cover 50% of the costs in the form of their deposit. The Rules further allow that non-payment of these separated deposits will result in the presumptive withdrawal of a claim, meaning that respondents cannot prevent a claimant from going ahead with a claim by making a large counterclaim and then refusing to pay the cost of their separated deposit.[53]

Point (c) of the same article makes provision that where a deposit is not paid within thirty days of receipt of notification of its falling due, the AMC shall send a further notification to both parties in order that one or the other may make the

47. https://www.wipo.int/amc/en/arbitration/fees/ (accessed 24 January 2020) point 1.
48. https://www.wipo.int/amc/en/arbitration/fees/ (accessed 24 January 2020) point 4.
49. Jennifer A Leitch, *Having a Say: Access to Justice as Democratic Participation* 4(1) UCL Journal of Law and Jurisprudence 76 (2015).
50. WIPO Arbitration Rules (2020) Article 72 (a)-(b).
51. *See* Chapter 14.
52. WIPO Arbitration Rules (2020) Article 72 (d).
53. WIPO Arbitration Rules (2020) Article 72 (e).

deposit.[54] This could potentially result in a circumstance in which access to justice is denied, as the claimant may not have sufficient funds to cover the full amount of the deposit required, rather than their own 50% share.[55] However, the same provision which allows the division of deposits where claims differ substantially retains a discretion for the AMC 'where it otherwise appears appropriate in the circumstances'. This discretion then allows for the separation of deposits in circumstances where there is no counterclaim, if the AMC feels that it is warranted, and avoids potential issues of access to justice through a respondent refusing to cooperate with an arbitration agreement. Thus, once again, while access to justice is not specifically referenced in the Rules, there are various mechanisms in place to protect the right of access to arbitral proceedings. These provisions would then have a 'chilling effect'[56] on disputants' efforts to delay or obstruct proceedings through placing undue financial burdens on their opponent.

[C] Emergency Relief Hearings

One criticism levelled against arbitration in general, which brings particular concerns for intellectual property disputes, which concern time-wasting assets, is the difficulty of obtaining interim relief.[57] Where immediate action is needed pending full settlement of a dispute, arbitral institutions sometimes do not provide for this, leaving parties forced to resort to national courts for interim provisions – this can impact on access to justice generally, and raises the same issues of difficulty for international disputes which may prompt disputants to select arbitration in the first place.[58]

Attempts at ameliorating this difficulty are clear in the construction of the WIPO Arbitration Rules. Article 48 sets out interim measures of protection and security for claims and costs, which empowers the Tribunal to take interim measures designed to protect the subject matter of a dispute. The Article allows the Tribunal to order the sale of goods which may be perishable, require the deposit of goods with a neutral third party, or make 'any provisional orders or take other interim measures it deems necessary...'[59] in response to a request by a party. The same provision is visible in previous iterations of the WIPO Arbitration Rules,[60] and is extensively discussed by comparison with other arbitral institutions in Horning, referring to the 1994 rules.[61] One failing of the thenArticle 46 (now Article 48) was that the interim relief needed to be ordered by the Tribunal. Thus, it was limited in terms of the relief it could offer as

54. WIPO Arbitration Rules (2020) Article 72 (c).
55. *See* Chapter 14.
56. *The Chilling Effect in Constitutional Law*, 69(5) Columbia Law Review 808 (1969).
57. Kevin J Brody, *An Argument for Pre-Award Attachment in International Arbitration Under the New York Convention*, 18 Cornell International LJ 99 (1985); Neil E McDonnell *The Availability of Provisional Relief in International Commercial Arbitration*, 22 Columbia Journal of Transnational Law 273 (1984).
58. *See* Chapter 1.
59. WIPO Arbitration Rules (2020) Article 48(a).
60. WIPO Arbitration Rules (1994) Article 46.
61. Richard A Horning, 'Interim Measures and Emergency Relief Rules' in Hans Smit (ed.) *WIPO Arbitration Rules: Commentary and Analysis* (2000 Juris Publishing).

it was necessarily restrained until after the Tribunal had been constituted. The 2014 revision (and consequently the 2020 version also) of the Arbitration Rules went further to provide for interim relief by further introducing emergency relief proceedings which can operate after the beginning of the arbitration (i.e., the request for arbitration being received by the AMC) and before the appointment of the Tribunal. Article 49 of the WIPO Arbitration Rules sets out emergency relief proceedings which parties can apply to the AMC to enact. It provides for the appointment of an emergency arbitrator[62] who will be empowered to order 'any interim measure it deems necessary'[63] and appointed usually within two days of a request for emergency relief.[64] The emergency arbitrator is then barred (unless otherwise agreed) from acting as a part of the arbitral Tribunal, and ceases to have any authority once the Tribunal has been constituted.[65] Access to justice is thus enhanced by the availability of protection measures from any point after the request for arbitration has been received.

However, there are some limits placed on the applicability of emergency relief, which preserve access to justice from the perspective of both disputants. Emergency relief is not available until registration fees have been paid and a deposit to cover the initial fees has been made in accordance with the schedule of fees.[66] Further, measures ordered by an emergency arbitrator cease to have effect if thirty days pass without the appointment of a full Tribunal.[67] Once the Tribunal has been appointed, it then has the power to affirm or remove the measures put in place by the emergency arbitrator.[68] Finally, and most importantly in ensuring access to justice, as this is a measure introduced only in the 2014 Arbitration Rules, it applies only to arbitration agreements entered into on or after 1 June 2014. Further, parties can elect to avoid the provisions of the article by mutual agreement.[69]

Thus, while arbitration through WIPO's AMC presents the same issues of access to justice through prohibitive costs as arbitration in general,[70] the WIPO Arbitration Rules present a thoughtful and considered arbitral scheme which prevents abuse of power and thereby prevention of access to justice for disputing parties through a range of considered and effective measures embedded throughout the Rules.

§13.04 THE ARBITRAL TRIBUNAL

Alongside costs, another crucial issue which can present issues of access to justice when selecting to arbitrate a dispute is that of the constitution of the arbitral Tribunal. Arbitration presents an alternative route to litigation which empowers disputants to

62. WIPO Arbitration Rules (2014) Article 49(e).
63. WIPO Arbitration Rules (2014) Article 49(i).
64. WIPO Arbitration Rules (2014) Article 49(e).
65. WIPO Arbitration Rules (2014) Article 49(l)-(m).
66. WIPO Arbitration Rules (2014) Article 49(d).
67. WIPO Arbitration Rules (2014) Article 49(j).
68. WIPO Arbitration Rules (2014) Article 49(m).
69. WIPO Arbitration Rules (2014) Article 49(a).
70. *See* Chapters 14 and 15.

'have a say' in the arbiter of their dispute and thus promotes access to justice.[71] However, it bears further investigation to what degree disputants are empowered to select the members of their arbitral Tribunal. Thus, this section considers the appointment of arbitrators to the Tribunal.

Composition and establishment of the Tribunal is dealt with in great detail in section iii of the WIPO Arbitration Rules. First and foremost in the section is the power given to the parties to decide the number[72] and procedure for appointment[73] of their arbitrators. Although the suggested clauses (as discussed above) limit the options to one or three arbitrators, the Rules do not place any limits on the number of arbitrators. Prioritising the ability of the disputants to set the method of selection for arbitrators promotes access to justice, and the rules also do not indicate that this decision must be made at the time of the arbitration agreement, but rather that the parties may come to an agreement at any point after the dispute has arisen. Nonetheless, to account for the fact that disputing parties may not be able to come to an agreement, the Rules make provision for default provisions to apply.[74] The WIPO Arbitration Rules' structures for appointment of arbitrators is in line with other arbitral bodies, and follows best practice by allowing joint appointment for single arbitrators and individual nomination for three-party arbitration, where the nominated arbitrators then select the third, chairing, arbitrator.[75]The Rules further protect access to justice by setting out procedures for default nomination of arbitrator(s) where the parties are unable to come to a decision.[76] By maintaining a list of suitably qualified persons, and enacting a default appointment structure, the Rules enshrine the need for the selection and appointment of arbitrators to be completed, in order to ensure access to justice for the disputing parties. Nonetheless, even the default appointment procedure contains provisions to ensure participation by providing for a list procedure and veto power for both disputants.[77]

The Rules further provide for access to justice by ensuring that there are robust provisions in place regarding nationality, impartiality and independence of arbitrators.[78] Finally, in order to promote and protect access to justice, the Rules provide for robust challenge procedures where the impartiality or independence of an arbitrator come into question. However, in order to prevent obstructive nominations followed by challenges to arbitrators nominated by parties, the challenge procedure is only effective where new information becomes known which could not have been known before the nomination by a disputant to a particular arbitrator.[79]

The Rules also comprehensively deal with how the arbitration should proceed when an arbitrator has been challenged and removed (or where an arbitrator requests

71. Leitch (*supra* n. 49).
72. WIPO Arbitration Rules (2014) Article 14.
73. WIPO Arbitration Rules (2014) Article 15.
74. WIPO Arbitration Rules (2020) Articles 14-18.
75. Toby Landau, 'Composition and Establishment of the Tribunal' in Hans Smit (ed.) *WIPO Arbitration Rules: Commentary and Analysis* (2000 Juris Publishing) 45.
76. WIPO Arbitration Rules (2020) Article 19.
77. WIPO Arbitration Rules (2020) Article 19(b)(iii).
78. WIPO Arbitration Rules (2020) Articles 20-23.
79. WIPO Arbitration Rules (2020) Article 24.

release[80]). A certain flexibility is present, as the appointment of a new arbitrator is envisaged,[81] but is not necessarily required in three-member tribunals, which may continue as truncated tribunals.[82] The reformed Tribunal then has the discretion to decide whether to re-hold any part of the arbitration, with due regard to the views of the parties.[83] This, too, promotes access to justice as it prevents an obstructive party from unnecessarily delaying the proceedings or increasing costs by demanding elements of the arbitration be repeated. At the same time, it continues to protect access to justice by ensuring that the views of disputing parties as to whether elements of the arbitration need to be repeated must be taken into account.

In sum, the flexibility, independence and impartiality of the arbitral Tribunal is maintained in order to promote access to justice, while also encouraging the participation of parties in the process as fully as possible. Access to justice is embedded throughout the process of establishing the arbitral Tribunal, and considered also in proceedings for modification of the Tribunal where necessary.

§13.05 THE OPERATION OF THE ARBITRATION

After the arbitral Tribunal has been constituted, the arbitration itself may begin. The Rules provide clear guidance on many aspects of the arbitration, creating a structure which is accessible, predictable and comprehensible. This section will discuss three specific aspects of the operation of the arbitration with reference to access to justice, and consider how the WIPO Arbitration Rules deal with issues thereof. First, the location and operation of the arbitration will be discussed, with particular reference to the mandatory preparatory conference and the possibility of arbitration without a physical hearing. Second, this section will discuss how the timescales of the arbitration are established and limited. The Arbitration Rules provide clear guidance on maximum timescales, while also allowing flexibility by mutual agreement. For parties who seek a speedy resolution to their dispute, the WIPO Expedited Arbitration Rules provide for a shorter timescale by limiting certain aspects of the arbitration.

[A] Place of Arbitration

The WIPO Rules make clear provision for the place of arbitration, while still allowing the parties to have control over the operation of their arbitral Tribunal. The Rules state first that the parties have the ability to select the place of the arbitration.[84] In the event that the parties have not selected a place of arbitration, however, the AMC retains the authority to do so.[85] The place of the arbitration is determined by the AMC, 'taking into

80. WIPO Arbitration Rules (2020) Articles 30-32.
81. WIPO Arbitration Rules (2020) Article 33.
82. WIPO Arbitration Rules (2020) Article 35.
83. WIPO Arbitration Rules (2020) Article 34.
84. WIPO Arbitration Rules (2020) Article 38(a).
85. *Ibid.*

consideration any observations of the parties and the circumstances of the arbitration'.[86] The arbitral award is deemed to have been made at the place of arbitration. However, a distinction remains: in Article 38, section (b), the Rules state that '[t]he Tribunal may, after consultation with the parties, conduct hearings at any place that it considers appropriate'.[87] This could potentially be interpreted to allow hearings to occur at a place other than the place of the arbitration, introducing a fourth location (after that of the two parties, and the place of arbitration). This uncertainty could lead to issues in access to justice for parties which may have difficulty reaching a specific location or could cause unreasonable financial burdens in placing additional travel requirements on parties. However, in the alternative, it is feasible that such a provision could enable access to justice in embedding the flexibility to allow for hearings to occur wherever is most appropriate. This could, for example, include a site visit to a subject of the dispute. Given also that the section mandates consultation with the parties, it is likely that this provision is more of an access route than a barrier to justice, as the requirement to consult would render an obstructive location difficult to justify absent compelling reasons from a party for why the hearings should take place there. Further, the second part of this subsection, which states '[The Tribunal] may deliberate wherever it deems appropriate' provides for access to justice in allowing the Tribunal to deliberate in a manner which is least difficult or expensive for the parties. Allowing tribunal members to decide where is most appropriate for them to deliberate can reduce travel and accommodation costs for arbitrators, and consequently lessen the barriers preventing access to justice for some arbitrating parties. Given that the WIPO Arbitration Rules are designed to deal specifically with international disputes, the ability to deliberate where appropriate is a welcome flexibility to enable access to justice in not mandating that deliberation take place at the place of arbitration.

[1] Preparatory Conference

One change introduced by the 2014 revision of the WIPO Arbitration Rules from previous versions was to introduce a mandatory preparatory conference. This is outlined in Article 40 of the Rules, and states that such conference must take place within thirty days of the establishment of the Tribunal.[88] Where previously the conference was optional, the 2014 rules amended this to require its operation, a change which was maintained in the 2020 Rules.[89] Preparatory conferences are a vital part of proactive case management, which is needed for efficient operation of arbitral proceedings, and thus access to justice.[90] The operation of an optional conference was found to be 'an important catalyst for the time and cost efficiency of proceedings'.[91]

86. *Ibid.*
87. WIPO Arbitration Rules (2020) Article 38(b).
88. WIPO Arbitration Rules (2014) Article 40.
89. WIPO Arbitration Rules (2020) Article 40.
90. Karl Heinz Bockstiegel, *Party Autonomy and Case Management – Experiences and Suggestions of an Arbitrator,* 11(1) Schieds 1, 2-6 (2013).
91. Christopher Boog and James Menz, *Arbitrating IP Disputes: the 2014 WIPO Arbitration Rules*, 24 Journal of Arbitration Studies 105 (2014), citing 'The 2014 WIPO Mediation, Arbitration,

This introduction is not out of line with other arbitral institutions at the time – the ICC Rules 2012 require a 'case management conference'[92], and the SIAC Rules 2013 make provision for a 'preliminary meeting'[93] as soon as practicable after the constitution of the Tribunal. In order to promote speedy resolution of the dispute, which is in itself an issue for access to justice, the mandatory preparatory conference is both a common and a sensible initiative.

While efficient case management is an issue for access to justice which is tackled by a mandatory case conference, the requirement for a further meeting can result in unnecessary burdens, adding travel costs and time costs to the existing costs of arbitration. However, the WIPO Rules account for this potential difficulty by granting the Tribunal the authority to conduct the conference as it sees fit.[94] This allows for the preparatory conference to be conducted via video conference, telephone, in a specified location, or in any other way which is most appropriate to the parties and the circumstances of the arbitration. This protects and empowers parties in enabling access to justice, as an initial online preparatory conference can then lead to a situation where the parties and the Tribunal can establish a structure and schedule for the arbitration which is time- and cost-efficient.

The flexibility of the preparatory conference and its impact on access to justice is carried through into other aspects of the arbitral process, specifically in envisaging both documentary-only arbitration, and virtual hearings.

[2] Online-Only Arbitration

The holding of a hearing is not a mandatory part of a WIPO Arbitration. Article 55 of the Rules lays out the specifics regarding this. If either party so requests it, a hearing for the presentation of evidence by witnesses and experts, or oral argument, or both, will be held. However, if neither party makes a request, the Tribunal retains the discretion to decide whether a hearing should be held. If there is no hearing, the arbitration will proceed on the basis of documents and other materials alone.[95]

The flexibility embedded in this article is an important component of accessing justice for both parties. Arbitration can be an expensive process, and the costs of arranging and attending a hearing can be a barrier to justice, particularly where the dispute is international. The possibility of arbitrating without a hearing or hearings will greatly reduce those costs, and therefore make the process more accessible for disputing parties of lower financial means. However, the potential need for a hearing or hearings is recognised in retaining the discretion on the part of the Tribunal to arrange a hearing. This avoids the possibility of justice being denied through absence

Expedited Arbitration and Expert Determination Rules' at www.wipo.int/amc/en/rules/newrules.html [no longer available].

92. ICC Rules Article 24.
93. SIAC Rules Article 16.3.
94. Specifically, the wording of the Rules states 'The Tribunal shall [...] conduct a preparatory conference with the parties in any suitable format ...' WIPO Arbitration Rules (2020) Article 40.
95. WIPO Arbitration Rules (2020) Article 55(a).

of a hearing where the dispute cannot be resolved without expert witnesses, oral arguments, etc.

A potential weakness of this structure may be that the Tribunal has no authority to deny a request to hold a hearing. This could lead to a scenario where one disputing party requests a hearing or hearings in order to artificially inflate costs for the other party and thus obstruct their access to justice, in a situation where documentary analysis would suffice. This could potentially be seen as a barrier for parties. However, there are competing interests to take into account here. Access to justice also requires that parties are given the chance to 'have their say'[96] and thus the possibility of a hearing should justifiably not be overridden by the other party or the Tribunal, if the first party requests it. The structure of this provision of the WIPO Arbitration Rules embeds access to justice in the process from the very beginning, allowing for diverse circumstances to be accounted for, and protecting the rights of disputing parties to access their choice of court.

If the decision is made (whether by the Tribunal or the parties) that a hearing should be held, the Rules still maintain adaptability which allows the process to truly embody access to justice. As discussed above, the Tribunal retains the discretion to determine how and where hearings and deliberations should be held.[97] Although not specifically mentioned in the Rules, this includes the possibility that hearings can be held via videoconferencing. Further, in encouraging access to justice, the AMC makes videoconferencing facilities available at no cost to disputants under WIPO Rules.[98] This enables technological solutions to replace the need for parties to be physically present in the same location, which can create a barrier to participation in international arbitration. The same consideration is given to appointing an emergency arbitrator in Article 49(g), which specifically mentions telephone conference as a potential avenue, but also maintains that each party should be given 'a fair opportunity to present its case'.[99]

Finally, parties to WIPO Arbitrations can elect to make use of the WIPO eADR system, which allows them to securely submit communications into an online docket, eliminating the need for multiple copies to be sent to the AMC, the Tribunal, and the other party, as well as minimising postal or delivery costs, which can increase rapidly in an international dispute.[100]

In sum, while the place of arbitration can present serious difficulties in access to justice, particularly in international arbitration, the Rules ensure that their arbitration process is accessible and fair for all parties. Justice and access to justice are threaded throughout the WIPO Arbitration Rules. While an international arbitration can present serious difficulties with access to justice, the WIPO Arbitration Rules and the operation of the AMC present a thoughtful and comprehensive response to these challenges and protect and embed access to justice throughout their processes.

96. Leitch (*supra* n. 49).
97. WIPO Arbitration Rules (2020).
98. https://www.wipo.int/amc/en/eadr/index.html (accessed 24 January 2020).
99. WIPO Arbitration Rules (2020) Article 49(g).
100. https://www.wipo.int/amc/en/eadr/index.html (accessed 24 January 2020).

[B] Timescales of Arbitration

Timescales of arbitration are often cited as a reason for selecting arbitration as a method of dispute resolution.[101] This is particularly applicable in intellectual property disputes, where the disputed subject matter is a time-wasting asset.[102] However, while the timescales of arbitration can be an asset, this is not to say that arbitrations concerning intellectual property disputes are always concluded speedily.[103] The timescales of arbitral proceedings are of particular concern for access to justice, as insufficiently long periods can prevent parties from being able to fully present their cases, whilst proceedings which proceed interminably place unreasonable cost burdens on parties, and can be utilised as a method of preventing access to justice by obstructive disputants. The WIPO Arbitration Rules lay out clear timescales for arbitral proceedings, envisaging most arbitrations to be completed within a twelve-month period. However, access to justice is also considered in granting authority to modify these time periods within the rules. Parties can extend or reduce specified time periods by agreement. The requirement for agreement means that parties are prevented from obstructing access to justice by suggesting unreasonably short or unreasonably long periods of time.[104]

Further protecting access to justice, the following section lays out the Tribunal's authority to amend time periods. While the Tribunal can, of its own accord, or at the request of one party, increase time periods, it cannot decrease them. This protects access to justice as it creates a system of checks whereby a party must consent to reducing their time in preparing for arbitration, but a judgement call can be made whereby periods can be extended if material is particularly complex, without the consent of one party. This allows for time to fully consider the issues and prevents an obstructive party from denying their opponent access to justice.[105] Access to justice is further enacted through the Article 65; where the final award has not been delivered within three months of closure of proceedings, the Tribunal is expected to provide regular reasons for the delay to the AMC.[106]

Where parties wish to resolve their dispute within a shorter period of time, rather than reducing the periods by mutual agreement under Article 4, they may elect instead to use the

WIPO Expedited Arbitration Rules.

101. *See* Chapters 1 and 3.
102. Hans Smit, General Commentary on the WIPO Arbitration Rules, Recommended Clauses, General Provisions and the WIPO Expedited Arbitration Rules', in Hans Smit (ed.) *WIPO Arbitration Rules: Commentary and Analysis* (2000 Juris Publishing) 5.
103. Tom Arnold, in his 1994 article, describes two particularly egregious examples: *Pilkington v. PPG*, which took seven years, and *Intel v. AMD*, which took 4.5 years. Tom Arnold *Why ADR? Booby Traps in Arbitration Practice and How to Avoid Them*, 5 American Review of International Arbitration 179, 187 (1994).
104. WIPO Arbitration Rules (2020) Article 4(f).
105. WIPO Arbitration Rules (2020) Article 4(g). *See* discussion in Smit (*supra* n. 102) 24-5.
106. WIPO Arbitration Rules (2020) Article 65(c).

[C] The Expedited Arbitration Rules

WIPO publishes and updates rules for an expedited arbitration procedure alongside its standard Arbitration Rules. Under this streamlined version of the standard rules, parties can elect to submit some or all disputes to expedited arbitration and follow a truncated procedure with a single arbitrator and reduced timescales. This comes with both advantages and disadvantages for access to justice. Expedited arbitration is not suitable for complex disputes,[107] but is particularly appropriate for financial disputes.[108] It is worth noting that the Expedited Rules limit hearings to three days,[109] and that expedited Arbitration Rules are not unique to WIPO.[110]

There are certain challenges to access to justice which can present in selecting fast-track arbitration. Due to the reduced hearing time, it is not suitable for dispute with lengthy discovery or evidentiary hearings. It is not necessarily suitable for disputes with multiple parties. Jurisdictional challenges may present difficulties – they are not heard separately, thus parties must still prepare arguments for full dispute as well as jurisdictional challenge. The reduced timescales may render parties less able to settle.[111] It can also be difficult to decide at time of contracting whether expedited or standard arbitral rules would be more appropriate.

However, expedited arbitration also offers some protections for access to justice. It is suitable for lower value disputes, and avoids time-wasting assets depleting pending full arbitration.[112] Parties can elect to submit certain types of dispute to expedited arbitration, increasing certainty.[113]

The AMC also provides clear and unambiguous flagging of the differences between arbitration and expedited arbitration, allowing parties to select the route most appropriate for their disputes.[114] Expedited arbitration protects the ability of parties to choose the most appropriate avenue for their disputes, provides alternatives for companies with limited time or financial resources, gives more certainty with fixed costs, and augments the standard arbitration by creating additional avenues to access dispute resolution.

107. Smit (*supra* n. 102) 27.
108. Pierre Yves Tschanz, *The Chamber of Commerce and Industry of Geneva's Arbitration Rules and their Expedited Procedure* 10(4) J Int'l Arb 51, 56 (1993), Lawrence W Newman & Michael Burrows, 'Fast-Track Litigation' NYLJ May 12, (1994) at 3, col. 1; John B Ballem, *Fast-Track Arbitration on the International Scene*, 2 American Review of International Arbitration 152, 153 (1991).
109. Smit (*supra* n. 102) 37-38.
110. *See* ICC Rules (2017), Article 30, SIAC Rules (2016), Rule 5; *See* more generally Irene Welser and Christian Klausegger, *Fast Track Arbitration: Just fast or something different?* 259.260 Austrian Arbitration Yearbook 267 (2009).
111. Smit (*supra* n. 102) 29.
112. Smit (*supra* n. 102) 5.
113. Smit (*supra* n. 102) 30. This is in line with other arbitral institutions, such as the AAA Commercial Arbitration Rules (2013) Rules E1-E10; *see also* Richard Akerman, *Rules for Expedited Arbitration Procedure*, (1995) 6 American Review of International Arbitration 301, 302 (1995) (SSC Expedited Procedures designed for 'minor disputes').
114. https://www.wipo.int/amc/en/arbitration/expedited-rules/compared.html (accessed 24 January 2020).

§13.06 CONCLUSION

This chapter has discussed in depth the embedding of access to justice through the WIPO Arbitration Rules, from its earliest version to the recently published 2020 Rules. This chapter analysed the access to justice provisions threaded through the WIPO Arbitration Rules from before a dispute arises, pointing out the accessibility, flexibility and most importantly comprehensive approach of the AMC to arbitration as a method of dispute resolution. From the provision of a sample clause generator to the possibility of submitting disputes to arbitration after they have arisen, the AMC and the WIPO Arbitration Rules ensure that access to justice through arbitration is available to all disputing parties, and justice is not denied by virtue of a lack of understanding, planning, or forethought on the part of either disputing party. The chapter discussed how access to justice is enacted in three specific portions of the rules, and how this affects the operation of the arbitration - costs, appointing the Tribunal and the operation of the arbitration itself. These measures contribute to breaking down the barriers which may act in impeding access to justice. However, the Rules are not oblivious to the context-specific requirements which impact each individual arbitration process, and maintains flexibility throughout.

Throughout this chapter, it is clear that access to justice has been a consideration of vital importance in all aspects of drafting the WIPO Arbitration Rules. Policies and procedures are clear and specific, and account for many aspects of access to justice, preventing obstructive parties from unduly delaying proceedings, and ensuring that the process is clear, open and comprehensible for all parties. Although the term 'access to justice' makes no appearance within the rules specifically, the principles of access to justice are firmly embedded throughout the AMC's arbitration processes, both under the Arbitration Rules and the Expedited Arbitration Rules. For parties, especially those with intellectual property disputes, international disputes, or international intellectual property disputes, the WIPO Arbitration Rules or Expedited Arbitration Rules provide an option which is robust, flexible, accessible and carefully constructed to protect access to justice for all parties involved.

CHAPTER 14

Advance on Costs under the SIAC Rules

Christine Sim

Access to justice in arbitration means that a claimant seeking to vindicate its claims should have free and fair access to arbitration. In practice however, the first step that a claimant must take is the full payment of the advance on costs for the arbitration—in simple terms, 'no money, no arbitration'. The advance on costs must cover the filing fee, the administrative costs and the tribunal's anticipated fees. This chapter explores how the arbitral advance on costs poses an obstacle to access to justice, and how institutions such as the Singapore International Arbitration Centre (SIAC) have balanced access to justice with its mechanism for payment of advance on costs. This chapter will discuss four practical issues. First, paying the advance on costs for an arbitration can be hefty. How do arbitral institutions determine the amount due for advance on costs? Second, a respondent can place additional hurdles in the way of the claimant succeeding in its claim by refusing to pay its share of the advance on costs. How do arbitral institutions deal with a respondent's refusal to pay its advance on costs? Third, what are the legal justifications for order to pay the advance on costs? Fourth and finally, is an order to pay an advance on costs enforceable?

§14.01 INTRODUCTION

Access to justice in arbitration means that a claimant seeking to vindicate its claims should have free and fair access to arbitration.[1] In principle, if there is an existing arbitration agreement, a claimant is free to commence an arbitration simply by giving notice to the respondent for ad hoc arbitrations and in institutionally administered arbitration, by filing a request for arbitration with the appropriate institution.

1. *See* the definitions of access to justice in Chapter 1.

In practice however, the first step that a claimant must take is the full payment of the advance on costs for the arbitration—in simple terms, 'no money, no arbitration'. The advance on costs must cover the filing fee, the administrative costs and the tribunal's anticipated fees. Paying the advance on costs is a prerequisite to the commencement of the arbitration.

This chapter explores how the arbitral advance on costs poses an obstacle to access to justice, and how institutions such as the SIAC have balanced access to justice with its mechanism for payment of advance on costs. This chapter will discuss four practical issues. First, paying the advance on costs for an arbitration can be hefty. How do arbitral institutions such as the SIAC determine the amount due for advance on costs? Second, a respondent can place additional hurdles in the way of the claimant succeeding in its claim by refusing to pay its share of the advance on costs. How do arbitral institutions deal with a respondent's refusal to pay its advance on costs? Which SIAC Rules and courts could offer relief? Third, what are the legal justifications for order to pay the advance on costs? Fourth and finally, is an order to pay an advance on costs enforceable?

§14.02 HOW IS THE AMOUNT OF ADVANCE ON COSTS DETERMINED?

Advance payments are intended to ensure that the arbitral institution holds sufficient funds to cover the next steps in the arbitration.[2] Paying a hefty advance on costs to commence arbitration can be a serious obstacle to access to justice, especially for individuals, small businesses or companies suffering from financial difficulties caused by the dispute.[3] Access to justice may be meaningless if the claimant is unable to pay the advance on costs required by the institution and the tribunal. The amount that a claimant has to pay just to start the arbitration, therefore becomes the price of access to justice—if it is too high, it could mean that the claimant becomes unable to commence an arbitration at all. According to the ICC's 2017 schedule of estimated fees, a case of disputed value of $2 million (which represents more than 60% of ICC cases) costs approximately USD 9,200 in administrative fees plus USD 100,000 in arbitrators' fees.[4] Similarly, SIAC fees for an SGD 2 million dispute amount to SGD 20,000 plus SGD

2. Gustav Flecke- Giammarco, 'The Allocation of Costs by Arbitral Tribunals in International Commercial Arbitration', in Jorge A. Huerta-Goldman, Antoine Romanetti and Franz X. Stirnimann (eds), *WTO Litigation, Investment Arbitration, and Commercial Arbitration* (Wolters Kluwer 2013).
3. *See* for example, the United States' federal draft Forced Arbitration Injustice Repeal Act, which seeks to prohibit pre-dispute arbitration agreements that force arbitration of future employment, consumer, antitrust, or civil rights disputes, and prohibit agreements and practices that interfere with the rights of individuals, workers and small businesses to participate in a joint, class, or collective action related to an employment, consumer, antitrust, or civil rights dispute, proposed by, U.S. Representative Hank Johnson (D-GA) and U.S. Senator Richard Blumenthal (D-CT), https://www.congress.gov/bill/116th-congress/senate-bill/610?q=%7B%22search%22%3A%5B%22Corporate+Governance+Fairness+Act%22%5D%7D (accessed 28 February 2019).
4. 2017 ICC Arbitration Rules, Appendix III, Article 3: Scales of Administrative Expenses and Arbitrator's Fees.

90,900 in arbitrators' fees.[5] Effectively, a claimant attempting to commence a claim to seek redress for its claim may have to first cough up approximately 5% of the value of its claim, merely for the right to be heard.

[A] Schedules for Advance on Costs

It makes a great difference to the ability of a claimant to raise sufficient capital to pay the advance on costs, that the claimant is given early notice of the amount that would have to be paid. Transparency in what costs are required to facilitate the arbitration is important to access to justice. Most established arbitral institutions are transparent about administration and arbitrators' costs. They regularly publish and update schedules setting out amounts that disputing parties expect to pay in for the administration and arbitrators fees, depending on the value of their dispute.

Generally, along with the Request for Arbitration, the institution would first require payment of a non-refundable advance on administrative expenses by the claimant. Next, a provisional advance is required in an amount intended to cover the costs of the arbitration until the tribunal's terms of reference or first procedural order. The provisional advance typically includes administrative expenses, the arbitrators' estimated minimum fees and reimbursable expenses. The provisional advance is usually in the range of 25%-35% of the advance as calculated for the entire arbitration.[6]

The advance on costs set by the institution is based on the estimated costs of the arbitration. In the case of an SIAC arbitration, the institution, taking account all claims and counterclaims, fixes the advance on costs payable in equal shares by the parties. Article 34.2 of the SIAC Arbitration Rules provides that unless the registrar directs otherwise, '50% of such deposits shall be payable by the claimant and the remaining 50% of such deposits shall be payable by the Respondent'. The advance fixed by the institution is calculated based on the administrative fees and arbitrators' fees for the entire arbitration.

As the difference between the stated maximum and minimum estimates in the schedules is significant, the arbitral institution often has broad discretion in the fixing of the exact figure for the advance on costs. However, in practice, absent special factors, established arbitral institutions such as the ICC Court would fix the initial advance on costs based on the scales, and the average between the minimum and the maximum fees to be charged by the arbitrators.[7]

Following the first advance on costs, the institution may readjust the advance on costs required to keep the wheels of the arbitration turning, based on whether the administrative fees and arbitrators' fees look set to exceed the amount in deposit.

5. SIAC Schedule of Fees, effective as of 1 August 2016, http://www.siac.org.sg/estimate-your-fees/siac-schedule-of-fees (accessed 4 June 2019).
6. *See* for example, ICC Secretariat, 'Costs and Payments', https://iccwbo.org/dispute-resolution-services/arbitration/costs-and-payments/ (accessed 4 June 2019).
7. Stephen R. Bond, Marily Paralika, et al., 'ICC Rules of Arbitration, Awards, Article 36 [Advance to Cover the Costs of the Arbitration]', in Loukas A. Mistelis (ed), *Concise International Arbitration* (2nd ed., Wolters Kluwer 2015) 430-437, 433.

Raising the advance on costs midway has an impact on a party's ongoing access to arbitration. The institution would issue a notice requiring that the parties pay an adjusted advance on costs. For instance, the SIAC's Practice Note provides that with regard to collecting 'Advances and Deposits', the SIAC would collect advances and deposits from the parties towards the costs of the arbitration, that the first tranche of advances and deposits is normally required from the parties shortly after the commencement of the arbitration or request for administration; and that the Registrar may from time to time request further advances and deposits from the parties.[8] Often, the filing of a counterclaim triggers the arbitral institution's request for further advances, as the quantification of the claims in dispute has changed. In the case of consolidation of several arbitrations, the institution may also find that the estimated costs are reduced and return the parties part of their deposited advances.

[B] Request for Division of Advance on Costs

A claimant may request that the advance on costs be divided differently between the disputing parties. When a respondent submits a counterclaim, it often pushes up the estimated costs of the arbitration depending on the value of the counterclaim. In such case, the administering institution would often adjust its estimate of the costs of the arbitration. Then, the parties would have to increase their deposits of advance on costs.

There is a risk that respondents file large counterclaims, thereby causing a significant increase in the advance on costs required for the claimant to continue the arbitration. If this is adopted by respondents as a litigation strategy, it could mean serious obstruction of the claimant's access to justice, as the claimant may be unable to pay the advance on costs that had been increased due to the respondent's counterclaim. In addition, a respondent might try to assert a very large set-off instead of a counterclaim to foreclose the possibility that a separate advance on costs is assessed on its disproportionately large counterclaim. The respondent may strategically decline to pay its share of the advance on costs, hoping that the heavy burden on the claimant to pay the full amount will hinder the arbitration.[9]

To mitigate such risk, arbitral institutions often provide that the institution may fix separate advances in respect of a principal claim and a counterclaim. The respondent-counterclaimant would be responsible for paying the advance on costs for its counterclaim, and the claimant would be responsible for the advance on costs required for its own claim. For example, the SIAC 2014 Practice Note provides that unless the registrar directs otherwise, advances and deposits shall be payable by the parties in equal shares. Further, the SIAC Practice Note reiterates that the registrar may

8. SIAC Practice Note for Administered Cases, paragraph 21, http://www.siac.org.sg/images/stories/articles/rules/Practice_Note_for_Administered_Cases_PN-01-14_2-January-2014.pdf (accessed 4 June 2019).
9. Richard H. Kreindler, *Impending Revision of the ICC Arbitration Rules Opportunities and Hazards for Experienced and Inexperienced Users Alike*, 13(2) Journal of International Arbitration 5, 76-77 (1996).

fix separate advances on costs for claims and counterclaims, respectively.[10] From an access to justice standpoint, this may seem fairer as each claimant and counterclaim is made responsible for putting money where their mouth is.

[C] What Happens If an Impecunious Claimant Is Bound to Arbitrate?

Access to justice suggests that an arbitrating claimant must be given the right to have its claims heard. However, this may not apply if the claimant does not have sufficient funds to pay the necessary advance on costs. The right to access to arbitration is not absolute. It must be weighed against the conditions under which the claimant consented to arbitrate.

Without other recourse, a disputing party that is unable to afford to pay the advance on costs to commence arbitration may apply for court assistance. State court judges are paid by the states to provide free dispute resolution services to the public. Generally, such requests should be directed to the courts of the seat of the arbitration. However, depending on the type of relief sought, a party may be seeking such relief before other courts, for instance, at the situs of property where such property is located, or the place where a contract-related tort occurred.

First, such a disputing party may seek to escape the arbitration agreement. The impecunious disputing party would submit to the court that the arbitration agreement is 'incapable of being performed' under Article II(3) of the New York Convention and Article 8 of the UNCITRAL Model Law on Commercial Arbitration.[11] The arbitration agreement is in reality incapable of being performed because the claimant is unable to pay the advance on costs necessary to commence the arbitration. However, claimants have not been successful in arguing that the arbitration agreement becomes 'incapable of being performed' without further proof that they had exhausted all attempts to obtain funding. In such cases, the claimant's free choice of arbitration represents the bargain between the parties, and thus justifies the enforcement of an arbitration agreement in spite of its impecuniosity.

In a Singapore court case, *Dyna-Jet Pte Ltd v. Wilson Taylor Pte Ltd*,[12] the Singapore High Court judge opined that an arbitration agreement is only 'incapable of being performed' if there is a contingency that prevents the arbitration from being set in motion. The court found that the defendant's financial circumstances did not amount to such a permanent contingency. Similarly, in *Amr Amin Hamza El Nasharty v. J Sainsbury Plc*,[13] the English Commercial Court ordered a stay of court proceedings as required by Section 9 of the 1996 English Arbitration Act, reasoning that the evidence as a whole fell far short of satisfying the English court that the claimant did

10. SIAC Practice Note for Administered Cases, paragraph 23, http://www.siac.org.sg/images/stories/articles/rules/Practice_Note_for_Administered_Cases_PN-01-14_2-January-2014.pdf (accessed 4 June 2019).
11. New York Convention, Article II(3); UNCITRAL Model Law on Commercial Arbitration, Article 8. *See* Michael Pryles, *When is an Arbitration Agreement Waived?*, 27(2) Journal of International Arbitration 105 (2010).
12. *Dyna-Jet Pte Ltd v. Wilson Taylor Pte Ltd* [2016] SGHC 238.
13. *Amr Amin Hamza El Nasharty v. J Sainsbury Plc* [2007] QB 920 (Comm), paragraph 40.

not have access to resources which would enable him to pursue his claims in arbitration. The English court focused on the claimant's choice to enter an arbitration agreement instead of his right to access to justice.

Similarly, French courts have expressed the view that impecuniosity of one party is not in itself sufficient to consider that the arbitration agreement is manifestly null or manifestly inapplicable. As such, the dispute reverts to being decided by the arbitral tribunal. In the *Lola Fleurs* case, the Paris Court of Appeal reaffirmed the negative effect of the principle of competence-competence even when one of the parties was impecunious. According to the Paris Court, the arbitrator is the sole judge of its own jurisdiction and court intervention is confined to situations where the arbitration agreement is manifestly void or manifestly inapplicable. In the *Lola Fleurs* case, a potential denial of justice that could result from financial incapacity did not make the arbitration agreement manifestly inapplicable. As a result, the court considered that the arbitral tribunal was the authority entrusted with guaranteeing access to justice.[14]

Second, a disputing party may seek court protection of their fundamental right to access to justice against the arbitral institution. Such impecunious party could plead that an arbitral institution's refusal to proceed, with registration and administration of the case, inhibits that party's access to justice and contravenes constitutional or fundamental rights according to the laws of the domestic jurisdiction. Under domestic constitutional law, this is often characterised as the fundamental principle of a fair trial.[15]

In *LP v. Pirelli*, the French Court of Cassation ordered that an impecunious party may be denied access to justice if an arbitrator refused to hear that party's claim because it could not afford to pay its advance on costs.[16] The respondent had submitted counterclaims, and the claimant requested that the ICC Court fix separate advance on costs. Despite submitting counterclaims, the respondent could not pay the advance on costs. As a result, the ICC Court decided that the counterclaims were deemed to have been withdrawn pursuant to the ICC Rules. Although the respondent was not precluded from presenting its claims in future proceedings, the Paris Court of Appeal set aside the final award as the tribunal had violated the respondent's right of access to justice and the principle of equal treatment guaranteed by Article 6 of the ECHR. However, the Court of Cassation qualified its decision by narrowing its finding to the situation where the counterclaims and claims appear to be inseparable.[17] It appears that the *Pirelli* case does not establish the positive rule that arbitrators must hear claims even if the advance on costs are not paid; but instead imposes a negative rule that arbitrators should not proceed to decide on issues related to a claim that has been deemed withdrawn.

14. Detlev Kühner, *The Impact of Party Impecuniosity on Arbitration Agreements: The Example of France and Germany*, 31(6) Journal of International Arbitration 807, 808 (2014).
15. *Ibid.*, 812.
16. *See LP v. Pirelli*, Paris Court of Appeal, 17 November 2011; *Pirelli v. LP*, Court of Cassation, Civ. 1re, 28 March 2013, no. 11-27.770; *Société Lola Fleurs v. Société Monceau Fleurs*, Paris Court of Appeal, 29 February 2013, no. 12/12953. (ICC Decisions on Costs, footnote 16).
17. Kühner (*supra* n. 14) 810.

Therefore, this is consistent with another case, where the French courts declined to rule that arbitrators must hear claims for which advance on costs have not been paid. In the case of *ICC v. S.A.R.L. Projet Pilote Garoubé*, the French courts opined that it was 'manifest' that Garoubé was facing financial difficulties and concluded that, taking into account the circumstances of the case and the financial situation of Garoubé, the decision of the ICC to withdraw the parties' claims represented an obstacle to Garoubé's access to justice. The ICC was thus ordered to reinstate the claims of Garoubé, lift the ICC Court's suspension of the proceedings, and to invite the tribunal to issue a partial award on liability. However, the French courts decided that it did not have jurisdiction to order the ICC to continue a claim where the disputing party was unable to pay the advance on costs.[18]

In contrast, under the 1998 German Arbitration Law, the German Federal Court considered that in case of party impecuniosity, the arbitration agreement became incapable of being performed and that termination of the arbitration agreement was therefore no longer necessary.[19] In another decision by the Cologne Court of Appeal, the court found that an arbitration agreement is incapable of being performed where one of the parties lacks the financial resources to cover the costs of the arbitration.[20] These decisions have been criticised.[21] Similarly, the Portuguese Constitutional Court found that the fundamental right of access to justice prevailed over the enforcement of the arbitration agreement as performance of the arbitration agreement had become totally impossible through no fault of the impecunious party. The court found that the parties' contractual agreement could not be enforced if it would result in breach of the right of access to justice.[22]

§14.03 WHAT CAN BE DONE IF A RESPONDENT REFUSES TO PAY ITS SHARE OF THE ADVANCE ON COSTS?

A respondent can deliberately place additional hurdles in the way of a claimant's access to justice by refusing to pay its share of the advance. In a particularly adversarial proceeding, a respondent typically questions why it should pay to be sued. A respondent's refusal to pay its share often vexes the claimant, who is then required to fully fund the arbitration until the final award. When the parties are bound by an arbitration agreement, the respondent's refusal to pay its share has direct implications on the claimant's right to access justice.

18. *ICC v. S.A.R.L. Projet Pilote Garoubé*, Paris Court of Appeal, 24 May 2016, no. 15/23553.
19. Kühner (*supra* n. 14) 815.
20. Juan Pablo Moyano, Impecuniosity and the Courts' Approach to the Validity of the Arbitration Agreement, 4(4) Journal of International Arbitration, 631-652, 637 (2017).
21. Kühner (*supra* n. 14) 816.
22. Moyano (*supra* n. 20) 637 citing Judgment No. 311/2008 of 30 May 2008, Case No. 753/07, Diário da República, 2a série, No. 148, 1 Aug. 2008 (Portuguese Const. Ct.) ('By admitting a power to judge parallel to the courts of the judiciary, the state does not resign from its role as the ultimate guarantor of the realization of justice . . . the only way to prevent the constitutionally unacceptable result, of denial of justice, is for the judicial tribunal to reassume jurisdiction.') (free translation). *A (Netherlands) v. B & Cia. Ltda., C et al.*, 647/02, 9 Nov. 2003, XXXII Y.B. Comm. Arb. 474(2007) (Portuguese S. Ct. 2003).

It is increasingly common for a respondent to refuse to pay its share of the advance on costs in an attempt to frustrate the arbitration. Such a strategy may risk negatively influencing a tribunal's views of the defaulting party. However, many respondents are still prepared to take this risk in order to create immediate financial pressure for the claimant. In some instances, the respondent has raised an objection to jurisdiction as a reason not to pay the advance on costs. Such a respondent would argue that it should not have to pay the advance on costs for an arbitration that should not have been brought against it in the first place. A claimant may have started an arbitration in a vexatious attempt to bring legal pressure on the respondent. In other cases, a respondent may simply be unable to pay because they are subject to domestic insolvency proceedings.[23] In the majority of the cases, a refusal to pay the advance is generally perceived as a tactic to delay the proceedings.[24]

Advances on costs are, as a general rule, paid by the parties in equal shares. However, from the perspective of the arbitrators and the arbitral institution, it does not matter which party pays the advance. Under Article 34.5 of the 2016 SIAC Rules, 'Parties are jointly and severally liable for the costs of the arbitration'. If one party fails to pay its share of the advance, the other party is free to pay the whole of the advance. In practical terms, the claimant has no choice other than to pay in lieu of the respondent if it wants the proceedings to move forward.[25] In the ICC's Decisions on Costs, it was noted that arbitrators have taken into account the respondent's unwillingness to pay the advance on costs, thereby forcing the claimant to pay the respondent's share of the advance.[26]

In an apparent effort to support access to arbitration, some arbitration rules may expressly provide that the respondent has a duty to contribute to the continuation of the proceedings. Therefore, such actions in frustrating the proceedings may be perceived as a breach of the arbitration agreement and a breach of the respondent's obligation to arbitrate in good faith.[27] In ICC Case No. 16812, the arbitral tribunal held that the reciprocal obligation of the parties to each pay half of the advance on costs does not only result from the application of the arbitration rules, to which the parties are

23. Venus Valentina Wong and Alfred Siwy, 'The Arbitrator and the Arbitration Procedure, Recalcitrant Parties and the Tribunal's Power to Order Cost Advance Payments', in Christian Klausegger, Peter Klein, et al. (eds), *Austrian Yearbook on International Arbitration 2014* (Manz'sche Verlags-und Universitätsbuchhandlung; Manz'sche Verlags-und Universitätsbuchhandlung 2014).
24. Micha Bühler, *Note—Sentence Partielle du 1er juin 2004 dans l'affaire CCI No 12491/KGA/EC*, 24(2) ASA Bulletin 290 (2006).
25. *Ibid.*
26. ICC Commission Report, *Decisions on Costs in International Arbitration* (2015) 2 ICC Dispute Resolution Bulletin, available at: https://iccwbo.org/content/uploads/sites/3/2015/12/Decisions-on-Costs-in-International-Arbitration.pdf (accessed on 10 January 2020) ('ICC Decisions on Costs'), p. 29, Case 7.
27. Thomas Rohner and Michael Lazopoulos, *Respondent's Refusal to Pay Its Share of the Advance on Costs*, 29(3) ASA Bulletin 549, 555 (2011).

contractually bound. It also results from the parties' obligation to execute their agreements in good faith.[28]

The central question is: who should bear the risk of paying arbitration costs? There are four parties that potentially have to bear this risk. First, it could be the other party, who would pay on behalf of the impecunious party, bearing the risk of being unable to eventually recover these costs when the award is enforced. Second, the arbitrators themselves may have to bear the risks of their fees being unpaid if they do not collect sufficient advance on costs. Third, the institution may have to bear the risks, by paying the arbitrators and waiting for the parties to pay at the stage of enforcement of the costs award. This is related to the fourth party, the users of the arbitral institution, who may have to indirectly subsidise the defaulting parties, through the institution setting up a special fund for cases involving an impecunious party.[29]

The principle of access to justice may require that the tribunal refuses to terminate the proceedings if the claimant has paid at least its own half share. In *Konsortium Oeconomicus v. the Czech Republic*, the tribunal decided that the proceedings could not be terminated in light of claimant's payment of its half share.[30]

A party may even attempt to seek an order that the respondent pay the advance on costs on behalf of the claimant. In *Rawat v. Mauritius*, the claimant took the further step of applying for interim relief requesting that the respondent be ordered to pay the whole advance on costs, including the claimant's share. The justification included that respondent's 'aims are preventing [him] from financing the arbitration proceedings and thereby from exercising his basic right to access justice'.[31] The tribunal decided that on the facts, the claimant had 'not sufficiently demonstrated that he has exhausted the options available to finance his case'.

Usually, if a claimant refuses to cover the costs of the arbitration, the arbitral institution and the tribunal will terminate the proceedings. A claimant who is unable to afford to pay advance on costs may attempt to seek the tribunal's assistance. However, at that stage, even if the claimant argues that the arbitration agreement should be given effect despite its failure to pay the advances on costs, the claim may be already suspended or terminated and it will no longer have an impact on the actions of the tribunal. Therefore, although the tribunal's authority to initially rule over cost related issues must be respected, it is unlikely in practice that the tribunal will get an

28. Nadia Darwazeh and Simon Greenberg, *No One's Credit Is As Good As Cash: Awards and Orders for the Payment of the ICC Advance on Costs*, 31(5) Journal of International Arbitration 557, 563 (2014).
29. Jaroslav Kudrna, 'Arbitration and Right of Access to Justice: Tips for a Successful Marriage', NYU Journal of International Law and Politics Online Forum—February 2013, p. 10.
30. Ivo Janda and Petr Polášek, *Konsortium Oeconomicus v. The Czech Republic, Decision for Termination of the Proceedings (5 Dec. 2011), Award on Costs (8 Feb. 2012) and Addendum to the Award on Costs (22 Feb. 2012)*, Case No. NN 452/FM, 5 December 2011. A contribution by the ITA Board of Reporters, Kluwer Law International, paragraph 39. The arbitration was later terminated on other grounds, due to the claimant's failure to submit its statement of claim and to pursue the case, *inter alia*.
31. *Rawat v. Mauritius*, PCA Case No. 2016-20, Decision on Interim Relief (11 January 2017), paragraph 90.

opportunity to decide on the validity of the agreement prior to suspension or termination.[32]

It can be particularly harmful to access to justice, in situations where the respondent's wrongful acts caused the claimant's cash flow problems, and therefore the claimant's resulting inability to raise the sufficient amount to pay the advance on costs. Widespread sentiment exists within the arbitration community that some form of redress should be immediately available to the claimant in the event that the respondent breaches its contractual commitment by refusing to discharge its share of the advance on costs.[33]

When refusing to pay its share of the advance on costs is increasingly adopted as a tactical move, some have argued that in order to restore a level playing field, the respondent must be ordered to pay its share of the advance costs. To secure access to justice, the tribunal or institution must be able to compel the respondent to pay its share of the advance, or to promptly reimburse the claimant for any payment it has made to cover the respondent's share.[34]

[A] Sanctions by the Arbitral Institution

How can a respondent be compelled to pay its share of the advance on costs to uphold access to justice? An arbitral institution often has no way to compel parties to contribute to the advance on costs. Unfortunately, the ultimate sanction that the institution can impose in the case of non-payment is to suspend administration of the claim and to consider the claim as being withdrawn. If the full advance on costs is not paid, under most arbitral rules, the institution reserves for itself the right to stop administering the claim. Article 34.6(a) of the 2016 SIAC Rules provides that the tribunal may suspend its work and the registrar may suspend SIAC's administration of the arbitration, in whole or in part. This remedy is inimical to the principle of access to justice.

Generally, the institution would take steps to suspend administration and discontinue the claim only if there has been a significant delay in payment. At the same time as the arbitrators are asked to suspend their work, the institution would usually issue a notice and grant the party or parties concerned a time limit for payment of the balance of the relevant advance on costs. Article 34.6(b) of the SIAC Arbitration Rules provides that the registrar may, after consultation with the tribunal (if constituted) and after informing the parties, set a time limit on the expiry of which the relevant claims or counterclaims shall be considered as withdrawn without prejudice to the party reintroducing the same claims or counterclaims in another proceeding. Similarly,

32. Moyano (*supra* n. 20) 644.
33. Mika Savola, *FAI Arbitral Tribunal's Separate Award on the Reimbursement of Advance on Costs*, Kluwer Arbitration Blog, 23 January 2018, http://arbitrationblog.kluwerarbitration.com/2018/01/23/fai-arbitral-tribunals-separate-award-reimbursement-advance-costs/ (accessed 4 June 2019).
34. Bühler (*supra* n. 24) 290-301.

Article 37(6) of the 2017 ICC Rules provides that the time limit is at least fifteen days. This is scant comfort to a claiming seeking access to justice.

Typically, the payment must be received by the institution. It may not be sufficient that payment is ordered or a cheque sent before the time limit expires.[35] If the time limit is not extended and it expires without the necessary payment being received or the relevant party objecting, the claims are considered withdrawn.

Many of the established institutions neither have power to make an order against the defaulting party, nor any power to decide that the defaulting party should thereby be somehow prejudiced in its substantive defence. Indeed, the institution and tribunal must remain neutral with regard to the substance of the dispute and must be careful not to prejudge the merits of the case. In ICC Case 13853, the tribunal decided that 'payment should be made direct to the claimants rather than to the ICC'. The tribunal accepted the claimants' submission that this is a contract debt: '[t]hat debt is owed to the Claimants and [...] it is they, not the ICC, who should receive payment'.[36]

For these reasons, prior to the constitution of a tribunal, the institution has little authority over the respondent's failure to pay its share of the advance on costs. The claimant often has no choice but to pay the share of the defaulting party to preserve its access to justice. As arbitral institutions consider improving users' access to justice, they should consider stepping in with better mechanisms to ensure that recalcitrant respondents pay their agreed share of the advance on costs. Occasionally, respondents who fail to pay their share of the advance on costs are also non-appearing respondents that have chosen not to participate substantively in the proceedings at all. Express rules exist regarding a party's waiver of its right to appoint an arbitrator when such party fails to submit its nomination on time. In this context, there may be room for arbitral institutions to develop more robust mechanisms to maintain access to justice, such as a rule providing for a party's waiver of the right to appoint an arbitrator in the event of non-payment of its share advance on costs.

[B] Court Orders Regarding Payment of the Advance on Costs

The party that has paid the other party's share of the advance on costs may consider starting parallel proceedings before the state courts to vindicate its right to access to justice; or in order to force the defaulting party to pay its share of the advance on costs.

If a claim was exaggerated or disproportionately large, and the advance on costs would be exceedingly high, a respondent may attempt to refuse to pay its share. In *Industrial Service & Machine Inc. v. Resin Systems Inc.*, in the Court of Appeal of Alberta, the claimant commenced court proceedings on the basis that the arbitration agreement had become inoperative. The respondent argued that the claimant had the option of advancing the entirety of the requested funds. The court refused to grant a stay in favour of arbitration. The court decided that the failure to pay an advance on

35. Bond (*supra* n. 7) 436.
36. Rohner (*supra* n. 27) 560.

costs was a breach of the applicable rules which rendered the arbitration agreement inoperative and invalidated the arbitration agreement based on a breach of contract.[37]

Courts protecting access to justice should be aware of respondents' sometimes cynical attempts to deny the claimant any access to a dispute settlement forum. In the United States, under Federal Arbitration Act, in *Sink v. Aden Enter, Inc.*, the claimant initiated court proceedings prior to the arbitration, which were then stayed at the request of the defendant. However, in an attempt to deny the claimant access to both the court and to arbitration, the defendant refused to pay its share of the arbitral advance on costs. The claimant requested that the court lift the stay, on account that the failure to pay the advance on costs constituted a waiver or breach of the arbitration agreement. The respondent attempted to delay the proceedings by arguing that it had to procure funding to continue the arbitration. The US courts concluded that this would lead a party into a cycle, to obtain a stay and then default in payment of the arbitral advance on costs. The court concluded that a party cannot compel arbitration where it has failed to pay the advance on costs for the arbitration, following a stay of proceedings. Similarly, in *Pre-Paid Legal Services, Inc. v. Cahill*, the claimant initiated court proceedings which were stayed in favour of arbitration. However, the respondent then refused to pay its share of the costs, which resulted in the termination of the arbitration. The courts concluded that failing to pay the advance on costs constituted a default under the United States Federal Arbitration Act.[38]

The same view has been adopted in France. In *Société TRH Graphics*, the respondent had failed to pay its share of the arbitration costs and the claimant refused to substitute payment. The respondent requested the French courts to refer the parties back to arbitration. However, the court refused and emphasised that the respondent had not provided an explanation for its refusal to pay its share of the advance on costs and had thereby unduly paralysed the proceedings.[39]

Seeking relief from courts to order that the respondent pay its share of advance on costs may not be immediately successful. In an English court decision, the judge found that the defendant was not in repudiatory breach by not paying the advance on costs of the arbitration. The English court reasoned that this is because the ICC Rules specifically contemplates such a scenario and provides that the claimant may pay the advance on behalf of the respondent first. The issue of the advance was in any event due to be addressed in a preliminary hearing for security for costs and the defendant had evidenced a clear intention to participate in the arbitration.[40]

Judicial support for access to arbitration varies across jurisdictions. The availability of recourse to the tribunal or a court depends in particular on the *lex arbitri* whether the non-defaulting party can obtain immediate recourse by requesting either

37. Moyano (*supra* n. 20) 640 citing *Resin Systems Inc. v. Industrial Service & Machine Inc.* [2008] A.B.C.A. 104, at 106 ('[T]he refusal to pay the costs makes the arbitration unworkable, and thereby inoperative, as there is no obligation on the other party to fund the defaulting party's share').
38. *Ibid.*, 640-641.
39. *Ibid.*, 631-652.
40. *BDMS Ltd v. Rafael Advanced Defence Systems* [2014] All ER (D) 244 ('BDMS'), paragraph 57.

the arbitral tribunal or the competent state court to rule on the defaulting's party obligation to advance the costs either before or after the payment of the other share.[41]

[C] Arbitral Tribunal Orders Regarding Payment of the Advance on Costs

In the alternative, once the arbitral tribunal is constituted, the paying party may seek an order from the tribunal that the defaulting party pay its share of the advance on costs. These proceedings may be accompanied by additional requests for security for costs which one or the other side may submit in order to prevent or reduce any potential enforcement problem.[42] In this way, tribunals themselves can ensure access to justice.

The legal basis for the tribunal's power to issue a partial award for immediate reimbursement of the advance on costs may be based on the arbitration rules. Article 27(g) of the 2016 SIAC Rules expressly empowers the tribunal to issue an order or award for the reimbursement of unpaid deposits towards the costs of the arbitration. Article 24(5) of the 2014 LCIA Rules[43] and Article 51(5) of the 2017 SCC Rules also expressly provides the tribunal powers to order a separate award for reimbursement.[44] Article 27(g) of the 2016 SIAC Rules provide that:[45]

> Unless otherwise agreed by the parties, in addition to the other powers specified in these Rules, and except as prohibited by the mandatory rules of law applicable to the arbitration, the Tribunal shall have the power to issue an order or Award for the reimbursement of unpaid deposits towards the costs of the arbitration.

Express reference to such powers by a tribunal is often welcomed by a compliant party as a tool that may be deployed against a recalcitrant party who refuses to pay for its share of the costs. Such express provisions allowing tribunals to issue an order or award for the reimbursement of any unpaid deposit resolve any ambiguity as to whether the tribunal has the power to make such order under the applicable laws of the seat of the arbitration. Clarity in the rules helps level the playing field against the tactics of non-paying respondents and improve access to justice.[46]

In the context of investor-state arbitration, Article 24(g) of the 2017 SIAC Investment Arbitration Rules also expressly provides that the tribunal may issue an order or an award for the reimbursement of unpaid deposits towards the costs of the

41. Valentina Wong (*supra* n. 23) 201-221.
42. Kühner (*supra* n. 14) 818.
43. 2014 LCIA Arbitration Rules, Article 24.5: 'the party effecting the substitute payment may request the Arbitral Tribunal to make an order or award in order to recover that amount as a debt immediately due and payable to that party by the defaulting party, together with any interest'.
44. 2017 SCC Arbitration Rules, Article 51(5): 'If the other party makes the required payment, the Arbitral Tribunal may, at the request of that party, make a separate award for reimbursement of the payment.'
45. 2016 SIAC Arbitration Rules, Rule 24(g).
46. Arthur Dong and Darren Mayberry, 'Corralling Defaulting Parties and their Unpaid Costs Deposits under the SIAC Rules 2016', Kluwer Arbitration Blog, 9 January 2017, http://arbitrationblog.kluwerarbitration.com/2017/01/09/corralling-defaulting-parties-and-their-unpaid-costs-deposits-under-the-siac-rules-2016/ (accessed 22 August 2019).

arbitration. In contrast, no such provision exists under the ICSID Arbitration Rules. Under 14(3)(d) of the ICSID Administrative and Financial Regulations, if the parties' advance payments were not received in full, the ICSID Secretary-General would inform both parties of the default and give an opportunity to either of them to make the required payment within fifteen days. If the advance on costs is not paid, the ICSID tribunal may stay the proceeding. Further, if the proceeding was stayed for non-payment for a consecutive period of more than six months, the tribunal might, after notice to and as far as possible in consultation with the parties, discontinue the proceeding. In *Burimi v. Albania*, the tribunal was requested to order that the respondent state pay its share of the advance on costs. The investment arbitration tribunal approached the question within the framework of a provisional measure, finding that 'there is no legal ground or precedent, in commercial or public international arbitration...for any such a measure against a Sovereign State before the issuance of any Award'.[47] In *Valle Verde v. Venezuela*, the investor argued that such an obligation arose from Article 61(2) of the ICSID Convention, ICSID Arbitration Rule 28 and ICSID Administrative and Financial Regulation 14.[48] Under the SIAC Investment Arbitration Rules, however, an award ordering reimbursement of the share of advance on costs paid by the claimant on the respondent state's behalf is immediately available.

The *Burimi v. Albania* tribunal further found that 'the measures requested by the claimants are not urgent because they can wait until the award is rendered'.[49] In contrast, some have argued that it is irrelevant that the final allocation of the arbitration costs between the parties will only be known at the time of the final award. It would be inconsistent with the purpose of the advance on costs to base the decision on reimbursement on the outcome of the final award. Its purpose is to finance the proceedings.[50] In *Valle Verde v. Venezuela*, the investor argued that Venezuela's disregard of its obligation to make advance payments for the proceeding put the investor in a 'critical financial situation, which seriously infringes on its right of defence and access to justice'.[51] The question whether an investor urgently needs a respondent state to pay its share of the advance on costs to secure access to justice remains debated.[52]

In addition, it has been doubted whether a claimant could base a substantive claim for repayment of the respondent's share on the arbitrators' contract.[53] According

47. *Burimi S.R.L. and Eagle Games SH.A. v. Republic of Albania* (ICSID Case No. ARB/11/18), Procedural Order No. 2 (3 May 2012), paragraphs 21-22, 46.
48. *Valle Verde Sociedad Financiera S.L. v. Bolivarian Republic of Venezuela* (ICSID Case No. ARB/12/18), Decision on Provisional Measures (12 January 2016), paragraph 57.
49. *Burimi S.R.L. and Eagle Games SH.A. v. Republic of Albania* (ICSID Case No. ARB/11/18), Procedural Order No. 2 (3 May 2012), paragraph 46.
50. Rohner (*supra* n. 27) 557.
51. *Valle Verde Sociedad Financiera S.L. v. Bolivarian Republic of Venezuela* (ICSID Case No. ARB/12/18), Decision on Provisional Measures (12 January 2016), paragraph 57.
52. Markus Altenkirch and Jan Frohloff, *The Advance on Costs in Investment Arbitration*, 33(3) ICSID Review 723 (2018).
53. Referred to in German as '*Schiedsrichtervertrag*'.

to some, such a claim cannot be raised before the arbitral tribunal, because claims deriving from the arbitrators' contract are outside the jurisdiction of the arbitrators.[54]

If the arbitral institution has made a decision on advance on costs, a tribunal may be reluctant to order otherwise. In ICC case 12491, the tribunal decided that the financial aspects of the arbitral proceedings are the exclusive province of the ICC Court, and that granting the claimant's application would interfere with such exclusive powers. The tribunal noted that this was a situation that 'the ICC Rules exactly seek to exclude'.[55] Further, it has been suggested that 'arbitral institutions can have the power to decide prima facie if the party has sufficiently demonstrated that it does not have enough funds to contribute to the advance on costs'.[56]

§14.04 LEGAL BASIS OF THE APPLICATION FOR PAYMENT OF THE ADVANCE ON COSTS

Depending on what legal grounds are relied on, and what remedy is sought, the legal test that a paying claimant must satisfy in order to obtain an order in its favour is fundamentally different. The legal basis of a paying the claimant's application for an order that the defaulting respondent pay its share of the advance on costs could be characterised as a breach of the arbitration agreement, a breach of the parties' procedural obligations, court assistance for the arbitration, or other substantive grounds available under the *lex arbitri* or governing law such as subrogation.

[A] Breach of the Arbitration Agreement

As a result of a breach of the arbitration agreement, a claimant may take different approaches depending on the law governing the arbitration agreement. For instance, under Swiss law, as damages are available for breaches of arbitration agreements *per se*, a claimant may argue that the respondent's failure to pay the advance on costs is a breach of contract for which the respondent is liable.[57] If the obligation to pay its share of advance on costs is expressly set out in the arbitration agreement, such a breach should be treated as substantive.[58]

If the contractual approach is followed, the respondent's failure to pay its share of the advance on costs would be a breach of contract, and the dispute will be limited to the amount of damages or the remedy of specific performance, if available, in final

54. Wong, Siwy, citing Hans Fasching, Kostenvorschüsse zur Einleitung schiedsgerichtlicher Verfahren, JBl 545, 550f (1993).
55. Partial Award No. 2 of 1 June 2004 in ICC Case 12491, reprinted in ASA Bulletin 2/2006, p. 281.
56. Mauricio Pestilla Fabbri, *Inapplicability of the Arbitration Agreement due to the Impecuniosity of the Party*, 15 (57) Revista Brasileira de Arbitragem 67, 80 (2018).
57. Matthew Secomb, *Awards and Orders Dealing with the Advance on Costs in ICC Arbitration: Theoretical Questions and Practical Problems*, 14 (10) ICC International Court of Arbitration Bulletin 59, paragraph 37 (2003).
58. Simon Gabriel, 'Chapter 13, Part XII: Damages for Breach of Arbitration Agreements', in Manuel Arroyo (ed.), *Arbitration in Switzerland: The Practitioner's Guide* (Kluwer Law International 2013) 1479-1480.

award. If, in contrast, the claimant seeks interim measures, the non-defaulting party must satisfy stringent requirements for interim measures of protection.[59]

According to the first approach, the failure to pay its share of advance on costs may be deemed a breach of the arbitration agreement. In *BDMS*, the English High Court recognised that that most arbitral and court decisions view a requirement to pay advance on costs in arbitration proceedings as a contractual obligation that one party to the arbitration owes to its counterparty in those arbitral proceedings.[60] The judge also recognised that the respondent's failure to pay the advance on costs breached the arbitration agreement, but found that the breach did not deprive the claimant of its right to arbitrate.[61] The court took the view that it was still open to the claimant to proceed with the arbitration by posting a bank guarantee for the defendant's share and then seeking an interim award or interim measure order from the tribunal that the advance be paid by the defendant.[62] An application based on a breach of contract, may also be viewed as a claim for specific performance, and not as a claim for damages.[63]

If the rules agreed by the parties do not provide for the claimant to cover the respondent's share of the advance, a respondent's failure to pay his share may amount to a repudiatory breach of the arbitration agreement, entitling the claimant to commence court proceedings to replace the blocked arbitration. In the context of the SMC-SIAC arb-med-arb procedures, there is no such express provision for the claimant to cover the respondent's share of the advance on costs. This reflects the common practice in mediation where both parties pay their share of the costs of the mediation voluntarily. The Singapore High Court found that since the respondent failed to pay its share of the deposit for the agreed med-arb dispute settlement procedure, and there was no express provision for the claimant to cover the respondent's share, the arbitration could not proceed. The respondent was deemed to have breached the arbitration agreement, and instead, the claimant was entitled to commence a court action.[64]

In *X (Cyprus) v. Y (Luxembourg) and Z (Luxembourg)*,[65] the tribunal decided that in principle, a claim for the reimbursement of the ICC advance on costs is a contract claim. The tribunal found that the general requirements for contractual

59. *Ibid.*, paragraph 7: 'the distinction between the two theoretical approaches has an important practical impact. The legal test that the non-defaulting party must satisfy in order to obtain an award or order in its favour is fundamentally different depending on the approach adopted. If the contractual approach is followed, the respondent's non-payment of the advance will normally be tantamount to liability for breach of contract, and the dispute will be limited primarily to the amount of damages or the availability of the remedy of specific performance. If, in contrast, the interim measure approach is applied, the non-defaulting party must satisfy stringent requirements for interim measures of protection.'
60. *BDMS Ltd v. Rafael Advanced Defence Systems* [2014] All ER (D) 244 ('BDMS'), paragraph 43.
61. *Ibid.*
62. *Ibid.*
63. Bühler (*supra* n. 24) 299. *See also* Secomb (*supra* n. 57) and Ibrahim Fadlallah, *Payment of the Advance to Cover Costs in ICC Arbitration: the Parties' Reciprocal Obligations*, 14(1) ICC International Court of Arbitration Bulletin 53, paragraphs 13-14 (2003).
64. *Heartronics Corporation v. EPI Life Pte. Ltd.* [2017] SGHCR 17 paragraphs 167-168.
65. *ICC Arbitration Case No. 17050/GZ*, 12 November 2010, *X (Cyprus) v. Y (Luxembourg) and Z (Luxembourg)*, paragraph 26.

liability were met: a contractual obligation existed; there was a breach of the obligation; and there was identifiable damage.[66] The tribunal found that the respondents had an obligation to pay the advance fixed by the ICC, and that they were in breach of their contractual obligation.[67] The claimant had made a payment of US$ 157,500 to cover the advance of costs payable by the defaulting respondents. The tribunal reasoned that if the respondents had abided by their contractual obligation, the claimant would not have had to incur this payment.

[B] Breach of a Procedural Obligation

The procedural aspects of an arbitration agreement may be distinguished from its substantive aspects. Thus, an ICC tribunal referred to the procedural aspects of an arbitration agreement as 'a separate contract which differs in its nature from a contract on the merits inasmuch as it is a contract of a procedural nature, but it is a contract nevertheless, giving rise to a procedural obligation to provide the advance on costs'.[68]

A party may apply to an arbitral tribunal for a procedural order specifically for the defaulting party to pay their share of the advance on costs. The claimant may frame his request as a request for interim measures. In ICC Case 13139 at paragraph 53, the tribunal considered that even if the parties' obligation to pay the advance on costs could only be considered as a procedural contractual obligation, it nevertheless has the power to issue a partial award for immediate reimbursement in favour of the party substituting the advance on costs on behalf of the defaulting party:

> As a matter of legal doctrine, the Arbitral Tribunal finds the conclusion inescapable that if a contractual obligation, even if it is a procedural contractual obligation, has been breached, it has jurisdiction to issue immediately a Partial Award in favor of the party that substituted itself for the defaulting party.[69]

In contrast, under German law, the parties, by concluding an arbitration agreement, are deemed to have assumed a substantive legal obligation owed to one another to pay their share in the advance on costs. This obligation is based on the (substantive) legal obligation to support and facilitate the arbitral proceedings deriving from the arbitration agreement.[70]

If such a procedural order is breached, the tribunal would face the question of how to enforce such an order. Apart from a request for interim measures, a claimant may seek a partial award from the tribunal that the respondent pays its share of the advance on costs. In *X (Cyprus) v. Y (Luxembourg) and Z (Luxembourg)*,[71] the tribunal

66. *ICC Arbitration Case No. 17050/GZ*, 12 November 2010, *X (Cyprus) v. Y (Luxembourg) and Z (Luxembourg)*, paragraph 35.
67. *Award in ICC Arbitration No. 13'439*, extracts published in Pierre Karrer, Naives Sparen birgt Gefahren, SchiedsVZ 3/2006, 113, 116.
68. Darwazeh (*supra* n. 28) 562.
69. Rohner (*supra* n. 27) 568.
70. Valentina Wong (*supra* n. 23).
71. ICC Arbitration Case No. 17050/GZ, 12 November 2010, *X (Cyprus) v. Y (Luxembourg) and Z (Luxembourg)*, paragraph 26.

noted that the claimant has not requested an interim measure but a partial award for breach of their contractual obligations by the respondents and that this request could be decided in an award, rather than in an order on interim measures. The tribunal further decided that this expenditure, albeit temporary, can be characterised as a damage. However, the tribunal was careful to state that this interim award was without prejudice to its ultimate decision on the allocation of costs.

Where the claimant has covered the respondent's share of the advance on costs, the claimant may wish to apply for a separate award for reimbursement of the payment.[72] Under Rule 27(g) of the SIAC Rules, a party may seek an order from the tribunal that the opposing party pay its share of the advance on costs. W.L. Craig, W.W. Park and J. Paulsson stated that '[a]ll of the conditions for an interim award seem fulfilled: immediate harm has been done on the non-defaulting party, the breach of the contractual obligation raises simple issues, the amount of damages [is] known and the claim is for a liquidated amount'.[73]

In ICC case 12491, the arbitral tribunal then considered whether the claimant's reimbursement claim could be based on the rules of subrogation. The subrogation of the non-defaulting party to the rights of the ICC against the defaulting party presupposes that the ICC has a right to require an advance payment from the parties. The tribunal held, inter alia, that the ICC Rules did not intend to create an actionable claim for the payment of the advance on costs. Indeed, the 'ultimate enforcement mechanism' of the ICC is Article 376) ICC Rules which provides for the discontinuation of the arbitral services.[74]

On the other hand, some courts have expressed doubt as to whether it has the power to assist the claimant by providing temporary relief. The Supreme Court of Sweden reasoned that since the final allocation of the arbitration costs between the parties remains uncertain until the decision on the merits of the case, a substitute payment of the advance on costs could only give rise, if at all, to a 'temporary right of recourse'. Therefore, the Swedish Supreme Court refused to create such a rule in light of the legal uncertainties that such a 'temporary right of recourse' would entail.[75] Similarly, the claim for costs in Austrian litigation is considered to be a procedural, not a substantive claim for which there is no access to courts.[76]

72. *See* Article 43(a) FAI Rules and Article 2.6 of Appendix II; *see also* Article 45(4) of the 2010 SCC Rules.
73. Bühler (*supra* n. 24) 292-293 citing W. Laurence Craig, William W. Park and Jan Paulsson, *International Chamber of Commerce Arbitration* (3rd ed., Oceana 2000) 267-270.
74. Bühler (*supra* n. 24) 297-298; 2017 ICC Arbitration Rules.
75. *Ibid.*, 294, citing *3S Swedish Special Supplier AB v. Sky Park AB*, judgment of the Supreme Court of Sweden rendered in 2000 in case T 5119-99, 2001:2 Stockholm Arbitration Report 75 (Annot. T. Jingzhou, A. Vincent, M. Polkinghorne).
76. Valentina Wong (*supra* n. 23) 201-221; Rober Fucik, Vor § 40 marg. no. 4, in ZPO (3rd ed., Rechberger 2006).

[C] Availability of Third-Party Funding

The claimant has a duty to enable its own access to justice. However, in reality, many cases will not fulfil the strict requirements for third-party funding.[77] Further, making the arbitral agreement dependent on the existence of third-party funding would subordinate its validity to an external contract, namely, the funding contract or equivalent financing instrument.[78]

Reliance on the availability of third-party funding mainly ignores the uncertainty the paying party faces when applying for financing. For example, where a dispute has already been initiated, various types of financing might not be readily available to the parties, although it is arguable that certain types of financial instruments, such as after-the-event insurance, might still allow for the parties to obtain funding where a dispute has already commenced. Ultimately, it is necessary to consider that the funder's decision to support a claim constitutes an investment assessment. Thus, it is unclear whether the possibility of external financing should control the decision of courts over the validity of the agreement.[79]

The party should not only be required to furnish prima facie evidence about the lack of funds but also that it would be entitled to legal aid in state court proceedings. To deprive the counterparty of its contractual right to go to arbitration is only justified if the impecunious party's right to present its case is in the particular case better protected in state court proceedings'.[80]

There are significant difficulties with proving that a claimant has suffered damage as a result of the respondent's failure to pay its share of the advance on costs, namely, the temporal nature of the restriction on the arbitration and the ability of the claimant to cure such a defect. Under the ICC Rules, the party which has paid its own share of the advance may post a bank guarantee to cover the remainder of the advance owed by the defaulting party.[81] As such, it may be argued that damages would be incurred, if at all, only once the ICC draws on the guarantee.[82]

Third-party funders are likely to play an important role in financing arbitrations as well as financing the enforcement proceedings for any partial awards for reimbursement of advance on costs. Where a claimant was forced to secure third-party funding to finance the advance on costs, a success fee payable to the third-party funding may be recoverable. In *Essar v. Norscot*, the tribunal considered that the respondent had set out to financially cripple the claimant, and as a consequence, the claimant had no

77. Kühner (*supra* n. 14) 818.
78. Moyano (*supra* n. 20) 649.
79. *Ibid.*, 649-650; Stefan Kröll, 'Bank-Related Instruments to Secure the Right to Arbitration Despite the Impecuniousness of a Party', in *Financial Capacity of the Parties: A Condition for the Validity of Arbitration Agreements?* 156 (German Institute of Arbitration ed., Peter Lang 2004). Susanna Khouri, Kate Hurford and Clive Bowman, *Third Party Funding in International Commercial and Treaty Arbitration—A Panacea or a Plague? A Discussion of the Risks and Benefits of Third Party Funding*, 4 Transnational Dispute Management 13 (2011).
80. Jonas von Goeler, *Third-Party Funding in International Arbitration and Its Impact on Procedure* (Wolters Kluwer 2016) 86; Kröll, n. 4, at 995.
81. 2017 ICC Rules, Article 1(6) of Appendix III.
82. Bühler (*supra* n. 24).

alternative, but was forced by the respondent's treatment to enter into litigation funding. The arbitrator also found that it was 'blindingly obvious to the respondent that the claimant ...would find it difficult if not impossible to pursue its claims by relying on its own resources'; and the arbitrator further found that the respondent 'probably hoped that this financial imbalance would force the claimant to abandon its claims'. The English courts agreed in principle with the tribunal's decision that success fees payable to a third-party funder could be recovered in costs awards.[83]

§14.05 IS AN ORDER FOR THE PAYMENT OF ADVANCE ON COSTS ENFORCEABLE?

The enforceability of an order for the payment of advance on costs depends in part on the form in which such an order is issued. The order may be issued as a procedural order, an interim award, a partial award or a separate award. If the order is issued in the form of an award, it may be immediately enforceable in New York Convention jurisdictions.

[A] Should the Order Be Made in the Form of an Award?

The form of the decision depends on how the relevant relief was characterised. As provided in Article 24(g) of the 2017 SIAC Rules however, the most effective form of such an order would generally be a partial award on costs. Such practice has been observed in earlier ICC partial awards. In ICC Case 13139, for instance, the arbitral tribunal held that 'the decision [...] must indeed be issued in the form of an award which deals in a final manner with a separate claim that is independent and not preliminary to other claims in this arbitration'. A similar view was taken in ICC Case 11330, where the arbitral tribunal found it appropriate to render a partial award instead of an order due to the 'independent and autonomous character of the parties' obligation'. Furthermore, in ICC Case 17050, the arbitral tribunal considered that a claim for the reimbursement of the advance on costs 'is a contract claim, and that it can be decided in an award, rather than in an order on interim measures'.[84]

On the contrary, the special circumstances of the case may require the tribunal to issue a different form of decision. In ICC Case No. 17233, the tribunal decided that, given the late stage of the proceedings, it was not prepared to rule on whether the respondent had violated a procedural obligation leading to a procedural order; or had violated a contractual obligation that should result in a partial award. Instead, the tribunal exercised its discretion to decide whether to render an award that puts the respondent under an immediate obligation to pay its share was appropriate given the dispute in question and present stage of proceedings. The tribunal took into account that the arbitration was only two months away from the main hearing and that, having paid the respondent's share of the advance on costs, the claimant was not deprived of

83. *Essar Oilfields Services Ltd v. Norscot Management Pvt Ltd* [2016] EWHC 2361 (Comm).
84. Rohner (*supra* n. 27) 557.

having its claims heard by the tribunal. Therefore, any possible detriment to the claimant in the tribunal choosing to render a procedural order rather than an award when the tribunal was close in time to issuing an award on the merits, was minimal.[85] In ICC Case No. 11392, the tribunal also observed that the remedy for non-payment of a party's share of the advance on costs was found in Article 23 of the 1998 Rules, relating to interim or conservatory measures issued by the tribunal. However, notwithstanding this observation, the tribunal ordered the respondent to pay its share of the advance on costs by way of an interim award.[86]

In addition, the arbitral tribunal in ICC Case No. 15072 had to determine the form of its decision. The tribunal surveyed that some past tribunals had considered claims for the reimbursement of the advance on costs as matters of interim relief to take the form of a procedural order. However, this tribunal recognised that this claimant's request for reimbursement was not aimed at a provisional or conservatory measure; but rather characterised the claimant's request as a breach of contract, and stated that its decision would constitute 'a final decision on a separate claim that is independent of the other claims raised in [the] arbitration'. As it was a final decision on a respondent's obligation to pay half of the advance on costs, the decision took the form of a partial award.[87] Approaching an order for reimbursement of the advance on costs as an interim measure has been described as a paradoxical situation:

> Imagine that a respondent subjects payment of its share of the advance to provision of security. This is refused because it provides no evidence of irreparable harm or urgency, and it is exempt from paying its share on the grounds that the other party has failed to provide evidence of these two prerequisites.[88]

[B] Is an Award for the Payment of Advance on Costs Enforceable?

At such an early stage of the proceedings, even if the tribunal makes an order that a defaulting party pays its share of the advance on costs, there are in reality very few avenues to enforce such an order.

First, the order may be 'self-enforcing', as the defaulting party facing such an order would not wish to defy the tribunal's order. The disputing parties should be concerned about being perceived in the eyes of the arbitrators, as 'good citizens' who respect their contractual commitments should be sufficient motivation for each party to comply with its duty to pay half of the advance on costs.[89]

Second, a successful claimant may also enforce such an order in a court with jurisdiction over the assets of the other party. If the tribunal's decision takes the form

85. Darwazeh (*supra* n. 28) 564-563.
86. *Ibid.*, 566.
87. *Ibid.*, 565-566.
88. Ibrahim Fadlallah, *Payment of the Advance to Cover Costs in ICC Arbitration: The Parties' Reciprocal Obligations*, 14(1) ICC International Court of Arbitration Bulletin 53, paragraphs 13-14 (2003).
89. Y. Derains & E.A. Schwartz, *A Guide to the New ICC Rules of Arbitration* (Kluwer Law International, 1998) 320.

of an award, the claimant may seek enforcement in New York Convention jurisdictions.[90] However, the enforceability of such an award varies across enforcing courts. The Swiss Federal Tribunal confirmed such view in a 2003 decision granting the enforcement of a French partial arbitral award rendered under the ICC Rules for the reimbursement of the advance on costs. [91]The Arbitration Court in St. Petersburg, Russia, took a similar view in 2009 regarding the enforcement of a partial award rendered under the SCC Rules for the reimbursement of the half share of the advance on costs, including accrued interest. The Russian court reasoned that the arbitral tribunal's decision regarding the parties' obligations to pay the advances on costs is a final award, regardless of a later decision on the final allocation of the costs of the arbitration between the parties.[92] Therefore, the SCC partial award was enforceable under the New York Convention.[93] Aside from these select jurisdictions, it is possible that other jurisdictions will refuse the enforcement of preliminary awards ordering the payment of an advance on costs.[94] The question remains open whether courts in various jurisdictions will consider that such an award is 'final' for the purposes of enforcement.

Complications may arise where the claimant seeks an award ordering the payment to an institution directly. The tribunal in ICC Case No. 12700 considered that questions might arise as to: who would be entitled to seek enforcement of such an award, and the arbitral tribunal's powers to render an award in favour of a third party.[95] However, such complications were averted in ICC Case No. 11866, where the tribunal took the view that it had the authority and discretion over the arbitral procedures, to order the respondent to remedy its breach of the arbitration clause during the arbitration proceedings. The tribunal ordered the respondent to pay directly to the ICC the amount corresponding to its share of the advance on costs within fifteen days of the notification of the award, and 'to do whatever is necessary to obtain the release by the ICC of the bank guarantee' which had been opened by the claimant to cover the respondent's unpaid share of the advance on costs.[96] Such an order may be characterised as an order for specific performance rather than an award of damages.

In reality, a partial award for the reimbursement of the advance does not have great practical value unless complied with voluntarily. A defaulting respondent is not likely to readily comply with such a partial award. At the same time, enforcement proceedings may take a significant amount of time—it may even still be pending when

90. Dong (*supra* n 46). *See* Y Lahlou, A Poplinger & G Walters, 'Other Issues in Enforcement Proceedings', in Frischknecht et al. (eds), *Enforcement of Foreign Arbitral Awards and Judgments in New York* (Kluwer 2018) 247; G Walters, 'SCC Practice: Separate Awards for Advance on Costs: 1 January 2007-31 December 2011' at 4 (2011) available at https://sccinstitute.com/media/56067/separate-award-on-advance-on-costs_gretta-walters.pdf.
91. Rohner (*supra* n 27) 558; Decision 4P.173/2003 of the Swiss Federal Supreme Court dated 8 December 2003; Decision A56-63115/2009 of the Arbitration Court of St. Petersburg dated 11 December 2009.
92. Rohner (*supra* n. 27) 558; SCC Case 142/2008 dated 4 June 2009.
93. Rohner (*supra* n. 27) 558.
94. Moyano (*supra* n. 20) 649.
95. Darwazeh (*supra* n. 28) 567.
96. *Ibid.*, 567.

the award on the merits is rendered.[97] In any event, the claimant will often face an insurmountable practical problem that the time limit set by the institution, usually fifteen days, would expire before an award enjoining the respondent to make the payment can be obtained and enforced.[98]

At the stage of the tribunal's final award on costs, a claimant may seek reimbursement for the advance on costs paid at the beginning of the arbitration in the form of a claim for damages. Under the SIAC Rules, the tribunal may award costs to the successful claimant, including for having to cover the respondent's share of the advance on costs. Non-compliance of orders under Rule 27(g) of the SIAC Rules would be taken into account by the tribunal in its assessment of costs.[99] Similarly, Article 28.4 of the LCIA Rules explicitly favours the general principle of apportionment by relative success on the merits. The tribunal may also take into account the parties' conduct in the arbitration, including any cooperation in facilitating the proceedings as to time and cost and any non-cooperation resulting in undue delay and unnecessary expense.[100] This may be the most practical solution to obtaining reimbursement of costs at the end of proceedings, but it does nothing to enable access to justice.

Finally, the question of interest remains. Is the claimant entitled to interest on the sum that it had to pay on behalf of the respondent? This may depend on whether the *lex arbitri* governs the issue of interest. In this regard, note that there is little consensus among jurisdictions on the question of what are the applicable interest rates for an arbitration; and in particular, whether any provision on interest in the applicable arbitration legislation applies to procedural issues. For example, a Finnish Arbitration Institute tribunal had found that the applicable arbitration rules did not preclude the tribunal from awarding interest to the claimant and decided that the issue of interest was governed by Finnish law. The tribunal concluded that under Finnish law, that the parties to arbitration are generally entitled to receive interest on defaulted payments.[101]

§14.06 CONCLUSION

In agreeing to international arbitration, the parties have clearly manifested their intention to take the dispute out of the jurisdiction of a domestic court. There are important policy considerations in enforcing the free choice of international parties with cross-border business to have their disputes heard in a forum perceived by both to be neutral. Therefore, some have argued that the threshold for access to justice to prevail should be lower in an international arbitration setting, as compared to the principle of access to justice before domestic courts. This is because the result of not enforcing an arbitration agreement would lead to the parties having to resort to a foreign state court,[102] which is the very situation they had intended to avoid.

97. Secomb (*supra* n. 57), paragraph 54.
98. Ibrahim Fadlallah (*supra* n. 88).
99. Dong (*supra* n. 46).
100. 2014 LCIA Arbitration Rules, Rule 28.4.
101. Savola (*supra* n. 33).
102. Kühner (*supra* n. 14) 816-817.

Respect for the principle of access to justice may be limited in practice when a claimant or respondent does not pay its share of the advance on costs. In order to promote access to justice in international arbitration, arbitral institutions could give more thought as to the mechanisms available to them in issuing orders prior to the constitution of the tribunal, tribunals could consider more thoroughly how orders for specific performance may be used in the context of ongoing proceedings, and third-party funders are likely to play an important role in financing arbitrations as well as financing the enforcement proceedings for any partial awards for reimbursement of advance on costs.

CHAPTER 15

Access to Justice and the Costs of ICSID

Duarte Henriques & Avani Agarwal

Access to justice has been recognised by the international legal community to be a fundamental right. The right deals with the ability of a person to ensure that their grievance is heard and appropriately redressed. This right is protected in investor-state transactions because states enter into bilateral investment treaties to provide investors with access to neutral arbitral tribunals. However, the costs of ISDS proceedings are so high, that they may negatively impact the ability of parties to approach arbitral tribunals. ICSID is one of the most significant institutions in the world for ISDS, thus making it crucial to consider its cost structure distinctly from average ISDS costs. This chapter looks at past empirical work dealing with ICSID proceedings in order to establish average costs. The ICSID Convention, the Administrative and Financial Regulations, the Schedule of Fees, as well as information about costs that has been made publicly available by the centre are all analysed. Lastly, various ICSID awards are studied along with prior literature, to ascertain the existence of any pattern in how costs are allocated. Not only can no such pattern be found, but different factors have been used with varying frequency by different tribunals, due to the amount of discretion provided to them. Such uncertainty is detrimental to the ability of parties to make informed choices about entering into ISDS proceedings. Based on these discussions, it is concluded that the right of parties to access justice is restricted by the increasing costs of ICSID Arbitration.

§15.01 INTRODUCTION

The international legal framework has recognised that there are some fundamental rights that belong to each human being, such as the right to a fair trial, the right to a proper medical care system, the right to employment, the right to a condign housing and many other rights recognised by international legal instruments such as the UDHR.

Among those rights one may also find the right to 'own property alone as well as in association with others' (Art. 17(1) of the UDHR). As a consequence, the principle that 'no one shall be arbitrarily deprived of his property' (Art. 17(2) of the UDHR) is a corollary of these fundamental rights.

These rights have also produced some crucial ramifications implied in international transactions, particularly the contractual freedom and the right to undertake in, promote and exploit investments in foreign countries. That is, not only is the right to invest and maintain investments in countries different from those of the national investor a recognition of the contractual freedom, but also and more importantly it is a recognition of the dignity of the human being and of the relevance of the relationships between sovereign states. In other words, international relationships between civilised sovereign states assume and promote the paramount importance of the contractual freedom, of the right to invest and maintain investments in foreign soil, and thus entail the need for a stronger protection of those investments.

As a consequence, many sovereign states enter into agreements for the protection of foreign investments with other states in order to secure equal status among nationals of both states. In this regard, the most popular instrument is the BIT, counting around 4,000 instruments as of today. Those treaties are designed to promote economic cooperation, stimulate the flow of capital and economic development of the parties, maximise the utilisation of resources, improve living standards, and 'providing effective means of asserting claims and enforcing rights with respect to investment under national law as well as through international arbitration'.[1]

Consistently, virtually every BIT contains provisions aimed at assuring a treatment to foreign investments equal to that conferred to national ones, obliging the compliance with international standards such as the 'fair and equitable treatment', and 'full protection and security' and the prohibition of expropriation except under strict circumstances and always against fair compensation. Along with these usual provisions, bilateral treaties and other instruments for the protection of investments also provide for the settlement of disputes via negotiation, mediation and, more frequently, ad hoc arbitration under the UNCITRAL Rules or institutional arbitration under ICSID Arbitration Rules, established under the 1966 Convention on the Settlement of Investment Disputes between States and Nationals of other States.

On the one hand, bringing forward a claim against a host state can be costly – extremely costly to be more precise – especially if considering the situation where foreign investors are deprived of all their assets as a result of expropriation measures without proper compensation or have become otherwise impecunious to pursue their claims, rendering almost impossible to get redress of their deprivation. On the other hand, the investor-state dispute settlement setting does not provide for 'legal aid' (except in the conspicuous case of the World Trade Organisation framework, which in any event is yet of too little help). Further, more often than not, resorting to local state courts is not a viable option (which may well happen for a number of reasons,

1. This language is borrowed from the "2012 U.S. Model Bilateral Investment Treaty" (accessible at https://www.state.gov/documents/organization/188371.pdf), but it can be found in virtually every other bilateral investment treaty, even if with some nuances in the drafting.

including those cases where the judicial system does not deliver a remedy in a timely manner).

This brings into question a potential violation of another equally crucial and fundamental right, that of access to justice. The right may be broadly defined as the 'ability of people to seek and obtain a remedy through formal or informal institutions of justice for grievances'.[2] It has been recognised in the EU Charter of Fundamental Rights (Article 47), the United Nations International Covenant on Civil and Political Rights (Article 2(3) and 14) and even the UDHR (Article 8). While the scope of the right has been restricted in these documents to instances where other fundamental rights are violated or where there is a threat of criminal sanctions, a broader construction has been recognised. Indeed, in the case of *Mondev International Ltd v. United States of America,*[3] an ICSID tribunal heard an argument premised on the denial of access to justice and found it to be viable.

The UN has acknowledged that one of the most significant obstacles in accessing justice is the cost of legal advice and representation.[4] Within the ISDS framework, these costs are compounded by the expenses of accessing and using the established mechanisms. It is therefore worth addressing the structure of these costs under the ICSID framework. In the following sections, we will address this topic and assess if and how it challenges the right of access to justice.

§15.02 COSTS IN THE ISDS FRAMEWORK

The first step in this analysis is to determine what is meant by costs. While each institution is likely to have its own definition, the UNCITRAL Rules, as updated in 2010, are reflective of the general standard. Article 40 defines costs as:

(a) The fees of the arbitral tribunal to be stated separately as to each arbitrator and to be fixed by the tribunal itself in accordance with article 41;
(b) The reasonable travel and other expenses incurred by the arbitrators;
(c) The reasonable costs of expert advice and of other assistance required by the arbitral tribunal;

2. *Necessary Condition: Access to Justice,* United States Institute of Peace, https://www.usip.org/guiding-principles-stabilization-and-reconstruction-the-web-version/rule-law/access-justice (accessed 18 March 2019).
3. *Mondev International Ltd. v. United States of America,* ICSID Case No. ARB(AF)/99/2 (Mondev International Ltd argued that it had been denied the minimum standard of treatment by the United States of America because the Supreme Court of Massachusetts departed from its established jurisprudence on contract claims without good reason, failed to remand necessary questions to the jury, and incorrectly extended statutory immunity for intentional torts to a public authority that was engaged in commerce, thereby denying justice. While the tribunal did not find the Court's decision to be so arbitrary as to constitute denial of justice, it agreed that a party who has suffered undue delay or *denial of access to the competent courts* or who has suffered a manifestly unjust judgment may invoke the doctrine of denial of justice. It also agreed that denial of justice violated the minimum standard of treatment as established under customary international law).
4. *Access to Justice,* United Nations and the Rule of Law, https://www.un.org/ruleoflaw/thematic-areas/access-to-justice-and-rule-of-law-institutions/access-to-justice/ (accessed 18 March 2019).

(d) The reasonable travel and other expenses of witnesses to the extent such expenses are approved by the arbitral tribunal;
(e) The legal and other costs incurred by the parties in relation to the arbitration to the extent that the arbitral tribunal determines that the amount of such costs is reasonable;
(f) Any fees and expenses of the appointing authority as well as the fees and expenses of the Secretary-General of the PCA.

This is taken to be an exhaustive list under the rules, since the article uses the word '*only*' before listing out the potential expenses.

Costs in investor-state arbitration may be classified into two main categories: arbitration costs, which include the costs of using an institution, fees paid to arbitrators and various administrative expenses; and legal costs, which include the parties' own costs such as legal fees. Most procedural rules in investor-state proceedings make it a point to distinguish between the two.[5]

The average costs of an investment arbitration have been estimated to be USD 10 million per case, with each party paying nearly USD 5 million, if an assumption is made that parties share these costs equally, at least before the award.[6] This has been recognised as a significant, staggering sum by commentators.[7] A survey conducted by the Corporate Council International Arbitration Group found that 100% of corporate counsel participants considered international arbitration to be too expensive, with much of the criticism targeted towards investor-state arbitration in specific.[8]

Based on a survey of publicly available information in 2012, commentators point out that combined costs exceed even USD 30 million in some cases.[9] For instance, in the case of *Abaclat v. Republic of Argentina,*[10] nearly USD 40 million was spent, with the claimant investor alone shelling out USD 27 million of the costs.

The largest component of these expenses are legal costs, estimated to average at 82% of the total costs of a case.[11] Arbitrator fees makes up for 16% while institutional costs usually amount to no more than 2% of the total expenditure.[12] In terms of average figures, legal costs are estimated to be anywhere between USD 4.4-4.5 million. Tribunal costs are estimated to fall around USD 750,000.[13]

5. Wendy J Miles, *Costs Allocation in Investor State Arbitration*, 80(4) The International Journal of Arbitration, Mediation and Dispute Management 413 (2014).
6. Matthew Hodgson, *Costs in Investment Treaty Arbitration: The Case for Reform*, 11(1) Transnational Dispute Management 1 (January 2014).
7. Lise Johnson & Lisa Sachs, *The Outsized Costs of Investor–State Dispute Settlement*, 16(1) AIB Insights 10 (2016).
8. Lucy Reed, *More on Corporate Criticism of International Arbitration*, Kluwer Arbitration Blog, http://arbitrationblog.kluwerarbitration.com/2010/07/16/more-on-corporate-criticism-of-international-arbitration/ (accessed 16 July 2018).
9. David Gaukrodger & Kathryn Gordon, *Investor-State Dispute Settlement: A Scoping Paper for the Investment Policy Community*, OECD Working Papers on International Investment 2012/03.
10. *Abaclat and Others v. Argentine Republic*, ICSID Case No. ARB/07/5.
11. Reed (*supra* n. 8).
12. *Ibid*.
13. Miles (*supra* n. 5).

The overall costs borne by investors and states are equivalent.[14] However, the impact of the high costs is felt disproportionately by some parties due to extraneous factors as well. For instance, studies note that developing countries may lack the requisite legal experience domestically and may have to bring in outside counsel. This in turn increases the legal costs they must incur.[15]

The high costs of the process also mean that some parties will be more likely to settle the dispute, often at values that they may not find to be just. A good example of this is the empirical study conducted by Anton Strezhnev, which proved that with an equivalent claimant firm, high-income respondent states were 22% more likely to receive a final award in comparison to low- and middle-income respondents.[16]

The average amounts awarded to successful claimants under the ISDS framework is nearly USD 76 million, with the median falling just around USD 10.5 million. If costs amount to USD 10 million, they are a massive and significant portion of the financial outcome.[17]

There have been some discussions in existing literature as to the reasons behind the high costs. Some explanations attribute the costs to the way lawyers deal with ISDS. It is argued that lawyers use expensive litigation techniques that have been borrowed from corporate practices or litigation before US courts (such as discovery), and bill up to USD 1,000 per hour. Further, lawyers must spend a substantial amount of time on researching and selecting arbitrators. Legal costs also increase due to the use of high-cost party appointed experts and detailed discussions of procedural and discovery-related issues.[18]

Another set of explanations focuses more on arbitration costs, discussing instead the limited availability of arbitrators and the tendency of parties to appoint from within the same pool of arbitrators, thus creating an asymmetrical market.[19]

Some other explanations also refer to the nature of cases and the law that is applicable, high damage claims that coincide with high tribunal costs as well as uncertain cost shifting rules.[20]

Further, it is crucial that parties considering entering into or responding to an ISDS proceeding know how costs will be distributed as this will allow them to make fully informed decisions about whether or not to enter into the proceeding, whether or not to accept a settlement offer, etc.[21] Two broadly defined approaches to cost allocation have arisen in international commercial arbitration: that each party bears its own costs; or that the successful party is reimbursed for its costs, thus encapsulating a

14. Eric Gottwald, *Leveling the Playing Field: Is It Time for a Legal Assistance Center for Developing Nations in Investment Treaty Arbitration*, 22 (2) American University International Law Review 237 (2006).
15. *Ibid.*
16. Anton Strezhnev, *Why Rich Countries Win Investment Disputes: Taking Selection Seriously* (2017), https://www.antonstrezhnev.com/research (accessed 18 March 2019).
17. Miles (*supra* n. 5).
18. Reed (*supra* n. 8).
19. *Ibid.*
20. *Ibid.*
21. Miles (*supra* n. 5).

notion that 'costs follow the event'.[22] In commercial disputes, successful parties tend to recover at least some of their costs.[23] This is a well-reasoned approach because it compensates the party while also discouraging 'unmeritorious actions'.[24] Unfortunately, in investor-state arbitration it is not a generally established practice to reimburse the winning party for their costs. Indeed, in a significant number of awards, the tribunal requires for the parties to bear their own costs.[25]

A review of 168 final awards, rendered between 2006 and 2013, reveals that ISDS has no specific approach to cost allocation.[26] Out of these awards, 47% compensated the prevailing party while 53% awards required that parties pay their own expenses.[27]

Tribunals have shown an inclination to awarding costs when claimants succeed, more often that when respondent states do. Even though claimants win only 41% of cases, they get a positive costs order in 53% of the disputes they win, compared to successful respondents who only get such orders in 38% of the cases.[28]

A direct consequence of these high costs has been that organisations such as the UNCTAD are starting to discuss how to replace investment arbitration with more effective alternatives.[29] This is incredibly unfortunate, considering the many advantages associated with arbitration as a dispute resolution mechanism.

§15.03 COSTS UNDER ICSID

ICSID is the world's primary institution in the field of international investment dispute settlement. It has administered a majority of all international investment disputes and features in most international investment treaties.[30] The centre has its own procedural rules, which are popularly referred to, and also administers cases under other rules. The number of cases registered by ICSID is only growing.[31] Thus, costs in ICSID arbitrations are likely to impact a large number of investors and states. Consequently, these costs must be examined in specific detail.

22. Gaukrodger & Gordon (*supra* n. 9).
23. S.W. Schill, *Arbitration Risk and Effective Compliance – Cost-Shifting in Investment Treaty Arbitration*, 7 J. World Investment & Trade 653, 665 (2006).
24. Susan D. Franck, *Rationalizing Costs in Investment Treaty Arbitration*, 88(4) Washington University Law Review, 769 (2011).
25. Miles (*supra* n. 5).
26. United Nations Conference on Trade and Development IIA, Issues Note 1, *Recent Developments in Investor-State Dispute Settlement, updated for the Multilateral Dialogue on Investment* (28-29 May 2013); Susan D Franck, *Rationalizing Costs in Investment Treaty Arbitration*, 88(4) Washington University Law Review, 769 (2011).
27. Kateryna Bondar, *Allocation of Costs in Investor-State and Commercial Arbitration: Towards a Harmonized Approach*, 32(1) Arbitration International 45 (2016).
28. Miles (*supra* n. 5).
29. *Investor–State Disputes: Prevention and Alternatives to Arbitration*, UNCTAD Series on International Investment Policies for Development, UNCTAD/DIAE/IA/2009/11 (accessed 1 August 2010).
30. *About ICSID*, ICSID, https://icsid.worldbank.org/en/Pages/about/default.aspx (accessed 17 March 2018).
31. *ICSID Releases 2018 Caseload Statistics*, ICSID, https://icsid.worldbank.org/en/Pages/News.aspx?CID=314 (accessed 29 January 2019).

In 2015, an effort was made to examine 138 ICSID arbitrations, concluded over the period of the five preceding years, in order to collect and evaluate data-related to costs.[32] This study revealed that on an average, the legal costs under ICSID for a claimant were approximately USD 5.6 million, with costs for respondents falling around USD 4.9 million. Additionally, tribunal costs came up to USD 882,668.[33]

It must be noted here that not only are the costs significantly higher than average ISDS costs, but there is also a significant disparity between the costs being paid by claimants and respondents. Further, data was not available for many of the 138 proceedings, thus limiting the scope of the study to a large extent.

ICSID tribunal costs are noticeably higher than the average costs arrived at by an Allen & Overy study conducted in 2012, which estimated them to be USD 769,000.[34] However, the same study noted that ICSID tribunal costs have the tendency to be 10% lower than costs under UNCITRAL Rules.[35] This is because ICSID has imposed a cap on arbitrators' fees.[36] Thus, it appears that the ICSID rules may have attempted to resolve some of the issues associated with costs.

ICSID administers cases under its own rules and also under other procedural rules. Under the ICSID Rules, costs consist of a party's private legal expenditures, the advances paid to ICSID for the fees and expenses of arbitrators as well as the centre's expenses and administrative charges, and the lodging fee that must be paid to institute proceedings.[37] There are also additional charges associated with special services or for the use of the Secretary-General as an appointing authority.[38]

As previously noted, legal costs in ICSID arbitrations are fairly high. These costs are not dealt with under the rules. Article 60 of the ICSID Convention provides a general framework related to costs and is a good starting point. It states that the tribunal shall determine fees and expenses within the limits that are laid out by the administrative council, after consultation with the Secretary-General. Alternatively, parties can agree with the tribunal in advance to fix the expenses payable to the members.

Thereafter, the Administrative and Financial Regulations need to be looked at to understand the cost structure. Regulations 14, 15 and 16 deal with the cost of a proceeding.

Regulation 14 refers to the direct costs of individual proceedings. Regulation 14(1) provides that each member of a tribunal, a commission or an *ad hoc* committee is entitled to receive a fee for each day on which he participates in meetings of the body

32. Jeffery P. Commission, *How Much Does an ICSID Arbitration Cost? A Snapshot of the Last Five Years*, http://arbitrationblog.kluwerarbitration.com/2016/02/29/how-much-does-an-icsid-arbitration-cost-a-snapshot-of-the-last-five-years/ (accessed 29 February 2016).
33. *Ibid.*
34. *Counting the Costs of Investment Treaty Arbitration*, Global Arbitration Review online news, https://globalarbitrationreview.com/article/1033259/counting-the-costs-of-investment-treaty-arbitration (accessed 24 March 2014).
35. *Ibid.*
36. *Ibid.*
37. *Cost of Proceedings*, ICSID, https://icsid.worldbank.org/en/Pages/Services/Cost-of-Proceedings.aspx (accessed 20 March 2019).
38. *ICSID Schedule of Fees*, ICSID, https://icsid.worldbank.org/en/Pages/icsiddocs/ICSID-Schedule-of-Fees.aspx (accessed 20 March 2019).

he is a member of (a), a fee for the equivalent of each eight-hour day for all other work performed in relation to the proceedings (b), a *per diem* allowance (c), travel expenses and (d) reimbursements for any direct expenses reasonably incurred. The amounts payable under (a) and (b) are determined by the Secretary-General, with the approval of the chairman, from time to time. The current fee is fixed as USD 3000 per day of participation in meetings and USD 375 for each hour of related work. If members wish to receive a higher amount, they must make a request for the same through the Secretary-General and the request must be approved by the disputing parties.[39] This is a significantly helpful measure as it puts a limit on the most significant portion of arbitration costs. The amounts under (c) and (d) are based on norms that have been fixed for the Executive Banks of the World Bank.[40]

Regulation 14(2) states that all costs and reimbursements related to members, witnesses, experts, the secretariat and hosts of proceedings held away from the centre will be payable only to the centre, which shall allot them. While this has no impact on the magnitude of the costs, it reduces the likelihood of costs being arbitrarily increased via private transactions as well as the loss of objectivity that such transactions can lead to.

Regulation 14(3) provides that the parties must make advance payments to the centre, instead of paying as and when costs arise. Costs likely to be incurred over three to six months are determined by the Secretary-General, in consultation with the President of the concerned body as well as the parties so far as it is possible. This mechanism, while administratively efficient, is detrimental to the idea of access to justice because during the institution of proceedings, the assets of investor parties may have been seized, or at the least negatively affected, and their financial capacity may have been reduced. They further have no binding say in the determination of costs. The first advance cost has been estimated to be USD 100,000-USD 150,000 per party.[41] The parties can also be asked to make additional supplementary payments if the Secretary-General and the President of the body believe this is necessary. However, before making such a demand, the Secretary-General is required to assess actual expenses incurred to ensure that more funds are actually needed. This prevents the parties from being made to pay excessively.

The costs governed by Regulation 14 are to be paid equally by both parties, although this arrangement may be changed during the final decision. All advances are payable the moment the Secretary-General makes a demand, and in whatever currency he denotes. The Secretary-General can stay the proceeding after forty-five days of non-payment, and can permanently discontinue the proceeding if it has been stayed for six consecutive months by reason of non-payment. This raises the concern that there may be situations where a state party can restrict the claimant's financial capacity for just long enough to avoid the proceeding.

39. *Schedule of Fees*, ICSID, https://icsid.worldbank.org/services/content/schedule-fees (accessed 1 January 2019).
40. Regulation 14, *Direct Costs of Individual Proceedings*, Administrative and Financial Regulations.
41. *Counting the costs of investment treaty arbitration* (*supra* n. 34).

The advance payable under Regulation 14 is inclusive of the administrative fee payable for use by the centre. Instead of charging based on actual use, the centre charges USD 42,000 as an annual fee, payable equally by both parties.[42] Since states are likely to make more use of the centre than individual investors, it is possible that this cost impacts investors disproportionately despite being objectively equal for both sides.

Regulation 15 deals with the fees for 'Special Services' that a party may want, such as translation or copies of documents. Special services will only be performed if the party concerned deposits the due fee in advance. The costs of such services are determined based on a schedule created by the Secretary-General and the parties or the tribunal have no say in the matter.[43] Services like translation are often crucial for parties to be fully able to participate in proceedings and this increased cost invariably means that some parties will find it tougher to take part in the arbitration than others will.

Regulation 16 describes the lodging fees payable for use by the centre. The party that wishes to institute arbitration proceedings, or to request a supplementary decision, rectification, interpretation, revision or annulment of an arbitration award or to resubmit a dispute to a tribunal after annulment, must pay a non-refundable fee to the centre. This fees under the current schedule is USD 25,000 for institution and annulment, and USD 10,000 for supplementary decisions, rectification, interpretation, revision and resubmission.[44] This cost remains the same even if the case is instituted under the Additional Facility rules, which deal with disputes that do not fall under the Convention.[45] This lodging fee must be paid along with the submission of the relevant request. For a post-award remedy, the fee must be paid within a prescribed time limit.[46] Additionally, while other costs of the proceeding, such as those of the centre and the tribunal, are split equally between the parties, the lodging costs are payable only by the party that files the request. This creates a situation where the party who seeks justice, or wishes to rectify perceived injustice, pays more. Given that claimants already have higher average legal costs, this additional expenditure only makes it harder for them to go through these proceedings.

When it comes to cost allocation, ICSID Rules have been called an 'outlier'[47] for being the most vague and uncertain. They neither provide a default position nor do they lay out the relevant factors that ought to be considered while determining who should pay what amount.[48] Article 61 of the Convention merely states that the tribunal will assess the expenses associated with the proceedings and decide 'how and by whom those expenses, the fees and expenses of the members of the tribunal and the

42. *ICSID Schedule of Fees* (*supra* n. 38).
43. Regulation 15(2), Administrative and Financial Regulations.
44. *ICSID Schedule of Fees* (*supra* n. 38).
45. *Overview of Arbitration under the ICSID Additional Facility*, ICSID, https://icsid.worldbank.org/services/arbitration/additional-facility/process/overview (accessed 24 March 2019).
46. *ICSID Schedule of Fees* (*supra* n. 38).
47. Miles (*supra* n. 5).
48. *Ibid.*

charges for the use of the facilities of the centre shall be paid'. This determination of costs is to be a part of the award. At the end of the proceeding, parties are invited to submit submissions on cost which include their arguments on how costs should be allocated along with an assessment of the costs they have incurred.[49] The Convention or any other rules do not provide any substantive criteria to guide the tribunal in cost allocation after parties have made their submissions[50]. The only exception to the absolute discretion given to the tribunal is if the parties manage to agree on how costs should be distributed.

The *travaux préparatoires* to the ICSID Convention complicates the matter of cost allocation further. Various drafts of the Convention contained an express rule that parties should pay their own costs, unless a party has instituted proceedings in bad faith.[51] However, this was removed from the final draft and a long process of negotiation.[52] During the negotiations it was often discussed that equal sharing of costs was 'consistent with the character of the ICSID regime',[53] which imagines friendlier proceedings.[54] However, various delegates from Latin America were in favour of extending the scope of cost recovery beyond bad faith actions.[55] It was feared by delegates that equal apportionment would discourage small- and medium-sized investors from submitting disputes to the tribunal.[56] This means that the influence of costs on access to justice was explicitly recognised by the drafters of the ICSID Convention. Unfortunately, it was dismissed at the time and delegates arrived at the conclusion that creating a limiting schedule of fees would sufficiently deal with the concern.[57] Since no consensus could be reached on cost allocation, Austria proposed that tribunals be allowed to make the decision on a case-by-case basis, unless parties agreed otherwise.[58] This proposal was accepted and included in the final draft of the Convention. As a consequence of the lack of instructions, no pattern in cost apportionment can be identified. Data suggests that 36% of awards compensate the prevailing parties while 63% awards make parties bear their own expenses.[59]

§15.04 ICSID DECISIONS RELATING TO COSTS

ICSID Decisions are reflective of how the centre's financial rules impact access to justice. For instance, in *Commerce Group Corp & San Sebastian Gold Mines, Inc. v.*

49. Rule 28 (2), The Rules of Procedure for Arbitration Proceedings (Arbitration Rules).
50. Miles (*supra* n. 5).
51. First Draft (Doc.43), dated 11 September 1964, Articles 62 and 64(3).
52. Miles (*supra* n. 5).
53. Miles (*supra* n. 5).
54. SID/63-16 (10 September 1963), *Memorandum of the discussion by the Executive Directors*, 10 September 1963, Discussion of the First Preliminary Draft Convention, p. 176.
55. *Consultative Meeting of Legal Experts* (Santiago, Chile, 3-7 February 1964), Summary Record of Proceedings dated 12 June 1964, p. 353.
56. *Consultative Meeting of Legal Experts* (Geneva, 17-22 February 1964), Summary Record of Proceedings dated 1 June 1964, p. 436.
57. *Ibid.*
58. *Ibid.*
59. Miles (*supra* n. 5).

Republic of El Salvador,[60] the tribunal discontinued an arbitration proceeding after over three years, because the claimants failed to pay the advance amount due. It was cognisant of the financial difficulties of the claimant as well as its numerous efforts to secure funding. The only decision where this factor was considered was the allocation of costs. The tribunal asked the parties to bear their own costs, despite the claimant having caused the cancellation, since it lacked monetary resources.

It has been argued that ICSID proceedings offer no predictability with respect to how costs will be allocated.[61] This section looks at available awards to see if a pattern can be identified.

As the tribunal in *Helnan International Hotels A/S v. Egypt*,[62] tribunals take various circumstances into consideration since the Convention provides no specific criteria for decisions on costs. It appears that when a tribunal asks parties to pay their own expenses, it normally does not provide any reasoning.[63] Some of the earliest examples of this are *Vacuum Salt v. Ghana*[64] and *Tanzania Electric Supply Co v. Independent Power Tanzania Ltd.*[65] In both these cases, the parties were asked to pay their own legal costs along with one-half each of the arbitration costs. This lack of reasoning suggests that tribunals accept this allocation to be the starting point.[66]

However, tribunals do sometimes provide reasons even when they do not adjust costs. A study of ICSID awards revealed that 15% of cases have used the reasoning that parties have acted in a bona fide manner and that worthy issues have been presented.[67] In *Atlantic Triton v. Guinea*,[68] the tribunal held that it was not adjusting costs because both parties had acted in good faith and cooperated with the tribunal. In *Wintershall*

60. *Commerce Group Corp & San Sebastian Gold Mines, Inc. v. Republic of El Salvador*, ICSID Case No. ARB/09/17 (Annulment Proceeding).
61. Miles (*supra* n. 5).
62. *Helnan International Hotels A/S v. The Arab Republic of Egypt*, ICSID Case No. 05/19, Award (3 July 2008).
63. *See Empresa Lucchetti S.A. and Lucchetti Peru, S.A. v. Republic of Peru*, ICSID Case No. ARB/03/4 Award (7 February 2005); *TSA Spectrum de Argentina S.A. v. Argentine Republic*, ICSID Case No. ARB/07/12 Award (19 December 2008); *CMS Gas Transmission Company v. The Argentine Republic*, ICSID Case No. ARB/01/8 Award (12 May 2005); *Joy Mining Machinery Limited v. Egypt*, ICSID Case No. ARB/03/11 Award (6 August 2004); *Mihaly International Corporation v. Sri Lanka*, ICSID Case. No. ARB/00/2 Award (15 March 2002); *Sempra Energy International v. Argentine Republic*, ICSID Case No. ARB/02/16, Award (28 September 2007); *Klöckner Industrie-Anlagen GmbH and others v. United Republic of Cameroon and Société Camerounaise des Engrais*, ICSID Case No. ARB/81/2 Award (21 October 1983); *American Manufacturing & Trading, Inc. v. Republic of Zaire*, ICSID Case No. ARB/93/1 Award (5 February 1997); *Cable Television of Nevis, Ltd. and Cable Television of Nevis Holdings, Ltd. v. Federation of St. Kitts and Nevis*, ICSID Case No. ARB/95/2 Award (13 January 1997).
64. *Vacuum Salt Products Ltd v. The Government of the Republic of Ghana*, ICSID Case No ARB/92/1, Award (16 February 1994).
65. *Tanzania Electric Supply Co v. Independent Power Tanzania Ltd*, ICSID Case No ARB/98/8, Award (12 July 2001).
66. Arthur W Rovine, 'Allocation of Costs in Recent ICSID Awards', David D. Caron, Stephan W. Schill, Abby Cohen Smutny & Epaminontas E. Triantafilou (eds), *Practising Virtue Inside International Arbitration* (Oxford University Press 2015).
67. Miles (*supra* n. 5).
68. *Atlantic Triton Company Limited v. People's Revolutionary Republic of Guinea*, ICSID Case No. ARB/84/1 Award (21 April 1986).

AG v. Argentina,[69] the tribunal dismissed the case for lack of jurisdiction but did not adjust costs because it found that the arguments were reasonable and were 'concisely presented to it by both parties'. Similarly, in *Compania de Aguas v. Argentina*,[70] costs were not adjusted because it was found that the claimant had 'raised a set of novel and complex issues not previously addressed'.

In the same study, it was found that 45% of the cases referred to relative success or failure as a rational for how costs were allotted.[71] In *SOABI v. Senegal*,[72] the tribunal cited the fact that neither party had been wholly successful while saying that costs will be shared equally. In *Tradex Albania v. Albania*,[73] the claimant won on procedural issues and the respondent prevailed on the merits. The tribunal used this to conclude that both parties should bear their own costs.[74] However, in *AAPL v. Sri Lanka*,[75] the tribunal found that neither party had been fully successful but treated the cost allocation differently. It allocated costs to reflect the relative success of each party, with the claimant paying 40% of the arbitration costs and one-third of its legal costs, and the respondent paying the remaining expenses.

There are also various awards where tribunals have shifted costs without much explanation.[76] An example of this is the case of *GEA Group v. Ukraine*,[77] where the state was awarded the entirety of its costs. The tribunal simply stated, '[w]ithout entering upon this debate here, the Tribunal considers that this particular case is an appropriate one for the exercise of its discretion ... in the Respondent's favour'.[78]

Alternatively, costs may be awarded with an intent to penalise the losing party. This has been used as the reason in 21% of all awards analysed in the mentioned study.[79] In *LETCO v. Liberia*,[80] the respondent did not participate in the proceedings and instituted a case with its national courts, in violation of Article 26 of the ICSID Convention. Consequently, the tribunal awarded full costs to the claimant in light of the respondent's 'procedural bad faith'. Similarly, in *Telenor v. Hungary*,[81] the respondent was awarded over USD 2.5 million, because the claimant's case was found to be

69. *Wintershall AG v. The Argentine Republic*, ICSID Case No ARB/04/14, Award (8 December 2008).
70. *Compañiá de Aguas del Aconquija S.A. and Vivendi Universal S.A. v. Argentine Republic*, ICSID Case No. ARB/97/3 Award (21 November 2000).
71. Miles (*supra* n. 5).
72. *Société Ouest Africaine des Bétons Industriels v. Senegal*, ICSID Case No. ARB/82/1 Award (25 February 1988).
73. *Tradex Hellas S.A. v. Republic of Albania*, ICSID Case No. ARB/94/2 Award (29 April 1999).
74. *Ibid.*
75. *Asian Agricultural Products Ltd. v. Republic of Sri Lanka*, ICSID Case No. ARB/87/3 Award (27 June 1990).
76. *Rovine* (*supra* n. 66).
77. *GEA Group AG v. Ukraine*, ICSID Case No ARB/05/16 Award (31 March 2011).
78. *Ibid.*
79. Miles (*supra* n. 5).
80. *Liberian Eastern Timber Corporation v. Republic of Liberia*, ICSID Case No. ARB/83/2 (31 March 1986).
81. *Telenor Mobile Communications A.S. v. The Republic of Hungary*, ICSID Case No. ARB/04/15 (13 September 2006).

vague and poor. In *Cementownia v. Turkey*,[82] the tribunal explicitly stated that 'ICSID tribunals can award costs against parties as a sanction against what they see as dilatory or otherwise improper conduct in the proceeding'. In that case, the respondent was awarded costs because the claimant had filed fraudulent claims, delayed the proceedings and tried to dispose of its assets during the proceeding.

§15.05 CONCLUSION

ISDS proceedings have been found to be expensive and studies have indicated that the costs are significant both in an objective sense but also in the opinion of arbitration counsel. Empirical data suggests that ICSID cases are more expensive than average ISDS disputes. While the centre has a comprehensive set of rules to deal with costs, the only rule that serves to limit costs is that tribunal fees cannot exceed the values set by the Secretary-General. An appropriate manner of cost adjustment can serve to reduce this issue. However, this raises additional questions.

It may be argued that if the winning party will be awarded costs, it can arrange for external funding with the certainty of repayment. However, there are multiple issues with this argument. First, *access* to justice deals with the ability of all parties to seek justice, and it cannot be ascertained by merely ensuring that the party that wins will *post facto* have the capacity to pay. Second, certainty of victory is, more often than not, only a theoretical possibility. Lastly, given that there are rising concerns of bias and external factors influencing the final award,[83] it may be considered inequitable and unjust to impose the entire cost of the process onto the losing party. This leads to the inference that parties should be made to pay for their own costs. There is evidence to suggest that this is the starting position for various tribunals. However, being compensated for costs may be really crucial for some prevailing parties, especially if they have had to source external funding. Indeed, as the discussion shows, both forms of cost allocation have been found to be unjust at different times. While the drafting committee was concerned that paying their own costs may be a hurdle to parties, a tribunal refused to adjust costs to the respondent due to the claimant's financial difficulties. Consequently, it appears that having a fixed method may not serve the interest of ensuring access.

At the same time, having some awareness about how costs may be allocated is incredibly crucial in allowing parties to make the right decisions and to negotiate better settlement options. Consequently, the best solution may be to provide criteria that will serve as a guide to the tribunal while still making cost allocation more predictable. An analysis of ICSID rules and cases reveals that such principles are neither found in the Convention nor can they be conclusively defined based on past cases.

82. *Cementownia 'Nowa Huta' S.A. v. Republic of Turkey*, ICSID Case No. ARB(AF)/06/2 (17 September 2009).
83. Sergio Puig & Anton Strezhnev, *The David Effect and ISDS*, 28(3) The European Journal of International Law 731 (2017); Anton Strezhnev, *Why Rich Countries Win Investment Disputes: Taking Selection Seriously* (2017), https://www.antonstrezhnev.com/research (accessed 18 March 2019).

Based on these factors, it may be concluded that costs under ICSID are high enough to create inequities and to dissuade parties from ensuring that they get the remedies they seek. This situation is not remedied in any significant manner. Thus, costs of proceedings under ICSID restrict the fundamental right of parties to access justice.

www.ingramcontent.com/pod-product-compliance
Lightning Source LLC
LaVergne TN
LVHW020644300926
849161LV00004B/810
9789403506913